LITURGICAL SUBJECTS

DIVINATIONS: REREADING
LATE ANCIENT RELIGION

Series editors:
Daniel Boyarin, Virginia Burrus, Derek Krueger

A complete list of books in the series
is available from the publisher.

LITURGICAL
SUBJECTS

Christian Ritual, Biblical Narrative,
and the Formation of the Self in Byzantium

DEREK KRUEGER

PENN

UNIVERSITY OF PENNSYLVANIA PRESS

PHILADELPHIA

Published by
University of Pennsylvania Press
Philadelphia, Pennsylvania 19104-4112
www.upenn.edu/pennpress

Printed in the United States of America on acid-free paper

1 3 5 7 9 10 8 6 4 2

Library of Congress Cataloging-in-Publication Data
Krueger, Derek.
  Liturgical subjects : Christian ritual, biblical narrative, and the
formation of the self in Byzantium / Derek Krueger. — 1st ed.
    p. cm. — Divinations : rereading late ancient religion
  ISBN 978-0-8122-4644-5 (hardcover : alk. paper)
  1. Orthodox Eastern Church—Liturgy—History. 2. Ortho-
dox Eastern Church—Doctrines. 3. Self—Religious aspects—
Christianity. 4. Byzantine Empire—Church history. I. Title. II.
Series: Divinations series
BX350.K784   2014
264'.0140956   2014012341

Once again for Gene

Bel contento già gode quest'alma
né più teme d'avere a penar,
che d'Amore la placida calma
il mio seno qui giunge a bear.

—Handel, *Flavio*, Act 1, Scene 4

CONTENTS

ABBREVIATIONS AND A NOTE ON TEXTS

AL   Armenian lectionary. Athanase Renoux, ed., *Le codex arménien Jérusalem 121*, 2 vols. Patrologia Orientalis 163, 168 (Turnhout: Brepols, 1969–1971) [cited by lection number in that edition]

ANF   Ante-Nicene Fathers

BBGG   *Bolletino della Badia Greca di Grottaferrata*

BHG   *Bibliotheca hagiographica graeca*, ed. François Halkin, 3rd ed., 3 vols., Subsidia Hagiographica 8a (Brussels: Société des Bollandistes, 1957; reprinted 1986)

BMFD   *Byzantine Monastic Foundation Documents: A Complete Translation of the Surviving Founders'* Typika *and Testaments*, ed. John Thomas and Angela Constantinides Hero, 5 vols. (Washington, D.C.: Dumbarton Oaks, 2000) [with continuous pagination].

BZ   *Byzantinische Zeitschrift*

CCSG   Corpus Christianorum Series Graeca

CSCO   Corpus Scriptorum Christianorum Orientalium

CSEL   Corpus Scriptorum Ecclesiasticorum Latinorum

DOP   *Dumbarton Oaks Papers*

FOTC   Fathers of the Church

GL   Georgian Lectionary. Michel Tarchnischvili, ed., *Le grand lectionnaire de l'église de Jérusalem (V^e–VIIIe siécle)*, 4 vols, CSCO 188, 189, 204, 204; Scriptores Iberici 9, 10, 13, 14 (Louvain: Secrétariat du CorpusSCO, 1959–1960) [cited by lection number in that edition.]

GRBS   *Greek, Roman, and Byzantine Studies*

Grosdidier de Matons, *Hymnes*
     Romanos le Mélode: Hymnes, ed. José Grosdidier de Matons, 5 vols., SC 99, 110, 114, 128, 283 (Paris: Cerf, 1965–1981)

JECS	*Journal of Early Christian Studies*
JÖB	*Jahrbuch der österreichischen Byzantinistik*
JThS	*Journal of Theological Studies*
LCL	Loeb Classical Library
LXX	Septuagint
Mateos, *Typicon*	*Le typicon de la Grande Église,* ed. Juan Mateos, 2 vols, OCA 165–66 (Rome: Pont. Institutum Orientalium Studiorum, 1962–1963)
NETS	*A New English Translation of the Septuagint,* ed. Albert Pietersma and Benjamin G. Wright (New York: Oxford University Press, 2007)
NPNF	Nicene and Post-Nicene Fathers
OCA	Orientalia Christiana Analecta
OCP	*Orientalia Christiana Periodica*
ODB	*Oxford Dictionary of Byzantium,* ed. Alexander Kazhdan, et al., 3 vols. (New York: Oxford University Press, 1991)
PG	Patrologia Graeca, ed. J. P. Migne
PMBZ	*Prosopographie der mittelbyzantinischen Zeit,* ed. F. Winkelmanns, Ralph-Johannes von Lilie, et al., 8 vols. (Berlin: de Gruyter, 1998–2013)
Romanos, *Hymns*	Paul Maas and C. A. Trypanis, eds., *Sancti Romani Melodi Cantica: Cantica Genuina* (Oxford: Clarendon, 1963)
SC	Sources chrétiennes
TLG	Thesaurus Linguae Graecae, <http://www.tlg.uci.edu>
TR	Triodion, Rome. *Triōdion katanyktikon: periechon apasan tēn anēkousan autō akolouthian tēs hagias kai megalēs tessarakostēs [Τριῴδιον κατανυκτικόν, περιέχον ἅπασαν τὴν ἀνήκουσαν αὐτῷ ἀκολουθίαν τῆς ἁγίας καὶ μεγάλης Τεσσαρακοστῆς]* (Rome, 1879).

I have cited the Psalms according the numbering of the LXX, supplying the Masoretic numbering in brackets. For translations of the Old Testament, I have used NETS, occasionally modified to enhance how Byzantine Christians would have understood the text. For the New Testament I have generally followed the New Revised Standard Version.

I cite Romanos according to the edition of Maas and Trypanis, Romanos,

Hymns. I have also consulted the SC edition, Grosdidier de Matons, *Hymnes.* Because the numbering in that edition differs from the Oxford edition, I have supplied the SC hymn number in parentheses at the first quotation of each hymn in each chapter.

For Andrew of Crete's *Great Kanon,* I have used the text in PG 97:1329–85. While the nine odes are numbered, there is no consistent system for citing the various stanzas, or troparia, and the PG supplies no numbers. After the ode number I have numbered the stanzas as they appear in that edition. I followed a similar logic for numbering the stanzas in the Stoudite kanons, for which I have used the received version as represented in TR as my text. For the sake of clarity, I refer to the biblical songs from the LXX book of Canticles (or Odes) as "canticles" and the division of Byzantine kanons as "odes," although they are both odes (ᾠδαι) in Greek.

In accord with emerging trends in Byzantine studies, I have cited Greek texts by English titles rather than Latin ones, and I have employed transliterations for unfamiliar Greek proper names used in the *ODB* rather than Latinizing them, even if this produces some inconsistencies.

CHAPTER 1

Shaping Liturgical Selves

Some time after the emperor Justinian's death in 565, Eutychios the patriarch of Constantinople added a new communion hymn for the celebration of the eucharistic liturgy on Holy Thursday, the annual commemoration of Christ's Last Supper. After a priest had consecrated the bread and wine and the Holy Spirit transformed them into the body and blood of Christ, a choir chanted, "At your mystical supper, Son of God, receive me today as a partaker, for I will not betray the sacrament to your enemies, nor give you a kiss like Judas, but like the Thief I confess you: remember me Lord in your kingdom."[1] In their song, the patriarch provided the laity with a ritual mechanism for identifying themselves as redeemable sinners. This self-conception employed two models drawn from the biblical narrative: one strikingly negative, the other rather more complex. Congregants should hope to approach the body of Christ not like Judas, with the kiss of betrayal (Mt 26:27), but like the Good Thief who had been crucified next to Jesus, and who, the Gospel explained, would be with him in Paradise (Lk 23:43). The hymn thus prepared Christians to approach Good Friday and Easter, or Pascha, understanding themselves as culpable and deserving of punishment while pardoned through Christ's sacrifice.

Changes to liturgy often meet with resistance, but also come with rationales. Those rationales reveal indigenous theories of ritual. According to the contemporary historian John of Ephesus, a non-Chalcedonian sharply critical of Eutychios, this innovation caused controversy and even unrest. John complains that Eutychios attempted to change the antiphon "which by ancient custom was in use in all the churches," mostly likely a verse from Psalm 148 that had served as the standard and fixed communion chant in the capital: "Praise the Lord from the heavens, praise him in the highest, Alleluia!" He circulated his new hymn, *At Your Mystical Supper*, "to all the churches," ordering that the old hymn "be suppressed and that his own be used, threatening those who would dare still to use the old one and omit his own." According to John of Ephesus, "The clergy of all the churches, the convents and monasteries of men and women" were alarmed and troubled and the whole city was in revolt. When Emperor Justin II himself demanded to know why Eutychios had made his innovation, "changing the ancient customs," the patriarch responded, "Lord, what I composed is far more suitable than the old one."[2] This liturgical substitution reveals aspects of Eutychios's view of the liturgy, namely that its texts should be "suitable," that is, that they should respond to the liturgical moment, situating each Christian with respect to the biblical narrative commemorated in the rites of the liturgical calendar.[3] To this end, the liturgy could be changed or augmented. The new hymn placed worshippers in the midst of the events of Holy Thursday and inserted them into the ritual drama. Eutychios's innovation also reflects broader shifts in Christian self-understanding and liturgical formation in the course of the sixth century, toward a greater emphasis on ritual performance as biblical reenactment.

The call to understand oneself in the role of the Thief reflects trends that transformed the Eastern Mediterranean Christianity of late antiquity into the Christianity of Byzantium. Between the sixth and the ninth centuries, the liturgical calendar increasingly brought the biblical narrative to life. Ritual practice rendered biblical and saintly characters present in both song and image. And clergy encouraged lay and monastic Christians alike to understand themselves through biblical models as the subjects of divine judgment and mercy. Scriptural narratives afforded opportunities to recognize oneself among the biblical sinners, for whom there was hope even in their sinful flaws. Near the turn of the eighth century the monastic teacher Anastasios of Sinai was asked, "Given that we often hear the word of God, but do not put it into practice [cf. Mt 7:26; Lk 6:49], [how] is it possible that we shall not be condemned?" At once stern and compassionate, he answered, "Even if we do not put it into practice, still it is not possible not to blame ourselves, because we hear and fail to listen. And self-blame [τὸ μέμψασθαι] is part of the business of saving ourselves."[4] The hearing and contemplation of scripture instilled an Orthodox guilt, both biblically informed and inwardly directed. But biblical sinners also offered the promise of forgiveness and the opportunity to participate in God's act of salvation. Anastasios was queried, "Is it possible to gain the remission of sins through one good work?" He answered with respect to biblical exemplars, "Yes, since the prostitute, Rahab, was saved because she sheltered the spies [Josh 2 and 6:25], and the Thief because of his faith [Lk 23:40–43], and the Harlot [i.e., the Sinful Woman of Lk 7:37–50] because of her lamentation."[5] Over the course of the liturgical year, and particularly during Lent, Byzantine clergy would appeal to a large cast of biblical characters, both male and female, to provide models of salvageable sinners, including Adam, Eve, and David, from the Old Testament, and the Prodigal Son, the Thief, the Harlot, the Leper, and Peter from the New. Such figures— and not Jesus or Mary—offered icons of moral development. Unlike hagiography, which routinely compared holy men and women to Christ's example, liturgy stressed the figures who needed and received his benefits.

*   *   *

In a 2006 book, liturgical historian Robert Taft explored how Byzantines saw the liturgy "through their own eyes," considering what they saw and heard primarily during the eucharistic liturgy, and how they participated in it and might have experienced it.[6] _Liturgical Subjects shifts this investigation to consider how Byzantine Christians came to view themselves through the liturgy._ My study begins at the height of the Byzantine Empire under Justinian I (527–565) and extends beyond the close of Iconoclasm in 843 to the turn of the eleventh century, around the year 1000, bridging the Christianity of late antiquity and medieval Byzantium. By highlighting major figures in the establishment and transformation of liturgical models for the self, and foregrounding ideas about interiority and identity, I trace continuities and developments across the so-called Dark Age. The sixth century effected a synthesis of the liturgy as a forum for the forging, expression, and transmission of a model self, reflected in hymns, sermons, the emergence of iconographic styles for representing key events in the life of Christ, and even in imperial legislation. By 1000, Constantinopolitan clerics achieved another synthesis, having fleshed out the liturgical calendar and the lectionary and edited and compiled the service books necessary for conducting an elaborate ritual cycle. Despite the dramatic geographical and economic transformations of the Empire after the rise of Islam, the long decline through the seventh and eighth centuries, and the slow renaissance of Byzantine culture in the course of the ninth century, I proffer a reading of the self and theories about the formation of the self in a long trajectory, from the hymns of Romanos the Melodist to Symeon the New Theologian's instructions for novice monks.[7]

This inquiry focuses on the ritual practice of the Byzantine Orthodox

Church, by which I mean the developing Byzantine liturgy of the Patriarchate of Constantinople. This church adhered to the councils of Nicaea (325)
and Chalcedon (451), and developed distinctive patterns for the liturgical
calendar and its celebration. Many aspects of its processional liturgy were
inextricably linked to the topography of the capital, as celebrants moved from
station to station along prescribed routes. Four key figures provide useful
lenses on liturgical innovations in the Byzantine traditions of the self: Romanos the Melodist, Andrew of Crete, Theodore the Stoudite, and Symeon
the New Theologian. The major authors covered here were all active, at least
for some phase of their careers, in and around the capital city. But the rites of
Constantinople were nourished in successive waves by the liturgical practice
of the Patriarchate of Jerusalem. This influence affected both monastic and lay
worship. The liturgical calendar of the Church of the Anastasis, or Resurrection, also known as the Church of the Holy Sepulcher, in the holy city itself,
offered a template for celebrating the life of Christ through the course of the
year, and the innovations of the monasteries of the Judean Desert, especially
the Monastery of Mar Saba, offered new prayers and new genres of hymns.[8]

Two of the Byzantine hymnographers whose poems help us chart the presentation of the self also came to Constantinople from the Levant. Romanos
the Melodist was born in the Syrian city of Emesa, and served a church in
Beirut before coming to the capital early in the sixth century. He perfected
the chanted verse sermon, later known as the *kontakion*, which owed much
to Syrian hymnographic styles. He composed during most of Justinian's reign.
Andrew, who later became the Metropolitan of Crete, was born in Umayyad
Damascus around 660. He received his education and was tonsured at the
Church of the Anastasis in Jerusalem. As a young man he made his way to
Constantinople, where he became the head of the orphanage attached to
Hagia Sophia and composed for its choir. He may have been responsible
for bringing the tradition of the hymn form known as the *kanon* to urban •
parishes.

The liturgical reforms of the ninth century brought additional Palestinian monastic disciplinary and worship styles to the capital. At the turn of
the ninth century, Theodore the Stoudite and his companions introduced
liturgies of the Judean desert monasteries to the Stoudios Monastery in the
capital, and created a potent synthesis of Hagiopolite and Constantinopolitan liturgical forms that would endure through the Fourth Crusade in 1204.
Among their many achievements, the Stoudites composed and assigned a
repertoire of hymns, especially kanons, for the season of Lent. Furthermore,

many of the artifacts and devotional objects that help us tell the story of the liturgical calendar disseminated from Syria and Palestine. To chart the history of the liturgical self in Byzantium, therefore, we must take an eclectic approach, considering the integration of words and images.

The scope of liturgy that concerns us also deserves remark. Although Chapter 4 addresses the celebration of the Eucharist, much of the evidence for the formation of subjectivity in Byzantine Christian ritual life derives from other services of the Church. Focusing on hymns means focusing on the services where they were sung. Our inquiry thus broadens beyond the Eucharist to consider the prayers of the daily office, both in churches serving the urban laity and in monasteries. Among all the services, the All-Night Vigil (*pannychis*, παννυχίς) of urban parishes and the celebration of Morning Prayer in the monastic office (observed also in lay parishes as the middle Byzantine centuries progressed) emerge as the most important occasions for the composition and performance of elaborate hymns. Over the course of the sixth through ninth centuries, Night Vigil and Morning Prayer developed by responding directly to the lectionary and liturgical season. Their structures reserved time for lengthy chants, and thus it was for these services that the most innovative composers created their most significant works.

While the lives and religious experiences of monastics and laity certainly differed, nevertheless, the models for the self often converged. Not only did hymnography mediate monastic styles of self-presentation to the laity, most hymnographic forms moved between the monastery and the parish church. Initially, in the course of the fourth century, Christians in the East developed two distinct liturgical types: one for monastic communities and one for lay congregations. The monastic liturgy emphasized the recitation of the Psalter in its entirety and filled the monastic day with prayer and meditation on scripture. The secular, or non-monastic, liturgy of cathedrals or parishes, often simply called by scholars the cathedral liturgy, celebrated the progress of the day and the shape of the liturgical year, included excerpts from the Psalms appropriate to the time of day and liturgical season, and featured processions with candles and eventually incense.[9] By the late fifth or early sixth century, on the eve of major festivals, the laity in Constantinople would gather for elaborate vigils that included the reading of scripture and its dramatic embellishment in lengthy sung sermons. In these hymns the biblical stories would come alive, reenacted and explored by such virtuosos as Romanos the Melodist.

Meanwhile, early on, in the deserts of Egypt and Sinai, some monks rejected hymnody as a practice more appropriate to the secular services conducted by urban clergy and attended by nonprofessionals.[10] But Palestine was different, and by the last decades of the sixth century, monks there had adopted traditions of adorning the liturgical hours with hymns of the sort sung at the Church of the Anastasis in Jerusalem. By this time, the singing of the nine biblical canticles during Morning Prayer was common to both monastic and cathedral rites in the Holy Land, and by the end of the seventh century, monastic composers embroidered this service with new hymns, known as kanons, that refocused the tradition of the biblical canticles to the themes of the liturgical calendar. In effect, a hybrid of the earlier monastic psalmody and the urban cathedral rite arose for monasteries, an urban-monastic office, still distinct from the rites sung for lay people, but one that increasingly borrowed from and was nourished by it.[11]

That said, the two hymn forms at the center of this study moved between lay and monastic realms. The kontakion, written for lay vigils in the sixth century, entered the monastic service of Morning Prayer by the ninth century, although in truncated form, and the kanon, which originated in Palestinian monastic communities in the late seventh century, quickly found its way into cathedral services in the course of a generation.[12] Mutual influence of monastic and lay services predated the pervasive monasticization of Byzantine parish liturgy in the course of the eleventh century. Laymen, including emperors, composed hymns that entered monastic service books.[13] In short, the two liturgical systems, monastic and lay, often celebrated in close proximity, and sometimes even by the same clergy, inevitably influenced each other, and thus did not remain entirely distinct.[14] Cantors and choirs sang hymns composed in monasteries during services for secular congregations, and lay people attended urban monastic churches.[15] The self mediated in these hymns emerges from both the specific contexts in which these compositions were first performed and the new contexts into which they were transferred. In the final analysis, monastic and lay selves drew on the same biblical types and tropes, and always resembled each other. This was never truer than during Lent, which imposed a sort of temporary monasticism on the laity. Nevertheless, after the sixth century, better documentation survives for monastic practices.

Working at the intersection of Byzantine Christian religious culture and contemporary critical approaches to the history of subjectivity, this book explores Orthodox liturgy as a mechanism for the formation of interiority. As a contribution to a cultural history of the Christian self, I investigate hymns, prayers, sermons, works of art, and catechetical instructions through which Byzantine clergy and artisans mediated Christians' approach to interiority, guiding how Christians might have access not only to God but to themselves. The turn to liturgy as a source for the self augments studies that treat subjectivity largely from the standpoint of intellectual history or as a philosophical problem or that treat self-consciousness or self-presentation in the literary works of prominent, elite men such as Gregory of Nazianzos or Michael Psellos.[16] Liturgical models for selfhood, authored by clergy and disseminated among the faithful in the context of worship, coexisted in Byzantium with other discursive subjectivities, including military and imperial selves; expected familial and gender roles; selves dictated by social station, guild, or profession; the selves of narrative fictions—including hagiography and the novel; and even Christian discursive selves beyond the liturgy. The liturgical self was only one of many contending in the broader culture, although it arguably had the greatest impact on Byzantine Christian self-conceptions across society.

We can say from the outset that access to the interior religious experience of Byzantine Christians proves difficult for two reasons. First, we lack direct evidence: no autobiographies exist explaining how Byzantine Orthodox Christians felt about themselves through their liturgical lives. Second, even if such sources existed, they would offer rhetorical constructs of piety, rather than incontrovertible evidence for the interior landscape of Byzantines at worship. And yet the Byzantine liturgy contains a good deal of first-person speech, either in the form of prayers offered in the first person plural, describing the moral condition and needs of the community or congregation, or the first person singular, particularly in hymns, that both expresses and inculcates appropriate habits of self-regard. Religious practices produce, articulate, and maintain norms for self-understanding and self-presentation. In a manner analogous to theater, ritual activities involve playing and ultimately inhabiting the mythic roles of sacred narrative. The interior lives of Byzantine Christians remain elusive, but hymns, sermons, ritual spaces, and religious artifacts offered templates telling Christians who they were in relation to God, each other, the church, and the state.

Attention to what lay and monastic congregants heard, said, sang, and did during liturgies, both the Divine Liturgy of the Eucharist, and the Liturgy of the Hours, sheds light on how participation in ritual events molded the worshipper by inculcating patterns of interior self-regard. Of particular interest are the psalms, hymns, and chants that the congregation sang, the prayers they recited, and the prayers said by the clergy to which the laity listened and to which they assented by saying "Amen." Moreover, liturgical texts, their modes of performance, and Byzantine reflections on the meaning and work of liturgy reveal a sophisticated, if largely unarticulated, indigenous Byzantine theory of how liturgy was expected to work, especially to work in producing Christians. Such a theory of the formation of subjects through ritualization reaches fruition in the instructions of the late tenth- and early eleventh-century abbot Symeon the New Theologian for his novice monks.

The lack in Byzantium of a text like Augustine's *Confessions*, which too many readers have assumed provides unmediated access to a real fourth-century Western Christian personage rather than a highly rhetorical literary portrait of one, is a much a boon as a burden. If we follow current trends in the history of subjectivity and understand the early Byzantine self as a rhetorical construct from the beginning, we can address the evidence that does, in fact, offer models for self-conception. We can also appreciate the role of clerical authors as the agents of liturgy. Liturgy was the place where Byzantine Christians learned to apply the Bible to themselves. Figures like Eutychios sought to frame and guide the formation of these selves. The greatest of the authorial voices of Byzantine hymnography, Romanos the Melodist in the sixth century, Andrew of Crete in the eighth, the poets of the Stoudios Monastery of Constantinople in the ninth, and others in their orbit such as the nun Kassia, scripted a typical Christian subjectivity in response to the lessons of the Bible. Exploring the "I" in their works thus involves the investigation not only of the persona of these poets but also of Byzantine models of the self. These poets produced a conception of the self that was at once distinctly penitential and grounded in a reading of scripture that emphasized a pattern of sin and redemption. In this sense, my project differs from those of modern scholars who might wish to understand personal or individual religion in Byzantium. Rather I seek to examine broadly disseminated and collective modes for constructing and expressing a common individuality that in its generic force is not quite individual at all.

Byzantium and the History of the Christian Self

The use of the term "self" to describe the "I"-speech and its interior operations in Byzantine liturgical texts requires some clarification and nuance. As Patricia Cox Miller has explained, contemporary critical theory understands that the "self" is "not an autonomous source of meaning but rather a con-struct, the product of systems of cultural convention." She continues, "The discourses of a culture not only set limits to how a self may be understood but also provide models or paradigms that are used to classify or represent that culture's understanding(s) of 'selfhood.'"[17] The selves on display in Byzantine Christian hymns, prayers, and sermons are neither historical selves nor tran-shistorical selves, but rather styles of self-presentation rooted in Byzantine religious culture. Moreover, even in their diversity, these selves tend toward a certain sameness, toward a generic vision of the Christian person, a typi-cal Byzantine Christian. Rhetorical criticism in the study of Mediterranean late antiquity and the Middle Ages has challenged the idea that the textual record provides unmediated access to Christians' interior realities. Indeed, it is now widely accepted that early Christian literature represents authorial vi-sions of reality, refracted through a variety of ideological lenses.[18] The hymns of Romanos the Melodist, Andrew of Crete, and the poets of the Stoudios Monastery display contingent selves, both the products of and paradigms for Byzantine cultural norms and values. The poems enact models for how listen-ers might understand themselves by presenting a culturally sanctioned image of the self, the subject of a particular style of self-regard, or subjectivity.[19]

The significance of this production of self-knowledge in the corpus of Byzantine liturgical poetry, for example, becomes apparent in light of schol-arly study of the emergence of supposedly distinctive Christian styles of the self. Generalizing broadly about the Christian self in premodernity, Michel Foucault wrote, "Each person has a duty to know who he is, that is, to try to know what is happening inside him, to acknowledge faults, to recognize temptations, to locate desires, and everyone is obliged to disclose these things either to God or to others in the community and hence to bear public or private witness against oneself."[20] The obligation to an inner truth required ritualized operations on the part of the Christian. The first involved the rec-ognition of oneself "as a sinner and penitent," while the second involved the verbalization of one's thoughts and desires to another. Foucault understood this second technique to have developed initially in fourth- and fifth-century monastic circles, where a disciple received spiritual direction from an elder.[21] In later centuries, and in the West particularly, Foucault argued that these technologies spread to the laity in the sacrament of confession and penance. Byzantine Christianity did not develop formal sacramental rites for confes-sion; however, monastic rules and instructions encouraged regular confes-sion of sin to one's spiritual father, and lay people were encouraged to confess major sins during the course of Lent.[22] Consideration of Byzantine liturgy as matrix for the self reveals both the power and the limitations of Foucault's genealogy of the Western Christian subject.

The first-person monologues in the corpus of Byzantine hymnography display a similar introspective subjectivity, attesting that such styles of the self were also available in the East and, furthermore, beyond the monastery. In a late fifth- or early sixth-century hymn *On Adam's Lament*, one of the earliest in a genre that would come in the ninth century to be called the kontakion, the anonymous poet imagines the first-created human's speech as he sits beyond the gates of Paradise. Adam serves as a stand-in for all humanity, lamenting the human condition as a Byzantine reader of Genesis would understand it: fear, drudgery, and trouble. Indeed, joining in the refrain, the lay congregation of an urban parish shared in Adam's voice, taking upon themselves his call for mercy and thus also his punishment in exile.

> I am polluted, I am ruined, I am enslaved to my slaves;
> For reptiles and wild beasts, whom I subjected by fear,
> Now make me tremble;
> > *O Merciful, have mercy on the one who has fallen.*
>
> No longer do the flowers offer me pleasure,
> But thorns and thistles [Gen 3:18] the earth raises for me,
> Not produce:
> > *O Merciful, have mercy on the one who has fallen.*
>
> The table without toil I overthrew by my own will;
> And now in the sweat of my brow I eat
> My bread [Gen 3:19];
> > *O Merciful, have mercy on the one who has fallen.*[23]

Although the congregants did not share Adam's specific deed of disobedience, the liturgical poet invited them to share his subjectivity and his perspective. Adam's sin was typical, and Adam a type for all humanity. Like Adam, all humanity joined in lamentation, called for forgiveness, and became salvageable sinners. Popular hymnography mediated Foucault's penitential subject even without a formal rite of confession and absolution. At the same time, the refrain invoked and constructed a God capable of a free act of mercy.

As we shall see in Chapter 2, the hymns of Romanos offered a performance of the self engaging in precisely these technologies: self-accusation and verbal confession, not merely in the voice of a biblical archetype. Significantly, he did so not in a monastic sphere or for a monastic audience, but rather at the urban Night Vigil, displaying this interior self-recognition before a primarily lay audience. Within the texts of his hymn, Romanos models the formation of the Christian subject. In the singing of his hymns, Romanos divulges his knowledge of an inner truth through public display; he declares himself a sinner. God and congregation witness the performance and see, in Romanos's expressions of conscience, something we might call a self. This Byzantine subject thus emerges in acts of confession, ritually articulated and liturgically performed. Moreover, this self forms in dialogue with constructions of biblical selves, a feature of Byzantine liturgical subjectivity perhaps most acute in the penitential masterpiece, the *Great Kanon* of Andrew of Crete, which works its way through the entire cast of biblical characters to create an abject Christian persona.

The emphasis on the human capacity for sinfulness reinforced an image of a broken self, damaged by personal history and potentially alienated permanently from God. In another context, Stephen Greenblatt has defined the self as "a sense of personal order, a characteristic mode of address to the world, a structure of bounded desires."[24] In Byzantine hymnography one finds styles of expressing the self that through their reiteration constitute a "characteristic mode of address." If, in his confession of inadequate bounds on his own desires, a hymnographer seems to present a sense of personal disorder, this is because sanctioned styles of self-display dictated the performance of a disordered self. Byzantine prayer engaged an aesthetics of subjectivity to display disappointment with the self. The discursive structure that we may regard as the Byzantine Christian self valued humility. It urged Christians to regard themselves as greater than no one and to attribute all virtuous action to the work of God. The script for the self required declarations of inadequacy and disarray.[25]

Most scholarship on subjectivity in premodern Christianity has described the making of the monastic self. Monastic subjectivities also figure prominently in the later sections of this book. The Byzantine evidence both confirms and challenges some of the trends in the academic trajectory. Following Foucault in *Discipline and Punish* and other works, scholars have stressed the place of the monastery in the history of the formation of Western subjects, particularly in the ritualization of obedience and the formation of the conscience.[26] Ascetic rigor and strict discipline effected the self because the

monk placed himself under constant surveillance. In addition to confessing
to his superior or spiritual advisor, he remained under their watchful eyes
and those of his fellow monks. Within the successful subject, this watchful-
ness ultimately became fully internalized and the monk became vigilant over
himself. Attempting to account for the performative qualities of subject formation, Talal Asad has suggested that "The program is performed primarily
not for the sake of an audience but for the sake of the performers."[27] In effect,
the monk performs the spectacle of his asceticism for himself. In the process,
"The monastic program that prescribes the performance of rites is directed at
forming and reforming Christian dispositions."[28] Byzantine liturgical materials augment these insights in several ways. Such a program for the formation
of subjectivity worked, in part, through the words of prayers and the singing
of hymns, through the adoption of subjectivating speech as one's own, that is,
as a coherent description of the self. Our Byzantine evidence will show also
that this ritualization to produce subjectivity functioned just as effectively for
lay people as for religious professionals, or at least that clergymen believed
this subjectivation could be similarly effective and so imposed it through
their compositions and chanted performances.

What did a Byzantine theory of religious practice look like? Within Byzantine liturgical thought, the subjectivation worked because of a strong confidence
in an external witness. In indigenous Byzantine religious discourses, ritual repetition formed the conscience and shaped self-recognition because God was
watching too. Byzantine theories of the formation—or reformation—of the
self depended on basic theological claims about God's omniscience and attention, claims that ultimately embedded the Christian in a narrative, funda-
mentally biblical in character, about the relationship between God and God's
people.[29] To understand Byzantines as theoretically informed agents of their
subjectivity, as Christians engaged in making and shaping themselves, we must
study the theological contexts in which they theorized themselves. Symeon the
New Theologian's attempts to instruct his monks on the making of themselves,
the subject of Chapter 7, make the centrality of such claims clear. Byzantine
Orthodox subjectivities formed in a Byzantine Orthodox theological context.[30]

For various reasons, the history of the Christian self has bypassed or
ignored Byzantium. Posing questions about Eastern Christian conceptions
of the self present in Byzantine liturgy disrupts characterizations of Byzantines that distinguish them from the trend toward increased interior anxiet-
ies among Western Christians, especially in the wake of Augustine and John
Cassian. That hymnographers such as Romanos, Andrew, and the Stoudites

offer such a model of a guilty conscience as normative to Eastern Christian audiences, both monastic and lay, may come as a surprise. Many scholars have held that the "introspective conscience" developed primarily—or even exclusively—in the Latin West or that it was a distinct product of late antique monastic culture. More problematically, some scholars of the medieval West, such as Colin Morris and John F. Benton, claimed the twelfth-century as the moment for an emergent awareness of the self as an individual, a conception of interiority predicated on later Enlightenment accounts of individual consciousness.[31]

Within the New Testament, the conscience [συνείδησις] features as an introspective capacity for moral discernment that can be either clear or troubled. For the most part, the assumption is that the Christian conscience is clear. Hebrews 13:18 states: "We are sure that we have a clear conscience, desiring to act honorably in all things." 1 Peter 1:14 calls on its readers, "Keep your conscience clear," and assumes that they can and that their abusing enemies will be thus put to shame. A passage in Romans 7 provides the most significant exception. Here, Paul illustrates a state of guilt-ridden interiority. "I do not understand my own actions. For I do not do what I want, but I do the very thing I hate. . . . I can will what is right, but I cannot do it. For I do not do the good that I want, but the evil I do not want is what I do. Now if I do what I do not want, it is no longer I that do it, but sin that dwells within me. So I find it to be a law that when I want to do what is good, evil lies close at hand. For I delight in the law of God in my innermost self [κατὰ τὸν ἔσω ἄνθρωπον], but I see in my members another law at war with the law of my mind [νοός], making me captive to the law of sin that dwells in my members. Wretched man that I am!" (Rom 7:15, 18–24; NRSV). In a landmark essay entitled "The Apostle Paul and the Introspective Conscience of the West," Krister Stendahl argued that in this passage, Paul was not speaking in his own voice, but rather impersonating the interior life of a gentile convert to Jesus when confronting Torah, thus presenting a fictive "I."[32] Subsequent scholarship in New Testament studies has generally confirmed that, in this portrayal of interior moral turmoil, Paul employs the rhetorical technique of "speech-in-character," that is, ethopoeia or prosopoeia, common in ancient rhetorical training.[33] Indeed, many late antique exegetes were unwilling to accept that Paul was speaking of himself; they preferred to read this as a fictive "I."[34] Models for representing the self-convicted mind abound in ancient tragedy, and students strove for the eloquent vocalization of a character's ethos [ἦθος]. But while Paul could imagine the guilty conscience, he did not claim it for himself or assume it to plague his converts. In most of Paul's writings, Paul exhibits what Stendahl called a "robust" conscience, confident that he was "blameless" with regard to righteousness under the law (Phil 3:6). Stendahl suggested that the introspective conscience, so typical of Roman Catholic and especially Protestant Christianity, did not originate with the letters of Paul, but rather with Augustine's interpretation of Paul, particularly Augustine's reading of Romans 7. Although in his conception of an "inner" human, Paul calls on traditions already present in Plato, for Stendahl and others, it was Augustine who "created from Romans 7 a normative model of the religious self that in Western culture has become the archetype for inquiry into the individual."[35]

This genealogy of the self, the result of Augustine's reading of Paul filtered through the Protestant Reformation, was not without consequence for views of Byzantium. Stendahl himself wrote that, "Judging at least from a superficial survey of the preaching of the Churches of the East from olden times to the present, it is striking how their homiletical tradition is either one of doxology or meditative mysticism or exhortation—but it does not deal with the plagued conscience in the way in which one came to do so in the Western Churches."[36] This view has persisted in histories of the Western self. Charles Taylor, in *Sources of the Self: The Making of Modern Identity*, located in Augustine the origins of an "inner person" and a concomitant "reflexivity" with respect to that inner person which he claims is "central to our moral understanding."[37] There are some problems with this account of the self. On the one hand, it is unclear whether Augustine's characterizations of interiority accurately reflect his own self-understanding, or, for that matter, that of late ancient Latin-speaking Christians generally, or whether it too is a form of speech-in-character presented as normative.[38] On the other hand, sufficient evidence survives in the Greek patristic tradition to depose claims of Western distinctiveness regarding the development of Christian ideas about conscience and the self. Byzantium has much to offer and to correct in the history of the self in Christian cultures.

A less superficial survey of Greek Christian literature shows agony over a guilty state of mind. Public sermons and ascetic instruction encouraged Christians in the eastern Mediterranean to discern the movements of their souls and to develop a discourse within themselves about their desires. Significantly, Athanasios and John Chrysostom encouraged their audiences, monks and lay people respectively, to keep a written diary of their sins, revealing that the act of introspection was conceived as an act of representation, the representation of the self to the self.[39] The role of the conscience (both

συνειδός and συνείδησις) in the formation of Christian self-conception features prominently in John Chrysostom's sermons and commentaries, where
the preacher accords the conscience an authority second only to God's for
judging the Christian.[40] A single passage from a sermon *On Lazarus* shows
how vividly Chrysostom conjures the guilty conscience:

> Even before the punishment to come, those who practice wicked-
> ness and live in sin are punished in this life. Do not simply tell me of
> the man who enjoys an expensive table, who wears silken robes, who
> takes with him flocks of slaves as he struts in the marketplace: unfold
> [ἀνάπτυξον] for me his conscience [συνειδός], and you will see in-
> side a great tumult of sins, continual fear, storm, confusion, his mind
> approaching the imperial throne in his conscience as if in a court-
> room, sitting like a juror, presenting arguments as if in a public trial,
> suspending his mind and torturing it for his sins, and crying aloud,
> with no witness but God who alone knows how to watch [these inner
> dramas]. The adulterer, for example . . . even if he has no accuser,
> does not cease accusing himself within. The pleasure is brief, but the
> anguish is long lasting, fear and trembling everywhere, suspicion and
> agony. . . . He goes about bearing with him a bitter accuser, his con-
> science; self-condemned, he is unable to relax even a little. . . . There
> is no way to corrupt that court. Even if we do not seek virtue, we still
> suffer anguish when we are not seeking it; and if we seek evil, we still
> experience the anguish when we cease from the pleasure of sin.[41]

Opening and inspecting the conscience divulges secret torment. In Chrysostom's juridical model, the conscience performs the work of informant, witness,
juror, judge, and jailer. Although he describes this model in the third person,
from the outside, his rhetorical performance encourages his audience to consider themselves within this model. The dramatization of the guilt-ridden
conscience functions as an opportunity for his listeners' self-recognition.

The writings of late ancient Greek Christians also include first-person
expressions of conscience, including sophisticated models for its operations
within the self and in the formation of the self. In a study of the discourses of
the self in the letters of Theodoret of Cyrrhus, Philip Rousseau has observed
the fifth-century bishop's use of the word *syneidos* in the literary display
of the author's inner world. Rousseau points to Theodoret's "inherent capacity for self-criticism."[42] Although it is impossible to bridge with certainty the gap

between the presentation of the self and its interior subjective experience, Rousseau shows how Theodoret's conscience represented both his moral self-reflection and the knowledge derived from it. Conscience thus functioned as a tool for knowing the self. Conscience participated in his ruminations as a witness of his actions both external and internal, and participated in a dialogue with God in which God could see Theodoret thinking. As in Chrysostom, conscience doubles and interiorizes the divine gaze.

One aspect of Paul's portrayal of the self not particularly prominent in Byzantium is his configuration of the divided "I." In Romans 7, Paul depicts an "I" that simultaneously knows what is right and fails to do it. Paul locates the struggle to do the right thing within the subject; and in some sense this struggle has split the subject.[43] Without reference to the vocabulary of Romans 7, Byzantine liturgical authors preferred to set up a division in the subject between the "I" and the "soul (ψυχή)," where the "I" blames the soul for sin and laments its disobedience to divine command. Here the "I," and not "the soul," serves as the seat of the conscience. Andrew of Crete casts much of the *Great Kanon* as the "I"'s address to the sinful "soul," although at other points, the "I" accepts responsibility for its own actions. The discourse with the soul—a dialogue within the self—thus ambiguates the dramatic trope, permitting internal dialogue and reproach. If this device attempts to shift or deflect blame, its abandonment constitutes an acceptance of blame and prompts another discourse of penitence, now a conversation between the "I" and God.

The lack of a single, simple word for "the self" in Byzantine Greek complicates but hardly foils an investigation of the self or selves emergent and displayed in Byzantine liturgical contexts. The pronouns *autos* (αὐτός) the "same" and thus the "self-same," and *heautos* (ἑαυτός), "himself, herself," almost always in oblique forms, establish linguistic identity with the subject or object of reference.[44] Something quite analogous to the self occurs ubiquitously as the subject of active verbs, the agent of deeds, thoughts, and emotions; or as the subject of middle voice verbs, and thus the subject of reflexive thoughts or actions. Locutions for the "soul," especially "my soul," or "you, O soul," provide a forum for discourses about interior life. And yet, as consideration of liturgical "I"-speech will reveal, Byzantine Christian models for the self tended toward conformity rather than individuation. Rather than being interested in how selves differed from each other, clergy promoted—and strove to inhabit—a model selfhood that recognized sin and called out for redemption. This self replicated itself through a biblical hermeneutic that read

Adam, David, and various sinners of the New Testament in a consistent light. Even with various linguistic structures and varied biblical stories, liturgical subjects converged on a single liturgical type.

Byzantine hymnography offered performances of the self where the singer modeled conscience-stricken interiority. In vocalizing such interiority, liturgical poets testify to a Byzantine Christian aesthetics of the self that proves to be relatively common. The corpus of Romanos, the subject of Chapter 2, helped develop an introspective conscience in Byzantium because it synthesizes the speech-in-character of the guilt-ridden Christian as normative speech. Romanos's "I" voiced a generalized model for Christian self-understanding. Later poets, such as Andrew (Chapter 5) and the Stoudites (Chapter 6) revised and sharpened this model, and their work reflects evolving conceptions of Christian self-formation as, at least in part, the sharing of this penitent voice. Moreover, this subjectivity took the stage in other liturgical forums to define both the individual and the collective. The flow of the liturgical calendar (Chapter 3) and the Divine Liturgy of the Eucharist (Chapter 4) formed penitent congregations engaged in ritual celebration to define and recognize themselves.

The Psalms and the Penitential Self

The biblical Psalms provided the most important repository of "I"-speech for Byzantine Christian religious life. As the primary prayer book of the Church, the Psalter exemplified Christian interior disposition, providing both its diction and its emotional range. In his *Letter to Markellinos*, a sort of liturgical guidebook on how to chant the Psalms, the fourth-century Patriarch of Alexandria, Athanasios, explained that the Psalms taught the Christian how to pray. Chanting the Psalms revoiced the words of David, and in the process one made the words one's own. According to Athanasios, once one set aside the prophetic passages in which the Psalms predicted the coming of the Messiah, one utters the rest "as his own words, and sings them as if they were written concerning him."[45] He promoted the chanting of the Psalms in part because they provided a script for understanding the self. "These words become like a mirror to the person singing them, so that he might perceive himself and the emotions of his soul, and thus affected, he might recite them." Moreover, these affects transmitted to listeners and changed their self-recognition and response to God: "For in fact he who hears the one reading receives the song that is recited as being about him, and either, when he is convicted by his conscience, being pierced, he will repent, or hearing of the hope that resides in God, and of the succor available to believers—how this kind of grace exists for him—he exults and begins to give thanks to God."[46] So the hearer also should be "deeply moved, as though he himself were speaking."[47] The multivocal words of the Psalms are at once David's and Christ's; written by the inspiration of the Holy Spirit, they are also the words of the inner self: "Each psalm is both spoken and composed by the Spirit so that in these same words . . . the stirrings of our souls might be grasped, and all of them be said as concerning us, and the same issue from us as our own words."[48] In this way, the ritual singing of psalms both expressed and shaped interior life.

The interiority that emerges in conformity to the Psalms proceeds not through a discovery of the individual, but by absorbing the subject into preexistent models. We can see this difference from modern and modernist theories of the self in early Byzantine understandings of appropriate and inappropriate dispositions. Far from charting a trajectory toward a spontaneous inner self or the revelation of an independent core identity, the practices of the monastic life proceeded according to biblical patterns. Referring to the great ascetic theorist Evagrios of Pontus (died 399), David Brakke has questioned the Foucaultian model for interior self-formation in late ancient monastic life. Rather than finding an interior self verbalized and renounced, Brakke stresses that for Evagrios, the thoughts that entered the monk's mind came not from within, but rather from exterior demons; indeed, in some important sense, they "were not in fact his thoughts at all."[49] Moreover, the remedy for these thoughts was not further introspection, but rather the recitation of biblical verses, including many from the Psalms, a "talking back," to ward off the evil demons. Evagrios's ascetic instruction thus moved away from developing a distinct self and toward constructing a biblically scripted, generic Christian identity. Such a theory of subjectivity undergirded lay formation as well; indeed, Athanasios probably composed the *Letter to Markellinos* for a layman. As in method acting, the goal was to become the speaker of the script.[50]

While the Bible could offer many models for accessing the self, Byzantine liturgical practice encouraged identification especially with penitential patterns. This narrowing focus on the self as sinner manifested most dramatically in the treatment of the Psalms. To be sure, these biblical prayers voice a range of emotions: they raise up shouts of joy and exultation; they offer praise and thanksgiving to God and consolation to the mournful; they celebrate divine victory and kingship.[51] And while Athanasios did not focus exclusively on penitential themes, subsequent Byzantines highlighted the Psalms' ability to shape feelings of inwardly directed grief, remorse, and contrition. Athanasios instructed that when someone sang Psalm 50 [51], he "spoke the proper words of his own repentance."[52] Thus psalm recitation conformed the self to scripture's voice because the Psalms stood at the center of prayer life for monastics as well as lay people, who chanted them either in private or in the services of the so-called cathedral rite of secular churches.[53] Thus to a great extent, the experience of praying the Psalms shaped the conception of the self in relation to God.

The practice of psalmody also reveals the complex gendering of the liturgical self. While the speakers of the biblical Psalms may seem on the page to be exclusively male, with most ascribed traditionally to David himself, in Byzantine Christianity, as in other liturgical traditions, both men and women chanted the Psalms. The Psalter and the Liturgy of the Hours belonged to monasteries and convents alike; lay men and women prayed the Psalms in private devotions.[54] Lay men and women worshiped together in cathedrals and parishes, although segregated by gender, with men usually in the central naos, or nave, and women in the side aisles or the upper galleries.[55] Hagiography regularly registers devotion to the Psalms as a mark of women's piety as much as men's.[56] Byzantine Christian women assimilated the voices of the Psalms as their own. About the disparate impact of such rituals we can, mostly, merely speculate. Liturgically sanctioned identities can only tell us so much about the interiority of actual people, whether male or female.[57] At the very least, we must understand that in practice, the speaker of the Psalms was both male and female, or either male or female, depending on performance contexts. Women took on the role of David, or possibly Christ, and in other contexts women identified with Adam, and men sang the Magnificat of Mary. The voice of abjection crossed gendered boundaries.[58]

Christians developed a variety of schemes for assigning the 150 Psalms of the Greek Bible, the Septuagint, to the separate prayer services of the day, although two systems eventually predominated in Byzantium. By the ninth century, the system of Hagia Sophia in Constantinople appointed the entirety of the Psalms over a two-week cycle, while in monasteries a system derived from Palestine divided the Psalter into twenty *kathismata*, "seatings" or "sessions," over one week.[59] Some psalms, however, took a more prominent role in shaping prayer life, both monastic and lay, because they were chanted or recited daily as fixed elements of the office. From the fourth century, monks and laity alike chanted or heard Psalm 50 [51], the voicing of one's own penitence, at every Morning Prayer service.[60] Tradition held that psalm as David's greatest expression of repentance, composed after the prophet Nathan had rebuked him for arranging the murder of Uriah the Hittite and taking Uriah's wife, Bathsheba, for himself. With its expression of abject contrition and petition for divine forgiveness, Psalm 50 provided the essential script for Christian confession:

> Have mercy on me, O God, according to your great mercy,
> and according to the abundance of your compassion blot out my
>   lawless deed [τὸ ἀνόμημά μου].
>
> Wash me thoroughly from my lawlessness [ἀνομία]
> and from my sin [ἁμαρτία] cleanse me
>
> because my lawlessness I know
> and my sin is ever before me.
>
> Against you alone did I sin [ἥμαρτον], and what is evil before you I did,
> so that you may be justified in your words and be victorious in your
>   judgment. (Ps 50:3–6 [51:1–4])

Later Byzantine hymnographers frequently quoted and adapted this so-familiar text, crafting their own expressions of repentance in close intertextual relation to this biblical template.

While these words shaped the penitential character of the daily office, they were by no means the only elements of fixed psalmody to effect such a subjectivity. Beginning in Palestine in the sixth century, monks adopted the practice of chanting a set of six psalms, known as the *Hexapsalmos*, at the opening of Morning Prayer, preceding Psalm 50. These consisted of Psalms 3, 37 [38], 62 [63], 87 [88], 102 [103], and 142 [143].[61] While these psalms touched on a number of themes and expressed a variety of affects, key verses illustrated a typical monastic subject's interiority troubled by guilt and imploring God for forgiveness. In fact, these psalms offered an affective itinerary, not so much a single state of mind as a sequence of dispositions.[62] Most likely the monks of the Stoudios Monastery in the early ninth century first brought this practice to Constantinople. That the Hexapsalmos was omitted only during the joyful week after Easter confirms that monks heard this grouping as particularly penitential.[63] Originally all the monks recited these psalms together: the Typikon, or rule, of the Stoudios Monastery indicates "*We* begin the six psalms,"[64] but eventually this duty fell to a single brother, a practice that had likely developed in Palestine by the eleventh century. Later rubrics instructed monks how to focus on the penitential aspects of these psalms by applying them to themselves: "The assigned brother chants the Hexapsalmos softly, with quietude and attention. So also all stand as though they were in the presence of God himself and praying because of their sins."[65] This instruction distinguished the Hexapsalmos from the collective chanting of the cycle of psalmody assigned in the Psalter throughout the week: for these, the monks were permitted [to sit. Instructions for the performance highlighted the solemnity of the practice and encouraged the application of the content of the six psalms to the entire community: "The brother must chant in a simple and humble voice, in such a way as to be heard by all."[66]

Many verses in the Hexapsalmos, whether chanted at the opening of Morning Prayer or occurring in the usual cycle of weekly or bi-weekly psalm assignments, portray a self fearful of a punishment deserved: "O Lord, do not rebuke me in your anger / or discipline me in your wrath" (Ps 37:2 [38:1]). Knowing God to be justifiably enraged prompts the subject to prepare for impending punishment and to confess: "I am ready for scourges . . . my lawlessness I will report, / and I will show anxiety [μεριμνήσω] over my sin" (Ps 37:18–19 [38:17–18]). Reciting or hearing such words should effect such an attitude toward one's self. Elsewhere in the set, the subject explains the wayward path taken away from God's commandments: "Because my soul was full of troubles / and my life drew near to Hell, / I was counted among those who go down into a pit" (Ps 87:4–5 [88:3–4]). But the narrative of descent leads to liturgy, as the recitation of the Hexapsalmos at Morning Prayer itself becomes the occasion to petition God for mercy:

> And I, O Lord, cried out to you
> and in the morning my prayer will anticipate [προφθάσει] you.
>
> Why, O Lord, do you cast off my soul,
> do you turn away your face from me?
> . . . .
> Your wrath swept over me; your terrors threw me in disarray.
>   (Ps 87:14–15, 17 [88: 13–14, 16])

Elsewhere in the sequence, the speaker pleads with God, "Do not enter into judgment with your slave, / because no one living will be counted righteous before you" (142 [143]: 2), and in another verse that would be especially poignant at the first service of the day, calls out, "Make me hear your mercy in the morning" (142 [143]: 8). The Hexapsalmos thus framed the practice of psalmody as a practice of petition—as set prayer rehearsing a speech-in-character applicable to each member of the community. But the abject appeal also takes place in a context that offers assurance. Psalm 102 [103] stresses God's pity and teaches that he judges humanity "not according to our sins . . . nor according to our acts of lawlessness" (Ps 102 [103]: 10).

> Compassionate and merciful is the Lord,
> slow to anger and abounding in mercy.
>
> He will not be totally angry,
> nor will he keep his wrath forever. (Ps 102 [103]: 8–9)

Within the structure of Sabaite Morning Prayer established at the Stoudios Monastery in the ninth century, the Hexapsalmos precedes the kathisma, the session or portion, of psalms appointed for the day, which are then followed by Psalm 50, perhaps the most abject expression of contrition. Thus these penitential verses bracket the variable parts of the service, confirming the penitential character of the whole service, and indeed of monastic life in general.

The speech of the Psalms thus defined the penitent subject, teaching the Christian how to pray, how to recognize oneself in one's iniquity, and how to call upon God for mercy. The Psalms also formed God as a character in the narrative of sin and redemption, calling on God to play the appropriate part. Psalm 6, not part of the Hexapsalmos but merely a psalm that appeared regularly in the rotation, richly illustrates the sinful subject's effort to define and script the relation between the human and divine subjects:

> O Lord, do not rebuke me in your anger
> nor discipline [παιδεύσῃς] me in your wrath.
>
> Have mercy on me, O Lord, because I am weak;
> heal me, O Lord, because my bones were troubled.
>
> And my soul was troubled very much,
> and you, O Lord—how long?
>
> Turn, O Lord; rescue my soul;
> save me for the sake of your mercy. (6:2–5 [1–4])

Commenting on these verses, Theodoret observed that David offered this supplication to God, "begging to be healed." "He does not beg to be censured in anger, nor does he plead not to be disciplined, but not to suffer it with wrath. Discipline me like a father, he asks, not like a judge; like a physician, not like a torturer. Do not fit the punishment to the crime; instead, temper justice with loving-kindness."[67] The Christian subject formed in the space between confidence and concern about an omniscient and all-forgiving deity. Moreover, this self was not static, assuming a single affective state, but rather the Christian subject experienced moral growth through a narrative of recognition and acceptance. Such a biblically sanctioned model for supplication shapes more than one liturgical subject, envisioning God as vividly as the self. Chanting the psalm co-positions the self and God, coaxing God himself to be a certain sort of subject, also a subject of prayer, formed as fatherly, compassionate, and merciful.

Sin and Human Nature

Byzantine Orthodox identification with biblical sinners and with the sin-recognizing "I"-speech of the Psalter raises questions about the place of sin in Byzantine religious thought. Historians of Byzantine theology have often stressed the absence of a doctrine of original sin in Orthodoxy. Free of the impact of Augustine's refutation of Pelagius and Julian of Eclanum, the Greek East never held that humans remained responsible for their first ancestor's transgressions, a sinful stain that Augustine held passed from fathers to their children genetically through semen.[68] Byzantine theologians tended to hold that humans were not intrinsically sinful by nature, since God created that nature. Rather, humans sinned by choice, through acts of will.[69] At the same time, while humans do not share Adam's sin, they share his mortality, the consequence of sin, and they certainly share in his proclivity for disobedience to divine command. Thus each human bears the weight of sin.

Such a conception of human sinfulness, or rather the human tendency toward sin, pervades the Byzantine hymnographic tradition. Liturgy thus disseminated broadly this view of the self responsible for sin, to monks and laity alike. Adam remained iconic. Andrew of Crete, in his *Great Kanon*, made a litany of his request that God take from him "the burdensome collar of sin."[70] He lamented,

Adam was justly cast forth from Eden, O Savior
for not keeping one commandment of yours:
what then shall I suffer, always setting aside your lifegiving words? (1.6)

In the *Lament of Adam*, quoted earlier, Adam provided the archetype of the human self. Humanity shared with Adam the need to lament and repent. As the seventh-century monastic teacher John Klimax wrote, "Adam did not weep before the fall, and there will be no tears after the resurrection when sin will be abolished, when pain, sorrow, and lamentation will have taken flight."[71] In the meantime, sin required compunction and tears. Liturgists sought to prompt compunction from all participants. And as John explained, "Compunction is an everlasting [ἀέvvαoς] torment of the conscience which brings about the cooling of the fire of the heart though spiritual confession [διὰ νοερᾶς ἐξαγορεύσεως]."[72] Later, Symeon the New Theologian would teach that Adam's gravest fault was not his disobedience, but his failure to repent.[73] Byzantine theological anthropologies, theories of the sinful self, often lie implicit in prayers and hymns.

In large part, Byzantine liturgy named the self as sinner. In their work on identity in modernity, Louis Althusser and Judith Butler have stressed the role of what they call "interpellation." In interpellation, the state or its organs call out a name, which provides identity as the subject identifies with that speech. In Althusser's classic example a policeman calls out to a person running away, "Hey you, there!" And the person hailed—*a presumed thief*—turns around, accepting the terms on which she has been hailed, forming her subjectivity in accepting guilt.[74] Byzantine prayers, hymns, and sermons ritualize interpellation, performing speech acts that call a sinful identity into being through accusation and its acceptance.

The Liturgical Calendar: Feasts, Lectionaries, and the Problems of the Evidence

While the Psalms scripted the subject over the course of the weekly cycle, and the Eucharist emphasized the identity of the Christian group through frequent repetition, the rhythms of the liturgical year played an equally significant part in the shaping of the Christian subject.[75] Even before the sixth century, the Byzantine liturgical calendar (the subject of Chapter 3) celebrated the life of Christ, with Christ's birth at Christmas on December 25; his baptism on Epiphany, or Theophany, on January 6, and Christ's entry into Jerusalem, his passion, death, and resurrection during Great and Holy Week and Easter. Lectionaries, or cycles of biblical readings, fit the right text to the right moment. On the major festivals, lections from the Gospels narrated the events celebrated. In late antique Jerusalem, these were often read where the events were believed to have taken place; elsewhere they were read from the church's pulpit or a public square in the course of a procession.[76] During the eucharistic liturgy in both Jerusalem and Constantinople, the account of the Nativity from Matthew 2 was read at Christmas, while the story of Christ's baptism in the Jordan from Matthew 3 was read on Epiphany.[77] On Great and Holy Friday, the passion narratives from all four Gospels were read out in the course of a long service.[78] Much of the hymnography for the festal cycle emphasized not so much the "I" as the "we," situating the entire congregation—itself a collection of "I"s—with respect to the biblical narrative and calling on Christians to identify themselves as a group as the objects of God's grace in his incarnation, suffering, and death.

The assignment of lections proper to specific days of the liturgical cycle differed from place to place and changed somewhat over time. Our early evidence for Jerusalem is much better than for Constantinople. Armenian and Georgian manuscripts provide excellent witnesses for the lectionary system in use in Jerusalem in late antiquity. Both the Armenian and Georgian lectionaries of Jerusalem are based on Greek originals, although both also show adaptation for the religious communities that used them. The Armenian lectionary reflects the lessons and psalms in use in the first half of the fifth century. The Georgian lectionary, as reconstructed from a number of manuscripts, witnesses the assignments in use around 700, although in most cases these assignments are obviously earlier.[79] For key feasts, the readings of Jerusalem influenced the selections in the capital, but for much of the year, Constantinople developed its own traditions of apportioning scripture. Reconstructing the cycle of readings in Constantinople in this period is more difficult. The two earliest manuscript witnesses to the cycle of readings in the capital date from the early and later tenth century respectively. Although these versions vary slightly, together they represent the lectionary or *Typikon of the Great Church*, the cycle of readings in use at Hagia Sophia by the early tenth century, which then became normative for the Byzantine Orthodox Church.[80] Some details of this set of propers had probably been established by the sixth century, as sermons or hymns sometimes confirm.

Lectionary systems could be especially sensitive to the progression of the festal cycle. Psalm verses in particular might provide an apt commentary on the liturgical moment: in ninth-century Constantinople for the Eucharist on Ascension, marking Christ's bodily departure on the Mount of Olives, the appropriate reading from Acts 1 narrating the ascension was preceded by Psalm 107:6 [108:5], "Be exalted to the heavens, O God, and over all the earth your glory." Then a verse from Psalm 46:6 [47:5], "God went up with a shout, the Lord with a sound of a trumpet," both preceded the parallel account of the ascension in Luke 24 and served as the hymn as people approached the sacrament of Communion.[81] Jerusalem developed and Constantinople adapted Vigil services featuring twelve (or more) readings from prophetic scriptures to anticipate both Christmas and Easter.[82] Because hymnography was keyed to the lectionary, knowing what was read on a given day illuminates the themes or biblical quotations chosen for a liturgical composition. Moreover, first-person speech in hymns varies with the liturgical calendar; like the lections, the hymns were assigned to specific days of the year. The self at Christmas varied from the progression of selves over the course of Lent. And at the same time, fundamental conceptions of the Christian person in relation to both God and the biblical narrative governed all these liturgical subjects throughout the year. In fact, as we shall see, the "I"-speech in Byzantine liturgy clustered especially around Lent. The penitential subject appropriate to the season of fasting and reflection predominated in Byzantine ritual performances of the self.

*   *   *

The pages that follow chart the performance and display of the Byzantine liturgical subject. This subject came into focus as the object of two gazes: both the inwardly directed vision of the subject over his or her own formation and the gaze of an all-seeing God. Christ looked upon the viewer at once in judgment and compassion. This bifurcation of Christ's aspect toward the self animates the famous portrait icon now in the Monastery of St. Catherine at Mount Sinai, probably painted in Constantinople toward the end of the sixth century (Figure 1). His right hand blesses the viewer, while his left holds a jeweled Gospel Book. His body is at once in motion and at rest. The slope and angle of his shoulders suggest that Christ has just shifted his attention toward the viewer. His face looks directly out. On the left side of Christ's face—the viewer's right—the brow knits as the eye narrows and the face darkens in shadow; the corner of the lip turns down in a scowl. The God of judgment

Figure 1. Panel icon of Christ. Sixth century. 84 x 45.5 cm. Holy Monastery of Saint Catherine, Sinai, Egypt. Photo: Agnieszka Szymańska.

looks out in wrath. But on the right side of his face, Christ's expression light-
ens and his mouth relaxes. His eye wells up with a compassionate tear.[83] Intimately, the image presents Christ as God of justice and mercy, both scolding
and comforting the viewer. It forms viewers as subjects of the divine gaze.
How did God see them? And how might they see themselves through God's
eyes?

The next three chapters address Christian identities and selfhoods in the
Byzantine Orthodox synthesis of the sixth century. The hymns of Romanos
give ear to Byzantine Christian voices, both spoken aloud publicly in the first
person singular and echoed within as internal speech. The celebration of the
liturgical calendar, by contrast, formed a communal identity of Christians
present to scriptural events as narrated in the lectionary, enlivened in hymns
and sermons, and imaged in artistic representation. The prayers recited at
the Divine Liturgy during the consecration of the body and blood of Christ
further interpreted the congregation as a community of sinners, each self a
penitent, and framed the Eucharist a penitential rite. The subsequent two
chapters carry this Byzantine self forward through the Dark Ages and into
the cultural renaissance of the ninth century. We shall watch and listen as
Andrew of Crete reinterprets the whole corpus of the Bible as a penitential
text. The production of a new hymnal for Lent at the Stoudios Monastery reveals the remarkable flexibility of Byzantine chant to shape interior lives and
instill emotions. Finally, we leave the realm of formal liturgy to explore the
repurposing of ritual behavior in the monastic exercises of Symeon the New
Theologian. Ultimately Byzantine Christians' theories about the efficacy of
liturgy reflected confidence about the shaping and making of the self.

CHAPTER 2

Romanos the Melodist and the Christian Self

Within his hymns, the sixth-century liturgical poet Romanos the Melodist gave voice to a wide range of biblical characters.[1] He composed dialogues, imaginatively reconstructing the interactions of biblical personae. In his Christological hymns, his audience might witness Christ's interaction with Mary, Peter, Thomas, or the Harlot who anointed Jesus while at supper.[2] In hymns on Old Testament themes, his listeners attended the narratives of Abraham and Sarah, Joseph, and Jonah. Keying his hymns to the events of the liturgical calendar, Romanos gave psychological depth to biblical heroes and villains, modeling a whole range of possible interactions both with the sacred stories and with God himself. Andrew Louth has written, "For Romanos the kontakion is a form of liturgical story-telling. In each case, an event, as related in the Scriptures and celebrated in the Liturgy, is retold in such a way as to enable those who hear it to enter into it."[3] And Georgia Frank stresses the hymns' articulation of the place of biblical narrative in early Byzantine ritual drama, arguing that "Romanos's hymns . . . represent the emergence of biblical epic in the context of Christian worship."[4]

Biblical characters, however, are not the only persons who sing in Romanos's hymns. The poet often gave voice to himself. In approximately half of the undisputedly genuine hymns, the cantor sings in the first person singular in the prelude, or prooemion [προοίμιον], or in the first and the final strophes.[5] The frequency with which Romanos sings himself within his poems prompts inquiry into the construction of the poems' "I." What is on display in these first-person passages? J. H. Barkhuizen took a formalist approach to the preludes and final strophes, cataloguing a variety of prayer types employed, including doxology, confession, and exhortation.[6] In their adherence to standard forms, these passages offer an important window on early Byzantine piety and self-expression. As the creation of a clergyman intending

to educate his flock, the "I" performs a type (*typos*) for the Byzantine Christian self that Romanos sought to impart. Romanos's hymns consist of a short
prelude and approximately eighteen to twenty-four strophes, called *oikoi*, or
houses (cf. Italian, *stanza*), of identical meter and melody. Unfortunately, the
original tunes for these compositions have been lost. For a third of the corpus
Romanos composed his own melodies, while for the rest, he used existing
tunes.[7] The last line of the prelude introduces a refrain that recurs at the end
of each of the subsequent strophes. Most scholars believe that the congregation joined in the refrain, which is usually fairly simple, although the congregants may have been aided by a choir that had practiced in advance of the
Vigil.[8]

    As a deacon in the church, Romanos's task lay not so much in form-
ing himself as in shaping the religious understanding and experience of his
congregants. The hymns, termed kontakia only in the ninth century, are
chanted verse sermons, keyed to the events of the liturgical calendar and the
emerging lectionary cycle of Constantinople. Most were performed during
the Night Vigils that preceded principal feasts. Attended by the laity, these
urban services included the chanting of psalms and readings from scripture,
apparently often the biblical lections appointed for the following day.[9] Although in the late fourth and early fifth centuries, John Chrysostom sought
to exclude women from attending vigils, worried in part about the safety of
women afoot in the city at night, other evidence firmly establishes the presence of women as well as men at such nocturnal services.[10] The biography of
the late fifth-century Constantinopolitan abbess, Matrona of Perge, reports
than when she was younger and married, "she was one of those women who
devoted themselves to all-night psalmody," although her husband "thought
she was living the life of a courtesan because of her frequent attendance at
all-night vigils."[11] The seventh-century *Miracles of Artemios* describes a number of women in attendance at night at that miracle-working shrine, where,
among other things, a cantor regularly chanted the hymns of Romanos.[12] Lay
men and women were thus both formed by what they heard.

    If the edges of these hymns form the "I," the core of the texts enacts the
stories of the biblical characters, the "I"s of the biblical past. Here too Romanos seeks to shape the Christian self. The men and women who interacted
with Christ serve as models for emulation. Minor incidents in the Gospels,
such as a healing or a conversation about redemption, provide entrees into
the minds of biblical figures. Romanos not only provides them with speeches
far beyond the few words afforded them in the Gospels, he often grants

them interior reflection. In their monologues, Romanos offers his audience a chance to ponder how biblical characters might have been present to themselves. However, in Romanos's hands this exploration of interiority eschews what we might term historical realism or even particularity. Rather than presenting a variety of personalities, Romanos portrays his biblical subjects as ideal Christian types whose thoughts pattern the way he would like his congregants' thoughts to proceed.

In their presentation of an ideal piety, the hymns of Romanos offer important evidence for the history of the self in Byzantium. Thus this chapter's investigation of Romanos's poetics of the self considers in turn Romanos's performance of his own subjectivity, his efforts to form the subjectivity of his congregants, and his representation of the inner experience of his biblical subjects, the characters from the Bible that he so vividly reinvents.

The Cantor's First-Person Speech

Romanos's first-person passages reveal the liturgical formation of the singer's identity and the poetics of the Christian self. In the final strophe of a hymn *On the Ten Virgins*, the wise among whom keep vigil during the night for the coming of Christ, Romanos turns to himself. Singing in his own voice, he situates himself within the divine drama, taking the role of a supplicant in need of God's help. He prays to be able to carry out the Christian teachings that he himself advocates even as he confesses his failure to do so.

> Release me, release me, Savior, condemned as I am by all men,
> For I do not do what I tell the people and advise them to do.
> And therefore I fall down before you; grant contrition, Savior, both
>   to me and to those who hear me,
> so that we may uphold all your commandments in our lives.[13]

Sometimes it is difficult to know which day of the liturgical calendar Romanos was writing for, since we do not possess a lectionary for sixth-century Constantinople, and the assignments in the surviving manuscripts of his hymns may rather reflect their placement in middle Byzantine liturgical practice. In this case, however, it seems most likely that Romanos chanted these verses for the vigil following Vespers on Tuesday of Holy Week. The eleventh-century manuscripts assign the hymn to that Tuesday, which corresponds both with the assignment of Matthew 24:36–26:2 to the service of Vespers in the tenth-century lectionary for Constantinople and the assignment of Matthew 24:3–26:2 in the late antique lectionary of Jerusalem.[14] The convergence in the two lectionary systems strongly suggests that some form of the lection was also in use in the capital in Romanos's time. This long reading from the Gospel encompasses Jesus' predictions of the coming of the End and of the Son of Man; the parable of the wise and foolish virgins; and the prediction that "after two days" the Son of Man will be handed over to be crucified. Thus the Gospel presents Jesus as speaking two days before his arrest on Thursday night. Romanos's hymn touches on each of these themes and highlights prophecies of the End.

In the context of Jesus' prediction of the coming judgment and the need to repent soon, Romanos presents himself among the unprepared, as an imperfect teacher, confessing that he does not practice what he preaches, in need not only of pardon but even of contrition. He rhetorically prostrates himself before God, verbally enacting the posture of penance. While the poet addresses God, his primary audience for this prayer for salvation is the gathering of lay Christians who have come to church to hear him chant. He prays not only for himself but on their behalf as well. He presents himself not so much to confess himself, but to model such a confessing self for his listeners.

Where he sings in the first person singular, the openings and closings of the hymns engage in the production of Romanos the Melodist. His persona emerges as an effect of these strophes. With reference to another early Christian author, Averil Cameron has written, "the self-conscious Christian creates his own self, and does so through the medium of texts, which in turn assume the function of models."[15] The "I" of Romanos's poems participates in self-presentation and self-disclosure. It engages in introspection and divulges its interiority. It identifies itself as the subject of interrogation and accusation. Generated through processes of confession, it names itself as sinner. Romanos's "I" is the product of a particular knowledge of the self, formed within a Christian narrative of fault and redemption. The poet, moreover, does not claim exclusive right over his conception of the self, but rather presents it with generalizing force: all those who hear him need God's assistance; all must inevitably acknowledge their sins.

The consideration of the self within the hymns of Romanos does not, in fact, entail the search for the biographical or historical Romanos within his corpus. Despite the frequent appearance of the "I" in the poems, Romanos left few traces of his life-story in his works. Nearly anything that might qualify as historical information about Romanos derives not from his poems, but rather from brief notices in middle Byzantine service books. It is here that we learn that the poet was born in the Syrian city of Emesa (modern Homs) and served as a deacon in the Church of the Resurrection in Beirut before arriving in Constantinople during the reign of Anastasios I, that is, before 518. These sources inform us that he served as a cantor and composer at the Church of the Theotokos in the Kyrou district in the northwest corner of the capital, where he was eventually buried.[16] Romanos wrote hymns for a wide variety of liturgical feasts during much of the reign of Justinian, of which at least sixty survive. He died sometime after 555. Attempts to situate Romanos within the political and religious contexts of Justinian's reign depend, albeit often quite reasonably, on inference and conjecture.[17]

In each of Romanos's hymns, the initial letters of each strophe form an acrostic, usually some variant of the phrase, "BY THE HUMBLE ROMANOS." Through these acrostics, which could not be heard in performance, Romanos attached his identity to the texts and identified himself—tacitly—with a principal Christian virtue, namely humility.[18] While the poet encrypted his identity as "the humble Romanos" into the hymns' acrostics, he scripted other aspects of his persona into the audible text, generating a performable identity, the subject of the poems' first-person singular speech. In some sense, then, the first-person passages in the opening and closing strophes are auto-biographical, scripting the self, but not because they provide historical details about the poet. Despite an outward display of inner turmoil, Romanos reveals no coherent individual narrative of the self, no story of Romanos. Here Romanos does not so much give evidence for the interior religious life of the Melodist, as provide a repertoire of performances of the self at prayer.[19] As in his treatment of biblical figures, these passages present characterizations. In his first-person speech, Romanos proffers a style of Christian self-presentation together with its implied patterns for Christian self-understanding.

The Prospect of Judgment and the Formation of the Conscience

One place to look for the self in the works of Romanos is in his characterization of the conscience, the interior dialogue about right and wrong. Romanos's performance of conscience-stricken self-regard animates his hymn *On the Second Coming*. The middle Byzantine manuscript tradition assigns the hymn to Meatfare Sunday, a week (that is, two Sundays) before the beginning of Lent, part of the introduction to the penitential season. Moreover, meditation on the Second Coming on this Sunday is attested both in the tenth-century lectionary for Constantinople, which assigns the reading of Matthew 25:31–46 and its description of the Great Judgment, and in the ninth-century service book for Lent, known as the Triodion, which includes a hymn attributed to Theodore the Stoudite on this very subject.[20] Even so, we cannot be entirely certain if this is the day for which Romanos composed his hymn, although he expands on precisely these themes. He quotes and alludes to a wide variety of apocalyptic passages from the Bible in the course of the hymn, and while the tenor certainly fits the mood of the run-up to Lent, which already in Romanos's time included these preparatory weeks, we cannot know precisely which lection Romanos responded to.[21]

Whatever the actual occasion, the poem engages in a sustained meditation on the end of time. In the first strophe, singing in the first person, Romanos frames a sinner's response to the prophecy of the Last Judgment.

> When I think of your dread tribunal, O Lord supremely good,
> and the day of judgment,
> accused by conscience [συνείδησις], I quake and tremble.[22]

Here Romanos becomes the exemplar of a penitent Christian, wracked with guilt at the prospect of eternal punishment. Already here on earth, his conscience makes its accusation in light of a juridical process to come.

> When you are about to take your seat on your throne [see Matt.
>   25:31] and make examination,
> then none will be able to deny their sins,
> where truth is the accuser and dread the warden (34.1; trans. Lash
>   221)

In the present, interior reflection acts as a stand-in for the principle of "truth," which will prosecute the sinner in the divine court of the age to come. Romanos dramatizes how the fear of judgment effects the formation of conscience.

Romanos depicts the Christian conscience as an interior courtroom. As the first strophe of the hymn indicates, the conscience convicts the self in anticipation of eschatological judgment. Toward the end of the poem, Romanos once again interjects himself, identifying as the subject of divine wrath:

At the home of judgment, how great and how many the lamentations
    of the condemned—
of whom I am one and the first. (34.22; trans. Lash 229; cf. 1 Tim 1:15)

And in the final strophe, Romanos models for the congregation petitionary
and intercessory prayer in light of his conscience's judgment:

All-holy Savior of the world, as you appeared and raised up nature
that was lying in offences,
    as you are compassionate, appear invisibly to me also, O
        Long-Suffering.
Raise me up, I beg, as I lie in many sins,
because what I say and advise for others I do not observe.
But I implore you, give me time for repentance,
and, at the intercessions of the Ever-Virgin and Mother of God,
    spare me
and do not cast me away from your presence,
    Judge most just. (34.24; trans. Lash, 230)

Here Romanos echoes the language and voice of the penitential psalms, especially Psalm 50:13 [51:11]: "Do not cast me away from you presence, and
do not take your holy spirit from me." Following a biblical model, Romanos
performs a troubled conscience praying for mercy, instilling practices of introspection and fear in preparation for judgment. Romanos thus cues not
only a reaction to biblical predictions of the judgment to come, but to his own
hymnographic explorations. Romanos's hymn should incite pity and fear and
trembling in the members of his audience as a sympathetic response to his
own self-performance.

    Perhaps the most elaborate performance of the self in the corpus of Ro-
manos's hymns is the *Prayer of Romanos*. The text survives only in a single
eleventh-century manuscript, which assigns it to the fifth Wednesday in Lent,
but this placement likely reflects other, later additions to the liturgy for that
week, including the eighth-century *Great Kanon* of Andrew of Crete to the following day.[23] Either Romanos composed the hymn for the season of Lent or he
intended to bring penitential themes to another moment in the year. Rather
than reflecting on a single biblical text or liturgical event, Romanos uses the
poem to take stock of himself and cultivate introspection. Once again, eternal punishment prompts the searching and exposure of the soul. Romanos

inscribes the conscience within an elaborate juridical model, one that oper-
ates in the present in anticipation of divine judgment and sentence. "Secretly
I forever flog myself, for my own conscience condemns me [τὸ συνειδὸς γὰρ
ἑαυτοῦ καταδικάζει με]" (56.12), he declaims. His conscience takes the parts of
both prosecutor and magistrate in an interior court. He declares,

> I have as tribunal [κριτήριον] my own reproach [ἔλεγχος] that pun-
>   ishes me
> before I will reach and suffer eternal torment. (56.12)

Subjected to his own trial and self-conviction, Romanos is vividly wracked
with guilt.

In the context of the Night Vigil, Romanos's performance of anxiety
models outwardly and liturgically what he believed should happen interiorly,
within the conscience of each person who heard him. Our poet-deacon models this interiority not for his own sake, but rather for the sake of his audience.
The hymns of Romanos demonstrate that early Byzantine lay Christians witnessed and were expected to apply models for articulating the self through
reflexive scrutiny. Romanos's discursive and performative presentation of the
self suggests ways that early Byzantine Christians might regard themselves,
indeed how they might be present to themselves as the products of their own
self-reflection.

The Typological Self

The early Byzantine self on display in the poems of Romanos, while affording
little access to Romanos the individual, grants a view of the Christian person
embedded in and responding to the lectionary and the liturgical cycle. The
self that emerges is a trope of the self, at once a generic Christian self and a
self listening to biblical narrative. Typically, Romanos contrasts himself to
the biblical exemplar discussed in a hymn, modeling self-consciousness as an
appropriate response to the sacred story. As a by-product of biblical exegesis, Romanos constructs this self in dialectical relationship with the biblical
lection.

In the first strophe of the same hymn *On the Ten Virgins*, most probably
written for the Tuesday of Holy Week, Romanos models for his audience how
to meditate on the meaning of the gospel passage:

> When I heard the sacred parable of the virgins, which is in the
>   Gospels,
> I stopped, stirring up reflections and thoughts [ἐνθυμήσεις καὶ
>   λογισμούς]:
> How was it that the ten possessed the virtue of immaculate virginity,
> and yet for five virgins the suffering remained fruitless
> whereas the others shone with lamps of humanity? (47.1)

Such passages have a hermeneutic function, as the poet guides his audience to contemplate the moral point of the passage. Romanos models devotional life in the moral exegesis of scripture. Scripture itself functions dynamically, able to effect "reflections and thoughts," not merely on the lectionary passage, but on the self. Scriptural readings thus have a reflexive function for the listener.

Romanos's self-insertion, his reflexive view of himself, usually consists in his recognition that he does not compare favorably with biblical exemplars. He expresses desire to imitate biblical models, and implicitly forms such desires in his listeners. But he fails to make the mark. In his liturgical reflection on the story of Abraham's sacrifice of Isaac, a hymn probably composed for the fourth Sunday of Lent as part of cycle of hymns on Old Testament themes for the penitential season, Romanos sings,

> I, a young man [ὁ νέος ἐγώ], wish to imitate you, old man
>   [Abraham]
> as you climb the mountain, but my legs are numb.
> Even if the spirit is willing, the flesh is weak.[24]

Quoting Jesus' warning to the disciples in the garden of Gethsemane (Mt 26:41; cf. Mk 14:38), Romanos invokes the same passage as the one that for Augustine prompted reflection on divergent wills within the human person.[25] Like Augustine, Romanos eschews a dualistic dichotomy between spirit and flesh, locating the problem in the soul, which needs encouragement to follow Abraham's example, even as it will fail to do so. The typological contrast between the "I" of the poem and the patriarch Abraham thus sets up the exegetical project as an exploration not only of the biblical story, but also of the failures of the self.

The exposure of truths about the self through biblical exegesis means that the self consists in an intertextual relationship to scripture. Stitched along the borders of the fabric of biblical narrative, the "I" in the initial and final strophes laments in self-knowledge. Exegesis affords an epistemology of the

self, a tool for self-recognition. More than a simple instance of the moral interpretation of biblical lessons, the interrogation of the self frames and guides
the exegesis within the poem. The goal, or *skopos*, of the dialogic exploration
of the Bible is a typological knowledge of the self.

The power of contrasting the self with biblical types in the formation of
a knowledge of one's subjectivity is acutely manifest in one of Romanos's two
hymns *On Joseph*, ascribed in manuscripts to Monday of Holy Week, and
probably composed as part of a Lenten cycle on Old Testament themes.[26]
Here, Romanos dramatizes Joseph's steadfast rejection of Potiphar's Wife's increasingly lurid sexual advances. In its emphasis on virtues of prudence and
self-control, the hymn, in fact, presents an extended discourse on conscience
and its relation to God's omniscience. The refrain stresses the subjectivation
of all people to divine surveillance: "*Because the eye that never sleeps sees everything.*" The refrain resembles the sentiments of Proverbs 15:3, "The eyes of
the Lord are everywhere, observing the evil and the good," and also echoes
Basil of Caesarea's formulation that "The unsleeping eye sees everything."[27]

As the poem progresses, and the audience observes Joseph persistently
rejecting his would-be seductress, Joseph also is watching himself internally,
observing his own thoughts.

> Even if those we live with do not see our act,
> For they are human and do not see what is hidden,
> Yet I have my conscience [τὸ συνειδός μου] for an accuser[28]
> if I should dare to do this lawless deed. (44.16)

Joseph's conscience is thus able to see what is hidden within himself and has
prosecutorial power to accuse him of sin.[29] The conscience functions as an
aspect of the self that mirrors or replicates the vision of God with respect to
the self. Moreover, this conscience does not work independently of God, but
rather functions entirely on the assumption of God and his divine knowing.
The strophe continues,

> And even if no one would convict [ἐλέγξει] me of adultery,
> I have a judge who needs no proof [ἐλέγχου].
> Always when I think of him [ἐνθυμούμενος], I shudder
> and I flee from shameful pleasures,
>   *because the eye that never sleeps sees everything.* (44.16)

Joseph's conscience thus acts within the context of the contemplation of God. Romanos presents Joseph as a moral model because of his double subjectivation; he lies under the purview of both his conscience and God. Both the conscience and God are able to see what is hidden, and the conscience acts on the soul in order to avoid divine opprobrium.

While Joseph's conscience remains clear, Romanos's does not. At the end of the hymn, the authorial voice engages in pointed self-accusation. Romanos contrasts himself with Joseph:

> When the lewd woman flattered him with word and deed,
> [Joseph] spurned all her shameless promises.
> He chose death rather than the dungeon of lust.
> But what shall I do, miserable and condemned I [ὁ ταλαίπωρος καὶ
>   κατάκριτος ἐγώ],
> since sin always clutches me in her hand? (44.22)

The first-person pronoun, employed with emphatic force at the end of the line, underscores the gap between Romanos and Joseph. Furthermore, the poet hypostatizes Potiphar's Wife as sin itself in all its seductive force. Even as the refrain posits the power of an external observer to shape the behavior of the observed, and even in light of Joseph's ability to employ internal observation to control himself, Romanos confesses a much more complicated relationship with his conscience. He is not like Joseph, who according to the prelude,

> was seen as righteous
> because he feared lest he sin [δεδοικὼς μὴ ἁμαρτῆσαι]. (44, prelude)

The repetition of the refrain through the following twenty-two strophes persistently reinforces the idea that the theater of human performance plays out in a divine panopticon. Within this context, the love of wisdom, *philosophia*, teaches humanity the virtues of "mindfulness," "courage," "prudence and justice" (44.1). Although the Melodist offers Joseph's habits of mind as a model for achieving self-control, he presents himself as an illustration of failure.

For Romanos, conscience, like exegesis, both guides and convicts. As Romanos sings at the end of in his hymn *On Doubting Thomas*:

I am frightened, for I know your counsels,
I know my works. Conscience [συνειδός] troubles me.
Spare me, my Savior.[30]

In contrasting himself with biblical exemplars, Romanos presents a subjectivity different from the subjectivity that he ascribes to the holy men of the past.
In doing so he offers a typology of the Christian self. Responding to scripture,
the "I" of the poems models typical styles of early Byzantine religious comportment, not the heroic patterns of the saints, but the reflexive subjectivity
of the ordinary Christian, one who recognizes himself as a sinner in need of
redemption. In this self-characterization, Romanos echoes trends among the
authors of early Byzantine hagiography, who often employed their prologues
and epilogues to contrast themselves with the saints they narrated.[31] In some
sense, Byzantine selves succeeded, not when they achieved the unattainable
level of the saints, but rather when they exhibited the compunction of the
hagiographer. In this case, Romanos provides the model of acceptable penitential self-regard.

If Joseph's heeding his conscience exemplifies the good, Judas's disregard
for the dictates of conscience instantiates an all-too-present evil. Romanos's
treatment of Judas suggests that Romanos's regular performance of moral im-
perfection was considerably better than some alternatives. Romanos's hymn
On Judas thematizes the consciencelessness of the apostle who betrayed
Christ in an extended invective, addressed directly to Judas in the second
person:

The receipt of the money in the purse, he gave to your trust,
and ungrateful [ἀσυνείδητος, literally "without conscience"] for all
      this you suddenly
appeared against him.[32]

The cantor rants at Judas in the vocative:

you ravenous, profligate, implacable,
shameless, and gluttonous, conscienceless [ἀσυνείδητε], lover of
      money![33]

Although the poem's refrain calls on God to be merciful and patient with the
congregation, Romanos does not, in the course of the hymn, connect Judas's

condemned conscience explicitly with his own or that of his congregants. On the surface, Judas stands beyond the pale. Later manuscripts' assignment of the hymn to Holy Thursday almost certainly reflects its original performance context.[34] Judas functioned not only as a powerful counterexample but also as a horrifying opportunity for Christian self-recognition on the eve of the crucifixion. Although Romanos never identifies with the arch-villain in *On Judas*, Judas's conscience functions much like his own. When he declares to Judas, "Your conscience condemns you [τὸ συνειδός σου κατακρίνει σε]" (17.22), his words recall his self-condemnation in the *Prayer of Romanos*, "my own conscience condemns me [τὸ συνειδὸς γὰρ ἑαυτοῦ καταδικάζει με]" (56.12).

As we have seen, Judas's role as anti-exemplar on Holy Thursday would be underscored in the decades after Romanos's death when, in either 565 or 577, the patriarch Eutychios added the new communion hymn, *At Your Mystical Supper*. The chant encouraged congregants to enter into the liturgical moment by identifying with the Thief, the redeemed sinner, and to reject the model offered by Judas.[35] When their lips made contact with the host, the body of Christ, communicants hoped to do so with a kiss of devotion, not betrayal. Judas offered the classic case of the negative type.

The Sinful Romanos

In contrast to Judas, whose betrayal of Christ lies strangely beyond Romanos's empathy, repentant sinners elsewhere in the New Testament provide Romanos with ample models for self-understanding. In relation to them Romanos articulates his identity as sinner: biblical typology and self-disclosing confession combine. The hymn *On the Harlot* illustrates ways that reflection on the biblical lection can contribute to a typological construction of the self.[36] Tradition conflated the Sinful Woman of Luke 7:36–50 with the woman who anointed Jesus during the supper at the house of Simon the Pharisee (Mt 26:6–13, Mk 14:3–9). Romanos and later Byzantine writers would often simply call her the Harlot (*pornē*).[37] In the sequence of events in Matthew, her story falls just before Judas's betrayal on the eve of the Passover. The manuscript tradition assigns the hymn to the Wednesday of Holy Week, an ascription that is almost certainly original.[38] The hymn calls listeners to self-examination and repentance in light of the biblical narrative. Romanos frames his reflection on the repentant harlot with a two-fold self-accusation. In the first strophe, he both identifies with her by confessing himself to be a fornicator, one of the *pornoi*, and contrasts himself with her in his failure to repent.

> Seeing Christ's words like sweet drops of fragrance
> raining down everywhere, and granting breath of life
> to all the faithful, the Harlot once
> came to hate the foul stench of her actions,
> as she considered her own shame
> and thought over the pain that had been brought about by them.
> For there is much affliction there [in Hell] for the fornicators,
> of whom I am one, and ready for scourges,
> which the Harlot quailed at and remained no longer a harlot.
> But I [ἐγώ], though I quail, I remain in
>   *the filth of my deeds.* (10.1; trans. Lash, 77)

By contrasting himself parenthetically with the sinful woman, Romanos stresses how he does not emulate her model of repentance, despite sharing her identity as fornicator and her terror in the face of eternal punishment. He contrasts her response to the words of Christ with his own recalcitrance. Through self-consideration, the woman was moved to conversion, a point to which we shall return below. But despite his own reflexivity, Romanos is stuck in his ways. The poem's "I" thus stands accused by the Harlot's story.

While Romanos offers the woman as a model, he presents himself to his audience as a counterexample, as one who hears the biblical verses, but does not properly respond. Both of the extant preludes to this hymn connect the model of the Harlot's compunction to the poet's call for forgiveness or deliverance. If only he could imitate the Harlot! The poem's second strophe continues the confessional mode of the singing self:

> I am never willing to abandon my evil deeds.
> I do not remember the dreadful things that I am going to see there
>   [in Hell].
> I do not consider the compassion of Christ. (10.2; trans. Lash, 78)

To his audience, Romanos offers himself as a mediating point between the successful penitent, represented by the biblical Harlot, and the self-accused sinner who has, as yet, failed to reform. The character "Romanos" functions as a stand-in for all Christians. Those singing the refrain, "*the filth of my deeds*," engage in self-accusation as a step toward repentance. The story of the penitent signals a path to righteousness for the self-accused. The poet encourages the congregation not only to model themselves on the sinful woman, but, at least initially, on the poet himself, who reflects the image of the Harlot, if imperfectly.

The liturgical function of Romanos's performance of self lies in his presentation of interiority. From the outset, Romanos entwines biblical interpretation with self-regard. In the final strophe, he seals his call to repentance by modeling Christian prayer. First, Jesus commands the penitent Harlot and Simon the Pharisee, now shriven:

> Depart. You have both been released from the rest of your debts.
> Go. You are exempt from every obligation.
> You have been freed.

Romanos then returns to himself and prays to have debts forgiven as well:

> Therefore, my Jesus, say the same to me,
> since I am quite unable to pay you back what I owe . . .
> as you are compassionate, pardon, forgive
>   *the filth of my deeds.* (10.18; trans. Lash, 84, modified)

The poem thus effects the formation of the self-accused subject, an identity that the singers of the refrain repeat for themselves. In scripting such a Christian self, Romanos constructs a model for piety in response to biblical narrative, a voicing of an imperfectly biblical self.

*   *   *

At the Night Vigil, Romanos instructed the faithful to keep watch on themselves. Through surveillance, they might come to conform to prescribed styles of Christian self-knowledge. By his own flawed example Romanos guided his audience to a generic model. Typology tends not toward individuality, but toward varieties of sameness.[39] Identity is relational; it is always a matter of identity with something else. Romanos supplies a biblical and confessional context in which listeners can identify themselves as just like him, as sinners in need of redemption. The first-person passages in the hymns of Romanos form the cantor as Christian subject, producing identity through exegesis and ritual. Sung in the course of the public liturgies of the Night Vigil, they disseminate an early Byzantine conception of the self.[40] In their confession of sinfulness without personal narrative, they engage in technologies of the self without disclosure of specifics. Before a captive audience, Romanos the Melodist becomes a Byzantine Christian Everyman. In the first person singular, he models styles of interiority and presence to self in the operations of his conscience, thus providing a template for how Byzantine Christians might know themselves. Romanos presents himself as an imperfect icon, the image of a Christian who recognizes his failings while celebrating and depending on God. Such an introspective self had become typical in Byzantium.

The Internal Lives of Biblical Figures

Romanos hoped that by hearing the cantor sing in his own voice and by accepting his invitation to enter the stories of the Bible, his Christian congregants would come to see themselves. And yet his models for self-regard—for the ways that Byzantine Orthodox Christians might have access to their own subjectivity—pose other challenges of interpretation. Often in Romanos's hymns, seemingly minor characters from the Bible take center stage, and he invites his audience to enter their stories; occasionally he attempts to enter their interior lives. While Romanos does not have a single term for interiority, he seeks access to a character's thoughts, mind, soul, or heart by reconstructing his or her interior monologues. These speeches, both inwardly expressed and externally vocalized, also employed the rhetorical art of ethopoeia, or "speech in character," a mainstay of late antique rhetorical handbooks, or *progymnasmata*, that involved putting oneself in the place of another to imagine and portray that person's thoughts.[41] Romanos had obviously mastered this technique, but his application of it raises questions beyond the literary building blocks that he employs.[42] His treatment of interior speech reveals concerns about how and by whom interiority might be knowable. His recreation of biblical characters embeds a discourse about access to another self or mind, and by extension about access to the mind of the Gospel text as well.

Romanos ponders how, and how much, those who knew Christ knew themselves, and how Christ knew them. The result does not precisely offer interiority; rather, it portrays the interiority of ideal types. What does Romanos think interiority looks like? What does he think it *should* look like? In the hymns, the exercise of exploring biblical characters' thoughts is always didactic. Romanos is, after all, delivering chanted verse sermons, interpreting the scripture to teach ethics and theology. His portraits of interior life both reflect and seek to shape a typological formation of the self. Repeatedly, Romanos's congregants are encouraged to identify their sins and seek forgiveness. By representing his biblical subjects' interior disposition, the Melodist seeks to form habits of personal religious reflection for men and women alike.[43]

The Soul in Doubt

In his hymn *On Doubting Thomas*, assigned to the Sunday after Easter, Romanos interrupts the action of the central scene of revelation and recognition, to penetrate the apostle's thoughts. Although the other disciples had seen the risen Christ, Thomas had not yet seen, and therefore did not yet believe.

> In the midst of the disciples [Christ] appeared when the doors were
>   shut.
> But Thomas when he saw him, bowed his face downwards,
> and in his soul [ἔνδον τῆς ψυχῆς] he was saying "What shall I do?"[44]

In Romanos's retelling, Thomas knows that this is his Lord and his God at sight, even before inserting his hand into Christ's body. Previously dubious about the resurrection, Thomas is now filled with doubt about himself and how he should act. In the moment that Christ appears before him, he worries about his own appearance in the eyes of his fellows:

> How shall I now make my defense to those I formerly did not
>   believe?
> What can I say to Peter? What to the others?
> Those whom I reproached before, how shall I now appease them and
>   cry
> *"You are our Lord and our God."* (7.7–10; trans. Lash 186)

He reproaches himself for not having simply kept silent about his unbelief. He confesses to having been angry [ὑπεκνίσθην] and jealous [ἐζήλωσα] when he saw the others' joy, especially "Peter, the denier." The epithet suggests that Thomas still seeks ways to distinguish his failings from theirs. Nevertheless he identifies and confesses his own sin within himself and asks forgiveness.

Through jealousy, then, I said what I said before.
Let me not be blamed, my Jesus, but be accepted. (8.8–9; trans. Lash
    186)

Romanos thus causes Thomas to exhibit a reflective conscience and contrition,
elements, as we have seen, central to appropriate Christian self-understanding.[45]

Even before Thomas's hand probes Christ's hands and side, the writer's
hand has probed Thomas's mind, seeking understanding. Thomas also has
access to this interiority; his interior speech shows self-recognition. But these
are not the only figures to have knowledge of the doubting apostle's inner
self. God has insight into Thomas's innermost thoughts. After Thomas has
reflected on his jealousy and his need for acceptance, Romanos says, "Thus
the Twin [that is, Didymus Thomas], speaking to himself, was speaking to
God" (10.1). His internal speech is always already a conversation with God.

He who examines the kidneys, seeing Thomas,
breaking his heart . . .
took pity and cried, "Bring your hand here.
Why do you doubt? Tell me you of little faith." (10.2–5; trans. Lash 187)

Here, Romanos adapts the language of Psalm 7:10[9]: "God is one who examines hearts and kidneys [ἐτάζων καρδίας καὶ νεφροὺς ὁ θεός]," a metaphor for
God's knowledge of the inner human. God's access to the mind thus figures as
access to the physical organs of the body, organs with moral implications. The
kidneys were traditionally the seat of one's conscience; the heart, the seat of
faith. God examines the soul the way a diviner examines entrails. As we shall
see, Romanos returns to this psalm verse elsewhere in his corpus as a prooftext when he enters the interiority of a character, stressing God's omniscient
access to his biblical subjects. But if God sees his biblical interlocutors as they
are present to themselves, Romanos's access to the self is less certain.

The Mind of the Harlot

A return to Romanos's hymn On the Harlot reveals that he is as interested in
presenting her interior life as he is his own. Early in the poem, Romanos expresses his desire to access the Harlot's subjective experience and understand
her thoughts:

I would like to search [ἐρευνῆσαι] the mind [φρὴν] of the wise
    woman
and to know how Jesus came to shine in her. (4.1–2)

When she hears that Christ was sitting "at table in the house of the Pharisee,"
whom Romanos will later identify as Simon, she hastens "driving her intent
towards repentance."[46] She speaks within herself to urge herself onward:

Come then, my soul, see the moment you were seeking,
The One who purifies you is at hand. Why do you stand fast in
    the filth of your deeds (4.6–11).

I am going to him, because it is for me he has come.
I am leaving those who were once mine, because now I long greatly
    for him.
And as the One who loves me, I anoint him and caress him,
I weep and I groan and I urge him fittingly to long for me.
I am changed to the longing of the One who is longed for,
and, as he wishes to be kissed, so I kiss my lover. (5.1–6)

Romanos presents a complexly eroticized desire for salvation, emotionally charged
with the Harlot's desire for contact and consummation with her beloved Christ.
Mixing love and remorse, the Harlot formulates and expresses her intentions. She
connects her interior disposition to the postures of her body, understanding these
exterior actions to be the signs of her soul that her divine lover desires:

I grieve and bow myself down, for this is what he wishes.
I keep silent and withdrawn, for in these he delights. (5.7–8)

Within her own thoughts, the Harlot engages in the practice of typological
exegesis. She invokes to herself a biblical precedent in the harlot Rahab, who
received Joshua's spies before the battle of Jericho. In this, the New Testament
Harlot demonstrates for Romanos's audience how to use biblical types in the
formation of the self—to meditate on the details of their stories as guides for
emulation. The Harlot thinks of Rahab as faithful to God's plan in her act of
hospitality, and thus "she found life as the reward for her reception" (7.2). She
wishes to follow Rahab's example even as she stresses the gulf between her
sexual sin and the purity of her beloved:

Then a harlot gave hospitality to chaste men,
now a harlot seeks to anoint with sweet myrrh a Virgin born from a
    Virgin. (7.5–6)

She also reflects on the prophet Samuel's mother, Hannah. When Hannah was
praying fervently but silently in the temple, the prophet Eli had first imagined
she was drunk, but she protested, saying, "No, my lord, I am a woman deeply
troubled; I have drunk neither wine nor strong drink, but I have been pour-
ing out my soul before the Lord" (1 Kgdns [1 Sam] 1:13–15). In Hannah, the
Harlot finds a type whose interior disposition is initially opaque to a male
religious authority. Eli does not know her as she knows herself—or as God
does. The New Testament Harlot reflects, God

took away the shame of the barren woman [Hannah]. Deliver a har-
    lot from
    the filth of her deeds. (8.10–11)

By the end of the hymn, the Harlot herself has become an exemplar. When
she anoints Christ's feet, Simon disapproves, and Christ scolds him:

Look at this harlot in front of you, as like the Church [καθάπερ τὴν
    ἐκκλησίαν], she cries out, "I renounce and I blow upon
    the filth of my deeds." (17.9–11)

In language that recalls preparation for baptism, the renunciation of the devil and
the exsufflation to exorcise him, the Harlot becomes a type for the Church. Romanos thus presents the Harlot's interiority—her anguish, her motivations, her
desires, and her ability to apply biblical types to her own situation—as a model
for the congregation to emulate. In the final strophe, he enacts this patterning
in himself, even taking on the words of the Harlot's interior speech, which have
served as the hymn's refrain. He calls on God in his compassion to "pardon, forgive / *the filth of my deeds*" (18.10–11). Romanos explores the mind of the Harlot
and discovers that it functions strikingly like his own. Like this most inventive
poet, she executes the processes of the typological mind, patterning her actions
and her self-understanding on earlier biblical figures. We shall return to this
hymn in Chapter 5, for it will show how Romanos's achievement in fleshing out
the interior life of his characters was occasionally recapitulated by later poets.

The Samaritan Woman's Theological Reflections
and God's Knowledge of the Self

If the Harlot's interiority presents Romanos with a model for emulation both
in life and composition, the thoughts of another biblical woman explore a
theological and epistemological conundrum. In the hymn *On the Samaritan
Woman*, Romanos problematizes the ways one can know the mind of another, including the mind of God.[47] The poem explores the repartee in John 4
between Jesus and a non-Jewish woman who has come to draw water at the
well of the patriarch Jacob. Where this lection occurred in the sixth-century
Constantinopolitan cycle is unclear, although the weeks after Easter, when
John was read sequentially, are most likely. The story plays on the woman's
misunderstanding of Christ's words and identity even as he knows a thing or
two about her, and thus raises questions of how one can know another, in this
case Christ. Romanos presents his speculations about the woman's interior
mental processes only after eleven strophes in which he follows the biblical
narrative closely. This recounting ends as Jesus reveals to the woman that he
knows her history with men.

Romanos uses Jesus' clairvoyance at the well to plumb the depths of her
mind, offering a tentative reconstruction of the woman's thoughts in her interaction with Christ:

When the holy woman understood the dignity of the Savior
from what had been revealed, she longed even more
to discover what and who was the one at the well
and perhaps [τάχα] was in the grip, not unreasonably, of thoughts
  like these [καὶ τάχα τοῖς τοιούτοις συνείχετο εἰκότως
  ἐνθυμήμασιν]. (15.1–4; trans. Lash, 69)

Whereupon, Romanos generates for her an interior monologue, in which she
puzzles out the theological paradox of her encounter with the Messiah. The
poet's pondering of her mind mirrors her reflection on the mind and works
of God as she attempts to discover the identity of Christ. Because she is a
type for the Church, her wonder and reasoning at the mystery of God incarnate model the thoughts Romanos regards as appropriate for Christian
consideration.

Is it God or man at whom I am looking? A being of heaven or of
    earth?
for see he makes the two known to me in one. (15.5–6)
. . . .
Is he then of heaven yet bears an earthly form? (16.1; trans. Lash, 70)

While Romanos qualifies his access to the woman's interior thoughts as
speculation—this is only perhaps what she thinks—God, by contrast, demonstrates complete knowledge. As the poet imagines her speaking to herself, she reflects that Jesus not only gives her to drink when he is thirsty,
but

          He shows me all my faults
   that I may receive
     joy and redemption. (15.8–10; trans. Lash 69)

Indeed, Christ knows of her succession of husbands and that she is not married to the man she now lives with.

   If then, being God and mortal, he has been revealed to me as human,
   and when thirsty he gives me drink as God and prophesies,
   . . .
   it was for him to know me and to proclaim to me what I am [αὐτοῦ
      ἦν καὶ εἰδέναι με καὶ κηρῦξαι ὃ πέλω]. (16.2–3, 6; trans. Lash,
      70)

In contrast to an all-knowing God, the Samaritan Woman's monologue im-
plies the limits of the poet's access to the thoughts of another:

   It was not for a human[48] to know my way of life and to imagine it
   but for the Invisible, who is now seen, to accuse and rebuke me.
      (16.4–5; trans. Lash 70)

Romanos cannot fully understand the mind of either of his characters, the
woman or Christ, and thus he undermines any assumption of his own authorial omniscience.

    Meditating on the divine-human paradox, and convicted by Jesus' knowl-
edge of her past, the Samaritan Woman demands further insight into him:

Son of a mortal, as I see you, Son of God as I understand you,
enlighten my mind [σὺ φώτισόν μου τὰς φρένας], Lord, teach me
who you are. (17.1–3; trans. Lash, 70)

. . .

Are you not the Christ who the prophets foretold was coming? (17.5;
    trans. Lash, 70)

She seeks theological instruction directly from this Christ in part because he
has perceived who she is, and she has perceived his perception:

For I see that indeed you know what I have done and all the secrets
of my heart. (17.8–9; trans. Lash, 70)

Romanos underscores Christ's access to the woman's interior life, describing
him as "the One who sees" and who

saw the ideas [διαλέξεις] of the wise woman
and the faith in her heart. (18.1–2; trans. Lash 70)

Her divine interlocutor's knowing crosses the boundary of her interior self,
making her the subject of divine knowledge, even if she remains the imprecise subject of Romanos's exegetical consideration. This woman is God's subject, not the poet's. In fact, Christ has "washed clean [her] mind" and has
come "willingly to dwell in [her]," invading her interiority with his salvific
presence, figured as the liquid from the source that can cross the limits of the
body. God is on the inside; Romanos is not.

As in *On Doubting Thomas*, Romanos invokes the verse from Psalm 7 regarding God's access to people's interior lives. In a witty transposition of her
biblical narrative, the Samaritan Woman

abandons her pitcher and takes upon the shoulders
of her heart the One who examines the kidneys and the heart
    [ἐτάζοντα νεφροὺς καὶ τὰς καρδίας]. (20.2–3; trans. Lash, 71,
    modified)

She takes within herself the one with insight into her innermost thoughts. In
fact, Romanos employs the same verse in the hymn *On the Harlot*, where he
identifies Christ as "the One who examines hearts and the kidneys" (10.13.5)

and therefore perceives the Pharisee's discontent at the welcoming of the woman to the banquet. But in that hymn, as if to stress the materiality of such knowing and its potential to affect the whole person, the woman herself has already declared Christ to be the one "who has set me entirely aflame, both my kidneys and my heart [τοῦ πυρώσαντός μου πάντα καὶ τοὺς νεφροὺς καὶ τὴν καρδίαν]" with his pure love (9.6). God's love and God's knowledge of the self are visceral.[49]

Earlier commentators on the biblical verse stressed God's access to the subject under judgment. In his *Commentary on the Psalms*, John Chrysostom wrote that God "said that he has no need of witnesses, nor of evidence, nor of proof, nor of documents, nor of anything else like that: he personally is in possession of knowledge of things beyond telling. . . . Now at this point he refers to unspoken thoughts of the mind as kidneys [νεφροὺς], to our most intimate and profound thoughts, hinting at this by reference to the position of organs."[50] In his fifth-century *Commentary on the Psalms*, Theodoret of Cyrrhus tied God's access to the entrails specifically to knowledge of sexual impulses. "He uses the term *kidneys* here for thoughts [νεφροὺς ἐνταῦθα τοὺς λογισμοὺς ὀνομάζει]: since the kidneys/entrails arouse the appetites of the abdomen [τὰς ὑπογαστρίους ὀρέξεις; literally those "below the belly"], from there our thoughts in turn give rise to desires." God is the one "who understands the hidden thoughts of people's mind [τοὺς κεκρυμμένους τῆς διανοίας τῶν ἀνθρώπων λογισμοὺς ἐπιστάμενος]."[51] In each of these hymns where Romanos himself searches the mind of a biblical figure, he cites the psalm to recognize God's superior knowledge. God has complete and certain access to human interiority.

As the poem on the cryptic dialogue between Christ and the Samaritan Woman reveals, the problem for the student of the Gospel is epistemological and exegetical. While God understands the organs of human desire, Romanos longs to divine the anatomy of scripture. He subsumes his examination of the woman's motivations, curiosity, bewilderment, and understanding within the larger project of biblical interpretation, the pondering of the story as a whole. Early in the hymn he invites the congregation,

> Having lately [ἄρτι] drunk[52] of the immortal waters,
> of which the faithful woman of Samaria has become like the finder
>   [ὡς εὑροῦσα]
> let us diligently search [ἐρευνήσωμεν καλῶς] all the channels
>   [φλέβας, literally "blood vessels"]
> let us briefly take up the words of the Gospel. (3.1–4; trans. Lash, 64)

The flow of the biblical narrative plays on the story's living water, the source of life flowing out in the text from a divine source. Romanos calls on the congregation to join the woman in her searching and discovery. The immortal waters flow through veins, suggesting that the life-giving liquid represents both the text of scripture and the blood of Christ. Thus the hymn seeks the interiority not only of the Samaritan Woman, but of the Bible itself. "What then," he asks, "does the Bible teach?" (4.1).

The Conscience of the Leper

The hymn *On the Healing of the Leper* underscores God's omniscient access to the interiority of the human person and makes this knowledge redemptive. Its assignment in Romanos's day is uncertain, although the single eleventh-century manuscript from Patmos in which it survives ascribes it to the second Wednesday after Easter, perhaps attesting an earlier series of lections in the weeks after Easter that demonstrated the power of Christ's divinity.[53] Romanos reads the Leper's physical ailment as a metaphor for moral blemish. In the prelude, the cantor prays to God,

> As you cleansed the Leper of his disease, O All-Powerful
> heal the pain of our souls,

and addresses Him as the "physician of our souls [ἰατρὲ τῶν ψυχῶν ἡμῶν]."[54] The hymn's original refrain is uncertain but probably was "*savior and alone without sin.*"[55] As in the hymn *On the Mary at the Cross*, Romanos uses medical imagery to describe Christ's saving work.[56] Of course, the verb *sōzō* and its derivatives can refer both to healing and to salvation, and yet Romanos's interest lies not in ambiguity but in treating the entire story of the Leper as an allegory for the communal and personal search for absolution. In the final strophe the poet calls on the Son of God,

> As you had mercy on the Leper, driving out his affliction with a
>   word, as you are powerful
> save [σῶσον] us also who approach your goodness
> and grant pardon of our faults. (18.2–4; trans. Lash, 58)

The story of the Leper and his healing informs practices of contrition. The Leper "was not ashamed to show everyone the defilement of his affliction"

(4.7). Falling to the ground in front of the crowd, he entreats God, "Like all the rest, save [σῶσον] me also, O Lover of Humanity" (4.9). The Leper models the call for the salvation that all Christians should seek, kneeling before God.

Romanos also gives the Leper a back-story, a process of reflective reasoning and preparation that Romanos seeks to put on display. He devotes four middle strophes to the Leper's internal dialogue as he considers his disease and determines to approach Christ in supplication. Here, Romanos constructs the interiority of the afflicted to prepare outward postures of repentance. "Warred on by the disease, the Leper lamented through his tears" (6.1). Romanos's approach remains tentative:

> He spoke words such as these [φησί τοιούτους λόγους]: "Alas, my
>   flesh has been dyed [ἀνεβάφη]
> by grave illness with a terrible dye contrary to nature [δεινῇ βαφῇ
>   παρὰ τὴν φύσιν],
> and like a stain it spreads over my whole body." (6.3–5; trans. Lash,
>   53)

The "stain" recalls common biblical vocabulary for sin, itself often figured as a mark or blemish, while the idea that it is "against nature" calls on Pauline and post-biblical ideas about the enormity of sin.[57] The Leper will soon declare, "For me the strength of the flesh rebels, contrary to nature [παρὰ φύσιν]" (8.7; trans. Lash, 54), a statement that recalls Paul's description of inner conflict in Romans 7:14–23 and connects deviance from divine law to the flesh itself.[58] Romanos's Leper thus practices the self-accusation appropriate within the conscience: His deformed skin has become a "hideous [ἄσχημος] sight" to him, a "dreadful decay." The Leper's language blurs desires for health and redemption. He declares,

>   I have not one single hope
> of salvation [σωτηρία] unless he grants it, the lover of humanity.
>   (6.8–9; trans. Lash, 53)

Even the Leper himself reads his illness within the framework of a doctrine of human sin.

In the next strophe Romanos causes the Leper to address his inner speech to his own soul, which he urges on by recalling a series of typological precedents for miraculous healing.

Hurry, then, my soul, go to Christ the Son of the Virgin,
that he may bring you healing [ἴασις] which you cannot receive from
    any human.
A blind man came [Jn 9:1–8], plunged in darkness from his mother's
    womb,
and what nature took from him, Christ gave to him.
He snatched the widow's son from death [Lk 7:11–17].
He made firm the limbs of the paralytic enfeebled for many years [Jn
    5:1–9].[59]

The Leper draws strength from the faith of the Hemorrhaging Woman, who "touched [Christ's] hem and was cured" (9.1). The Leper reasons that Christ has the power to cure maladies that doctors cannot because, in part, he is "above all nature [ὑπὲρ φύσιν πᾶσαν]" (8.8), as demonstrated by his birth from the Virgin's womb. This allows Christ to counter what is against nature in the human body and soul. Like that of the Harlot, the Leper's interiority encodes the poet's own patterns of thought, the practice of reasoning through typology which marks his own compositions. For Romanos all the biblical healings—the blind man, the widow's son, the paralytic, and the woman with the issue of blood—figure as types for the salvation of the sinner. Because he consistently allegorizes physical illness as moral turpitude, the physically afflicted receive a penitent's interiority. Fortified by biblical exemplars—as Romanos hopes his audience will also be—the Leper determines to run to Christ with his entreaty.[60] For his faithful practice of a penitent's heart, Christ relieves him of his affliction (13.1), saving him from the shame of his blemish.

Epistemology and the Hemorrhaging Woman

Romanos's interest in contrasting God's knowledge of interiority with his own more limited powers of perception colors his hymn *On the Hemorrhaging Woman*. In the biblical narrative, a woman who has bled for twelve years, presumably vaginally, and therefore ritually defiling her, approaches Jesus in a crowd and touches the hem of his garment, causing him to turn and ask, "Who touched me?" (Mk 5:25–35; Lk 8:43–49). In keeping with much late ancient exegesis of the story, Romanos's Christ "knows all things before their origin" and "was not ignorant beforehand of what had happened."[61] Unlike the situation in Mark's version of the story, reproduced in Luke (but see Mt

9:20–23), this Jesus always knows who it is that has touched him. Instead, Jesus poses the question of who touched him to the disciples to demonstrate the limits of their understanding. In this way, the poem contrasts various levels of knowledge and the parallel roles of poetry and interior imagination that access it.

Early on, the authorial voice within the hymn addresses Jesus in the second person, creating an odd situation where Romanos begins to narrate to Christ an event at which he was present. Romanos does not tell Jesus anything that he does not already know. The poet tells Jesus that because of his reputation as a healer, the Hemorrhaging Woman approached him,

> silent in sound
> but crying out eagerly to you with her hand
>   *Savior, save me.* (12.2.4–6)

The hymn stresses that she came secretly and furtively touched the hem of Christ's garment (12.3.1–3). She approaches in stealth not to steal power from an unsuspecting Jesus, but rather to keep "the enemy" from knowing her intentions and out of fear of the reaction of the crowd. Far from being stalked unknowingly, Jesus hears the silent call for help embodied in the woman's gesture.

Once again, Romanos attempts to enter his biblical character's train of thought, and once again, her healing stands in for salvation. In contrast to the closely related hymn *On the Leper*, where the man's affliction is a type for human sinfulness, this woman bleeds because of her own moral fault.[62]

> Most likely [εἰκός] the bleeding woman not only was reasoning
>   [thus] but said to herself
> "How shall I be seen by the All-seeing One, bearing the shame of my
>   sins [πταίσματα]?
> If the blameless one sees the flow of blood, He will draw away from
>   me as impure,
> And this will be more terrible for me than my affliction,
> If he turns away from me as I cry out to him:
>   *Savior, save me.* (12.5)

For seven strophes the woman debates silently with her interlocutors. In the course of her reflections, Romanos creates for the woman a sort of psychological depth: like his Thomas, the Melodist's Hemorrhaging Woman worries not only about the thoughts of God but about the thoughts of others. She now reconstructs in her head a dialogue between herself and the assembled crowd, whose thoughts, as she represents them to herself, are unkind and shaming. She anticipates that these people would push her away and demand, in accord with Levitical law, that she first purify herself with immersion in a ritual bath to rub away her stain before approaching Jesus (12.6). But with gumption (in her head at least), she advocates for herself:

> Perhaps [τάχα] you men are determined to be harder on me than my
>   condition [is].
> Do I take control [κεκράτημαι] now out of ignorance? I know that he
>   is pure.
> For this reason I have come to him, to be delivered from both the
>   reproaches and the defilement.
> Do not then hinder me from gathering [my] strength. (12.7.1–4)

She accuses the crowd of jealousy and of not wishing her redemption (12.8). "The spring's flowing gushes for everyone! For what reason [χάριν τίνος] do you stop it up?" (12.9.2). When they see God healing her, she tells them, then *they* will feel shame (12.9.5).

By focusing on the silent woman's interiority, Romanos illustrates how a Christian might claim agency in the face of societal opposition (12.10.4), and thus sets a model for Christians to summon the audacity to approach Christ. Romanos emulates her pluck in entreating God in his own voice in the prelude and first strophe. He also emphasizes his imaginative affinity with his heroine, as she too invents conversations. When his recreation of her inner dialogue concludes, he writes, "The bleeding woman, perhaps [τάχα], spoke such speeches, to those who wanted to scare her away" (12.12.1). Both Romanos and the Hemorrhaging Woman reconstruct speeches in the realm of perhaps. Finally, in showing the woman's construction of the crowd and its opposition, Romanos raises the implicit point that no human can actually know the mind of another, can properly assess another's intentions and motivations. Christians ultimately cannot know the selves of others, and therefore they must not judge.

Jesus, by contrast, knows exactly what has happened when the woman touches him. He turns to his disciples to instruct them.

By whom was this done? You ought to know, my friends.
I just now made known the drama's plot [δραματούγημα], and now I
    shall reveal to you how the one who stole
made use of my power; voicelessly she came to me crying,
And laying hold of my robe like a letter,[63]
she plucked healing, calling to me
    "*Savior, save me.*" (12.14)

Moreover, and unlike the disciples at this point, she has not only touched his robe, she has grasped, Jesus explains, his divine nature (12.15).

    The following strophe returns to the woman and her internal thoughts:

When she perceived that she had not escaped notice, the woman
    reasoned to herself [συνελογίζετο] thus.
She said, "I will be seen by my savior Jesus, now that I have been
    cleansed of my stain.
For I am no longer afraid. For by his will I have accomplished this."
    (12.16.1–3)

It is clear here that the woman is thinking within herself, since she refers to Jesus in the third person. Romanos departs from the tradition of the Gospel of Mark, where the text reports that the "woman came in fear and trembling, fell down before him, and told him the whole truth (Mk 5:33)" and the Gospel of Luke, where "she declared in the presence of all the people why she had touched him and how immediately she had been healed" (Lk 8:47). Romanos is more interested in interiority than in public attestations of divine power. Moreover, the first line of the strophe that introduces her speech is ambiguous. Who is speaking here? Has Romanos's authorial voice reclaimed the narrative, having ended Jesus' speech to the disciples and having abruptly returned to narrating about the woman without a clear transition? Or is it Jesus himself, continuing to lecture the disciples, who illustrates for them the woman's interior life over the course of three strophes, and who has complete knowledge of her sense of accomplishment and relief? Then she seems to address him, perhaps aloud: "I fled to you for refuge, good doctor. . . . Do not rouse your anger against me" (12.18.1–2). After the speech, Christ responds to the woman directly, praising her faith; but he has not (only?) heard her voice, rather, he has read her thoughts. As she herself says to him,

You knew my heart as I cried out to you,
  "*Savior, save me.*" (12.18.5–6)

In the end, only Christ is omniscient, while the crowd and the disciples misunderstand, and the woman and the poet can only conjecture about the minds of others.

The Identity of the Self

Romanos leads his congregants into the minds of those who encountered Christ, and he presents in the self-exposure of the first person singular a troubled conscience praying for mercy. In this variety he provides a range of identities and occasions for shaping the subject through liturgy. Or does he? The corpus of Romanos provides multiple but ultimately convergent subjectivities. Often writing for Lent, Romanos invents interior lives for his biblical subjects, creating Thomas, the Harlot, the Samaritan Woman, the Leper, and the Hemorrhaging Woman in his own image. They become, with him, models for and models of Christian typological thought: his exploration of their thoughts demonstrates how Christians should think within their own minds, at once present to the story, the characters, God, and themselves.

Considering the interiority of his biblical subjects, Romanos discovers a remarkable degree of conformity and surprisingly little depth. As he questions what might be going on in their heads, he reveals inner lives imaginative and normative. Plumbing the souls of the Bible engages in ethopoeia but not in the creation of individual ethos or character. Rather, the hymnographer illustrates variations on a single and ideal ethos, a pattern for introspection. The exercise in searching the mind of another models biblical exegesis in the formation of the self. Romanos teaches by example how to perceive and shape human subjectivity, to strive to know oneself as God does. How then to assess one's access to the self? Is one's interior life, so accessible to God, merely a matter of conjecture? Or is it a matter of melding the self to the pattern? In the end, the self that matters is the self in relation to God, the self as suppliant, dependent on God for salvation, an identity that everyone shares, or should share. The poet's search for interiority uncovers not how early Byzantine Christians were present to themselves, but rather how this preaching deacon, on behalf of the church, thought they should be present to themselves, understanding themselves as biblical subjects.[64]

At this point, it should be clear that Romanos's interiority is not the same as a modern psychology. But it is also rather different from what Krister Stendahl termed "the introspective conscience" he thought typical of the Christian West, and which he tied to Augustine's reading of Paul. In the lack of individuation among his biblical characters, Romanos does not call on the Pauline models so prominent in Augustine, both in the *Confessions*, his heavily rhetorical portrait of his own interiority, and in his accounts of sinful conscience in the later anti-Pelagian writings. Throughout the corpus, Romanos does quote from Paul, especially from Romans and 1 Corinthians, but nowhere nearly as often as from the Gospels. For the most part he quotes phrases about salvation, especially from 1 Corinthians 15's account of resurrection and new life.[65] Romanos quotes from Romans 7 only twice, never employing Paul's distinctive language of interior conflict and turmoil, where Paul talks of himself as not understanding his own actions, and of not doing what he wants, but rather "the very thing" that he hates (7:15), nor does he talk of "sin that dwells within [him]" (7:17). He never speaks of Paul's conception of the "inner human" or the "human within" [κατὰ τὸν ἔσω ἄνθρωπον]," usually translated into English as the "inmost self" (Romans 7:22), that delights in the law of God, but struggles in conflict with the "law" governing his members. In only one place, and in the formally distinct *Prayer of Romanos*, where the poet sings only in the first person, does the hymnographer echo Romans 7:

> But I, wretched one, warring against you, became a captive
>   [αἰχμάλωτος, cf. Rom 7:23] and a slave
> Sold to barbarous sin [cf. Rom 7:14].[66]

Here, Romanos adopts Paul's model of the human battling God, but *not* the human battling within himself. Instead, the self is lured away from God by "the wicked one," the Devil (56.6). The turbulent construction of authorial voice and subjectivity so critical to Augustine's self-portrayal in the *Confessions* and so important for the West simply does not figure in Romanos's discourse of the self.

It is unclear how Romanos might have treated Paul himself, either drawing on the epistles or on the Lukan narrative in Acts. To be sure, Romanos quotes the Pauline letters and occasionally cites Paul by name. No poems survive dramatizing an episode in Paul's life, perhaps because the lectionary assigned the reading of Acts to the place of the Epistle—and not of the Gospel—in the weeks following Easter, although it is unclear whether this practice, attested in the tenth-century lectionary of Constantinople, and likely established by the late ninth, extended back into the sixth century.[67] Or perhaps Romanos's liturgical calendar simply did not celebrate festivals dedicated to the life of Paul other than as one of the group of apostles, so there was no occasion to celebrate his story in a vigil.[68] In any case, in the surviving poems Romanos shows little interest in plumbing Paul's mind. In the hymn *On the Adoration of the Cross*, the calling of Paul (Acts 9:1–22) serves as an illustration that God

> does not hesitate to go out
> and summon the elect and the chosen to life [eternal],
> just as long ago he sought Paul and found and called him
> and showed him forth as his herald and apostle.[69]

More significant, in his hymn *On the Mission of the Apostles*, possibly written for the Feast of Holy Apostles on June 30, which has as its refrain, "*Who alone knows what is in the heart* [τὰ ἐγκάρδια]," Romanos sees Christ explaining that he will replace Judas, the betrayer, with Paul among his disciples, implying that he knows the interior lives of both.[70] Romanos has reverence for Paul, but is not particularly interested in understanding Christian subjectivity through him or his writings.

More prominent for understanding the Christian self are penitential passages from the Psalms. This biblical prayer book largely shapes his expressions of grief and joy. In sixty hymns he quotes or echoes the Psalter over 300 times, with a tag from nearly every Psalm.[71] Romanos quotes or echoes Psalm 50, David's confession of sin, ten times; Psalm 102, a prayer in affliction, five times. The hymns share with Augustine's *Confessions* the strong intertextual reliance on the language of the Psalms in the scripting of the self. Could it be that because of the influence of the Psalms, and in the absence of much interest in Romans 7, Romanos's Christian subjectivity emerges not in internal struggle but in penance? Perhaps he finds the self at a later stage of a process of self-recognition, but he demonstrates little interest in dramatizing conversion beyond depicting the conception of self sufficient to understand the necessity of penance. It is worth remembering that in Byzantine Greek *metanoia* (μετάνοια), etymologically a "change of mind," means "repentance," and not "conversion." By the sixth century, it also referred to the posture that expressed repentance, namely prostration.[72]

In his *Letter to Markellinos*, offering advice on the recitation of the Psalter,

Athanasios taught not individuality but rather identification with the speaker of the Psalms, encouraging a performance that melded the self to the biblical model.[73] Romanos's hymns exhibit a similar technology for the formation of identity. Despite his interest in redemption, he shows little interest in the details of a sinner's life. In the hymn *On the Harlot*, Romanos does not rehearse the Harlot's change of heart. The story lacks the enumeration of deeds that one receives in Augustine's *Confessions* or the seventh-century *Life of Mary of Egypt*, where the author has the heroine recount her life before conversion in remarkable and shocking detail.[74] Instead, Romanos portrays the Harlot only after she had "come to hate the foul stench of her actions" (10.1). He limits himself to creating for her an interior monologue that occurs after she has determined to approach Christ as a penitent. This allows for an elaborate performance of contrition, but it does not engage in a narration of her life in sin. Romanos is less interested in what she did than in the structure of her interior self-regard once she has resolved to seek forgiveness. In this way, the Harlot's performance mirrors Romanos's own. In his first-person performances, instead of specificity or individuality, Romanos proffers something both public and generic. The self on display is both broadly applicable and broadly applied. The performance of self-identification functions as a species of typology: The sinful woman compares herself to Rahab the Harlot who gave refuge to Israelite spies within the walls of Jericho (10.7), and Romanos compares himself to the New Testament Harlot. He too gives no specifics about his transgressions, but merely supplies the names of sins and the types of sinners with which he identifies.

It is through the lens of penance that Romanos envisions the corpus of scripture. In a hymn *On Repentance* that takes as its point of departure the story of Jonas's prophetic call to the Ninevites, the poet presents a list of biblical penitents to call the people of Constantinople to imitation. The single manuscript witness assigns to the hymn to Wednesday of the first week of Lent, although this may reflect a later placement. First Romanos addresses God:

> Putting aside the despair of Nineveh
> You abandoned the threat that had been proclaimed
> and, O Lord, your mercy conquered your anger.
> Even now have pity [σπλαγχνίσθητι] on your people and your city.[75]

He enjoins God to receive the inhabitants' repentance, but he also exhorts his congregation to see their spiritual healing.

Come!
Let us rush thence to receive strength for our soul!
For there the Harlot gained health [ὑγίανεν];
There also Peter put away his denial;
There David broke down the pain of his heart.
And there the Ninevites were cured [ἰατρεύθησαν].
Let us not hesitate but arise,
let us show the wound [τραῦμα] to the Savior and receive the salve
     [ἔμπλαστρον]. (1.1–8)

Humanity's sin is a serious injury that requires treatment. The patient might be afraid to go to the doctor, but the Bible is full of exemplars who have courageously gone to the divine clinic. Moreover, God requires no recompense: he heals for free. Romanos only recommends that people "give tears in return for the gift" (2.5). Just as he invites people to attend the Nativity and Ascension (as we shall see in Chapter 3), he invites them to their own healing.

The self portrayed in Romanos, then, is hardly static; rather, Romanos depicts a subjectivity in motion, progressing from self-recognition to repentance. He observes the development of the self in his biblical figures, as they grow in their knowledge of themselves. In this way he stages the formation of selves among his audience, encouraging depth and change. However, in this scheme, he presents himself differently from the reformed sinners of the Gospels. He maintains a gap between his portrait of himself and his scriptural exemplars. As a liturgical voice, he remains an incomplete project, one whose conscience and patterns of thought might serve as a catalyst for Christian transformation through example and experience. In a second hymn on the theme of the Ten Virgins, Romanos's own speech models the disposition and desires of the Christian on the verge of repentance, engaging in confession and prayer, fumbling for words even as God already knows and understands.

Open, Lord, open for me the door of your mercy
before the time of my departure.
For I must go and come before you
and render an accounting for everything,
that which I said in words and accomplished in deeds,
and contemplated in my heart.
For the murmurs of muttering are not hidden from your ear.

Romanos then invokes a phrase from Psalm 138 [139]:13, which in the Septuagint reads, "Because it was you who possessed [ἐκτήσω] my kidneys, O Lord,
you supported me from my mother's womb," and thus emphasizes God's
knowledge of the self. He writes,

> "You have possessed my kidneys," David cries out to you in his
>   psalm,
> and "in your Book all is written" [Ps 138 (139):16].
> Reading in it [the Bible] the marks [στίγματα] of my evil deeds,
> engrave on your cross that in it I boast, crying to you,
>   "Open!"[76]

Curiously, God knows the self not only through reading interiority, but through
reading scripture. Thus, one's own knowledge of the self and sin can proceed
through a parallel exegesis of Bible and soul. Conflating knowledge of scripture,
viscera, and the sinful self, Romanos affixes all to the cross of Christ, the death
of sin, and the promise of resurrection. Convicting the conscience, scripture
crucifies, but it also points the way toward Paradise and opens its gates. On the
verge of confession and in prospect of judgment, the self progresses.

*   *   *

In Romanos, we observe the dissemination of monastic epistemologies of the
self among the early Byzantine laity. Just as his contemporary Dorotheos of
Gaza (505–565) stressed the cultivation of the conscience and the practice of
self-accusation in the monastery, Romanos imparted these technologies to
the urban crowds.[77] This discovery should not surprise us: Romanos composed many of the hymns we have just considered for the seasons of Lent and
Holy Week; and nearly all of them were assigned to this penitential period in
eleventh-century service books, where they continued to shape the experience of Lent in the cathedral office of the middle Byzantine period. These
were times in the year when Byzantine Christians perceived themselves more
acutely as the subject of God's gaze. Romanos's performance of an introspective conscience coheres with the laity's temporary asceticism during Lent. Although ordained a deacon, Romanos himself was apparently never a monk.
In his hymn *On Life in the Monastery* Romanos positions himself outside
the monastery looking in.[78] He imagines his audience interrogating him, "if
not in mouth, at least in spirit" (55.9), about how he is able to teach about

the virtues of asceticism if he himself has not renounced the world. Like the examples provided by most of his biblical characters, the monks present Romanos with a model against which to measure himself.

Romanos models a strategy of biblical interpretation and response to biblical narrative that precipitates his self-designation as sinner. He draws his listeners to self-recognition through biblical narrative, ascetic models, and the preacher's own example. His Christians come to knowledge of themselves through conformity to types. In accord with early Byzantine discourses on virtue, this self was inflected by humility: that is, by patterns of Christian self-regard that valued the effacement of self. In part because Romanos had produced himself as a generic Christian, his persona detached easily from his person. Just as he sang the words and thoughts of his biblical characters, cantors other than Romanos sang his hymns and thus not only give voice to his wide range of biblical figures, but impersonated him as well. Three papyrus fragments and one parchment, all dating from the late sixth or early seventh century, together with a poem by Dioskoros of Aphrodito that employs the name "Romanos" in an acrostic, attest to the dissemination and popularity of his compositions during and shortly after his lifetime.[79] The *Miracles of Artemios* (18) reports that during the reign of Heraclius (610–641), one of the recipients of that saint's miracles was "a certain man who from a tender age used to attend the all-night vigil of the Forerunner and who sang the hymns of the humble Romanos among the saints, right up to the present day [probably c. 660]."[80] This cantor, who the text explains had lived on his own for more than fifty-two years, appears to have had a very long career performing Romanos's hymns at the Church of St. John the Baptist in Oxeia in Constantinople. Such ongoing performances—in a different church from the one where Romanos had originally performed—strongly suggests that by the seventh century the hymns had achieved canonical status. Manuscript evidence suggests that many of the kontakia continued to be performed in their entirety during the vigils of the cathedral liturgy, and thus before lay audiences, into the eleventh century.[81] By the ninth century, monks sang excerpts from the kontakia during Morning Prayer. These truncated versions, inserted after the sixth ode of the morning's kanon hymn, usually consisted of Romanos's prelude and the first one or two strophes, that is, the parts of the hymns where the cantor sang in the voice of Romanos.[82] From the moment the historical Romanos sang his hymns, and for centuries thereafter, Romanos was one of the characters in the liturgy and one of the classic Christian selves.

a

b

c

Figure 2. Cast bronze censer with
scenes from the Life of Christ, depicting
the Annunciation (a), Nativity (b),
Baptism (c), Crucifixion (d), and
Woman and Angel at the Sepulcher (e).
Late seventh or early eighth century.
11.43 x 12.07 cm, 50.80 cm with chain.
Virginia Museum of Fine Arts,
Richmond. Adolph D. and Wilkins C.
Williams Fund. Photo: Travis Fullerton
© Virginia Museum of Fine Arts.

d

e

CHAPTER 3

Calendar and Community in the Sixth Century

While liturgy shaped interiority, it also formed collective identity. Some stories in the lectionary cycle prompted introspection, but others, particularly the key events in the life of Christ, encouraged Christians to gather as witnesses to their own salvation. In the sixth century, hymnography, preaching, and the visual arts converged to construct Christians within a single imaginary that presented the Gospel in cyclical time. As the liturgical year became biography, the Christian calendar placed the liturgical subject within the biblical drama. From Christmas to Pentecost, the self emerged in the communal experience of feasts and fasts.

Over one hundred cast bronze censers depicting the life of Christ survive from the sixth to the tenth centuries, suggesting that such objects abounded in early Byzantine churches, at least in Palestine, Syria, and Egypt, and that their form, iconography, and popularity survived the iconoclasm of the eighth and early ninth centuries. The majority of these censers show from four to six scenes, although some later ones have as many as twelve. One example in the Virginia Museum of Fine Arts depicts the five most common scenes in charming, if chunky style: the Annunciation, the Nativity, the Baptism, the Crucifixion, and the Holy Women at the Tomb (Figures 2, 3).[1] In the Annunciation, the angel Gabriel, his wings outstretched, greets the Virgin, who is sitting in a high-backed chair, holding a distaff as she spins wool. In the Nativity, the Christ child lies swaddled in a manger, as the heads of an ox and an ass peer in with curiosity. The Virgin reclines on a mattress to the right, while Joseph, to the left, sits with his head resting on his arm. In the Baptism, John the Baptist stands above the River Jordan, placing his hands over the head of Christ, who is mostly submerged in the water, as the Holy Spirit descends from heaven in the form of a dove. An angel stands in attendance on the right bank of the river. In the Crucifixion, Christ's arms

Figure 3. Line drawing depicting in projection the scenes from the life of Christ on the Virginia Museum of Fine Arts censer. Drawing by John C. Gibbs.

stretch out on the cross beneath the sun and the moon.[2] His mother, Mary, and his beloved disciple, John, stand beneath the cross, while the two thieves executed with Christ frame the scene, each lashed to a post. In the final scene, Mary Magdalene approaches the Holy Sepulcher from the right, where she encounters an angel, seated at the left, who points to the empty tomb, indicating that Christ is not here, as he has risen from the grave. In five scenes, the censer epitomizes the Gospels.

More than a simple biography of Christ, the scenes adorn a liturgical object with a liturgical sequence. Each of these vignettes depicts an event imaged and imagined in the early Byzantine liturgical calendar. Wrapping around the censer in a continuous ring, the scenes present the life of Christ as a cycle of observances at which a censer might swing. The artisan who executed the censer has considered the convex shape of the object and has placed the heads of the major figures above the curve, where they can catch the light. For early Byzantine Christians, incense symbolized prayers rising up to heaven, an understanding reinforced by a verse from the Psalms that opened the Vespers service: "Let my prayer rise as incense before you, a lifting up of my hand as an evening sacrifice" (Ps 140 [141]:2). Filling the church with sacred smoke, the censer and the story it depicts contributed to the sanctification of the congregation, reminding worshippers who they were in relation to the biblical narrative and thus to God.[3]

An arrangement of similar scenes adorns the underside of the sliding lid of a wooden reliquary box now in the Vatican Museums (Figures 4 and 5).[4] Dating from around 600, the box contains stones and fragments of wood that a pilgrim collected while on a visit to the Holy Land. Some still bear simple Greek inscriptions that indicate the places where they were obtained. One sliver of wood reads "from Bethlehem [ΑΠ ΒΗΘΛΕΕΜ]," presumably a relic of Christ's cradle. Three of the stones say "from [Mount] Zion [ΑΠ ΣΙΩΝ]," "from [the place of] the life-giving Resurrection [ΑΠ ΖΩΟΠΟΙΟΥ ΑΝΑΣΤΑΣΕΩΣ]," and "from the Mount of Olives [ΑΠ ΟΡΟΥΣ ΕΛΑΙΩΝ]." The illustrations expertly painted on a gold background coordinate with the items to trace the pilgrim's itinerary through the events of the gospel narrative. Reading from lower left to upper right, the lid depicts Christ's nativity at Bethlehem, his baptism at the Jordan River, his crucifixion at Golgotha, the women arriving at his empty tomb, and Christ's ascension into heaven on the Mount of Olives. The iconography of the first four of these scenes strikingly resembles the representations on the censer. The medium of paint permits a greater level of finesse and detail on the Vatican panel than the censer's cast bronze does. The crucifixion, for example, portrays men on either side of Christ, one raising a sponge with vinegar for him to drink, the other piercing his side with a lance, in keeping with the Gospels' accounts. The figures on the left and right in the Nativity and the Visit to the Tomb reverse the censer's arrangement, but retain the same basic composition. The Vatican box's Visit to the Tomb includes, in addition to the small peaked building, or aedicule, also on the censer, a rotunda covering that structure. As others have noted, this architectural environment does not look like the rock-cut tomb with a stone rolled from its entrance, as described in the Gospels. Rather it resembles the Church of the Anastasis (Resurrection) in Jerusalem as it had appeared since the fourth century, when, under the patronage of the Emperor Constantine I and his mother Helena, it became a pilgrim shrine. The Vatican box figures the women approaching the aedicule not merely as those of the Gospels, but also as the late sixth-century pilgrims who visited Jerusalem, one of whom commissioned the box.[5] Their destination likewise becomes both the empty tomb of the Bible and the covered tomb of pilgrimage.

While on the road, the pilgrim had journeyed through the events of Christ's life, collecting tokens at each sacred site. But this was not the first time that the pilgrim had trod such a path. The desire to see the places where the events of Christ's life had taken place had been formed at home, in the

Figure 4. Reliquary box with stones and slivers of wood from the Holy Land. Circa 600. Painted wood, stones, wood fragments, plaster. 24 x 18.4 x 3 cm. Photo: Vatican Museums © Vatican Museums.

Figure 5. Underside of the lid of the reliquary box from the Holy Land, with scenes from the life of Christ. 1 cm thick. Circa 600. Photo: Vatican Museums © Vatican Museums.

pilgrim's local parish church, where over the course of many years, through the cycle of feasts, the story of Christ's life had come alive in liturgical celebration.[6] Attending church, Christians heard the various elements of the narratives read out to them in the lectionary, expounded in sermons, and elaborated in hymns. Most never went on pilgrimage to the Holy Land, but all had sojourned through the story. The scenes painted on the reliquary lid thus carried multiple referents with respect to time and space: the gospel narratives, the experience of pilgrimage, and the flow of the liturgical year.

Both the censer and the reliquary box employ iconography for each of the individual scenes that had emerged and become quickly standardized over the course of the sixth century. Such images appeared on pilgrims' tokens, jewelry, and amulets, and in gospel books and lectionaries. Although it is unclear whether they derived first from the Holy Land or from Syria, these iconographic types enabled early Byzantine viewers to picture events of the Bible that were at once localized in the Holy Land in the past, and celebrated in the church and in the home in the liturgical present. The iconography served to illustrate each part of the story. The liturgy recruited the past and co-opted the landscape, placing the ritually formed viewer among the narrative's elements. On the lid of the Vatican box the sequence carries the viewer's eye and mind upward, from the Christ's earthly birth in the lower left to his heavenly ascension, both a temporal trajectory and a theological anagogy, leading to realities beyond time. On the censer, the sequence repeats in the round. Together, the censer and the reliquary box attest an experience of biblical time both linear and cyclical.[7] Time past combines with time present to position the Christian worshipper within the story of salvation.

A Church Present to the Life of Christ

By the sixth century, Byzantine Christian liturgy and art converged to bring the biblical narrative to life in a liturgical present. Together, hymns, prayers, sermons, and images encouraged Christians to visualize themselves as witnesses to biblical events and to understand themselves as the objects of God's work on earth. The resulting religious synthesis reveals the role of liturgy in the formation of communities and selves, and in defining the identity of the Christian "we." This mapping of the biblical narrative into liturgical time was by no means unique to Byzantium, and developed also among Syrian, Coptic, and Latin Christians, between late antiquity and the Middle Ages.

One might regard this aspect of the calendar as broadly typical of liturgical Christianities, even if only the Byzantine trajectory pertains to our inquiry here.[8] Two clerical authors, active in the capital during the mid-sixth century, help capture the character of these celebrations. In his hymns composed for festivals of the Christian year, Romanos the Melodist not only animated the narrative sequence of Christ's life; he invited congregants to enter the world of the Bible. Based in the suburban church of the Virgin in the Kyrou district in northwest Constantinople, he composed for the popular Night Vigils on the eve of major feasts from the 520s through about 555.[9] Just as Romanos's career was ending, a priest known as Leontios the Presbyter began to write and preach homilies for a small congregation elsewhere in the capital, although which church he served is unknown. Likely between 552 and 565, during the last years of Justinian's reign and Eutychios's first period as patriarch, he delivered sermons on major feast days to a lay congregation made up of ordinary artisans. In his preaching he shifted effortlessly between exegesis of a biblical past and vivid excitement about a biblical present.[10] Read in parallel, the works of Romanos and Leontios reveal the work of the clergy in shaping the experience of the liturgical calendar.

The precise dating of the standard iconographic types represented on the censer and the reliquary box is unclear; many devotional objects bearing such images appear to date from the second half of the sixth and the early seventh century. Their wide dissemination suggests a slightly earlier origin, contemporaneous with Romanos's productive years, perhaps, although likely in a different region. We cannot know whether Romanos's poems influenced the artists' rendition of the same events or whether Romanos came to visualize these events through the new iconographic forms; there may have been no direct influence between them. The immediate impact of Leontios's sermons is less clear, although his sermons appeared in a number of middle Byzantine homiletic collections.[11] We can however say that Romanos, Leontios, and the artisans who made devotional objects depicting scenes from Christ's life engaged a shared aesthetic. Each sought to make the stories of the Bible present to sixth-century Christians by offering points at which Christians could insert themselves into the biblical action.

Long before the iconoclastic controversy of the eighth and ninth centuries prompted elaborate theories of how Christ and the saints might be present in their images, ancient viewers expected that artistic representations rendered their subjects available. As Jaś Elsner has explained, "real presence in pre-Christian antiquity was both assumed and undertheorized, so that ancient

theorists would not have been entirely clear (should they have thought to
ask) in what sense, to what extent, and in what way a person's memory or a
god's divinity was contained inside an image."[12] Pre-iconoclastic Christianity in Byzantium operated under similar, if imprecise, assumptions. Just as
the image of the emperor presided over late Roman courts, standing in for
his presence and indicating his authority over legal proceedings, Christ was
simultaneously present in his image and in some sense absent.[13] More important, Christ's presence manifested itself in the experience of the viewer,
whether the viewer thought Christ inherent in the representation or not.
The image called Christ to mind; Christ could be profoundly present for the
viewer when she looked at and thought about him.[14] While a frontal image
of Christ, such as in the Sinai icon (Figure 1), might invite an experience of
direct communication between Christ and the viewer, narrative scenes posed
at once more complex and more bounded opportunities for engagement with
their subjects. In a representation of Christ's baptism, for example, Christ was
perhaps present in his image, but the larger interest was how the event of the
baptism—a moment in Christ's narrative—might be present. Here too, the
viewer's response to the image might render the event not merely presented
but present, both as the subject of memory and reflection and as a catalyst
for emotional engagement. Thus festal images, liturgical hymns, and sermons
invited Christians to experience the biblical narrative by rendering events
available through artistic and literary representation.

    In the previous chapter, we saw that the first-person singular passages at
the beginnings and endings of many of Romanos's hymns illustrate a generic
Christian individual formed in dialectic with biblical stories. Other passages
encourage the formation of the community as a group. For Christmas, Epiphany, Annunciation, Palm Sunday, Good Friday, Easter, Ascension, and Pentecost, Romanos wrote dialogues to dramatize the key stories and inserted
his sixth-century Christians as a congregation into the action as witnesses
and participants.[15] Much of his exhortation involves inviting people not only
to hear the events of the ritual drama but to see them. In contrast to those
hymns where Romanos sings as a single self, an "I," here the cantor performs
his role as deacon, calling his audience to prayer and directing their attention
to the liturgical moment. In composing his hymns, Romanos authored the
"we" that he invited Christians to identify with. Thus he shaped them as the
subjects of the liturgy, not merely in their roles as listeners to the strophes and
singers joining the refrain but as the recipients of the divine grace dispensed
through the biblical action.[16] In contrast to most of the hymns we discussed

in the previous chapter, where the hymns' placement in Romanos's sixth-century calendar remains a matter of some uncertainty, the assignment of the hymns for major festivals is obvious from their opening lines. And while we cannot know when, over the course of his long career, Romanos composed any of the individual festal hymns, or the order of their composition, his festal cycle as a whole exhibits a unified vision of how hymnography makes the year a liturgical experience. As a group, the hymns carry the congregation through the sequence of the biblical narratives as presented in the lectionary on holy days. In a similar fashion, Leontios the Presbyter delivered his sermons during the eucharistic liturgy, immediately after the biblical readings. Guiding the congregation's response to the lections, his preaching combined scriptural exegesis and moral exhortation with rhetorical flourishes designed to heighten the emotional engagement with the day at hand. With repeated phrases, rhythmic prose, and chains of association, he transmitted enthusiasm to his listeners, encouraging sentiments appropriate to the various deeds of God.

Time and the Liturgy

Within the sequence of festal hymns, Romanos employed a variety of techniques to encourage reflection on biblical celebrations. Often in a hymn's prelude and first strophe, the present tense and the word "today [σήμερον]" render the action of the Bible as if happening in the "here" and "now." Leontios worked similarly, creating a liturgical time that collapses the worshippers' present with the Bible's past. In effect these writers created a biblical and liturgical present.[17] In other places in their hymns and sermons, the biblical events have taken place in the past, but the festival affords the opportunity not only to recall the stories but to respond to them with both the appropriate interior comportment and outward expression, ranging from grief to jubilation. Thus Romanos and Leontios employed liturgical writing, hymnography and homiletics, to shape emotional responses to scriptural events. As a survey of these hymns and sermons demonstrates, their task involved instructing their congregants how to react to the Bible and its liturgical commemoration. By coordinating their festal compositions with images on sixth-century devotional objects, we can see how art and hymnography performed similar tasks.

What Romanos and Leontios accomplished in the mid-sixth century, calling congregants to the biblical action, was not entirely new, but rather

marked a stage in a long development of attitudes about how Christian liturgy might work.[18] On the one hand, liturgical historians Paul Bradshaw and
Maxwell Johnson have argued that the fourth-century liturgy was largely "a
historical remembrance and commemoration of the *past*."[19] Even the liturgies
in and around Jerusalem, celebrated on the spots where the biblical events
were believed to have taken place, recalled the biblical narrative without re-
enacting it, "remind[ing] worshippers of the story to bring it alive for them."[20]
On the other hand, the homilies that Gregory of Nazianzos composed in the
380s for various festivals of the church engage in a mixture of what Nonna
Verna Harrison has characterized as "festal anamnesis" and "festal mimesis,"
both the retelling and the reenactment or re-presentation of biblical events, a
strategy similar to Romanos's. In Gregory's festal homilies, the events of salvation history occur in the present: on Christmas, "Christ is born. . . . Christ
is on earth"; on Epiphany, "Christ is illumined. . . . Christ is baptized"; and
at Easter, "Christ is risen from the dead. . . . Christ is freed from the tomb."[21]
These sermons became canonical readings for various feasts by the ninth
century, but their immediate impact on late-fourth- and fifth-century Christians is more difficult to gauge.[22] One homily by the fifth-century patriarch
Proklos of Constantinople (c. 390–c. 446) on the Nativity repeatedly pairs the
word "today" with the past tense, while another prefers the present. A homily
on the crucifixion regards that event as in the past.[23] The early sixth-century
Syriac hymnographer Jacob of Sarug (c. 451–521) composed a homily for the
Great Sunday of the Resurrection that speaks of "today" (*b'yoma, yoma ha,
b'hana yoma*) in the past tense, treating Easter as a day to remember the great
events of salvation.[24] In his sermons Leontios the Presbyter oscillates between
treating biblical events in the past tense, drawing meaning out of the words of
scripture, and declaring the events present in their liturgical celebration. As
in Romanos's treatment of these observances, we see an eagerness to meld the
past and present, thus grafting the community onto the biblical events that at
once had redeemed and were redeeming them.

Christmas

By the sixth century, the main holidays observing events in Christ's life had
been in place in Constantinople for some time.[25] With one possible exception,
Romanos's poems did not introduce new festivals, but rather sought to frame
the experience of those already familiar. On Christmas, Romanos invited

Figure 6. Pilgrim flask depicting the Adoration of the Magi and Shepherds (obverse); and the Ascension of Christ (reverse). Palestine. Sixth-seventh century. Tin-lead alloy. Grabar no. Monza 1. Museo e Tesoro del Duomo di Monza, Italy. Photo: Foto Marburg/Art Resource, NY.

Christians to visualize the events as if on a visit, constructing the congregation as liturgical pilgrims. The hymn *On the Nativity* begins,

> The Virgin today [Ἡ παρθένος σήμερον] gives birth to him who is
>   above all being,
> and the earth offers a cave to him whom no one can approach.
> Angels with shepherds give glory,
> and magi journey with a star,
> for to us there has been born
>   *a little Child, God before the ages.*
>
> Bethlehem has opened Eden, come, let us see [δεῦτε ἴδωμεν];
> we have found delight in secret, come, let us receive [δεῦτε λάβωμεν]
> the joys of Paradise within the cave.[26]

The poet lures the listeners as a group into the narrative—"Come let us see," "Come let us receive"—presenting the annunciation to the shepherds and the adoration of the Magi as if these were happening in the very moment and as if each listener might join in. The congregants travel with the Magi to Bethlehem, now situated in the present. Western Christians will be familiar with a similar technique in the Christmas carol "Adeste Fideles," "O Come All Ye Faithful," most likely composed in the eighteenth century. Here too, the hymn invites the congregation to journey to Bethlehem to behold the Christ child.[27]

Romanos's words describe a scene familiar in later sixth-century depictions of the Adoration of the Magi, such as we find on a pilgrim's flask collected in Jerusalem and once filled with holy oil from the Church of the Anastasis, or Holy Sepulcher (Figure 6), now in the Cathedral Treasure in the Italian town of Monza.[28] The encircling inscription reads, "Oil of the wood of life of the holy places of Christ." The flask depicts Mary enthroned with the Christ child beneath the star of Bethlehem. Angels above lead the Magi (left) and the shepherds (right) to venerate the Virgin and child. The Magi's Phrygian caps indicate that they come from the East and have traversed afar. Gary Vikan has argued that pilgrims saw themselves in this iconography, that "Pilgrims in effect *became* Magi."[29] Pilgrims imagined themselves imitating these biblical travelers: they too came to the Holy Land to worship Christ. Similarly, when they visited the Holy Sepulcher, they imitated the Marys who visited Christ's tomb on Easter Sunday and found it empty.

And yet, Romanos's hymn makes it clear that such an experience of visiting a biblical place in the company of biblical characters was not reserved to pilgrims alone. The liturgy in one's home church could render biblical events present far from Jerusalem. Romanos even saw the parallels from one calendrical reenactment to another: in one of six surviving hymns *On the Resurrection*, written for Eastertide, the women approaching the tomb speak to each other,

> Come let us hurry, like the Magi
> let us adore and let us offer
> sweet spices as gifts [Mt 2:11] to the One who is now wrapped,
> not in swaddling clothes, but in a shroud.[30]

The Marys imitate the Magi, and both become types for the celebrating Christian. Thus Romanos engaged in a depiction of biblical events that drew the congregant, as a viewer, into the action. The Monza flask underscores the liturgical associations of its iconography. Beneath the scene of adoration, and above a lower register full of the shepherds' flocks, the inscription reads "Immanuel, God is with us [EMMANOYHΛ MEΘ IMΩN O ΘΣ]," a quotation from Matthew 1:23, a verse that in turn quotes and explicates Isaiah 7:14.[31] ("'A virgin will conceive and bear a son, and they shall name him Emmanuel,'

which means 'God is with us [μεθ' ἡμῶν ὁ θεός].'") Both the late ancient Jerusalem lectionary and the middle Byzantine typikon for Hagia Sophia assign
Isaiah 7:14 to the Vigil preceding the Feast of the Nativity and Matthew 1:23 to
the readings for Christmas morning.[32] Romanos echoes the verse from Isaiah
in the first strophe of his hymn *On the Nativity* (1.1.7) and quotes the gloss
from Matthew in a hymn for Epiphany, "God is with us, nations, / know and
understand" (6.11.2). We can be reasonably confident that a Greek-speaking
pilgrim from anywhere in the Eastern Mediterranean would understand that
the inscription revoices words familiar from the liturgies where the nativity
of Christ and the adoration of the Magi were envisioned. That is, liturgical
participation framed the pilgrim's experience.

Romanos's hymn also prompts theological reflection on what his congregants observed. Listening to the cantor sing and joining in on the refrain, the
congregation first overhears the Virgin Mary's speech to her infant son, as she
expresses her amazement at the incarnation and the virgin birth and wonders
at God's purpose: "Maker of heaven, why have you come to those born of
earth?" (1.3.2). Then they are present as the visitors from the East approach
her door and ask Mary questions:

> "Who are you,
> that you have borne such a child?" (4.5–6)

In the midst of the action, the Christmas Vigil becomes an occasion to puzzle
at the mystery of salvation. Joining in the refrain to the numerous strophes,
the congregation sings along with Mary, the Magi, and with the narrator, the
"I" of Romanos, participating in the reenactment: *"a little Child, God before
the ages."*

By contrast, Leontios the Presbyter focused on the consequences of
Christ's birth, declaring ecstatically thirteen times in the opening of his Nativity sermon, "Christ has been born! [ὁ Χριστός ἐγεννήθη]."

> Christ has been born and Adam has been recalled.
> Christ has been born and Eve has been ransomed from grief.
> Christ has been born and the snake has disappeared.
> Christ has been born and Paradise has been restored.[33]

The savior's advent reverses humanity's expulsion from the Garden of Eden.
For Leontios, Christ's birth has also caused the decline of Judaism and set

Christianity on a firm foundation. Furthermore, the nativity of the savior
has affected the experience of Christian worship in smell and sight as well as
sound. The rhetorical repetition of the declaration of the savior's birth ends,
"Christ has been born and the church has been perfumed. Christ has been
born and the light has been added."[34] The sweet odor and divine light that
have come to the whole Christian world are present among the congregation in the liturgical celebration of Christmas: in the smell of incense and the
light from the candles lit in the middle of the year's darkest night. Leontios
declares, "Today there is both an increase of material light and an illumination of spiritual light."[35] Later in the sermon, Leontios subtly shifts an event
in the past into the liturgical present. Commenting on the lection from Matthew 2:12 about the Magi coming from the East—"You have just heard the
evangelist Matthew saying,"—he renarrates the key elements of the story with
present tense verbs and in rhythmic cadence:

> "In Bethlehem of Judea [Mt 2:1]" Christ the Master is born,
>   and is seen before all by Magi.
> In the days of Herod [Mt 2:1]"
>   and he who is without a beginning makes a beginning to his days.
> He is born in a cave
>   and bears everything in his hand.
> He is placed in a manger,
>   and becomes food for all [i.e., in the Eucharist].
> He is wrapped in swaddling-clothes,
>   and bestows release from sin.

If the event is past, its implications manifest themselves in the triumphant
present for all congregants, the subjects of God's salvation, through his incarnation and through the distribution of his body and blood.

A gold medallion now in the British Museum highlights the salvific and
protective effects of the incarnation. An intimate object, 5.8cm in diameter,
its loop indicates that it was worn around the neck, a piece of jewelry that
functioned as an amulet (Figure 7). In an abbreviated version of the scene
on the Monza flask, the obverse depicts the three Magi approaching an enthroned virgin and child; a star and an angel guide them. Of course, one finds
no angel in Matthew's account of the Magi's visit, only in Luke's story of the
Shepherds, and the angel is probably a holdover from the more complete depiction of the subject, as on the Monza reliquary flask (Figure 6). As on that

Figure 7. Gold medallion depicting the Adoration of the Magi with the inscription "Lord help the bearer, Amen" (obverse); and the Ascension of Christ with the inscription "Our peace we leave with you" (reverse). Sixth/seventh century. 68 x 58 mm. © The Trustees of the British Museum [1983,0704.1].

flask, the reverse depicts the Ascension of Christ. To some extent the two scenes book-end Christ's life on earth from his infancy to his departure for heaven, much as in the lower left and upper right of the Vatican reliquary box (Figure 5). Both scenes show others interacting with Christ: either approaching him from afar or looking up in wonder. Both the Magi and the Apostles offer points of insertion for the viewer into the image and the scene displayed. Below the Adoration on the medallion the inscription offers a simple prayer in somewhat irregular Greek, "Lord help the bearer, Amen." The participle is feminine (ΦΟΡΟΥΣΗ), indicating that the amulet was worn by a woman. In effect, she approaches the Lord much like the Magi, but in an act of supplication, asking for divine assistance. The power of biblical iconography and the events it called to mind could provide physical protection in the course of this life and offer the promise of salvation in the world to come.

Epiphany

Twelve days after Christmas, on January 6, the manifestation of Christ's identity at his baptism, celebrated on the Feast of the Theophany, or Epiphany, also takes place in the liturgical present.[36] Romanos's hymn *On the Holy Theophany* begins,

> You have appeared today [Ἐπεφάνης σήμερον] to the inhabited world
> and your light, O Lord, has been signed upon us [Ps 4:6],
> who, with knowledge, sing your praise, "You have come, you have appeared,
> *the unapproachable Light* [1 Tim 6:16]."[37]

On the one hand the hymnographer asserts that the congregation's own baptism, commonly called in Greek "illumination" or "enlightenment" [φωτισμός], has been sealed in the very moment of Christ's encounter with John at the Jordan.[38] The congregation sings its refrain in the present tense, offering its own liturgy as an immediate response to the event. On the other hand, Christ's baptism serves as a prompt for each Christian to take on Christ as a covering. Christ, "a great light has shone . . . blazing out of Bethlehem," his rays dawning "on the whole inhabited world" (5.1.2–5). Romanos invites Christians,

> Therefore let us all, Adam's naked children,
> put him [Christ] on that we may be kept warm;
> for as a covering for the naked and a light for the darkened
> you have come, you have appeared,
> *the unapproachable light.* (5.1.6–10; trans. Lash, 39)

Identified with Adam's nakedness after the Fall and at the same time with their own stripping in preparation for baptismal initiation, those assembled should respond to Christ's baptism by clothing themselves with Christ (Gal 3:27; Rom 13:14).[39] On a cold, dark night in early January, as they witness Christ's extended dialogue with John about the implications of his baptism for the salvation of the world, Romanos places his congregants into the story and calls them to participate in their own salvation, to cover and warm themselves in the new brightness. He recalls to them their own baptism, the ritual process which defined and defines them as Christian. This celebration of Epiphany reinforces each Christian as the subject of baptism and salvation. Both the historiated censer (Figures 2, 3) and the Vatican reliquary box (Figure 5) depict the precise moment of Christ's baptism with remarkable efficiency: with Jesus naked in the water between them, John places his hand on Christ's head. The dove descends from heaven, manifesting Christ's divine identity as the Son of God. But the feast celebrating this event encouraged viewers not only to see God in Christ but to see Christ's baptism as a type for their own initiation, to see themselves as recipients of divine enlightenment in God's sealing grace.

John the Baptist provides a more complex point of comparison for Christians, as Romanos encourages sympathy with his thought patterns and identifies him with their parish clerics. Much of the hymn deals with John's reluctance, even his fear, to baptize Jesus, who coaxes him,

> Do not hesitate, baptize me. Just lend me your right hand.
> I dwell in your spirit and I possess you wholly.
> Why then do you not stretch out your palm to me?
> I am within you and outside you. (5.9.5–8; trans. Lash 43)

Having lent his power to John's right hand, Jesus explains that he will hand this power on to the apostles and subsequently to priests, thus prefiguring the role of priests in baptizing others. Romanos links this power explicitly with the action celebrated in the liturgical feast and presents it as something visual and audible:

> I am showing you clearly the Holy Spirit,
> I am making you hear the voice of the Father
> as it declares me his true Son. (5.13.6–8; trans. Lash 45)

When Romanos narrates the baptism itself, he shifts into the present tense and emphasizes its sacerdotal quality:

> [T]he son of the priest in the office of a priest
> stretches out his palm and lays his hand on Christ. (5.15.1–2; trans.
> Lash 45)

In response, John declares,

> I sense
> that I am more than I was before.
> I am something else. I have been changed, I have been glorified,

for I am seeing, I am baptizing
the unapproachable light. (5.16.6–10; trans. Lash 46)

In his imagining of Christ's baptism, Romanos has prompted his listeners to consider John's transformation and their own. But if baptism has begun the work of salvation, it is not yet complete. Romanos ends his second hymn on the baptism of Christ with the following prayer:

I sang a hymn [ὕμνησα] of your Epiphany; give me a clear sign;
Cleanse me of my hidden sins [Ps 18 (19):13], for my secret wounds
  destroy me.
. . . .
I uncover my suffering, I shall find you for my salvation,
  who appeared and illumined all things. (6.18.1–2, 8–10)

As witness to the Lord's baptism and a participant in its liturgical celebration, the singer recalls his own shame and the cleansing and healing it will yet take to make it right. Even as Romanos positions the subject in the liturgical present at the banks of the Jordan, he orients the Christian looking simultaneously inward at the sinful self and forward toward a salvation still in the future.

Annunciation

The other major Christological event fixed in the calendar is Annunciation, celebrated on March 25, a feast that usually occurs in the midst of Lent. Among the major feasts on Romanos's calendar, this was the comparative newcomer, perhaps originating in the early sixth century in Palestine and introduced to Constantinople in 550. It is certainly possible that in this instance Romanos wrote to promote a new observance.[40] While this event falls peculiarly with respect to the progress of the narrative of Christ during the course of the year—after Christ's Baptism and, usually, before Holy Week—its placement is fitting, occurring nine months before Christ's birth on December 25. The Annunciation begins the cycle of images on the Virginia Museum censer (Figures 2, 3). The scene also appears alone, as on a simple terra cotta token dated to the late sixth or early seventh century at the British Museum (Figure 8). The dissemination of the image in a variety of media suggests that the festival quickly became popular. About the size of a dime, this token was part of a trove of some eighty tokens that depict scenes from the Gospels, found near the column of St. Symeon the Stylite in northern Syria and made of local clay. Associated with pilgrimage to Symeon's shrine at Qal'at Sem'an, their local production precludes interpreting them as referring specifically to pilgrimage to Jerusalem. Rather, their primary referent is liturgical. Here Mary is seated on the right, spinning wool with a spindle and distaff, indicating that she is preparing to weave the body of God. From the left, beneath a cross, the Angel Gabriel gestures toward her in the midst of his speech.[41]

In a hymn *On the Annunciation*, one of two of his that survive on this subject, Romanos encourages the congregation not only to see the scene from the outside but to enter into it:

> With the angel Gabriel come [δεῦτε], and let us accompany him to
>   the Virgin Mary,
> and let us greet her as mother and nourisher of our life.
> For it is not only fitting for the general to greet the queen,
> but also possible for the humble to see and salute her.[42]

Thus the congregation joins the angel and imitates his address to the Mother of God, who by nursing the Christ child will offer the milk of everlasting life to all. Rehearsing both Mary's words in the Magnificat and Gabriel's salutation, "Hail (Lk 1:28)," Romanos guides collective exclamation as a repetition of the angel's veneration.

> As mother of God [μητέρα θεοῦ] all generations call you blessed (Lk
>   1:48) and call out,
> "Hail undefiled! Hail maiden called by God!
> Hail holy, hail delightful, hail beautiful!
> Hail comely, hail seedless, hail chaste!
> Hail mother who knew no man!
>   *Hail unwedded bride.*"[43]

Through their own singing, the congregation enters the soundscape of the Annunciation. Joining their voices with the archangel's, the congregation should marvel at the paradox of the incarnation. Liturgical singing thus bridges the gap between the present and the past, allowing something more than a reenactment of the ritual drama. Romanos employs voices as a medium through

Figure 8. Terra cotta token depicting the Annunciation, found at Qal'at Sem'an, Syria. Sixth/seventh century. 17.5 mm. © The Trustees of the British Museum [BM 1973,0501.1].

which to enter a biblical reality. Later, testimony during the sixth session of the Seventh Ecumenical Council at Nicaea in 787 expresses how such an opportunity for engagement with the story might lie inherent in a visual depiction: "When we see in an image [or: on an icon] the angel bringing the good news to the Virgin, we must certainly bring to mind that 'the angel Gabriel was sent from God to the Virgin. And he came to her and said: "Hail, O favored one, the Lord is with you, Blessed are you among women [cf. Lk 1:26–28]."' Thus from the Gospel we have heard of the mystery communicated to the Virgin through the angel, and this way we are reminded of it. Now when we see the same thing in an image [or: on an icon] we perceive the event with greater emphasis."[44] Well before debates about iconoclasm, hymnography and art converged in representing the event to draw renewed attention to the Gospel text.

Palm Sunday

Similar techniques shape the moveable feasts. Romanos's hymn *On the Entry into Jerusalem*, written for the Vigil of Palm Sunday, both melds and divides the past and the present to place the worshipper both within the action and beyond, responding to it with the benefit of hindsight. Christ's arrival in Jerusalem "carried on an ass" gains meaning in light of the coming crucifixion, and thus the palms celebrate a salvific event in both the action's future and the congregation's past.

> Since you have bound up Hades and killed Death and resurrected
>   the world,
> the children with palm branches shout to you, Christ, as to a
>   conqueror
> calling out to you today, "Hosannah to the Son of David."[45]

The children's acclamation, drawn from Matthew 21:9 and 15 and Mark 11:9, was heard also the following morning in the lectionary assignment for Morning Prayer and acclaimed during the processional liturgy at the Eucharist, where at least since the time of Egeria's visit to Jerusalem in 384, children participated in the festivities.[46] The hymn's refrain reveals that Christ comes not merely to be crucified, but "*comes to call Adam back*."

As the poem progresses, Romanos mixes his tenses. In some places the action is very much in the present:

> Behold our king, gentle and tranquil, seated upon an ass,
> comes in haste to suffer and to cut off suffering. (16.2.1–2)

Yet elsewhere Romanos narrates, "With palm branches the babes sang hymns to you, fittingly calling you Son of David" (16.6.1). This shifting of the entry into Jerusalem into the past, however, makes the liturgical reenactment an opportunity to join the chorus, as the cantor eventually sings in his own voice:

> Give me the skill to cry out [δεῖξόν με καλλίεργον βοᾶν], "Blessed
>   are you,
>   *who comes to call Adam back.*"[47]

When the congregation join in the refrain, they too yearn to participate appropriately in praising God, to take the acclamation of the innocent children—
occurring in a conflated past and present—as their cue for celebration.

A sermon by Leontios the Presbyter for Palm Sunday, by contrast, follows
the Constantinopolitan lectionary's assignment of John 12:1–18 to the Divine
Liturgy, although Leontios also plays with the concept of temporality.[48] The
sermon reflects on the verses, "The next day [i.e. Sunday; six days before the
Passover] the great crowd that had come to the festival heard that Jesus was
coming to Jerusalem. So they took branches of palm trees and went out to
meet him, shouting, 'Hosanna! Blessed is the one who comes in the name of
the Lord—the King of Israel'" (Jn 12:12–13). Although the Gospel's account
sets the event in the past, Leontios shifts it into the present and melds it with
the near and distant future. He repeats "already" and uses verbs with continuous aspect: "Already the favors of the Lord's celebration are peeping out;
already the signs of the most blessed feast [i.e., Easter] are running in anticipation . . . already the pleasures of the general resurrection are blooming in
anticipation as in the spring." Palm Sunday looks forward not only to Easter
but also to the end of time. Meanwhile, Christ's entry into Jerusalem becomes
present both in consideration of the reading from John, which the preacher
reminds his congregation they have just listened to, and in its liturgical reenactment: "Already the faithful crowd, running forward to meet the Lord,
shouts, as you have heard, 'Hosannah in the highest! Blessed is the one who
comes in the name of the Lord, the King of Israel.'"[49] Leontios exhorts his
congregation to "Listen to the day and seek it," for it provides an opportunity
"to cleanse yourself in advance from every blemish," "to undo enmity," "put
a stop to anger," "check slander," "bind fast love," and "increase your love for
the poor."[50] The short time before Good Friday and Easter thus provides an
interval for heightened attention to moral improvement. The congregation
runs forward, like Peter toward the tomb, eagerly preparing for Christ's resurrection and their own.

In another sermon for Palm Sunday, presumably preached in a different
year, Leontios glossed the lection and the liturgical acclamation of the "hosanna," saying, "The hymn-singing [ἁρμόζουσα] was truly suited to the Savior; the blessing was appropriate to the one who had won trophies. The song

of the crowd was a triumphal ode [ἐπινίκιον], for they had already caught the scent of the life-giving perfume of Christ, which clearly shows the defeat of death."[51] Leontios combines the royal ceremonial of the emperor's adventus into a city in victory with the incense of holiness redolent even within the church, able to cover the stench of impending death.[52] In this fashion, Leontios links the lection to the pageantry of the liturgical action. Palm Sunday looks backward to the time of Jesus, forward to the resurrection, and inward toward the self, encouraging moral progress.

Even images in nonliturgical books can indicate this liturgical dynamic. Just after the midpoint of the sixth century, around the time that Leontios preached, an artist depicted such a celebration of Christ's adventus in the luxurious Rossano Gospels codex (Figure 9).[53] The composition of the page overlays the liturgical celebration, the procession, and the lectionary readings appointed for the day. Here Jesus rides sidesaddle and is greeted by a crowd of men. Two cast down cloaks before him; others carry palm branches. Apostles gesture toward the Son of David. Children climb a tree (left) or the towers of the city gate (right) to catch a glimpse. The image draws elements from both the Synoptic Gospels, where the crowd spread their cloaks and lay down branches, and the Gospel of John, in which they lay down palms. But none of the Gospels mentions children at this point. They appear only later, in Matthew 21:16, a passage also part of the Jerusalem lections for the day, crying out, "Hosanna to the Son of David," after Jesus has cleansed the temple of the money changers and healed the blind and the lame. The depiction would seem, however, to be as much influenced by a sixth-century Palm Sunday processional liturgy as by the narrative accounts. Within the manuscript, the illumination is one of twelve scenes from Christ's life, including some of Jesus' miracles and parables, the trial before Pilate, and the Lord's Supper. These are collated at the beginning of the manuscript, which today contains only Matthew and most of Mark, but which originally must have contained all four Gospels. Likely used for continuous reading of the Gospels outside a liturgical setting, not as a lectionary, the images nonetheless present the stories through a liturgical perspective, in many cases coordinating the scenes with Old Testament prophecies that the events fulfill. Underneath the depiction of the Entry into Jerusalem, four prophets, depicted in bust, gesture toward the action. In three cases, their texts featured in the liturgy for Palm Sunday in late antique Jerusalem, as attested by the Georgian Lectionary. Two of these are quoted in Romanos's hymn *On the Entry into Jerusalem*, attesting their use in the capital, a practice later witnessed in the tenth-century

Figure 9. Christ's Entry into Jerusalem with the attestation of Old Testament prophets, from the codex known as the Rossano Gospels. Sixth century. Painted purple vellum. 11 x 10 ¼ in. Biblioteca Arcivescovile, Rossano, Italy. Photo: Scala/Art Resource, NY.

Constantinopolitan lectionary. The first text, under a portrait of King David, is Psalm 117 [118]:26, "Blessed is the one who comes in the name of the Lord," also quoted in each of the Gospels. The second bust is Zachariah, with the text of Zachariah 9:9, also quoted in Matthew 21:5 "Tell the daughter of Zion, your king comes to you . . . humble and mounted on a donkey and on a colt, the foal of a donkey." The Georgian Lectionary for Jerusalem assigns both that psalm verse and a snippet from Zachariah to the processional liturgy for Palm Sunday. The longer reading from this chapter of Zachariah was heard the previous Wednesday in Jerusalem and on the even of Palm Sunday in the Typikon for the Great Church in Constantinople.[54]

The third text is again from the Psalms, Psalm 8:3[2]: "Out of the mouths of babes and nurslings you furnished praise for yourself." It is unclear whether this verse was sung in Jerusalem, although the Georgian Lectionary assigns the preceding verse, Psalm 8:2[1], before the reading of the pericope from Matthew 21 that includes the episode where Jesus quotes this verse while speaking in the Temple. The verse does show up in the tenth-century Constantinopolitan Typikon as one of the Palm Sunday communion hymns, along with Psalm 117:26.[55] In the Gospel of Matthew 21:15, Jesus himself quotes this verse after casting out the money changers and performing miraculous healings. In any case, within the manuscript, the text serves as license for the prominent presence of children, both in familiar Palm Sunday processions and in the painted image. One finds a similar expectation of the centrality of children in an early ninth-century hymn by the Carolingian Theodulf of Orleans (c.750–821), familiar to Protestants in the translation of John Mason Neale:

Glory, and laud, and honor,
To Thee, Redeemer King
To whom the lips of children
Made sweet Hosannas ring.[56]

The last prophet, mislabeled Malachi, offers Zachariah 14:9, "And the Lord will become king over all the earth," which in the context of the Rossano Gospels presents the procession as a royal adventus, much as Romanos and Leontios do, although the passage does not occur in the Jerusalem lectionary until Good Friday.[57] The artist has melded the sights and sounds of the festival to render his Entry into Jerusalem a portrait of the pageantry of the church. He, like Romanos and Leontios, sought to convey the excitement of Christ's arrival in the Holy City and to anticipate its numerous consequences.

Great and Holy Friday

After the procession with the palms, Holy Week becomes more somber. In a homily for Good Friday, Leontios shifts once again between past and present tense in explaining the significance of the day: "When did the Lord pray for his enemies? When? On this present [παρούσῃ] Friday, when he was present [παρέστη] on the cross. For today, as you know, the judge of all is crucified."[58] Marking the cosmic drama, Romanos's hymn *On the Passion of Christ* narrates the death of God on the cross in its prelude as an event that has occurred "today," that is, in the very proximate past, and then calls for a cosmic response to the calamity in the immediate present.

> Today the foundations of the earth quaked;
> the sun, unable to endure the sight, hid itself:
> the source of all life lay stretched on the cross.
> Paradise had been opened to those locked in primeval sin.
>   *Only Adam dances for joy.*

> Draw back today [Ἔκστηθι σήμερον] in terror, heavens; sink into
>   chaos, earth;
> do not dare, sun, to gaze upon your Master
> willingly hanging on the cross.
> Let rocks be shattered: the Rock of Life is pierced by spikes.
> Let the veil of the Temple be split in two: the Master's body
> is being ripped by the lance of the lawless.
> Let all creation shudder and groan at the Creator's suffering.
>   *Only Adam dances for joy.*[59]

Invoking an apocalyptic scene based on biblical accounts of the aftermath of the crucifixion in Matthew 27:51–53, Romanos prompts an affective response: each Christian in attendance should recoil in terror, should shudder and groan. Collectively they should experience a violent sympathy with Christ's suffering and death. Romanos thus renders the action vivid to shape their emotional disposition.

While Adam, presciently, rejoices in his coming salvation, the Christian subject, at this moment, should feel and express grief and horror. In effect, Romanos supplies the congregation with their stage directions for participating in the subsequent scene. Later in the hymn, following the course of the passion narratives of the Gospels, Romanos recreates the crowd's taunting of Jesus, the High Priest's condemnation, the mob's call—"savage, bloodthirsty" (20.13.1)—for Jesus' crucifixion, and Pilate's washing of his hands. Framing this action, Romanos also affirms, in the first person singular, the benefit to each Christian from the death of Christ on the cross.

> O my Savior, you have taken my [nature] so that I may possess
>   yours.
> You accepted your suffering so that I could now
> scorn suffering; by your death I live again.[60]

Each person is thus implicated in the gift of new life resulting from Christ's death, and therefore becomes a more interested witness to the Passion. At the end of the hymn Romanos cues an additional response, calling on each, in the vocative and second person singular, to participate in the liturgical celebration of Christ and his sacrifice:

> O earthborn one, sing hymns to him; tell of the one who suffered
> and died for you (sing.). Receive him into your soul,
> whom you will see living once again after a little while. (20.23.1–3;
>   my trans.)

In expectation of the resurrection, the Christian self prepares joyfully for Christ to dwell within. Romanos thus calls the subject into formation in the trauma and the promise of Good Friday. The censer (Figures 2, 3) and reliquary panel (Figure 5) depict the essential elements of the scene, with Christ's arms stretched out on the cross, crucified between two thieves, while Mary and John stand on either side of the crucified Lord. Like Romanos's hymn, these images invite the viewer to witness the Son of God's sanctifying suffering. On the painted panel, the crucifixion occupies the entire middle register, dominating the visual field, thus placing the events of Good Friday at the center of Christian attention.

Easter

Two of Romanos's poems *On the Resurrection* adopt the central declaration of the Easter liturgy for their refrain, "The Lord is risen [Ἀνέστη ὁ κύριος]!," explicitly linking hymnography to the established liturgical form.[61] In their treatment of the resurrection as an event both past and present, they echo the discovery of the empty tomb on a late sixth-century pilgrim's ampulla (Figure 10).[62] The tin-lead flask, now flattened, once contained holy oil obtained at the Church of the Anastasis in Jerusalem. The scene is captioned with the same liturgical motto: "ΑΝΕΣΤΙ Ο ΚΥΡΙΟΣ," "The Lord is Risen." As in the biblical narrative, the two Marys approach the tomb and are greeted by an angel who tells them the tomb is empty. But the women do not carry a spice jar, as indicated in the narrative; rather, one swings a censer of the sort familiar in contemporary Christian liturgical celebrations. As on the censer (Figures 2, 3) and the reliquary panel (Figure 5), the flask depicts the scene familiar to pilgrims: the small aedicule with a peaked roof and a grilled gate under a large rotunda supported by tall columns. But the referent is not merely the Church of the Anastasis. The image conflates the sixth-century pilgrim's experience of a holy place with the experience of the liturgy commemorating the resurrection of Christ. The caption places the event in a conceptual Easter at once biblical, liturgical, and immediate. Long before the pilgrim had set foot on the road, she had experienced the joy and discovery of the risen God at Easter in her home church on a sixth-century Easter Sunday.[63] Liturgy had already conflated the past and present before the pilgrim journeyed to see the place where the events had happened.

Given their pronouncement that Christ has already risen from the grave, it is unlikely that either of these two hymns with "*The Lord is Risen*" as their refrain was sung at the Paschal Vigil beginning on Holy Saturday, which anticipated the lighting of the paschal flame.[64] Perhaps they were sung not at a Night Vigil at all, but during daylight. In the first of these hymns, the prelude exclaims triumphantly about Christ's rising as an event in the past that demands the refrain as a liturgical response in the present:

Death was swallowed up in victory [Is 25:8; 1 Cor 15:54]
by your rising from the dead, O Christ our God.
Therefore, we, exulting at your passion,
rejoice, forever celebrating,

Figure 10. Ampulla depicting the Women Discovering Christ's Empty Tomb. Jerusalem (?). Sixth–early seventh century. Lead. Diam. 4.6 cm. © Dumbarton Oaks, Byzantine Collection, Washington, D.C.

and cry out with jubilation,
  "The Lord is risen."[65]

The congregation joins the chorus with liturgically cued joy. The remainder of the hymn dwells on the request to Pilate to send soldiers to make sure the tomb was not raided and Jesus' body stolen. Framed by the repetition of the boastful refrain, these events serve to prove the resurrection and cause further exultation. Even with no surviving melody, one senses that the tone is giddy.

The second hymn with this refrain offers a chance for a personified Hell to have his say, and for much of the poem, the declaration that the Lord is risen falls perhaps unhappily on the lips of the vanquished. On the other hand, the refrain supplies Hell's punch line for nine of twenty-two strophes; thus the congregation gets to sing the victory over Death, perhaps even drowning out the voice of the adversary with this declaration.[66] Even so, Romanos opens the poem not in the first person plural or with an invitation to the collective. Instead, he sings in the first person singular, modeling the appropriate piety:

I venerate your cross, Christ my God,
and I shall glorify your tomb, Immortal One,
and celebrating your resurrection, I cry out to you,
  "The Lord is risen."[67]

Even the interrogation of Hell is prompted within the self, as the poet reasons
with Christ that only Hell would understand Christ's descent, "since [Hades]
was able from what he saw and what he suffered to learn of [God's] power"
(1.2). The hymn enacts intellectual curiosity and the pondering of the story
of the harrowing of Hell, as the "I" asks Hell for an explanation before turning to the guards, the human witnesses to the security of the tomb. Initially,
the "I" expresses doubts: even though he knows "exactly how [Christ] was
resurrected," he wants to ask the guards, "Who stole [Christ's] body?" (1.4),
and later,

Who rolled away the stone
and carried off the dead? (13.6–7)

The congregation thus becomes witness to a forensic investigation, one that
will reinforce faith in the resurrection with the gathering of the facts. Nevertheless, having opened the hymn in the first person singular, after the detec-
tive work is over and the "sweet word" (21.6) of the Lord's rising has been
confirmed, Romanos returns to himself, once again as the penitent. Looking
forward to the Second Coming, he closes the hymn with a prayer:

In the last hour, when you come to resurrect me—
for you will come, my Savior, not as now from the tomb, but from
      the firmament,
. . . .
then do not judge me, I pray, so that I may say, "Not for [my] pun-
      ishment but to redeem me,
  "The Lord is risen." (21.3–4, 6–7)

Even in the festive hour, now past the Lenten afflictions, the narrator's "I"
enacts the sinner seeking forgiveness. Easter merely offers a prism through
which to refract the penitential subject through the promise of salvation.

Leontios the Presbyter, preaching on Easter Day, emphasizes another element of the Easter liturgy, the psalm verse that served as an antiphon, and which he reminds his congregation has just been chanted responsively that morning, probably just before the epistle: "This is the day that the Lord has made; let us rejoice and be glad in it [Ps 117 (118): 24]."[68] He remarks:

> This is the day which is named after the Lord [*kyriakē*, that is, Sun-
>   day], of triumph,
> which is the cradle of the resurrection,
> which embellishes itself with grace,
> which is the banqueting house of believers,
> which is the dismembering of the spiritual lamb [Ex 12:8–11],
> which gives milk to those who are born again;
> which is [a day] of rest for those who are weary.[69]

In fact, while he encourages them to feast on lamb, he reminds them not to run off to taverns but to martyr shrines; not to celebrate in drunkenness but in moderation; "not exulting like Jews, but reveling like apostles," and by singing psalms at home.[70] Here the clergyman sought to regulate the celebration with proper comportment, emphasizing Christian self-control, because "on this day Adam was freed, Eve was released from suffering, humanity was redeemed from its distress. Today Christ our Master rose up from the dead in the night, appeared to Mary Magdalene and the other Mary first of all, and said to them 'Rejoice [Mt 28:9], and through all your sex.' 'Rejoice,' said the Lord to the women."[71] Easter was first and foremost a chance to celebrate redemption from sin. And thus Easter was always framed by the proper self-conception of each Christian as a sinner in need of this redemption.

Ascension and Pentecost

The two subsequent major festivals of the Easter season play on themes of presence and absence, raising questions about the availability of God to humanity and simultaneously forming and quelling Christian anxiety about separation from God. Forty days after Easter, Romanos's efforts to place the congregation within the biblical narrative involve inviting them to engage their imagination to visualize themselves in the midst of the story. In his hymn *On the Ascension of Christ* the cantor sings,

Let us imagine [Νομίσωμεν] we are standing on the Mount of Olives
and that we bend our gaze on the Redeemer,
as he rides upon a cloud.[72]

The poet directs their glance upward; so did sixth-century visual representations of the ascension. The Christian woman's gold medallion from the
British Museum provides a lively and dense depiction of the ascension of
Christ on the Mount of Olives (Figure 7).[73] Christ, seated in a mandorla,
is born aloft by angels while the disciples and Mary look up and gesture
in astonishment. The inscription at the bottom echoes Jesus' words at the
Last Supper (albeit in mangled spelling), where he explains to his disciples
that he will leave them, but that the spirit of God will abide with them:
"Our peace I leave with you [Jn 14:27]." Lest the viewer be worried about
divine absence after divine ascent, the image and inscription reassure that
God will remain present. More important, the apostles' gestures, with outstretched arms and raised hands, together with the angels' flight, guide the
viewer's eye upward, encouraging her to see Christ ascending. The medallion's rendering of Jesus' last act on earth employs the same iconography
as that found on the pilgrim's flask from Monza (Figure 6) and on a manuscript page from a sixth-century lectionary, now interleaved in the Rabbula
Gospels (Figure 11).[74]

Romanos's sensory engagement with the event inserts the congregation
into the action of the ascension. The eyes' upward glance figures the contemplation of higher matters.

Come, let us return to our senses [δεῦτε, ἀνανήψωμεν] and raise on
high our eyes and minds.
Let us mortals make our sight together with our senses
fly to heaven's gates.[75]

The liturgical self ascends bodily through ritual participation. Romanos also
emphasizes the apostles' distress, their grief, their weeping, and their groaning as they ask Jesus, "Are you leaving us, O compassionate one? Parting from
those who love you?" (4.4; Lash 197). Like the inscription on the gold medallion, the poem assumes a fear of absence. In fact, every strophe ends not only
with the refrain but with the identical line preceding it, as Jesus repeats to the
disciples, and thus to the Church,

Figure 11. The Ascension of Christ, now interleaved in the Rabbula Gospels (cod. Plut. I, 56), Syria, sixth century, folio 13b. © Biblioteca Mediceo Laurenziana, Florence, Italy. Reproduced with permission of the Italian Ministry of Culture. Any publication without permission from the ministry is strictly prohibited.

> I am not parting from you.
> *I am with you and there is no one against you.* (4.13–14)

But the repetition itself prompts the need for such comfort: Romanos moves the congregation to share the disciples' anxiety about Christ's departure.[76]

In the hymn *On Pentecost*, Romanos troubles the Christian subject with God's absence after his ascension. He bids God to "give swift and stable comfort," to his servants, "when our spirits are despondent."[77] "Be near us," he prays, "be near, you who are everywhere" (1.5). Quelling such worries, Romanos allows his congregants to hear him reminding God, "You were not parted from your disciples, Savior, when you took the road to heaven," and "not one place is separate from you." Indeed the apostles "had you in their souls" (2.6). Just as the disciples rejoiced "dancing and singing and glorifying" (2.8) after the ascension, the descent of the Spirit on Pentecost demands a liturgical response, one which has already been set up in the hymn's prelude. For Romanos, Pentecost is the typological reversal of the Tower of Babel in Genesis 11:5–7. In the first instance God "came down and confused the tongues," dividing the nations. But with the descent of the Holy Spirit, God "divided out the tongues of fire," and "he called all to unity." The cantor cues the congregation's refrain:

> and with one voice we glorify
> *the All-Holy Spirit.* (prelude)

Over the course of the hymn's strophes, the cantor manages the congregation's emotions and understanding, recounting the events of Acts 1 and 2 as the unlearned disciples prepare to receive the Spirit and then marvel at the gift of languages.[78] Romanos takes on a variety of clerical roles: raconteur of the biblical narrative, scriptural exegete, prayer leader, and doctrinal teacher. Thus he implicitly constructs the congregation not only as recipients of the Spirit but also as the recipients of the deacon's instruction in matters biblical and theological.

Leontios's two sermons on Pentecost interpret readings from John 7 and Acts 2, the lections appointed for the Divine Liturgy.[79] The reading from Acts recounts the descent of the Holy Spirit fifty days after Easter and the way in which the apostles began to speak in a variety of tongues. In one of these sermons, Leontios uses the word "today" thirty-five times. In one passage he slips effortlessly from what happened on this day in the past to reconfiguring it as something present.

Today the apostles had steadfastness;
today the fisherman are sophists;
today the ignorant are teachers;
today the ones who have one language have several languages;
today the inarticulate speak good Greek [ῥωμαΐζοντες].[80]

Treating the apostles as unlettered fishermen, Leontios follows Acts 4:13, which describes them as "witless and unskilled."[81] Tongues of fire have transformed them; today they are aflame and spread the word of the Gospel.

Following themes present in Romanos and on the gold medallion Ascension (Figure 7), Leontios's other Pentecost sermon negotiates the exchange of the Son for the Spirit.[82] He begins by "calling out quite loudly," a verse from Psalm 46, encouraging liturgical exuberance. "All you nations, clap your hands! Shout to God with a voice of rejoicing [Ps 46:2 (47:1)]." This psalm, in fact, had long associations not with Pentecost, but with Ascension, especially for a later verse: "God went up with shouting, the Lord with a sound of a trumpet [Ps 46:6 (47:5)]."[83] But why, asks Leontios, should the congregation rejoice? "Because the Lord of glory has ascended into heaven and the Holy Spirit has come down on earth."[84] Considering the Church as the bride of Christ, the preacher continues, "Because Christ the bridegroom has been taken up, [but] we have not endured widowhood."[85] Once again the descent of the Spirit happens in the present: "Today the Holy Spirit, as you have heard, opened heaven, filled tongues, enlightened the world, shone brightly on the apostles, put the Jews to shame, confused the Gentiles, was added to things below, but was not separated from things above." As so frequently in his sermons, Leontios reminds his congregation that their identity differed from that of both Pagans and Jews. Christians, and not Jews or Pagans, receive God's salvation as the subjects of God's grace.[86] Finally, Leontios shifts from narrative to catechesis, reminding his congregation, "[The Holy Spirit] proceeded from the Father, but it was not removed from the Father. It was sent by the Son, but did not change its place. The difference in the modes of expression comes from the hypostases, not from the one essence of the Godhead. We are taught as we can hear; we are not able to see how God is."[87] Thus the descent of the Spirit on Pentecost recapitulates the eternal outflowing of the Spirit from the Father. Leontios subsumes ritual time into the timelessness of God's interior life.

* * *

The sixth-century festal cycle helped Christians understand God's work-
ings in and out of time and situate themselves toward God within the life of
Christ. Romanos invited congregants to identify themselves not merely as
witnesses to the biblical narrative but as objects of God's purpose in enduring
incarnation, suffering, death, and resurrection. Leontios generated affective
responses to the narrative sequence that brought about Christian salvation.
In the course of his festal hymns Romanos took his congregation to a variety of biblical scenes. His hymns for the major feasts of the life of Christ
invited the whole assembly to join Romanos in witnessing the events being
celebrated. He invited them to "come" in the second person plural and prayed
on his and their behalf as "we" and "us." Present to the biblical narrative, he
encouraged lay Christians to watch the drama unfold, ponder the theological
paradoxes, and learn about their own place in salvation history.[88] Attendant
to the liturgical drama in the festal calendar, Romanos's and Leontios's congregants learned to place themselves within the action as recipients of divine
grace, as ones for whom the story was happening.

The singer and the homilist exhorted their congregants to listen, to watch,
and to sing along, forming them as the Church that God loved and chastised,
a communion of Christian selves, a collective subjectivity. These Christian
subjects inhabited multiple temporalities by engaging the biblical narrative.
Thus the preludes and the opening and closing strophes of Romanos's festal
hymns oriented Christians as a group toward the Bible, not only as participant witnesses but also as the subjects of God's interaction with humanity.
Slipping effortlessly between the present and past tenses, Leontios and Romanos encouraged immediacy in the subject's interaction with God's earthly
biography. Each Christian journeyed through the life of Christ; each self
formed in dialectic with the stories of the Bible. In the chanting and preaching, time past and time present meld to demand affective responses: joy at
the incarnation and resurrection, remorse at the crucifixion. Even on Christmas and Easter, our clerical authors reminded early Byzantine Christians that
their sin catalyzed the action, was the problem that God sought to solve, and
that Christ's suffering on the cross lay at the center of his saving deeds.

The centrality of the crucifixion within the narrative, where Christ gave
his life for the life of the world, would figure prominently in a new arrangement of liturgical scenes that gained popularity in the later eighth and early
ninth centuries, both during and in the wake of the debates about images, perhaps even influencing attempts to theorize how images might work. Pectoral
crosses with gospel iconography protected their wearers in both this world

Figure 12. Reliquary cross. First quarter of the ninth century. Constantinople. Silver with gold and niello. Now at the Pieve di Santa Maria, Vicopisano, Italy. Photo: Michele Bacci.

and the next by calling to mind not only Christ's saving passion but also other liturgical elements of his narrative. A silver cross from first quarter of the ninth century once enclosed a relic of the True Cross, a sliver of wood associated with Christ's crucifixion at Golgotha (Figure 12). Produced in Constantinople, the cross now belongs to a small church in the town of Vicopisano in Italy.[89] Illustrated in niello and gold on both sides with iconography mostly familiar since the sixth century, the cross supplements the scene of the crucifixion with a cycle of festal images, presenting a synoptic view of place, time, and space. At the center of the obverse, Christ hangs on the cross beneath the sun and the moon, flanked by Mary and John. Inscriptions nearby abbreviate Jesus' words to them: "Behold your mother" and "behold your son" (Jn 19:26–27). Above the crucifixion, the Angel Gabriel (*right*) salutes the Virgin in the scene of the Annunciation. The left arm of the cross depicts the Nativity, with the Virgin lying horizontally beneath a swaddled infant in a manger. Joseph appears below with his head in his hand, watching as the Christ Child

receives his first bath. The right arm illustrates the Presentation of Christ in
the Temple forty days after his birth, in accord with Jewish law regarding the
bringing of offerings and the purification of mothers after childbirth: at the
altar, Mary lifts her son toward the prophet Simeon (see Luke 2:25–35), an
event celebrated in early February from the later fourth century in Jerusalem
and introduced to Constantinople during the reign of Justinian I.[90] Beneath
the crucifixion, the lower arm depicts the Baptism of Christ.

The reverse depicts only two scenes. The lower arm depicts Christ's Resurrection, or Anastasis, employing a new iconography that replaced the visit
of the women to the tomb. Here, as in one of Romanos's Easter hymns, Christ
rises from up from Hell, trampling Death, personified under his feet. He has
burst the gates of Hell, suggested here as one door flies above his head, another behind his back. He lifts Adam and Eve (*right*) from their graves, while
David and Solomon peer out of a sarcophagus (*upper right*). An intimate object worn on the owner's chest, most likely under clothing, the cross's iconographic arrangement places the Baptism and the Anastasis back to back,
joining the viewer's own baptism to Christ's death and its promise of resurrection to new life.[91] The rest of the reverse is taken up with an artful distribution of the elements of Ascension iconography, with Mary prominent at the
center of the cross and the apostles arrayed horizontally along the left and
right arms. On top, Christ rises into heaven, completing a vertical movement
that begins at the bottom of the cross with the harrowing of Hell.

In a treatise defending images, roughly contemporaneous with the production of the Vicopisano cross, the ninth-century patriarch of Constantinople, Nikephoros I (806–815), discussed such gold and silver crucifixes, which
he asserted Christians had made "from the beginning." His remarks reveal
expectations about wearing such historiated phylacteries: "We Christians
wear [them] suspended from the neck and hanging down over the breast for
the protection and safeguarding [πρὸς φυλακὴν καὶ ἀσφάλειαν] of our lives
and for the salvation of our souls and our bodies; for which reason they have
received the name [phylactery], for curing our sufferings and for averting at-
tack by unclean demons. We believe [them] to possess these [properties], especially those on which the passion and miracles of Christ and his life-giving
resurrection are often shown in images. And there is an infinite multitude of
these found among Christians."[92] Offering its owner the protection inherent
in the Christological narrative as a whole, the Vicopisano cross condenses
the Gospels, the liturgical calendar, the wearer's earthly wellbeing, and her
eternal salvation. The cross's very form shapes this reiteration of the story of

Christ. Nikephoros remarked, "We see in a great number of places the cruci-fixion of the Lord depicted in an image [ἐν εἰκόνι]. . .the body suspended, the hands stretched out and pierced by nails; by means of all these is the saving passion of Christ depicted for us, that most marvelous miracle and the most significant way in which we have been saved."[93] Situating the atonement at the center of the account, the Vicopisano cross shapes the meaning of all the other episodes. Much as the liturgical calendar situated the Christian congre-gant with respect to the New Testament story, the cross in turn defines the viewer as one in need of its protection, pardon, and redemption.

CHAPTER 4

Eucharistic Prayers: Compunction
and the History of Salvation

The broad sweep of the annual liturgical cycle was hardly the only place where Christians found themselves read into the events of biblical history. Eucharistic prayers recited at the consecration of the host situated Christians in the long sweep of linear time, inviting the community's self-recognition as the children of Israel and as a church of sinners. In contrast to the annual liturgical cycle that inserted the congregation into different moments in the life of Christ throughout the year, the liturgical prayers of offering over the bread and wine incorporated Christians into the Old Testament narrative of Creation, Fall, Law, and Prophets, and the New Testament story of redemption at every celebration of the Eucharist. The liturgical year stretched out the New Testament story, from the birth of Christ to the descent of the Holy Spirit on the apostles, over half the year, from late December to the verge of summer. The Divine Liturgy, by contrast, presented the broad outlines of the entire biblical narrative in a single invariable prayer.

Here too sixth-century liturgists associated liturgical participation with the shaping of affect and identity. In 565, the final year of his reign, the Emperor Justinian published a law that reveals the penitential character of the early Byzantine Eucharist. The law ordered "all bishops and presbyters to say the prayers used in the divine oblation [προσκομιδή] and holy baptism not silently [κατὰ τὸ σεσιωπημένον], but in a voice that can be heard by the faithful people [λαῷ] so that the souls of those who listen may be moved to greater compunction [εἰς πλείονα κατάνυξιν] and raise up glorification [δοξολογία] to the Lord God."[1] Robert Taft notes that New Law 137 is the "only Late-Antique source . . . to show any concern that the people hear, understand, and interiorize the anaphoral prayers," but in fact the law codified Byzantine clerics' expectations about how liturgies effected the formation of self-regard among the laity.[2] It also asserted both the church's and the state's interest in shaping their subjects' interior religious disposition. Accounts from Constantinople in the subsequent decades attest that attendance at eucharistic services could be quite high, with large numbers of the laity receiving communion. Eustratios's *Life of Eutychios* relates that so many people attended the liturgy upon the patriarch's return to the capital in 577 that the distribution took "from the third to the ninth hour, because everyone yearned to receive communion from him." And at Easter shortly before his death in 582, "he gave the immaculate and life-giving body of our Lord Jesus Christ to all the lay faithful."[3] The Eucharist provided an important opportunity for liturgical instruction and formation of the self.

The prayer of divine oblation in question, also known as the anaphora [ἀναφορά], or prayer of "offering," is the rough equivalent of the Western Christian canon prayer. Recited over the bread and wine, the anaphora included an encapsulation of salvation history from creation to the incarnation, the description of the Last Supper ("On the night before he died for us . . ."), and the invocation of the Holy Spirit to transform the bread and wine into the body and blood of Christ. By the middle of the seventh century, and for the subsequent history of Byzantine Orthodoxy, the custom was for the priest to recite the anaphora in such a way that the congregation could not hear it. A slow shift toward a silent or inaudible anaphora seems to have begun in the early sixth century in Syria.[4] At the very end of Justinian's reign the practice had spread widely enough to be the object of imperial opprobrium. Part of the problem lay with the education and preparation of the clergy. The law's preface complains that some clerics "do not know even the prayer of the holy oblation (τῆς ἁγίας προσκομιδῆς) or of holy baptism." It is most likely that a party of church leaders requested the ruling and had a hand in shaping its text. The preface cites "various complaints" regarding "clerks, monks and certain bishops" who have not observed church canons. Moreover, provincial governors are directed to compel "metropolitans and other bishops" to convene synods to enforce the law (137.6.1). Church leaders would insure that the right words were said and the right feelings instilled.

From the legislation's point of view, the anaphoral prayers served to form the conscience of Christian listeners: they prompted congregants to recognize themselves as sinners in need of salvation and to express gratitude toward God for their redemption. While the law of 565 offers solid evidence that some churchmen in the mid-sixth century were reciting the anaphora silently, or in a manner inaudible to the congregation, it also confirms that the practice was far from universal. Furthermore, the effect of the sanctions enumerated in the legislation likely—if briefly—curtailed the liturgical innovation of silent praying that it cited as an abuse. Embedded in the legislation's concern for the clergy's competence and audibility lies a theory of ritual efficacy and a conception of how the eucharistic rites of the early Byzantine church ought to work on the assembled laity. We might call this an early Byzantine emic or indigenous theory of religion.

During the reign of Justinian the eucharistic prayer of the Divine Liturgy was doubly productive. Its epiclesis, the prayer invoking the presence and work of the Holy Spirit, served to confect the body and blood of Christ. And at the same time the prayer scripted and produced the conscience of the ideal Christian. With the promulgation of the law requiring an audible anaphora, the state expressed its interest in the successful formation of the liturgical subject, an introspective and penitent subject who, as we have seen, was modeled also in the first-person singular speech in the hymns of Romanos. The liturgy thus engaged in interpellation, calling the subject into linguistic existence through speech.[5] That is, the prayers of offering constituted a speech act effecting the production of ritualized subjects, subjects who identified themselves with the biblical narrative as recipients of divine grace. Indeed, the lay participant in the eucharistic rite was doubly subject, both to the law of the state and to the interpellative force of the liturgical service. The state, following the church leaders who initially complained about the eclipse of the audible anaphora, viewed the liturgy as an effective instrument in the formation of its subjects.

In publishing the law, the state expected that hearing the anaphora would stir the listener to greater compunction (κατάνυξις). The term *katanyxis*, compunction or contrition, derives from the church's discourse regarding the necessity of penance, not from standard legal vocabulary. Like its Latin counterpart *compunctio*, *katanyxis* indicates a puncturing or pricking of the heart or the conscience. This goading serves as a motivation to repentance. Despite the legal tradition's interest in punishment and reform, this is the only occurrence of the term "compunction" in the entirety of Justinian's *Corpus of Civil Law*.[6] "Compunction," however, appears a dozen times in the hymns of Romanos, suggesting that mid-sixth-century liturgists viewed the cultivation of compunction as one of the desired effects of participation in Christian ritual activity in general, not just the Eucharist. In fact, New Law 137's linkage between the soul's compunction and the glorification of God echoes the final strophe of one of Romanos's hymns for the season of Easter.

> Grant compunction to our souls [κατάνυξιν ταῖς ψυχαῖς ἡμῶν], O
>   merciful One,
> so that we might glorify (δοξάζωμεν) you,
>   *the Life and the Resurrection.*[7]

In preludes to the hymns *On the Harlot, On the Hemorrhaging Woman,* and one of the hymns *On the Prodigal Son,* the cantor "cries out" to God "in compunction" for salvation, modeling in the first person singular remorse as a proper response to sacred stories.[8] In *On the Mission of the Apostles,* the cantor's prayers express fervent desire for compunction:

> Make clear my tongue, my savior, open wide my mouth
> and fill it. Prick [κατάνυξον] my heart
> so that I might follow what I say and be the first to do what I teach.[9]

Elsewhere he calls on God on behalf of the congregation: "Grant compunction to your servants."[10] He invites his listeners to engage in the practices of repentance. A prelude for a hymn *On the Ten Virgins* (which may not be part of Romanos's original composition) warns that the "judge is at the door" and encourages hearers,

> Let us go fasting, and let us offer
> tears, compunction, and alms
> crying out, "We have sinned more than the sands of the sea."[11]

In *On Repentance* Romanos offers biblical types of the repentant community:

> Let us then lament from the heart
> as the Ninevites in compunction opened heaven
> and were seen by the Deliverer and he accepted their repentance
>   (μετάνοια).[12]

Thus the corpus of Romanos demonstrates a clergyman's desire to inspire feelings of compunction in the congregation though the experience of the liturgy, and offers a context in which to understand clergy complaints that if parishioners could not hear the anaphora, they might miss an opportunity to be coaxed toward repentance. And not long after Justinian's death, the Patriarch Eutychios introduced his communion hymn for Holy Thursday, *At Your Mystical Supper*, encouraging people to receive communion while identifying with the Thief, the saved sinner, and not with Judas. Clerics were the agents and authors of a liturgy of compunction.

The Eucharist had become in essence a penitential rite, even if one prepared for it by confessing and purifying the conscience. Although early Byzantine religious leaders believed that there was an eternal liturgy of some sort in heaven, not all believed that it included a sacrificial offering. The heavenly liturgy might consist of glorification without compunction, because in heaven compunction was unnecessary. Some aspects of the eucharistic liturgy clearly linked earthly practice with the eternal liturgy in heaven. Early in the anaphoral prayer, the priest cued the congregation to join the nine ranks of angels, and especially the Cherubim and Seraphim, in the Sanctus hymn. By the end of the fourth century, Eastern Mediterranean liturgies adopted an expanded version of the Septuagint text of Isaiah 6:3, where the winged creatures sang antiphonally before the throne of God: "Holy, holy, holy, Lord Sabaoth, heaven and earth are filled with your glory. Hosanna in the highest."[13] The correspondence between earthly and angelic singing was reinforced with Justin II's introduction of the *Cherubic Hymn*, which the twelfth-century historian George Kedrenos dated to 573/4. Sung during the Great Entrance, the procession of gifts toward the altar, the hymn identified the congregation in their liturgical participation as "We who mystically represent the Cherubim and sing the thrice-holy hymn [i.e. the Sanctus] to the life-giving Trinity."[14] But even though the congregants might represent the angels in singing the eternal hymn, they did not necessarily emulate the angels when they offered the eucharistic elements.

Some Byzantine Christians believed, moreover, that the sacrificial liturgy would come to an end. The *Hexaemeron* of Anastasios of Sinai, most likely composed in the last decades of the seventh century, reflects the view that the eucharistic offering was necessitated by the fall into sin. A monastic teacher who had lived in Cyprus and Palestine before he entered the monastery at Mount Sinai, Anastasios looked forward to the life of the Resurrection: "This will be a day free of servitude, when sacrifice and the liturgical service for our sins are no longer offered to God."[15] In his *Questions and Answers*, Anastasios repeats the view of an unnamed monk who explained, "All the services and liturgies and feasts and communions and sacrifices take place for this purpose, that one may be purified from sins, and that God may dwell in that person."[16] In the previous century, Romanos had expressed the view that the earthly liturgy would come to an end at the time of tribulation, in the hymn *On the Second Coming*, which closely follows a homily of the Greek Ephrem. At that time, "The Holy Things [τὰ ἅγια] will be taken away," he says, using the same term the priest uses at the elevation of the consecrated bread: "Holy things for the holy!"[17]

> And so all who await Christ will die persecuted,
> psalms and hymns will cease,
> nor will there be liturgy [λειτουργία] or consecration [ἁγίασμα], of-
>   fering [προσφορά] or incense [θυμίαμα]. (13.1–3; trans. Lash,
>   226)

Relying on a prophecy in Daniel 9:27 predicting the cessation of sacrifice at the last times, Romanos conceives that the eucharistic service will not persist in eternity, neither its sacred actions, nor its prayers, nor its appurtenances. Furthermore, Romanos's expectations about the "psalms and hymns" may point beyond the eucharistic liturgy to the Liturgy of the Hours, including Morning and Evening Prayer, and even the Night Vigil itself. All sacrificial worship of God will come to an end, in part because of the reign of the anti-Christ, but also in part because the conditions that require its offering will no longer obtain. When God Incarnate comes on the clouds to reign,

> the ranks of all the angels
> and archangels praise you as they run before your throne, Lord.
> . . . .
> Cherubim and seraphim minister with trembling
> and ceaselessly give glory, as they sing the Thrice Holy Hymn.
>   (16.2–3, 6–7)

The Sanctus prayer persists, but at this hour it is too late for repentance (22.1–9) and apparently Eucharists never resume. While this construal may not have been universal, it follows logically from the assumption that the Eucharist itself was a rite performed under conditions of sin.

If, in Romanos, compunction and doxology served as the desired responses to biblical stories and their exegetical expansion in hymnody, what was it in the anaphoral prayers of the eucharistic liturgy that might prompt the same interior religious disposition and practice? What was it that sixth-century Byzantine clergymen thought needed to be heard "so that the souls of those who listen may be moved to compunction," so much so that they sought assistance from the legal apparatus of the state? Answering this question would prove easier if we knew with precision the prayers of oblation that the authors of New Law 137 had in mind. A variety of anaphoral forms were in use throughout the empire in the sixth century. Many of them derived from liturgical traditions associated with Antioch and Western Syria in the fourth century, including forms in the trajectories of the Liturgy of Basil and the Liturgy of James. Some form of the Liturgy of Basil had become standard in Constantinople before the beginning of the sixth century, although the received text of the Byzantine Liturgy of Basil derives from a later date. The earliest surviving manuscript witness, in the Barberini Euchologion (Barberini gr. 336), dates from the 790s. The text breaks off toward the end of the recitation of salvation history. From this point, our earliest witness is Grottaferrata Γβ VII of the tenth century.[18]

Liturgies of the West-Syrian type, including the Liturgy of Basil, emphasize the history of salvation and include encapsulations of the biblical narrative from creation to redemption. This narrative includes the fall of humanity and the calling of the prophets. Such focused reshaping of the Old Testament story functions to explain the necessity of Christ's advent and sacrifice. Perhaps most significantly, the anaphora identifies the congregation as the subject of biblical narrative. It all happened to a congregational "us." I would argue that it was the recitation of salvation history in particular that Justinian's law expected would prompt compunction. As in the hymns of Romanos, exposure to biblical narrative effected the pricking of the heart or conscience and inaugurated processes of moral reflection and repentance. The law of 565 thus confirms the essentially penitential character of early Byzantine eucharistic worship. Hearing the narration of salvation history in the anaphora would also move Christians to glorify God; but the context for this doxological response lay in Christians' interiorization of their identity as contrite sinners. The ideal subject of the liturgy offered glory to God in gratitude for a much-needed salvation.

Even with the great variety of forms in use in late antiquity, at the center of all eucharistic liturgies lay the recollection and reenactment of Jesus' deeds at the Last Supper in the offering of bread and wine as his body and blood. With the repetition of the words of institution ("This is my body . . .

Figure 13. Paten with the Communion of the Apostles (Riha Paten), said to be found at Riha near Aleppo, Syria. 565–577. Silver, gilding, and niello. 35 x 35 x 3.18 cm. © Dumbarton Oaks, Byzantine Collection, Washington, D.C.

This is my blood") and the attendant priestcraft, the historical anthropologist can envision a Christian melding of myth and ritual.[19] A silver paten from Northwest Syria, crafted during the reign of Justin II, underscores the early Byzantine synthesis of rite and history (Figure 13).[20] Fashioned to hold the eucharistic bread, the paten illustrates the Communion of the Apostles. Christ is depicted twice, distributing both the bread and the wine to his disciples. Not merely an event in the past, the scene offers a foundation or type for the ceremony in which the object itself was used. Jesus does not sit, as in the gospel accounts, but stands behind an altar table laid with a sumptuous cloth. Behind him an architectural setting suggests a chancel screen. The event takes place in a church, and on the altar are a chalice, a paten, and two wineskins. Jesus presides at once over the historical Last Supper and over the Church's Eucharist, the later rite that developed to commemorate, reenact, and repeat the event. The paten's viewers, seeing the scene outside of the service itself when the paten was not in use, would understand themselves to participate in the same rite when they took communion. The Eucharist thus caused participation in the central New Testament event and liturgical rite in which Jesus fed himself to his followers.

But the predominant Eastern Christian eucharistic liturgies also emphasized an earlier past, a past that spanned the time from Creation and the Fall through the Law and the Prophets, thus setting a historical context for God's acts of salvation in the person and work of Jesus Christ. Unlike the variable preface prayers of the Roman and other Western liturgies that focused the celebration of the mass on the liturgical season, in Byzantium the anaphora did not vary throughout the year. These Eastern liturgies invariably set the eucharistic sacrifice within the huge sweep of time from creation to redemption. During the introspective season of Lent, the celebratory triumph of Eastertide, and the long months after Pentecost, the anaphora served to form repentant subjects in response to the sweep of biblical history.[21]

The anaphoras of the so-called West Syrian type, including those associated with the development of the Liturgy of Basil, constructed a biblical past not only through ritual reenactment but also, and perhaps primarily, through the ritual recitation of the history of salvation. From the late fourth century to the early seventh—that is, before the advent of the silent anaphora—when Christians assembled for the Divine Liturgy in congregations throughout the eastern Mediterranean, they tended to hear encapsulations of biblical tradition during the anaphora. The eucharistic prayers provided a liturgical mechanism for teaching a sacred history. They constructed a Christian identity grounded in an interpretation of the biblical past that, through ritual participation, Christian congregations came to inhabit. The contrast between the story telling of the biblical narrative and the re-presentation of Christ's Last Supper raises questions about the relative importance of narration and performance in late ancient Christian ritual. These questions move beyond the shape of the liturgy to the goals and priorities of the shapers of the liturgy and the effects of the liturgy in shaping Christians.

Anaphoral Practices

The emphasis on the narration of the biblical past before the consecration of the bread and wine was especially prominent among a family of liturgies that scholars have termed West Syrian: the earliest extant example derives from the region of Antioch in the late fourth century.[22] At its first textual appearance, in a compilation known as the *Apostolic Constitutions*, the form shows ample evidence of prior development, indicating that the basic outlines are much earlier. The most enduring member of this liturgical family is the Byzantine Liturgy of Basil, some form of which had become standard in Constantinople before the early sixth century and remained the principal liturgy of the Byzantine Orthodox church until the eleventh century, when it was replaced by the Liturgy of John Chrysostom at all but ten services per year. Within this family, the placement of the historical narrative varies, sometimes occurring before the Sanctus prayer, and sometimes after it. In either position, the recitation of biblical history frames the re-enactment of the Last Supper and participation in communion.

After the Sanctus prayer, the received form of the Byzantine Liturgy of Basil has the priest recount to God the history of the creation and fall of humanity: "For you took dust from the earth and formed the human; you honored him with your image, O God, and set him in the paradise of pleasure, and promised him immortality of life and enjoyment of eternal good things in keeping your commandments. But when he had disobeyed you, the true God who created him, and had been led astray by the deceit of the serpent and had been subjected to death by his own transgressions, you, O God, expelled him in your righteous judgment from paradise into this world and turned him back to earth from which he was taken."[23] This protological account ends with a foreshadowing of redemption, reminding God that he was also already dispensing to humanity "the salvation by rebirth which is in your Christ."[24] The historical sweep then moves quickly through the shape of the Old Testament narrative as read through a Christian lens: "You sent forth prophets; you performed works of power through your saints." And at this point, the prayer introduces the first-person plural, the congregational "we," making the congregation, indeed the whole Church, the object of God's work of redemption. "You spoke to us through the mouth of your servants the prophets, foretelling to us the salvation that should come; you gave the Law for our help; you set angels as guards over us."[25] The liturgical repetition of the narrative thus constructs and interpellates the congregants as the "us." Through ritual narration, the text identifies the Christian community as the ones upon whom God has acted. Only after this biblical story forms them do the participants reenact Christ's last supper. Unfortunately, for our purposes, this version of the prayer occurs for the first time in the late eighth-century manuscript of the Barberini Euchologion, where the rubrics preceding the anaphora direct, "the priest says [the following prayer] silently [ὁ ἱερεὺς μυστικῶς λέγει]," raising the possibility that the text of this anaphora as preserved in the manuscript was never recited audibly, even if it developed from a prayer once pronounced regularly with a full voice.[26] This text is not a certain witness to what a sixth-century Byzantine heard.

An overview of earlier anaphoral practice compared with this later Byzantine Liturgy of Basil, however, permits us to interpolate the likely outlines, character, and principal elements of the sixth-century prayer of concern to New Law 137. Moreover, the broader development of eucharistic prayers in early Christianity offers some perspective on the particular features of the Liturgy of St Basil's narrative and historical emphases. Scholarly attempts to identify Basil of Caesarea himself as the author or redactor of the prayer type rest more on tradition and piety than on hard independent evidence.[27] Basil's name is associated with *a* liturgy in sixth- and seventh-century sources, and the Barberini manuscript ascribes this liturgy to Basil, while the liturgy generally attributed to John Chrysostom appears there without attribution. But, as we shall see below, other related liturgies also circulated in Basil's name. We can only say with certainty that early Byzantines believed this liturgy and others to have been composed by Basil. At the same time, scholars generally agree that the form contained in the manuscript had its origins in the late fourth or the fifth century, as related liturgical prayers can demonstrate. The text contained in the Barberini Euchologion marks the culmination of a trajectory from improvised to set prayers, and from the audible recitation of these prayers to a silent anaphora.

Anaphoral prayers were initially extemporaneous and of varying lengths, although church authorities expected them to conform to guidelines regarding their content.[28] Writing around 150, Justin Martyr explains that after receiving the bread and wine, the man presiding over the congregation "offers up prayers and thanksgiving to the best of his ability"; he also says that these prayers were "lengthy."[29] The *Apostolic Tradition*, once attributed to Hippolytus of Rome, and now believed to date from the third or fourth century, contains a set prayer for the anaphora but states that it is not necessary for the bishop "to say the same words we gave above, as though striving [to say them] by heart, when giving thanks to God; but let each one pray according to his ability." While the bishop might even offer a shorter prayer, the author of the *Apostolic Tradition* requires that "his prayer be soundly orthodox."[30] We should note that worshippers and church authorities could neither appreciate the varying content of these prayers nor assess their orthodoxy unless celebrants offered them aloud.[31] The *Life of Melania the Younger* reports that while the saint was on her deathbed in 439 she asked Gerontios to celebrate "the holy offering [τὴν ἁγίαν ἀναφοράν]" on her behalf (66). Gerontios (died 485), himself the author of the *Life*, relates that his grief was so great that he was unable to speak up. When Melania could not hear him, she said, "Raise your voice so that I will hear the epiclesis [ἐπίκλησις: literally, the 'invocation' or the 'naming']." Robert Taft has shown that, in keeping with contemporary usage, "'epiclesis' refers in this instance to the entire eucharistic prayer, not just to the anaphoral invocation of the Holy Spirit."[32] Obviously both Melania and Gerontios expected the prayer to be audible, as had Justin and the author of the *Apostolic Tradition*.

While the third- or fourth-century *Apostolic Tradition* presents the option of a set anaphoral prayer, evidence that fixed prayer was the standard custom emerges late, with firm evidence only from the middle of the sixth century on. Moreover, the proliferation of different anaphoras between the fourth and eighth centuries confirms that even as churches, dioceses, and patriarchates moved toward set prayers, these prayers varied from region to region and from one doctrinal community to another.[33] In its concern to root out those priests who said the prayer incorrectly, Justinian's legislation of 565 assumes that the text of the anaphora was fixed and expresses the desire that it be said consistently, each time the same prayer in the same way. However, Justinian's law desires uniformity in an age and in jurisdictions where there was a variety of fixed forms. The law does not seem to seek to impose a Constantinopolitan prayer on communities using alternate prayers, nor does it seek to distinguish orthodox forms from forms that the state regarded as heterodox or belonging to heterodox communities. The law merely requires that the "prayer of offering" be recited aloud so as to be audible. It does not require or request that those hearing the anaphora take communion.

Additional evidence for a general custom of set anaphoral prayers comes indirectly in hagiographical accounts composed in the early seventh century. John Moschos's *Spiritual Meadow* contains a miracle story in which an unordained monk recites the words of the anaphora while carrying bread from the village back to the monastery, thus effecting its canonically irregular transformation into the body of Christ. In another story, Moschos tells how when children were playing a game of "church" with loaves on a flat rock, one child recited the words of oblation (προσκομιδή), which he had learned by heart. Both stories depend on the use of a set and audible prayer that could be memorized.[34] In the story of the children's game, the text supplies that that "it

was the custom in some places for the priests to say the prayer aloud," probably indicating that the early seventh century was a period of transition from
an audible to a silent anaphora and that Moschos assumed that his audience
might find an audible anaphora unusual. It is however possible that this is
a later gloss on the text, explaining an archaic practice. At the same time, it
remains unclear which anaphoral prayer Moschos, who died in 619, or his
travelling companion Sophronios, the future Patriarch of Jerusalem, who
died in 638, would have expected this memorized prayer to be: the anaphora
of the Byzantine Liturgy of Basil, or one of its prototypes, or perhaps a version of the related Liturgy of James, which was common in Jerusalem and
Antioch through the seventh century and remains in use among the Syrian
Orthodox.[35]

For most of late antiquity, then, the anaphoral prayers of the eucharistic
liturgy, whether extemporized or fixed, and varying from place to place, were
recited aloud. Were the people listening? For the most part, they could hear.
The spaces where Christians attended their liturgies were not obstructed by
tall barriers separating the sanctuary from the nave of the church. In most
places a low screen, or *templon*, separated the laity from the celebrants during this phase of the ritual action, but the ritual action of the liturgy of the
faithful remained visible, unscreened by curtains or veils.[36] While in large
churches, such as Hagia Sophia, the priest's recitation of the anaphora may
well have been hard to hear, in general, Christians in the late ancient world
could both see and hear the offering.[37] Participation in communion remained
high, especially on feast days, through the seventh century, after which point,
the numbers of those taking communion—although not necessarily those in
attendance—declined.[38]

So how much attention did the laity pay during the service? To be sure,
John Chrysostom's late fourth-century sermons lament his congregation's
wandering minds, boredom, talking, and milling about.[39] Such activity likely
persisted everywhere from time to time.[40] But the complaints also suggest
that church leaders expected lay congregants to be attentive. As a Syrian
church order composed in the sixth century for a bilingual Syriac and Greek
congregation demonstrates, those in attendance at the liturgy chanted the
Kyrie during processions, joined in responses to the psalm between the Old
Testament lesson and the Epistle (which responses often included the first
six verses of the penitential Psalm 50), and were exhorted to listen to the
readings.[41] The *Narration of the Abbots John and Sophronios* reveals that near
the turn of the seventh century, the people attending the Liturgy of James

sang a variety of hymns and *troparia*, including the "Holy God," the *Cherubic Hymn*, and the communion psalm, or *koinonikon*.[42] Indeed, the end of antiquity marks a high point in lay participation at the Eastern Orthodox eucharistic service. People must have been paying some attention. The Barberini Euchologion has the people responding "Amen" to various prayers, including the anaphora. Indeed, its late eighth-century rubric requires that the priest raise his voice at the end of the prayer ("Εκφώ[νησις], pronounced aloud") in order for the people to know when to respond with the "Amen" that had been their standard practice at the end of the anaphora from the time of Justin Martyr.[43] When these prayers were audible, the laity must have listened at least some of the time; and the repetition of set patterns and, eventually, fixed prayers, meant that congregants would have become very familiar with their content over time. As to whether the average churchgoer would have understood what she or he was listening to, it is worth observing that the language of the Liturgy of Basil, while full of biblicizing turns of phrase, did not diverge significantly from the late ancient Greek found in contemporary saints' lives; furthermore, Justinian's law expects that the prayer is sufficiently comprehensible to compel the listeners to feel compunction and glorify God.[44]

Salvation History in the West Syrian Anaphoral Tradition

Earlier extant liturgies of the West Syrian family confirm the predilection among many late antique liturgists and congregations for a ritualization of the Old Testament past in the eucharistic prayers. A form known as the Egyptian Anaphora of Basil attests an earlier moment in the trajectory of the Byzantine Liturgy of Basil.[45] This prayer, still in use in Arabic in the Coptic Church, survives in its entirety in Bohairic Coptic, although it was originally composed in Greek. A Sahidic Coptic manuscript from the first half of the seventh century confirms the antiquity of this eucharistic prayer, although in this witness the first third of the prayer is missing. (The Sahidic fragment begins with Christ's descent into Hell, resurrection, and ascension, immediately before the words of institution.)[46] Scholars tend to agree that this prayer derives from the late fourth or the fifth century and that the anaphora of the Constantinopolitan Liturgy of Basil expands either this text or, more likely, a common ancestor. The Egyptian Basil first invokes creation after the Sursum corda ("Let us lift up our hearts"). Addressing the prayer to God, the priest intones, "you made heaven and earth and the sea and all that is in them" as well as "all things visible and invisible."[47] A naming of ranks of the angels and a description of the Cherubim and Seraphim sets up the Sanctus.[48] The subsequent post-Sanctus salvation history is brief: "You formed us and placed us in the paradise of pleasure; and when we had transgressed your commandment through the deceit of the serpent, and had fallen from eternal life, and had been banished from the paradise of pleasure, you did not cast us off forever, but continually made promises to us through your holy prophets."[49] This encapsulation of an Old Testament past, with its first-person plural insertion of the congregation into the story (although at a point different from Byzantine Basil), functions as prologue to Christ's work of salvation. The Greek and Bohairic versions include rehearsal of the "transgression of your commandment through the deceit of the serpent," the expulsion from Paradise, and the calling by the prophets, before declaring the incarnation of "our Lord and God and Savior Christ at the End of Days" by the Holy Ghost and the Virgin Mary.[50] The Egyptian Basil thus confirms the emphasis within this liturgical tradition on shaping the congregation as the subjects of the entirety of salvation history; but this earlier and shorter prayer also permits an appreciation of the work of the liturgists who produced the expansion of the narrative in the Byzantine Basil.

A general rule in the study of liturgical history states that over time shorter forms get elaborated and expanded, but this is not always the case.[51] The church order known as the *Apostolic Constitutions*, compiled toward the end of the fourth century probably near Antioch, contains the earliest surviving nearly complete text of a Christian eucharistic liturgy.[52] Its particularly lengthy anaphoral prayer demonstrates the composer's interest to integrate history and ritual.[53] The extensive renarration of Old Testament history occurs before the Sanctus. After the Sursum corda (here, "Up with your mind"), the prayer recounts the creation of the world and the history of Israel through the battle of Jericho over the course of twenty-two paragraphs.[54] This entire pre-Sanctus narrative is addressed in the second person to God, raising questions about why a fourth-century West Syrian congregation or polity would offer God such an extended *logos*. The length of the anaphoral prayer has raised some doubt as to whether the form was ever actually used, but Louis Bouyer estimated that the entire prayer might take about fifteen minutes to recite, well within the liturgical tolerance of worshippers in late antiquity.[55] This deployment of Israel's history is likely in part polemical: in a region that into the fifth century continued to contain significant populations of both

Jews and Marcionites, the liturgical repetition of Old Testament narrative asserted its relevance to the formation of the Christian community.[56] Scholars have identified possible elements of a Jewish liturgy for the Day of Atonement in the eucharistic prayer.[57] But even beyond competing claims about and over the Old Testament, the lengthy anaphoral history in the *Apostolic Constitutions* reinforces the relation of a biblically grounded account of salvation to the eucharistic rite by ritualizing the past.[58]

The eloquent reshaping of Old Testament narrative in the *Apostolic Constitutions*, part of the West-Syrian anaphoral trajectory, extends well beyond the possible content of the anaphoral prayer in use in Constantinople. But it also reveals the longue durée of the Eucharist as a forum for shaping Christian community and instilling a penitential disposition through a recapitulation of the Bible. The story of creation recalls the celebration of God as creator in Psalm 104, but also bears marks of the Christianization of this narrative observable in roughly contemporaneous Christian cosmological literature, such as the *Hexaemeron* of Basil of Caesarea.[59] Under the rubric "it is truly fitting and right to praise you before all things" (8.12.6), the anaphora lauds God who "brought all things from non-existence into existence through your only-begotten Son" (8.12.7). God "made all things through him . . . and through him [he] granted existence" (8.12.8). Before all other things, God made heavenly Powers, here enumerated in all their ranks, and thereafter "the visible world and all that is in it" (8.12.8). God "set out the heavens . . . established the earth . . . fixed the firmament . . . arranged night and day" (8.12.9) and created the sun and moon. The protological narrative continues, citing God for making water "for drinking and cleansing," life-giving air "for breathing in and out, and for the production of sound through the tongue striking the air and for hearing which is aided by it to receive the speech which falls upon it" (8.12.10). In this case, the celebrant's production of sound has barely begun. After recounting the creation of the other elements, fire and earth, the prayer turns to the creation of animals and plant life with a rhetorical flourish before narrating the creation of humanity: "not only have you fashioned the world, but you have made man in it, the citizen of the world, displaying him as the ornament of the world" (8.12.16). Creation is thus the prehistory of the story of humanity.

The prayer's author reveals a flair for drama in setting up the fall in the garden. For although this man had "an inborn law, that he might have in and of himself the seeds of the knowledge of God" (8.12.18), he "neglected to keep the commandment and tasted the forbidden fruit, by the deceit of the serpent and the counsel of the woman," and was "justly [driven] out of the Paradise" (8.12.20). The subsequent encapsulated history of early humanity and of Israel recalls Nehemiah 9 and Hebrews 11. Stating as a general principle its view of Christian history, "You glorified those who remained faithful to you, and punished those who rebelled against you," (8.12.21) the prayer reminds God that he accepted Abel's sacrifice but rejected Cain's; that he received Seth and Enosh, "and translated Enoch" (8.12.21). The prayer recalls the flood, the salvation of Noah, the destruction of Sodom, and the survival of Lot. The celebrant recounts, "It was you who rescued Abraham from the godlessness of his forefathers and made him inheritor of the world; and you revealed your Christ to him; you chose Melchizedek to be high priest of your service" (8.12.23). After the patriarchs, the prayer turns to Moses and Aaron: God prevented the Hebrews from "destroying the law of nature" (8.12.25) through idolatry and polytheism, and revealed the law to Moses. "You glorified Aaron and his descendants with the honor of priesthood, you punished the Hebrews when they sinned, and received them when they turned back" (8.12.25). The text then flashes back to Egypt to recall the ten plagues and the Exodus, ending with the call of Joshua and siege of Jericho (left unnamed in the text), where "you laid walls low without machines or human hands" (8.12.26). The text thus highlights the rejection of paganism, God's providential relationship with those who have served him, and the punishment or rejection of the wicked.

The historical narrative comes to an abrupt stop at this point in order to set up the Sanctus, shifting from worldly affairs to the "unnumbered armies of angels . . . eternal armies . . . myriads and myriads of angels" (8.12.27) who sing the biblical Trisagion unceasingly. But the sentences immediately after the Sanctus return to establishing a historical context, although this time to offer an exegesis for the coming of Christ: "He did not despise the race of men as it perished; but after the law of nature and the warnings of the Law and the reproofs of the prophets and the guardianship of angels, when they were violating the natural and the written law, and casting out the memory of the Flood, the burning [of Sodom], the plagues of the Egyptians and the slaughter of the Palestinians, and were all about to perish as never yet, by your counsel it pleased him who was maker of man to become man, the lawgiver to be under the law, the high priest to be the sacrifice, the shepherd to be a sheep (8.12.30)." Here, perhaps, the author of the anaphora in the *Apostolic Constitutions* offers his most concise explanation for his own insistent renarrations of the history of Israel: it is precisely when the race of men were "casting out the memory" of God's punishments of the wicked that they were in greatest peril of annihilation. Forgetting or not knowing the biblical story could lead to death. This lengthy anaphora endeavors to produce a community liturgically reminded of and thus liturgically formed by the past. This prayer itself does not appear to have been in wide use beyond the region of Antioch or in use for a long period. The text's greatest value is in attesting the coverage of salvation history possible and even desirable in an era when anaphoral prayers were still often extemporized. And while this thorough-going Christian recital of Old Testament history does not find its way into the Byzantine Liturgy of Basil, the technique of rereading the sweep of salvation history to instill compunction and gratitude would reemerge in the massive liturgical hymn, the *Great Kanon* of Andrew of Crete, in the early eighth century. The Old Testament was the history of the need for salvation.

The anaphoral prayers of the West Syrian type considered here: the Byzantine Liturgy of Basil, the Egyptian Basil, and the extensive eucharistic prayer contained in the *Apostolic Constitutions,* all feature theologically inflected narratives of a Christian and biblical past. Emphasizing the pattern of creation, fall, law, prophets, and redemption through the incarnation, suffering, death, and resurrection of Christ, these prayers construct and impart a salvation history to a ritually formed community. These anaphoras both produce a past and produce a people whose past it becomes. It was such a history—not just a past but an interpretation of the past—that New Law 137 sought to insure the faithful laity would hear. Churchmen and the state apparatus understood that such a narrative would "move listeners to greater compunction," simply because that is what the Christian view of history did. Hearing the history of salvation triggered feelings of remorse. Justinian's law simply assumes this effect of the anaphora's text.

Rite, Creed, and Disposition

In later centuries, the most significant audible repetition of salvation history in the eucharistic liturgy occurred during the congregation's recitation of the Nicene Creed, which contains an encapsulated narrative of the birth, life, death, and resurrection of Christ. As the words of the received text of the Niceno-Constantinopolitan Creed put it: "He came down from heaven, and was enfleshed by the Holy Spirit and of the Virgin Mary, and became human. And was crucified for us under Pontius Pilate; suffered and was buried. And rose on the third day according to the Scriptures; he ascended into heaven and is seated at the right hand of the Father."[60] The regular recitation of the creed in the course of the Byzantine liturgy began in the early sixth century in Constantinople. The *Ecclesiastical History* of Theodore Lector relates that Timothy, patriarch of Constantinople from 511 to 518 and a non-Chalcedonian, "ordered the symbol of faith of the 318 fathers be recited at each synaxis [eucharistic liturgy]. . . . Formerly it was recited only once a year, on Good Friday, during the bishop's catechesis."[61] When Chalcedonians regained the patriarchate, they retained the recitation of the creed, and it continues to be recited aloud in liturgical traditions to this day. However, between the late fourth and the early to mid-sixth century, in congregations where a West Syrian-style anaphora was either extemporized, read, or recited from memory, the laity and clergy alike absorbed their salvation history, not from the ritual recitation of the creed, but from hearing an anaphoral prayer pronounced over the bread and wine during the liturgy of the faithful. The sixth century thus emerges as a relatively brief period when both the anaphora and the creed were said aloud during the course of the liturgy.

That the introduction and spread of the recited creed occurred early in the same century that also saw the shift toward a silent anaphora raises questions about their relative functions as ritual narrations of salvation history. In his *Mystagogy*, an explanation of the various elements of the liturgy, Maximos the Confessor, writing around 630, says that the "divine symbol of faith [the creed] signifies (προσημαίνει) the mystical thanksgiving (εὐχαριστίαν) to perdure though all eternity for the marvelous principles and modes by which we were saved by God's all-wise providence on our behalf."[62] By terming the creed a sign of an eternal *eucharistia*, Maximos connects the ritual recitation of the Nicene Creed, and particularly its brief history of salvation, with the offering of the thanksgiving, or eucharistic prayer. Both texts, the anaphora and the Creed, engage in the narration of salvation history as a form of thanksgiving.[63] This is all the more significant, given that Maximos does not discuss the content of the anaphora in his commentary, presumably because in his experience, it is no longer recited aloud.[64] After the eclipse of the audible anaphora, the function of guiding the thankful recollection of biblical events fell to other liturgical elements, especially the Creed.

So long as the anaphoras of the West Syrian type could be heard, they shaped a congregation's understanding of and relationship to the past. The celebrant recited an epitome of the Old Testament over the bread and wine prior to their transformation into the body and blood of Christ. At the same time as the prayer offered thanksgiving to God for the dispensation of biblical history, it offered the congregation a Christian past rooted in biblical narrative. Significantly, the prayer did not treat the Old Testament narrative typologically, as a series of events that prefigure more relevant, and more real, events to come. The narrative treats the divine dispensation as a coherent whole. This history is not strictly speaking supersessionist, replacing Judaism with Christianity, although the effect is similar.[65] Instead, the anaphora defines the congregation collectively both as humanity, created and fallen, and as Israel, the chosen people of God to whom God sent prophets and gave the Law. In the context of the ritual recitation, the biblical narrative recounts Christians' own past, not someone else's.

In the Byzantine Liturgy of Basil, a shorthand recounting of the life of Christ follows the Old Testament précis. The prophets and the law (in that order in the Barberini Euchologion) precede the "fullness of the times" when God the Son became incarnate.[66] The New Testament narrative contained in the anaphora is slightly longer, recalling the incarnation and virgin birth and Jesus' commandments. This narration includes events pared away in the spare outlines of the creed. "[He] cleansed us with water and sanctified us by the Holy Spirit, he gave himself as a ransom to death." After the crucifixion, Christ descends into hell and rises again on the third day. Echoing Paul in referring to Christ as the "first fruits of those who had fallen asleep," the text glances eschatologically to the time when the "us" of the prayer would themselves experience resurrection. The anaphoral prayer thus frames the liturgical action of the recollection and re-enactment of the Last Supper and the consecration and distribution of the elements with an overarching narrative, a history both past and future. In this liturgical form, the community received definition through both its ritually enacted meal and its ritually recounted history. Moreover, the text of the anaphora recounts the biblical narrative in a dense fabric of quotations and echoes of scripture.[67] Both the story and the language of the Septuagint and the New Testament render the central ritual of Christian practice an elaborate intertextual repetition of the Bible.

The part of the anaphoral prayers that invoked the Holy Spirit, the epiclesis, likely enhanced the formation of a penitent subject. In the version of the Liturgy of Basil first witnessed in a tenth-century manuscript at the Monastery of Grottaferrata, the epiclesis is framed by the priest's confession of his unworthiness: "We also, your sinful and unworthy servants, who have been held worthy to minister at your holy altar, not for our righteousness, for we have done nothing good upon earth, but for your mercies and compassions which have poured out richly upon us, with confidence approach your holy altar."[68] But by the time this prayer was added to the text, the priest was likely reciting the entirety of the prayer silently, and only he might be aware of its content. The Egyptian Liturgy of Basil reveals that the epiclesis was originally framed with a reminder of the congregation's unworthiness. After "our re-membering his holy sufferings for us, and his resurrection from the dead, and his ascension into heaven," and looking forward to "his glorious and fearful coming again to us," the prayer invokes the Holy Spirit on behalf of all as-sembled: "And we, your sinners and unworthy servants, pray you, our God, in adoration that in the goodwill [GK: εὐδοκία] of your goodness your Holy Spirit may descend upon us and upon these gifts." And the epiclesis ends bidding God, "Make us all worthy to partake of your holy things for sancti-fication of soul and body."[69] I suspect that this or a similar statement of col-lective guilt, not merely the priest's guilt, framed the epiclesis known to the mid-sixth-century legislators, thus reinforcing the formation of compunction in the conscience of lay participants.

The persistent recollection of biblical history in West Syrian anaphoras provides important evidence for the ways that late ancient Christians thought about their rites. Modern theorists have long debated the relationship be-tween narrative and action, or myth and ritual, in religious celebrations throughout the world.[70] In many instances, of course, rituals enact myths; and this is clearly the case with the repetition of the Last Supper in the words of institution, and the distribution of the elements in the eucharistic service.[71] The anaphoras considered here, however, give evidence of a late ancient the-ory of ritual that emphasized the role of telling a story alongside acting one out. The recitation of salvation history not only provided the context for the Eucharist, but worked independently to shape its participants. Authorities composing the liturgies and legislating their performance expected the ritu-alization of communal memory to instill feelings of guilt and gratitude, to prompt introspection and praise. For the idealized subject of these liturgies, the eucharistic rite used salvation history to effect interior self-reflection and a contrite disposition in a biblically formed people. In recounting a Christian and biblical past, the anaphora had the power to produce a Christian and biblical self.

Preparing for the Eucharist

In the shift to a silent anaphora, the offering prayer of the Eucharist lost its function as an instrument of communal formation, but the Eucharist retained its character as a penitential rite. In the course of the fourth century, after the conversion of Constantine, church leaders cultivated among their congregations an increased sense of awe for the consecrated elements, instilling a fear of their holiness and their potential danger for those unworthy. At the end of that century, John Chrysostom stressed that congregants should take the Eucharist only in a state of purity, even as he bemoaned that some avoided it, and he encouraged people to take communion frequently. "I observe many partaking of Christ's Body lightly and incidentally [ὡς ἔτυχε], and rather from custom and form, than consideration and understanding. When, one says, the holy season of Lent sets in, however he may be, he partakes of the mysteries, or, when the day of the Epiphany comes. And yet it is not Epiphany, nor is it Lent, that makes a fit time for approaching, but it is sincerity and purity of soul."[72] Preaching a high regard for the holiness of the sacrament, he upbraided them: "How shall you present yourself before the judgment-seat [τῷ βήματι; also 'the chancel'] of Christ, you who presume upon his body with polluted hands and lips? You would not presume to kiss a king with an unclean mouth, and the King of heaven do you kiss with an unclean soul? It is an outrage [ὕβρις]!"[73] Such regard meant that Christians needed to prepare for the Eucharist by recalling and repenting their sins. Post-communion prayers asserted that even after communicating, one was still a sinner. In late antique Syria, bishops such as Theodore of Mopsuestia, who died in 428, and Philoxenos of Mabbug, writing around 500, encouraged Christians to pray to the Eucharist itself after receiving communion, not only adoring the body of God, first in their hands, and then in their own bodies, but by confessing their sinfulness and acknowledging their unworthiness to receive it.[74]

Clergy and monastic leaders called Christians to self-examination before taking communion, encouraging them to determine whether they were spiritually pure. Writing just after the mid-point of the sixth century, Cyril of Scythopolis described how in the previous century, the great Palestinian monastic founder Euthymios was able to discern the moral state of his monks. The abbot taught, "Frequently, when distributing the holy sacrament to the brethren, I have seen some of those who approach illuminated by communion and others condemned." He enjoined them, "Attend to yourselves, brethren and fathers, and let each of you 'examine himself and so eat of the bread and drink of the cup,' as the Apostle says, for he who does this unworthily 'eats and drinks judgment upon himself' [1Cor 11:28–29]."[75] The risk lay not in the defiling the sacrament, which was holy in itself, but in further defiling the communicant who lacked contrition. Anastasios of Sinai, permitting frequent communion as appropriate, warned against those who communicate "with contempt, allowing more room in their souls to Satan, as happened with Judas," whom, "Satan entered into [Jn 13:27]," along with the bread.[76] As in the hymn *At Your Mystical Supper*, one prayed not to partake of the host with the kiss of betrayal.

Sinners, however, were encouraged to communicate, as the rite had the power to forgive sin. At some point in the second quarter of the sixth century, a troubled monk wrote a letter to the monastic sages Barsanouphios and John requesting advice about whether to take communion. He had had a sexual dream at night and presumably had experienced an issue of semen. The response underscored the curative value of the Eucharist: "Let us approach with all our wounds and without any contempt, as people who are needful of a doctor; then, he who healed the woman with the issue of blood [Mt 9:22] will also heal us. . . . When you are about to take communion, say: 'Master, do not allow these things to be unto my condemnation but unto purification of soul and body and spirit.' Then, you may approach with fear, and our Master, who is kind and loving, will work his mercy with us."[77] Reflecting on one's moral state prepared one to attend the liturgy and to receive the sacrament. The sixth-century eucharistic prayer thus reinforced the self-acknowledgment as sinner cultivated in the exhortation and advice of religious professionals.

In the course of the middle Byzantine period, long after the eclipse of the audible anaphora, confessionary prayers recited privately to prepare for communion became common and standardized. Scrolls dating from the eleventh through early thirteenth centuries attest primitive versions of a prayer, attributed in the tradition to John of Damascus and still recited by Orthodox Christians among their pre-communion petitions. "Master, Lord Jesus Christ, our God, you alone have the power to forgive sins: since you are good and love humans, forgive me all my transgressions, committed knowingly and unknowingly, involuntarily and voluntarily, in deed, word, and thought, and without condemning me deem me worthy to partake of your divine, precious, and immortal mysteries, not as a burden, punishment, and increase of sins, but as sanctification, illumination, support, a token of eternal life, a shield against every opposing power and an expiation of my many transgressions."[78]

Through its ritual actions and its rites of preparation, the Byzantine Eucharist identified and encouraged a subjectivity formed in self-accusation, created through periodic and structured occasions for the self-attribution of guilt. The hearing and the recitation of prayers materialized conceptions of the self in human persons, producing compunction in the subject and producing the subject in and through the recognition of compunction. The Eucharist thus had the power to provide knowledge and understanding of the self. The following chapters trace this subject through subsequent eras, beyond the early Byzantine period, through the so-called Dark Ages and into the next great liturgical synthesis of the middle Byzantine centuries, where liturgists continued to employ biblical narrative and ritual action to identify and shape the self as sinner.

CHAPTER 5

The Penitential Bible and the *Great Kanon* of Andrew of Crete

Liturgy provides a great deal of information about the models for introspection available to Byzantine Christians. As we have seen in the previous chapters, in the prayers and hymns, clergy encouraged congregants to pattern their self-reflection, providing forms through which they might have access to themselves. Compositions for Lent, in particular, deployed liturgical experience in the production of a penitent self. As the works of Romanos and the prayers of the anaphora demonstrate, this self was not unique to any individual. Rather, through the liturgy the clergy sought to reproduce this self in each participant. Byzantine liturgy thus provides access to the self as institutionally formed, not individual but typical. This self is not an autonomous religious self but rather a cultural product, the subject of liturgy. Perhaps more than any other work of Byzantine hymnography, the *Great Kanon* of Andrew of Crete, composed in the late seventh or early eighth century, has come to typify the Lenten self, the subject of lament and reproach. Through its capacious juxtaposition of the biblical narrative and the soul-accusing self, the *Kanon* reveals the underlying structures of the liturgically encouraged self and the exegetical mechanisms deployed to produce it.

Andrew of Crete's massive penitential poem, still chanted in Orthodox churches during Lent, marks an important moment in the Byzantine deployment of biblical narrative to form Christian subjectivity.[1] Organized into nine odes, the *Great Kanon* introduces Old Testament personages in the first eight odes roughly in the order of their appearance in the biblical text or according to Byzantine conceptions of the course of history. The ninth ode moves chronologically through a harmonized narrative of the New Testament Gospels. Today the hymn is sung among Orthodox Christians in its entirety at

Morning Prayer (*Orthros*), or Matins, on Thursday of the fifth week of Great Lent and also in four portions at Compline (*Apodeipnon*), the last office of the day, from Monday to Thursday during the first week of Lent.[2] Indeed, the original performance context was almost certainly during a single Matins service and, given the penitential content and the focus on Genesis, most probably during Lent, although the day is uncertain. When the *Great Kanon* first appears in service books associated with the Stoudios Monastery of Constantinople, it does so during Matins or Vespers on various days of the fifth week of Lent.[3] The method of original performance remains uncertain, although we shall see in the next chapter that, by the end of the eighth century, kanons were usually performed chorally. It is unclear whether Andrew wrote the *Great Kanon* for choral performance or to be chanted by a single cantor, and I have striven to consider the poem as an expression of a Byzantine voice, rather than to assume solo or choral performance of that voice.

The goal of Andrew's biblical survey is to inspire repentance. The poem opens with the question, "Where shall I begin to lament the deeds of my wretched life?" (1.1). The answer lies at the beginning of human history, with Adam, and from this beginning, the poet proceeds chronologically through the whole of the biblical narrative. In the course of 250 stanzas the poem's "I" employs a long series of biblical characters to accuse and convict himself of sin. The scriptural narrative provides both negative examples that the subject has imitated and positive examples that the subject has neglected. In the middle of the eighth ode, at the point where Andrew shifts from a chronological treatment of Old Testament figures to a consideration of characters from the New Testament, he explains the point of his endeavor:

> I have brought before you, O Soul, all those from the Old Testament for a model [πρὸς ὑπογραμμόν]: imitate the pious deeds of the righteous, and on the contrary flee from the sins of the wicked. (8.12)

The whole of the biblical corpus offers urgent moral instruction.

Andrew's exegetical method can be seen already in the opening ode in his consideration of the story of Cain and Abel from Genesis 4. The poet sings,

> I have followed after Cain's bloodguilt, by deliberate choice; by giving life to the flesh I have become a murderer of the conscience of my soul (συνειδότι ψυχῆς), and I have gone to war against it by my evil deeds.

I have not resembled Abel's righteousness, O Jesus; I have never
brought you acceptable gifts, nor godly deeds, nor a pure sacrifice,
nor a life unblemished. (1.7–8)

The juxtaposition of Abel's offering of first fruits with Cain's act of fratricide offers Andrew the opportunity to contrast a negative exemplar with a positive one.
The poet limits himself to the elements of the story as narrated in the biblical
text. In fact, he appears to make little use of earlier commentarial traditions,
including earlier sermons on Genesis.[4] In contrast to Cain's murder of Abel,
Andrew's murderousness is reflexive; he has entertained fleshly thoughts and
thus committed spiritual suicide. Throughout the poem, Andrew reads scripture
against himself to prompt contrition and to seek God's forgiveness. Assurance
of God's mercy frames the exercise from the start, as he petitions in the first
stanza, "But as you are compassionate [εὔσπλαγχνος], grant me forgiveness of
transgressions [παραπτωμάτων]" (1.1). In its bravura performance of a Christian
conscience, the poem illuminates how the institutional church shifted its liturgical apparatus to shape the interior religious life of Christian persons.

Only the bare outlines of Andrew's biography can be known with any
certainty. Andrew was born in Damascus around 660. In his youth, he joined
the monastery of the Church of the Anastasis in Jerusalem, where he received
an education that would have included biblical studies and theology. Indeed,
in Byzantine tradition he is often called Andrew of Jerusalem. In 685, he journeyed to Constantinople, where he subsequently served as a deacon at the
Church of Hagia Sophia and administered an orphanage and a poorhouse. At
some point between 692 and 711 he became metropolitan of Crete and bishop
of its capital city, Gortyna, on the island's southern coast. Although he was
tonsured at a young age, he spent much of his career serving and leading lay
people, attached to urban cathedrals. He died in 740 on the island of Lesbos,
on his way home from a visit to the capital.[5] Among his surviving works are a
number of liturgical hymns in the form of the *kanōn* for use during Morning
Prayer and exegetical sermons keyed to specific liturgical feasts, including
those dedicated to Mary: the Nativity, Dormition, and Annunciation.[6]

Andrew is often credited with inventing or perfecting the kanon, a new
type of liturgical hymnody that replaced the sequence of nine biblical odes
chanted at Morning Prayer.[7] Other early practitioners of the form included
John of Damascus and Kosmas of Maiouma, both associated with the monasteries of the Judean desert, including Mar Saba, indicating that the kanon had
its origin in the region around Jerusalem.[8] Andrew seems to have brought

this budding tradition to the capital. To date, most scholars have assumed that kanons were originally intended for monastic use.[9] This assumption deserves reconsideration. By the late seventh and early eighth centuries, the chanting of the biblical canticles was common both to monastic Morning Prayer and to the Morning Prayer service of the so-called cathedral hours in urban churches attended by the laity.[10] Indeed, Andrew's compositions may show how kanons with their series of new odes came to replace the canticles in lay worship even before the monasticization of the cathedral liturgy that began in the ninth century, when Sabaite liturgical forms spread throughout the Byzantine church under the influence of the Stoudios Monastery in Constantinople.

It is unclear whether Andrew composed the *Great Kanon* in Constantinople or later on Crete.[11] The best evidence for assigning the *Great Kanon* to Constantinople is the prayer in the final stanza to the Theotokos for the protection of the city (9.27), but these verses could just as easily have been written on Crete. Twice in the poem, the singer refers to his old age (1.13; 8.6), making a strong case for composition on Crete, although this claim might simply be a trope of penitential literature.[12] Since the *Great Kanon* expands the form to its limits, it is unlikely to have been an early work. Given Andrew's posts at Hagia Sophia and on Crete, it seems more likely that Andrew wrote not for a purely monastic audience, but for a congregation of clerics and laity assembled for the liturgy in major urban churches.[13] Thus, like the great sixth-century hymnographer Romanos before him, Andrew deployed the biblical narrative to model a style of interiority for a Christian congregation.[14]

The interior religious lives of Byzantine Christians at the end of antiquity and into the so-called Dark Age of the late seventh and the eighth centuries are difficult, if not impossible, to access. This is especially the case for lay people, who have left few sources. Outside of monastic literature, Christians rarely speak in their own voices about themselves. Letters, such as those found among the sixth-century correspondence of Barsanouphios and John of Gaza, occasionally reveal the troubled layman confessing to a wise monk or seeking guidance on a moral matter.[15] Hagiography narrates the lives of holy men and women, but rarely concerns itself with character development and gives little insight into ordinary people's self-reflection. The absence of early Byzantine autobiography is a mixed blessing: while it deprives scholars of a strong individual voice, such as Augustine's in the West, it prevents Byzantinists from taking an idiosyncratic and heavily rhetorical voice as typical. And if letters and hagiography survive for earlier and later periods, the

century and a half after the Arab conquests of the mid-seventh century witnessed a significant drop in the production of literature.[16]

The *Great Kanon*, on the other hand, dramatizes the recognition of the
self. Within the *Great Kanon*, the recollection of biblical exemplars generates
contrition or compunction, *katanyxis* [κατάνυξις] in Greek, most literally the
puncturing or wounding of the self.[17] As Andrew begins his accounting, he
encourages himself,

> Come, wretched soul, with your flesh, confess [ἐξομολογοῦ] to the
> Creator of all, and from now on, leave your past folly and bring to God
> tears in repentance [ἐν μετανοίᾳ]. (1.2)

It is precisely this self-recognition that provides Andrew with access to himself. The cataloguing of biblical figures thus becomes a Foucaultian "technology of the self," a mechanism for confession.[18] Of particular importance
to Foucault were practices of *exomologēsis*, or confession, which produce a
knowledge of the self in which one recognizes oneself as a sinner and penitent.[19] In such a process, one becomes the subject of one's own reflection.

As we have already seen in Romanos, Byzantine liturgy mediated this
practice beyond the confines of spiritual direction in the monastery. Andrew's
Great Kanon illustrates and dramatizes a style of the self formed in a typological and dialectical relationship with the biblical narrative, particularly as that
narrative might be experienced liturgically. Explaining his method in Ode 9,
Andrew prefaces his harmony of the Gospels thus:

> I bring before you the examples [ὑποδείγματα] from the New Scrip-
> ture, to lead you, O soul, to contrition [κατάνυξις]. (9.4)

The litany of biblical figures throughout the poem prompts interior self-
reflection and both frames and guides the formation of the self as a penitent
subject. The hymn's performance of interiorly directed biblical exegesis thus
provides critical evidence for the history of the self in Byzantium.

Accusing the Self

The pioneering historian of Byzantine music, Egon Wellesz, declared Andrew
"indefatigable in turning scriptural examples to the purpose of penitential

confession."[20] The poet laments and accuses himself in the first person, a generic "I" with totalizing force. As in the opening and closing strophes of the kontakia of Romanos the Melodist, Andrew's "I"-speech is not autobiographical in the strict sense; it is not the lament of a narrated or historical self. The poem names not specific sins but categories of sins in thought and deed. The result is a virtuoso performance of penance without the individual content that would make it the repentance of a particular person. Like the first-person speech in Romanos, Andrew uses the cantor's voice to typify a troubled Christian conscience. He exclaims,

> There is no sin in life, nor deed, nor wickedness that I, O Savior, have not committed, in mind, and in word, and by choice. In intent, will, and action [καὶ θέσει, καὶ γνώμῃ, καὶ πράξει], I have sinned as none ever has before.

> Therefore have I been judged, and therefore have I been convicted, wretch that I am, by my own conscience [συνείδησις], than which there is nothing in the world more rigorous. O Judge, O Redeemer who knows me, spare and deliver and save me, your servant. (4.4–5)

In fact, this self-assessment and its reliance on the model of an interior courtroom where the conscience is put on trial is consistent with depictions of self-accusation and conviction in the hymns of Romanos, where the penitent serves as the subject of his own judgment.

As the hymn progresses, the self bifurcates, with the "I" of the poem accusing and berating his "soul," whom he addresses in the second person. "Give heed [ἐνωτίζου, cf. Lat. *notare*], O my soul, to the cry of the Lord: and separate yourself from your former sin" (2.31). "To whom can I compare you, O soul of many sins?" (2.31–32). Recalling the punishment of the wicked in the Deluge in the time of Noah, he accuses,

> It is you, alone, O soul, who opened the floodgates [καταρράκτας, cf. LXX Gen 7:11] of the wrath of your God, and who poured [it] down as upon the earth, upon your flesh, and your deeds, and your life, and you remained outside the Ark of salvation. (2.34)

Invoking the destruction of Sodom by fire from heaven, he declares, "you have kindled, O soul, the fire of hell, in which you also shall be burned bitterly" (2.39). In this manner, much of the poem is cast as a dialogue within the self—between the cantor and his soul. Frequently he exclaims, "You have heard, O my soul." Thus the singer calls the soul both to the recollection of biblical narratives and to their application to the self as a paradigm of failure. This soul as subject is the product of both biblical memory and reflexive judgment. In this sense the soul becomes the subject of biblical narrative, but only in a particularly self-accusing mode. The "I" uses the Bible to convict the soul through a consistent set of operations in which both the accusing Bible and the convicting conscience converge to produce knowledge of the self.

Traditions of penitential practice were already well developed in early Byzantine monasticism, although they did not constitute a sacrament (as they would in the West) or have a formal rite.[21] By the early ninth century, handbooks enumerated sins, especially sexual ones, and assigned penitential programs to each.[22] Monastic theoretical sources tended to distinguish between *metanoia* (μετάνοια), repentance for specific sins; and *katanyxis* (κατάνυξις), "compunction/contrition," or *penthos* (πένθος), "inwardly directed sorrow," a more generalized repentance of one's sinful nature or habits.[23] During the course of late antiquity, baptismal preparation, spiritual direction, hagiography, hymnography, and sermons mediated these concepts and habits of self-regard to the laity.[24]

The oldest set prayers for penance and confession in the Byzantine tradition appear together in the Barberini Euchologion (Barberini gr. 336), a Constantinopolitan service book that dates from the 790s.[25] In a study of prayer and penance in Byzantium, Robert Phenix and Cornelia Horn have considered the place of these forms in the trajectory toward a developed confessional rite in the tenth or eleventh century.[26] The prayers to be recited by a cleric "for those who are repenting [ἐπὶ μετανοούντων]" and "for those who are confessing [ἐπὶ ἐξομολογουμένων]" appear independent of a set liturgy; that is, they belong to no penitential rite or formalized practice of confession. Instead, they seem to be for occasional use as the need arose.[27] The first prayer over penitents incorporates Old Testament types, establishing biblical precedents for the remission of sin: "O God our savior, who through your prophet Nathan granted remission to David who repented for his own faults, and accepted Manasseh's prayer of repentance, also the very same, your servant N. [αὐτὸς καὶ τὸν δοῦλον σου τόνδε] who repents of his own transgressions [μετανοοῦντα ἐν τοῖς ἰδίοις παραπτώμασι], accept him according to your habitual love of humanity, ignoring his offenses."[28] Although Phenix and Horn rightly tie these references to narrations of the repentance of David in 1 Chronicles 21 and Manasseh in 2 Chronicles 33, the prayer's immediate referents are more likely liturgical than purely scriptural. The reference to David recalls Psalm 50 [51], David's song of repentance heard regularly at the opening of Morning Prayer. The invocation of Manasseh most likely recalls the Septuagint's Prayer of Manasseh, usually grouped in manuscripts among the book of Canticles, although not one assigned to the early Byzantine cycle of canticles at Morning Prayer.[29] In the *Great Kanon* Andrew alludes to Manasseh's prayer, bidding himself to "fervently rival his repentance [μετάνοια] and gain [his] contrition [κατάνυξις]" (7.16).

The Euchologion's prayer over those confessing, by contrast, invokes types not from the Old Testament, but from the New. "Lord our God, who granted remission of sins to Peter and the Harlot [ἡ πόρνη] through their tears and who justified the Tax Collector [ὁ τελώνης] who recognized the transgressions of his way of life, also accept the confession of your servant N."[30] As Phenix and Horn point out, Peter and the Harlot, together with the Prodigal Son, occur frequently as biblical exemplars of penance in Syrian Christian prayer and hymnography.[31] Both figure in hymns of Romanos as well. Thus both prayers call on biblical types for repentance and forgiveness that had become common in liturgical usage.

Significantly, Andrew occasionally removes figures from their biblical order, even though he also treats them elsewhere in their proper sequence. Peter, the Harlot, the Tax Collector, and the Prodigal Son step out of their places in the New Testament narrative to provide a counterpoint to the march of history, to provide models for repentance.[32] Thus, near the beginning of Ode 2, before an extended meditation on Adam, Andrew invokes both Peter and the Harlot:

> The storm of evils surrounds me, O compassionate Lord: but as unto Peter, so unto me, stretch forth your hand.
>
> The tears of the Harlot, I also set before the one who pities. (2.4–5)[33]

The New Testament figures, men and women alike, are thus not merely historical examples of virtue and vice, but also types for the penitent Christian that illustrate proper comportment before God during the penitential season of Lent. The only Old Testament figure that Andrew dislodges from his putative historical context is David (2.23; 7.17), who like the New Testament exemplars offers a model of repentance. In a particularly moving sequence he laments in successive verses, "I have sinned, like the Harlot I cry out to you" (2.22). "I have fallen like David licentiously and fouled myself [βεβορβόρωμαι]" (2.23).[34] "Be merciful, as the Tax Collector I cry out to you" (2.24). Thus, like the emergent liturgical prayers, Andrew favors the concatenation of a familiar repertoire of penitent types, in this case without regard to historical sequence.[35]

In imposing the thoroughness of biblical chronology, however, Andrew moves beyond the invocation of classic penitential types to prompt and model repentance and confession. Now the entire narrative corpus of scripture convicts. He summarizes his literary practices and purposes toward the beginning of his ninth and final ode:

> I have brought before you, O soul, Moses' story of the creation, and after that, all the canonical scripture [πᾶσαν ἐνδιάθετον γραφήν] recounting for you [ἱστοροῦσάν σοι] about the righteous and the unrighteous; O soul, you have imitated the second of these, not the first, and you have sinned against God. (9.2)

The Bible as a whole has taught him that he is a sinner and that he has not followed the good example of scripture. Despite his epic treatment of biblical history, his soul has remained unmoved to repentance:

> The Law is enfeebled, the Gospel idle, in you all the scriptures are neglected, the Prophets and every word of the righteous man have lost their power. Your wounds, O soul, have multiplied; there is no doctor to heal you. (9.3)

In Andrew's hand, the Bible in its entirety provides the measure of personal sin, an anthology suitable for gauging individual disobedience. Running through a gallery of negative and positive examples, the *Great Kanon* reconfigures the entire corpus of the Bible as a penitential text.

Canticles and Odes

The *Great Kanon* recounts the major events and personages of the Bible to accuse the conscience of sin and to prompt the soul to seek divine rescue. In the course of 250 stanzas, or troparia, organized into nine odes, Andrew rehearses the entire scope of biblical history in loosely chronological if not strictly canonical order. Each ode has its own meter and tune called an *irmos* (εἱρμός; plural *irmoi*), introduced in the first stanza and repeated. The second, third, and sixth odes are divided into two sections, with different irmoi, perhaps allowing Andrew a greater variety of chant melodies to break up what might otherwise become monotonous.[36] The irmoi exhibit a variety of meters and stanza lengths, although each form depends on conveying sense relatively simply, through short metrical units with little enjambment. The language is direct and broadly accessible, drawing on biblical and liturgical vocabulary. Andrew clearly wished his congregation to understand the hymn and absorb its implications for their understanding of themselves. Although hymnographers, including Andrew, usually wrote their kanon odes to preexistent melodies and accent patterns, Andrew may have set the odes of the *Great Kanon* to canticle melodies he had composed himself. Most probably the earliest example of the hymn is found in a tenth-century manuscript, copied in the calligraphic style of the Stoudios Monastery in Constantinople and now at the Monastery of St. Catherine in the Sinai (Sinai gr. 735, f. 69r., Figure 14). Here the texts of the irmoi are drawn from the canticles. For example, Ode 1 is to be sung to an extant tune for Exodus 15:2, "The Lord is my help and my defender [Βοηθός καὶ σκεπαστής]," the canticle it either follows or replaces. Eleventh-century service books, known as heirmologia, contain the irmoi needed for all kanons in the repertoire with musical notation. Here, the irmoi for the *Great Kanon* are attributed to Andrew, although this could perhaps simply indicate that their use in the *Great Kanon* was the most familiar.[37]

In the course of the composition, Andrew treats Adam and Eve (Ode 1 and 2); Cain and Abel (Ode 1); the generations from Cain to Noah and the tower of Babel (Ode 2); Sodom and the story of Lot (Ode 3; first irmos); then Abraham, Isaac, Ishmael, through Jacob (Ode 3, second irmos); Jacob, Esau, and Job (Ode 4); Joseph and his brothers, and Moses (Ode 5); the exodus from Egypt and the wandering in the desert, and Joshua (Ode 6, first irmos); the book of Judges, then Hannah, Samuel, and David (Ode 6, second irmos); the dynastic history of kings and prophets from David through Ahab, including Elijah (Ode 7); further prophets, repeating Elijah, then Elisha, Jeremiah, and Jonah (Ode 8); and a quick encapsulation of the Gospels (Ode 9).

The placement of Job between Jacob and Joseph reveals that Andrew proceeded not according to a plan that strictly followed the order of the figures' appearance in the biblical canon, but rather according to a "chronological plan" invoking figures as they had occurred in the course of human "history." Andrew places Job in Ode 4, after Esau, and before turning to Joseph in

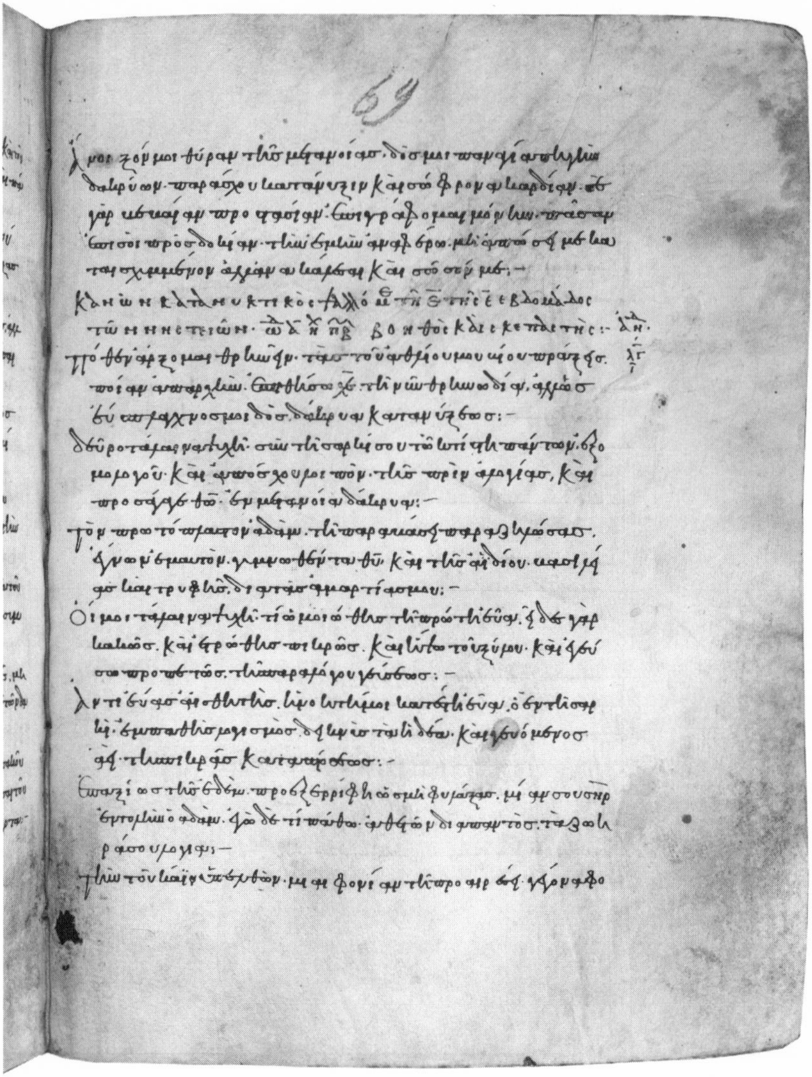

Figure 14. The opening of Andrew of Crete's *Great Kanon* in the manuscript Sinai graecus 735 of the tenth century. The poem's title appears in the sixth and seventh lines as "Penitential Kanon [Κανών κατανυκτικός] sung on Thursday of the fifth week of the Fasts." This is followed by the indication "Ode 1 in the second plagal mode" and the first words of the irmos, which is drawn from Canticle 1, the Song of Moses in Exodus 15. An abbreviation of Andrew's name (as Andrew of Jerusalem) appears in the *right* margin. Sinai graecus 735, f. 69r. Photo by permission of Saint Catherine's Monastery, Sinai, Egypt.

Ode 5. Additions to the Septuagint text of Job 42:17 identified Job with Jobab (Genesis 36:33) and claimed he was a great-grandson of Esau.[38] The result is a compendious treatment of the biblical history as a whole in the formation of the penitent subject, who regards the narrative with compunction and responds with contrition.

The nine odes of Andrew's *Great Kanon* replaced the nine biblical canticles of the Morning Prayer service with new exegetical hymnography and refocused the liturgy on penitential themes.[39] In the fifth-century Codex Alexandrinus and other early Greek Bible manuscripts, the biblical book of Canticles or "Odes" follows after the Psalms. Although the number of canticles in the manuscripts varies from nine to fifteen, from at least the fifth century a group of nine canticles provided a cycle of biblical songs for liturgical use that were distributed throughout the week, one per day, with the Magnificat recited daily; three canticles were chanted on Sunday. These canonical canticles include

1. The First Song of Moses (the Song of the Sea; Exodus 15:1–19)
2. The Second Song of Moses (at the end of his life; Deuteronomy 32:1–43)
3. The Prayer of Hannah (LXX 1 Kingdoms [1 Sam] 2:1–10)
4. The Prayer of Habakkuk (Habakkuk 3:1–19)
5. The Prayer of Isaiah (Isaiah 26:9–20)
6. The Prayer of Jonah (Jonah 2:3–10)
7. The Prayer of Azariah from the Greek book of Daniel (LXX Daniel 3:26–56)
8. The Song of the Three Holy Children, also from Greek Daniel (LXX Daniel 3:57–88 with three extra verses);
9. The combined songs of the Virgin (Magnificat) and of Zacharias (Benedictus) from the Gospel of Luke (Luke 1:46–57 and 68–79).[40]

Robert Taft has suggested that their use as a complete cycle at Morning Prayer, with all nine canticles chanted in order, originated in the monastic office of *agrypnia* or the Saturday Night Vigil. Such a practice was known to John Moschos and his companion Sophronios in the late sixth or early seventh century in Palestine and Sinai. Not long thereafter the nine canticles entered the cathedral rite of Morning Prayer.[41]

Replacing the canticles at Morning Prayer with new odes keyed to the liturgical season was a new practice in the late seventh and early eighth centuries. This shift from canticles to kanons was surely gradual, and the increased liturgical activity during Lent and on key festival days provided opportunities for liturgical poets like Andrew to replace familiar biblical songs with new texts. We should assume, however, that throughout Andrew's life the cycle of canticles was still in use on most days of the calendar and was deeply familiar not only to Andrew but also to a significant part of his congregation. Most surviving early examples of the kanon are shorter than the cycle of canticles, and tend in each of their odes to make sustained reference to the texts they are replacing or, more likely, supplementing. Such is not the case with the odes of the *Great Kanon*, which both are longer than the canticles they replace and depart from their themes. Andrew's odes reproduce the sense of chronological movement through the events of the Bible and salvation history that structures the original selection and organization of the canticles. But at most, Andrew has been inspired by their roughly chronological sweep through examples of biblical hymnody.

The relationship with each of the original canticles, however, is loose to nonexistent. Andrew's odes proceed through the biblical narrative at a different pace as well as with different emphases. The first biblical canticle sings triumph and thanksgiving for deliverance from the Red Sea. Andrew's first ode reflects on Adam and Eve's fall in the Garden and then on the contrast between Cain and Abel.

The second canticle is the song of Moses at the end of his life—a text that in fact recounts some biblical history as it enumerates Israel's faithlessness; but Andrew's second ode is still meditating on Adam and the fall from grace in the garden. Indeed, the odes would seem to supplant the original canticles, since the juxtaposition of the original canticles with his new odes would be quite jarring.

In aggregate, the original cycle of biblical canticles is not particularly or primarily penitential. The words *katanyxis*, *penthos*, and *metanoia* do not occur in any of the canticles. In places, the canonical cycle does address themes of sin. The Second Song of Moses (Cant 2) contrasts God's faithfulness with Israel's faithlessness and recounts some biblical history, while the Prayer of Azariah (Cant 7) includes a confession of collective sin: "For we have sinned and broken your law in turning away from you; in all matters we have sinned grievously. We have not obeyed your commandments; we have not kept them or done what you have commanded us for our own good (LXX Dan 3:29–30)." But overall, the *Great Kanon* replaces hymns praising God with narratives accusing the self, doxology with penance. In exchanging scriptural canticles for a sweeping biblical survey, Andrew provides a liturgical meditation on salvation history appropriate to the season of Lent.[42]

The Old Testament, the Lectionary, and Lent

Eight of Andrew's nine odes treat the Old Testament. The focus on the Old Testament is significant, given the paucity of Old Testament readings in the emerging Byzantine lectionary system.[43] While some monks, clergy, and educated laymen with access to books might have been familiar with entire books of scripture, the vast majority of Christians encountered the Bible chiefly when they heard it read out in church during the eucharistic service of the Divine Liturgy, during sermons, or during prayer hours. Their Bible and their knowledge of it were determined by the appointed readings. By the ninth century, the standard service book containing passages from the Old Testament, known to modern scholars as the Prophetologion, assigned lections from Old Testament texts primarily during Lent and on principal Christological and Marian festivals, but this system must already have taken shape earlier, perhaps in the sixth century.[44] Only a small percentage of the Old Testament (less than 15 percent) would be heard in the course of the liturgical year, and the lectionary includes brief excerpts from only about half of the Old Testament books.[45]

Old Testament readings had fallen out of use in Constantinople during nearly all celebrations of the Divine Liturgy by Andrew's time. In fact, it remains a matter of scholarly debate whether or for how long earlier Constantinopolitans had heard more of the Old Testament during the eucharistic service, in a pattern similar to the Western Christian practice of having three readings during the Liturgy of the Word, usually a reading from the Old Testament, followed by a reading from an Epistle and a lection from the Gospels.[46] The Armenian witnesses to the lectionary in use in Jerusalem in the first half of the fifth century and the Georgian witness to the lectionary in use there around 700 attest readings from the Old Testament through much of the year, although more heavily during Lent and on major feasts.[47]

Within Byzantine lectionaries in Andrew's day, the greatest exposure to the Old Testament occurred during Lent and came from just three books: Genesis, Proverbs, and Isaiah. On weekdays throughout the Great Fast, lections from these books proceeded according to a system of continuous reading, although none was read in its entirety; as Lent progressed much of each book was passed over. Moreover, the excerpts were read not during the Eucharist, but Genesis and Proverbs during Vespers (*hesperinos*) and Isaiah during the mid-day prayers.[48] For Holy Week itself, these texts gave way to passages from Exodus, Job, and Ezekiel respectively. The overwhelming prominence of Genesis among Old Testament lections during Lent may reflect an expansion of a primitive Easter Vigil that highlighted the events in biblical history relevant to understanding the incarnation, death, and resurrection of Christ.[49]

Andrew's treatment of Old Testament narratives reflects the centrality of Genesis in the Lenten lectionary. Odes 1 through 5 handle figures from Genesis, from Adam to Joseph. His order of presentation does not strictly proceed through the canonical order of the book's chapters. In Ode 3, for example, he opens with an extended meditation on Lot and Sodom (Genesis 19) before returning to Noah (Genesis 7 and 8), whom he had already introduced in Ode 2. As Ode 3 progresses, he treats the binding of Isaac (Genesis 22) before the story of Ishmael and Hagar (Genesis 16 and 21); and invokes Jacob's ladder (Genesis 28) before Melchizedek (Genesis 14). He returns to Lot and Sodom at the end of the ode. Some of these stories do not appear in the Prophetologion, including the story of Lot and Sodom in Genesis 19 and the story of Jacob and the angels in Genesis 32:22–32. Andrew is clearly working here from a complete text of Genesis and a more thorough knowledge of its stories than one might glean even from regular church attendance. At the same time, the lectionary does govern to some extent the treatment of individual figures, as the handling of Job illustrates. The Prophetologion assigns readings from Job for Vespers from Monday through Thursday of Holy Week, covering Job 1:1–2:10 (the opening narrative before the book's lengthy speeches); Job 38:1–23 (part of God's answer to Job); and Job 42:1–5 (Job's reply to God).[50] Andrew's treatment of Job invokes details from Job 1 and 2 only and thus most probably reflects or demands a familiarity with Job from the liturgical readings alone.

Andrew's handling of the remainder of the Old Testament proceeds more quickly. Part way through Ode 5, more than halfway through the poem (at stanza 132 out of 250), Andrew proceeds from the stories of Joseph and his brothers in Genesis to the story of Moses in Exodus. He does nothing to mark the shift to a new biblical book, but moves seamlessly from Joseph in the pit to Moses in a basket, suggesting a greater interest in the progression of history than in divisions within their Old Testament sources. The treatment of

Moses and Exodus carries over into the first irmos of Ode 6, with reference to the manna from heaven and the fleshpots of Egypt, both drawn from the book of Numbers. To the extent that members of the audience knew most of the stories from Genesis and the story of Moses, the effect of Andrew's poem was to focus the exegesis on the implications of each relatively familiar biblical story for self-regard.

However, from this point until the last section of Ode 8, Andrew's invocation of Old Testament figures (with the notable exception of David and perhaps Elijah) moves far beyond the familiarity with biblical stories one might expect from the lectionary. At the end of Ode 8, Andrew invokes figures familiar because songs from their books were used liturgically as biblical canticles: Jonah, Azariah, and the three Boys in the Furnace (LXX Dan 3); and the prophet Jeremiah, from whose book the Byzantine lectionary tradition assigns readings for Holy Thursday, Friday, and Saturday. Here however, Andrew is no doubt relying on his monastic formation and his study of scripture—especially Genesis—in monastic settings. As the poet rather rapidly surveys figures drawn from Judges and 1–4 Kingdoms [1 and 2 Samuel and 1 and 2 Kings], none but the very learned would know what he was talking about. Instead, the message would be an overwhelming sense that the whole of scripture—even its most obscure corners—converged to convict the conscience of sin. Indeed, as the lectionary confirms, Lent was a season of heightened interest in the Old Testament; this meant that the Old Testament would tend to be read as a penitential text.

In subsequent centuries, knowledge of Old Testament history in Byzantium would be mediated in part through Andrew's *Great Kanon*. Manuscripts of Old Testament books in their entirety, let alone complete Old Testaments, were relatively rare. In contrast, the lectionaries and service books necessary for conducting the liturgy were relatively common. This meant that, in addition to those narratives transmitted through the Prophetologion, the *Kanon* provided the most familiar and available access to biblical history before the time of Jesus. In fact, the author of a curious renarration of Old Testament history known as the *Palaea Historica*, composed no earlier than the ninth century, cites Andrew as an authority more than any text outside the Bible, terming him variously "Andrew," "the Cretan," and "the wise man."[51] A learned commentary on the *Kanon* in the thirteenth century by Akakios Sabaites further demonstrates that the poem's extensive sweep of biblical history remained attractive to Byzantine intellectuals.[52]

Old Testament Exemplars

Andrew's treatment of specific biblical figures illuminates his techniques and objectives. Because he aims to draw a moral judgment on the narrating self, his engagement with the biblical narrative remains fairly basic. He does not appear to draw significantly from ancient commentarial traditions. He refers to enough details in the story to make the contrast between what his soul has been doing and what it ought to have been doing, but he eschews a deeper inquiry into the text so typical of Jewish and Christian exegesis in late antiquity. He does not expand the narrative by adding additional, extrabiblical details, in the mode of midrash, nor does he compose additional dialogue giving depth to the characters as in earlier liturgical hymnography, such as in the Syriac *soghitha* or Greek kontakion. He generally avoids a typological reading of Old Testament figures and episodes as prefiguring Christ. Instead, the Bible comes mediated only by a hermeneutic of self-accusation.

Adam and Eve serve to illustrate Andrew's theology of human responsibility in the fall from Paradise and the expulsion from Eden, thus beginning a chronicle of human sin and disobedience to divine will. They also offer an opportunity for the singer to reflect on his own sinfulness by reading his own sins as reproductions of biblical sins.[53] The story of Adam and Eve and their expulsion from the garden was familiar from the lectionary as well as from more general Christian lore: the Prophetologion assigns Genesis 2:20–3:20 (from the creation of Eve from Adam's rib through God's pronouncement of punishment) to Friday of the first week of Lent, and Genesis 3:21–4:7 (from God's making of leather tunics for Adam and Eve through the middle of the story of Cain and Abel) to Monday of the second week.[54] As appropriate to his sequence through biblical literature, Andrew addresses the first humans at the beginning of his survey, in Ode 1.

> I have rivaled in transgression (τῇ παραβάσει παραζηλώσας) the first-created Adam, and I know myself stripped naked of God and of the everlasting kingdom and [its] delight because of my sins. (1.3)

Already here, Andrew finds the vocabulary for his presentation of the self in the biblical account. He applies Adam's nakedness to himself and invokes the "delight [τρυφή]" of Paradise in Genesis 3:23 from which he too has been exiled. Eve also provides an exemplum:

Alas wretched soul! How much are you like the first Eve! You saw
evil and you were grievously [πικρῶς] wounded, and you grasped
the tree [ξύλος] and rashly tasted the food of unreason [παράλογος].
(1.4)

Andrew's life of sin becomes a reenactment of Eve's story in the Garden, seeing the fruit, touching and eating it.

Andrew returns to Adam in the second ode, where in a sequence of nine
stanzas he further allegorizes elements of the story of Adam's fall, rendering
Adam's narrative a script through which the poet rehearses his own fall into
sin. By reassembling key details, Andrew spiritualizes the story and performs
exegesis on himself. He laments,

Now I have rent my first robe [στολή] which the Fashioner
[Πλαστουργὸς] wove for me from the beginning, and so I lie naked.
(2.7)

Focusing on Adam's clothing and nakedness, Andrew depends on earlier
and widely familiar exegetical and hymnographic traditions that in the fall
Adam and Eve were stripped of their original and beautiful raiment or "robe
of glory."[55] This widespread tradition in Jewish and Christian exegesis stands
in tension with the statement in Genesis 2:25 that after their creation Adam
and Eve were "naked . . . and not ashamed," but emphasizes the rupture into
mortality that Adam and Eve's sin entails.[56] Andrew himself is responsible
for the destruction of his God-given garment. The next stanza continues the
theme of Adam and Eve's clothing to narrate the self:

I have clothed myself in the rent tunic [χιτών], which the serpent
wove for me with [his] counsel, and I am ashamed. (2.8)

In contrast to the text of Genesis 3:21, where God makes tunics of skin or
leather [χιτῶνας δερματίνους] for Adam and Eve after he sentences them to
travails and labor, here the serpent weaves the debased textile with his subtle
enticements. In shifting responsibility for this second and lesser garment to
the serpent, Andrew reprises Eve's own attempt to displace blame for disobedience in Genesis 3:13: "The snake tricked me, and I ate," just as Adam himself
had sought to blame Eve.[57] Andrew also attempts to escape responsibility. In
a subsequent verse, the textile production shifts again:

The sin stitched for me tunics of skins [τοὺς δερματίνους χιτῶνας],
having stripped me of the first robe, woven by God. (2.12)

The plural "tunics" derives directly from the biblical verse indicating both
Adam and Eve's postlapsarian costume, even as Andrew assigns the garments'
manufacture to his own transgression. Ultimately, then, Andrew accepts responsibility for his spiritual clothing:

I am clothed in the raiment of shame [τὸν στολισμὸν τῆς αισχύνης]
    as with fig leaves.
I am dressed in a tunic of disgrace [κατεστιγμένον χιτῶνα].
I have soiled the tunic of my flesh and fouled, O Savior, that [which
    was] in accord with the image and likeness. (2.13–15)

Andrew has debased not just his clothing but God's own creation—the image
of God in which he was created.

Andrew's shame recapitulates the fall of Adam, not because all have
sinned in and through Adam, as the Western doctrine of original sin might
argue, but because Adam functions as a type for the sinful individual. In fact,
Andrew's freedom with the biblical story and the shift in agency for the tunic
of skins clarifies responsibility for Andrew's own fall. In the course of these
verses, Andrew accepts that he has been the agent of his own sins. Metaphori-
cally, and with some creative reworking of the story's details, Adam serves
Andrew as a biblical pattern through which to recognize himself. Biblical
clothing, of course, prompts other associations, and just two stanzas later,
Andrew alludes to Joseph's garment (Gen 37:3) in a similar vein:

I adorned the statue of the flesh [σαρκὸς ἀνδριάντα] with the many-
colored coat of shameful thoughts [λογισμοί], and I am condemned.
(2.18)

Throughout the poem, Andrew's sins occur in the realm of the mind, as an
engagement with shameful thoughts and sinful desires. In this register, Andrew abstracts a spiritualizing interpretation from the flesh of the text. With
reference to Adam's sin in the garden, Andrew reflects on himself:

I looked at the beauty of the tree, and I deceived my mind [νοῦς], so I
lie naked and ashamed. (2.9)

And earlier in the poem, in the first ode, Andrew declares,

> Instead of the Eve of sensory perception, I have the Eve of the mind
> [Ἀντι Εὔας αἰσθητῆς, ἡ νοητή μοι κατέστη Εὔα], the passionate
> thought in the flesh, suggesting sweet things, but always tasting bitter
> when gulped down. (1.5)

In contrasting an Eve of the flesh with an Eve of the mind, Andrew's exegesis
thus recapitulates the physical and fleshly sins of the Old Testament figures in
the movements of his own mind, particularly in his desires for fleshly things.

This shift in concern from physical sins to their mental contemplation, common in Christian moral reflection, finds its biblical warrant in the Sermon on the
Mount, where Jesus equates angry thoughts with murder and lustful thoughts
with adultery (Matthew 5:21–32). The use of philosophical vocabulary, such as
the distinction between an aesthetic and a noetic Eve, is rarer in the *Kanon*. Yet
occasionally Andrew draws on monastic moral and philosophical discourse, part
of Byzantium's Evagrian legacy. Later in the poem, in Ode 4, he introduces additional categories derived from moral theology in his allegorizing treatment of
Jacob and his wives, where Leah and Rachel come to represent action (πρᾶξις)
and knowledge (γνῶσις). Like the monastic John Klimax, Andrew reads Jacob's
ladder as a pattern or model (δεῖγμα) "of mounting through action and ascent
through knowledge" (4.6) that should prompt a reformation of the self:

> If then you wish to live in action and knowledge and contemplation
> (θεωρία), make yourself anew. (4.6)

Theōria, "contemplation," serves two functions, to describe a life of moral
discernment through contemplation of God and to introduce the exegetical
approach of allegorical reading. Andrew uses *theōria* in this more technical
sense two stanzas later in his allegory of Leah and Rachel.

> Think for me of the two wives as action and knowledge in contemplation [ἐν θεωρίᾳ]. Action for Leah as (she had) many children; knowledge for Rebecca as (the result of) many labors. For without labor,
> neither deeds nor contemplation, O soul, will be successful. (4.8)[58]

The allegorical treatment of Jacob's wives, however, is exceptional within
the poem, as is the focus on theoretical distinctions between action and

knowledge. For the most part, Andrew engages in a more straightforward moral exegesis of the biblical stories, where biblical figures provide examples to imitate or avoid.

If Adam and Eve are the standard types for the fall from grace into sin, King David exemplifies the penitent sinner. Having slept with Bathsheba and arranged the death of her husband Uriah (2 Kingdoms [2 Sam] 11), David is guilty of both adultery and murder. These most famous aspects of the story of David were not read out from the lectionary in the course of the liturgical year, but more likely remained familiar because of David's importance as the composer of the Psalms, and particularly Psalm 50 [51], the penitential Psalm par excellence. According to an ascription that had become part of the Psalm's text in the Septuagint, David composed the Psalm "when the prophet Nathan came to him, after he had gone in to Bathsheba" (LXX 50:2). In fact, David's prayer of repentance had been one of two possibilities for use as the opening psalm at Morning Prayer since the fourth century.[59] By the late sixth century Psalm 50 preceded the nine canticles in the monastic communities of Palestine and Syria and quite likely preceded the original performances of Andrew's kanons.

In a series of stanzas in the seventh ode, Andrew sings of "David, the father of God [πατρόθεος (or: 'ancestor')]" who sinned twice, "pierced by the arrow of adultery"—an allusion to the weapon of Eros—and "captured by the spear of murderous vengeance." Reflecting on himself in light of David's faults, the poet accuses his soul, "But you are more grievously ill because of your impulsive will [ταῖς κατὰ γνώμην ὁρμαῖς] than your deeds" (7.4). While David, "mixed adultery with murder," he "at once demonstrated a double repentance" (7.5; cf. 2 Kingdoms [2 Sam] 12:9, 13. Thus David, whose sins become paradigms of the worst of human desire, especially in light of Jesus' remarks about anger and lust in the Sermon on the Mount (Mt 5:21–30), should serve to prompt penance, but Andrew has willfully failed to seek God's forgiveness.

In his capacity as the composer of the Psalms, David provides Andrew with another sort of model for himself, although the connection remains implicit. "David once composed a hymn [ὕμνος], painting as in an image [συγγραψάμενος ὡς ἐν εἰκόνι], by which he exposes [ἐλέγχει] the deed which he did" (7.6).[60] The "hymn" in question is Psalm 50 [51], David's great penitential prayer for forgiveness. Andrew continues, "He [David] cried out, 'Have mercy on me [Ἐλέησόν με, Ps 50:3 (51:1)],' 'for against you alone have I sinned [Ps 50:6 (51:4)],' the God of all. 'Cleanse me yourself [Ps 50:4 (51:2)]'" (7.6).

Here Andrew quotes David, or nearly so, adjusting his wording slightly to fit his meter. At the end of the seventh ode, Andrew once again weaves David's lament with his own, naming his source and model: "But in pity restore to me the joy, as David sings" (7.18). The reference is to Psalm 50:14 [51:12], "Restore to me the joy of your salvation." And in the following stanza he cries out, "O only Savior, you yourself have mercy on me, as David sings, according to your mercy"(7.9), quoting David's words that open the Psalm, "Have mercy on me, O God, according to your great mercy" (Ps 50:3 [51:1]). Thus Andrew revoices the psalmist's words, striving to imitate David's act of composing a hymn, as well as his tuneful confessing of sin and penitential disposition.[61]

New Testament Exemplars

Throughout the hymn, the singer laments that his litany of Old Testament exemplars has failed to bring about his repentance or reform. Perhaps New Testament models will be more effective. In some sense, he already imitates them, as a stanza in Ode 8 demonstrates. He compares himself to a list of savable sinners from the Gospels.

> Like the Thief I cry out to you: "Remember" [Lk 23:42]. Like Peter I weep bitterly [Mt 26:75; Lk 22:62; cf. Mk 14:72]. "Forgive me, O Savior," I call out like the Tax Collector [cf. Lk 18:13]. I shed tears like the Harlot [cf. Lk 7:38]. Accept my lament, just as once [you accepted] the Canaanite Woman's [Mt 15:22].[62] (8.14)

Each biblical figure provides a phrase or action, or both, to which the poet joins his own expressions of regret and atonement. The self presented in the stanza and from the pulpit thus reenacts a pastiche of biblical penitents at their moment of entreaty.

In contrast to many of the Old Testament figures invoked earlier in the poem, most of these New Testament types would have been familiar to Andrew's late seventh- or early eighth-century congregants from their appearance in the Lenten and Holy Week lectionary. The late antique Armenian and Georgian lectionaries for Jerusalem both assign the reading of Matthew's account of Peter's denial of Christ and his bitter weeping (Mt 26:69–75) to a cycle of Passion readings on the eve of Good Friday.[63] The story of the penitent thief crucified next to Jesus, who would be with him in Paradise, unique to the Gospel of Luke (23:39–43), was appointed for Vespers the following day.[64] Andrew would have known this practice while at the Church of the Holy Sepulcher in his youth. Later witnesses to the Constantinopolitan lectionary reflect the influence of Jerusalem's reading cycle and assign Peter's denial to the Eucharist on Holy Thursday and Luke's account of the Thief to Vespers on Good Friday.[65] This same lectionary assigns Matthew's story of the Canaanite woman (Mt 15:21–28) to the thirty-second Sunday after Pentecost and Luke's Parable of the Pharisee and the Tax Collector (Lk 18:10–14) to the thirty-third Sunday after Pentecost, that is, to the eucharistic liturgies for weeks just prior to the beginning of Lent, although the placement of the Parable of the Pharisee may have occurred after Andrew's time.[66]

Congregants' familiarity with these stories, however, was likely grounded in or enhanced by the cycle of liturgical hymns composed in previous centuries, which had become canonical or were in widespread use. Every one of these figures appears in the hymns of the sixth-century poet Romanos the Melodist, some as principal characters in his midrashic expansions of their narratives.[67] Andrew is quite fond of his New Testament penitents, and he includes all but Peter in his chronological harmonization of the Gospels in Ode 9. And as we have seen, he also invokes Peter, the Harlot, the Tax Collector, and the Thief in the earlier odes, relieving his survey of Old Testament figures with a catalogue of redeemed sinners who interacted directly with Jesus in order to encourage repentance. Perhaps more than any other biblical personages, these are the people he wishes to identify with and emulate.

The Harlot from Romanos to Andrew and Kassia

A focus on Andrew's treatment of the figure he consistently calls "the Harlot [ἡ πόρνη]" illuminates how Andrew constructs his appeal to New Testament models. Comparison with Romanos's kontakion on the same woman, discussed in Chapter 2, allows us to chart important differences between the two hymnographers' handling of scriptural narrative. Furthermore, consideration of a ninth-century hymn attributed to the nun Kassia affords perspective on how the Harlot became a canonical type for all Byzantine Christians. Although we have attended to the story earlier, the shape of the gospel traditions themselves reveals Andrew's marked conservatism. The Gospel of Mark recounts a meal that Jesus took in the house of Simon the Leper two days before Passover (Mk 14:3–9). During the meal, a woman approaches

Jesus with an alabaster jar full of expensive scented oil, or *myron*, breaks the jar, and pours the perfume on his head. Matthew follows this source rather faithfully, but Luke's account places the story much earlier in the narrative, at the home of a Pharisee, and adds details that reshape the woman as a penitent sinner; it is this version, with subsequent Christian interpretations, that captures Andrew's interest. Luke writes, "And behold, a woman of the city, who was a sinner [ἁμαρτωλός], when she learned that he was at table in the Pharisee's house, brought an alabaster jar of scented oil [ἀλάβαστρον μύρου], and standing behind him at his feet, weeping [κλαίουσα], she began to wet his feet with her tears [τοῖς δάκρυσιν], and wiped [ἐξέμασσεν] them with the hair of her head, and kissed his feet, and anointed them with the scented oil (Lk 7:37–38)." When the Pharisee objects, Jesus chastises him and explains, "Therefore I tell you, her sins, which are many, are forgiven, for she loved much; but he who is forgiven little, loves little." He then tells her, "Your sins are forgiven" (Lk 7:47–48). John 12:1–9 recounts a similar story about a dinner at the home of Mary and Martha, in which Mary pours *myron* on Jesus' feet; but the hymnographic tradition leading up to Andrew, including Romanos, does not identify the sinful woman with Mary the sister of Lazarus. It fell to the commentators and hymnographers to identify the woman's sin as harlotry.

As Susan Ashbrook Harvey has shown, this sinful woman was especially popular with the authors of dialogue hymns. Extensive poetic explorations of her tale survive in Syriac by Ephrem and Jacob of Serug, and in Greek in the corpus known as Greek Ephrem and in the hymns of Romanos the Melodist.[68] A glance at Romanos reveals both Andrew's debt to this earlier tradition and his departures from their midrashic methods. Romanos, in his typical fashion, opens the story up, giving dialogue to each of the participants. In the manner of a Method actor he provides the woman with an extensive back-story and a variety of psychological motivations. As we saw in Chapter 2, he "search[es] the mind of the wise woman" (10.4.1–2).[69] He invents a scene in the market where she converses with the perfume merchant. Romanos compares her to other persistent women, including the Canaanite Woman, Hannah the mother of Samuel, and Rahab the Harlot. Moreover Romanos plays jauntily on themes of harlotry and desire, calling the *myron* a "love potion" (10.10) and constructing Jesus as the woman's true lover: "I break with past lovers, that I may please my new love" (10.10).

The contrast with Andrew's treatment is stark. In the two stanzas where Andrew reflects further on the Harlot, he adheres to the biblical account.

Shortly after his list of figures whose words and deeds he imitates, Andrew returns to the Harlot to compare himself again with her.

> As I empty out an alabaster jar of tears like scented oil, O Savior, upon your head, I call out to you like the Harlot, seeking mercy. I bring to you entreaty, and I beg you to give me release.[70]

Here the basic elements of Luke's text suffice. He maintains Luke's vocabulary: tears, alabaster, scented oil. Andrew permits himself an unoriginal pun and an elegant effect: When he compares himself to her in "seeking mercy [ἔλεον]," he uses a homophone of the word for olive oil [ἔλαιον]. And he imitates the Harlot by emptying on Jesus a jar filled not with oil but with tears. This is not, however, the first time in the poem that he has made this transposition. When he mentions the Harlot much earlier in Ode 2, he declares, "I have sinned like the Harlot. . . . O Savior, accept my tears as scented oil" (2. 22). Having landed on this evocative substitution, he has stuck with it.

In Ode 9 the Harlot appears for a final time in the *Great Kanon*, this time in her chronological order within Andrew's survey of gospel personages. Once again, Andrew hews closely to the account in Luke, maintaining much of its vocabulary, recasting Luke's words as necessary to the metrical scheme.

> O my wretched soul, you have not emulated the Harlot, who took the alabaster jar of scented oil, and with her tears anointed the Lord's feet. She wiped them with her hair.[71]

We have again the scented oil, the alabaster jar, the tears, and the feet of Jesus. All the vocabulary comes directly from the biblical text.

The various details of this treatment do not amount to exegesis in the sense of approaching the text to discover something within it, but rather function to invoke literary epithets or visualize an iconography, identifying a figure according to biblical conventions. Indeed, Andrew persists in this practice throughout the hymn, reproducing the language of the Bible to form the penitent subject and restating biblical elements to smooth or flatten the biblical variety for a single purpose. In great contrast to Romanos, Andrew employs the woman not to plumb the depths of the narrative or the mind of the woman but to accuse the hearer and himself. Andrew allows the woman not merely to wet Jesus' feet with tears, but to "anoint" them [σὺν δάκρυσιν ἤλειψε]. But even here, the anointing of feet acknowledges Luke's version and the story in John, where Mary uses the jar of scented oil to anoint Jesus' feet, rather than his head. In effect, the poet repeats the story; he does not retell or rethink it.

Romanos, on the other hand, performs extensive metrical exegesis of the story with varied diction, even avoiding some of the key words in the biblical account. He never uses the word for "alabaster jar [ἀλάβαστρον]"; he uses the verb "to weep [κλαίω]" only once, when the woman is describing her own motivations for approaching Jesus; and he uses the word for "tears [δάκρυα]" only twice in eighteen stanzas, both times in Jesus' mouth describing the woman and her actions. Like Andrew, Romanos also frames his treatment of the Harlot by focusing on himself.[72] In the first stanza, he declares that he too is a fornicator, and that while "the Harlot quailed" at the threat of eternal punishment, he "remain[s] in the filth of his deeds" (10.1). In the eighteenth and final stanza, he prays that he too will have his debts forgiven, extending the fiscal metaphor:

> Relieving me of the capital of my soul and interest of my flesh,
> as you are compassionate, pardon, forgive
> *the filth of my deeds.* (10.18)

But Romanos uses self-reflection to enlarge and open the narrative, whereas Andrew uses self-reflection to focus it.

Perhaps the most famous treatment of the Harlot in all of Byzantine liturgical poetry is the shorter sticheron, or versicle, by the ninth-century nun from Constantinople, Kassia.[73] Born into an aristocratic family, Kassia wrote both secular and religious verse, and corresponded with the great monastic leader, Theodore the Stoudite, before entering religious life.[74] Likely composed to be performed between sections of psalms at Morning Prayer on the Wednesday of Holy Week, the hymn opens describing the woman briefly in the third person. The framing verses blur the moment of the Harlot's appearance at the dinner in the home of Simon the Pharisee with the moment when the Marys approached Christ's tomb to anoint him in death. Moreover, both of these events are folded into the liturgical present.

> Lord, a woman who fell into many sins,
> Recognizing your divinity,
> Took up the myrrh-bearer's office,
> And with tears brings you myrrh before your entombment.

Although in the biblical accounts, the women at the tomb are led by Mary Magdalene, the poem does not name her, and this association is lacking in earlier Byzantine hymnography.[75] The rest of the poem reimagines the woman's own voice in the first-person singular, addressing her prayer to God in a speech-in-character. Like Romanos, Kassia enters the woman's interior life as she crafts a typologically complex entreaty. The third-person frame, which does not reappear at the end of the hymn, eases the transition from the singer's own persona into the role of the Harlot, as she laments her transgressions and bids Christ for forgiveness.

> "Ah me!" she says, "night is upon me,
> The goad of incontinence, gloomy and moonless,
> To lust after sin.
> Receive my streams of tears,
> You who feed clouds to draw the water of the sea;
> Bend to my heart's groans,
> You who bent the heavens with your ineffable abasement [κενώσει]."

Assuming her subjectivity, the singer compares her tears with God's oceans, and her humiliation with God's self-emptying in the incarnation. She thus imitates him in miniature, conforming herself to his expansive and magnanimous example, and thus seeks his acceptance.

In the following verses, the speaker moves from a description of anointing Christ's feet with her hair to another association with the feet of God, and thus pulls herself toward another sinful woman, Eve, who did not present herself in repentance but rather hid from the divine presence in the Garden of Eden.

> I shall cover with kisses
> And wipe again
> With the hair of my head
> The immaculate feet of you,
> At whose footfalls echoing in her ears,
> Eve in paradise at even-tide hid herself in fear.

The poem closes as the Harlot's prayer tends toward a more generic confession and entreaty, a petition appropriate to the penitential season:

Soul-saving savior, who will track down
The numbers of my sins and the depths of your judgments?
Do not overlook me your servant,
You who have pity without measure.

Thus, without returning to the voice of the frame narrator, the poem leads
the singer through the role of the Harlot to a model for the Christian self,
but without breaking character. In contrast to Romanos's and Andrew's treatments, Kassia does not focus on the interiority of the opening narrator, an "I"
beyond the biblical context. Where the earlier poets use the Harlot as a lens,
among many, through which to view the self, Kassia fuses the singer's subjectivity entirely with the Harlot; the singer becomes her, even as she emulates
Christ and contrasts herself with Eve.

It is reasonable to assume that Kassia wrote her hymn *On the Sinful
Woman* to be performed by the nuns of her monastery. In such instances, the
voice of the frame and the voice of the Harlot are women's voices. A singing
nun assumes the identity of a penitent biblical woman. But the earliest manuscript appearances of the hymn suggest additional forms of reception. Perhaps because of Kassia's presence in Constantinople and her association with
Theodore the Stoudite, the hymn entered the tradition of the Triodion, the
Lenten service book that is the subject of the following chapter. The earliest
example of the hymn is found in the manuscript Sinai graecus 734–735, which
also contains the earliest witness to Andrew's *Great Kanon*. The Stoudite editors included Kassia's hymn as the eleventh of twelve *stichera idiomela*, that
is, short hymns composed to their own melodies rather than to model tune
types, appointed for Holy Wednesday.[76] An eleventh-century Triodion copied
in southern Italy at Grottaferrata and now in the Vatican Library, Vaticanus
graecus 771, includes Kassia's hymn as the last in a series for the same day.[77] In
both cases, the hymn appears without attribution to any composer or author,
which is not unusual in these manuscripts, although some hymns, especially
longer kanons, are provided with their author's names. These manuscripts indicate that from an early period, Kassia's hymn *On the Sinful Woman* was also
sung by men, rendering the frame in a male voice, a gendering perhaps reinforced if someone using the manuscript did not know the poem was by Kassia. The male singer then shifts into the voice of the Sinful Woman, much as
the cantor of Romanos's kontakion, engaging in an apparently commonplace
liturgical transgendering. Singing Andrew, one compared him- or herself to

men and women of the Bible, but singing Romanos or Kassia, singers of both genders *became* the men and women of the Bible. In short, the penitential imaginary of Byzantine hymnography encouraged movement between and across genders in the quest for an appropriate subjectivity.

Andrew of Crete and the Aesthetics of the Self

Considering the kontakion of Romanos, the *Great Kanon* of Andrew, and the sticheron of Kassia, we witness differences in genre based on liturgical placement and function. Through much of the reign of Justinian, Romanos composed his lengthy verse sermons for All-Night Vigils on Saturday nights, the eves of major festivals, and during Lent. The Vigil service included psalms, hymns, and the reading of scriptural passages relevant to the liturgical season, including also those appointed in the lectionary for the following day. Romanos's kontakia thus commented through expansion on biblical texts that had just been heard. His works are verse homilies, and this function accounts for their approach to scripture. The kanon, by contrast, supplemented the biblical hymnody appointed for Morning Prayer. Rather than functioning as sermons, kanons provided a series of liturgical reflections in the form of prayerful song. Mary Cunningham has characterized the kanon as "meditative rather than didactic" and their form "more as soliloquy than as dramatic dialogue."[78] Kanons were also keyed to the liturgical season and could reflect the lectionary, as Andrew Louth has demonstrated regarding John of Damascus's kanons for the feasts of Easter, Transfiguration, and the Dormition of the Theotokos, and, as we shall see in the following chapter, in the hymns of the Stoudite reform.[79] But the models remained the canticles themselves, first-person hymns of praise, thanksgiving, and repentant self-reflection. Kassia, on the other hand, wrote in a genre of short hymns that punctuated the appointed psalmody with reference to the day's lections. In that sense, her work was like Romanos's but in miniature, a poignant character sketch.

In the *Great Kanon*, Andrew preferred a survey of biblical types more like a catena than an interpretation. In this, he borrows from the use of exemplars or types in prayer forms, including, for example, the penitential prayers in the Barberini Euchologion or in the anaphora of the *Liturgy of Basil*, which recounts much of sacred history in the process of giving thanks over the bread and wine. In the *Great Kanon*, Andrew gathers the sweep of salvation into a single literary unit, bringing the entire cast of the biblical narrative to bear on the formation and wounding of the Christian conscience. But the difference also seems to indicate a difference in liturgical aesthetics, away from the exegetical and toward litany. By assembling biblical events into a single penitential hymn, Andrew achieves an aesthetic result not unlike those emerging roughly simultaneously in Jewish liturgical poems, called *piyyutim*, for the Day of Atonement, suggesting a shared approach to biblical narrative as a repository for moral instruction and the formation of the penitent subject.[80]

If we can recognize differences in artistic styles, for example, between late Roman naturalistic painting and middle Byzantine frontal and more static iconic representations, we should also be able to examine and describe changes in liturgical styles. While Romanos fleshes out the background of each biblical figure, Andrew presents a surprisingly uniform gallery of biblical types. Kassia's portrait is, in some sense, also iconic, focusing on one figure, although that figure then engages in her own exegesis of biblical self-identification. While Romanos expands the biblical narrative, Andrew refocuses the entirety of the Bible on a single self-accusing operation. Kassia's Sinful Woman reads the Bible in a similar fashion. Thus from Romanos to Andrew to Kassia we can chart a difference not only in the representation of the self but in the mechanisms employed to coerce the formation of this self. Romanos opens the biblical narratives to explore them, to place the congregants within the narratives as witnesses to the drama, creating a feeling of immediacy, as if one were there.[81] Andrew places the subject at a greater distance from the narrative—hearing about it, recalling it, but ultimately absorbed within the act of self-reflection—not so much present to the Bible as present to the self as subject. Kassia's hymn shows how these operations might coexist, compressing an exegesis of self and scripture into very few lines.

While it might be tempting to posit a tendency toward dramatically increased introspection over time—from the early Byzantine liturgical drama of Romanos, to the interior anxiety of the contemporary Christian in the *Great Kanon*, and then, perhaps, to Kassia's focus on the Harlot's exegetical interiority—these differences may have more to do with developments of their respective literary genres and hymn forms than with broad and consistent changes in the conception of Byzantine selfhood. Our evidence is fragmentary, and my analysis selective. Moreover, for much of Byzantine history, the use of these genres overlapped. In Andrew's own day, this shift from biblical exegesis to self-reflection may not have been so momentous. It is nearly inconceivable that Andrew would not have known the corpus of Romanos's hymns, which had become canonical in some churches by the late sixth or early seventh century. The *Miracles of Artemios* attests the cantor at the Church of John the Baptist in Constantinople who spent 52 years singing the hymns of Romanos at weekly Night Vigils throughout the liturgical year.[82] Andrew arrived in the city only twenty years later. A careful study by Alexander Lingas has refuted the notion, once standard in music history, that the kanon replaced the kontakion in the course of the seventh and eighth centuries. These musical forms always belonged to different services: the kontakion to the sung office of the Night Vigil, the kanon to Morning Prayer; the first a popular service of urban cathedrals; the second, I would argue, a form shared in its basic outline by monastics and laity alike.[83] Lingas has shown on the basis of manuscript evidence that the cathedral Night Office persisted in Constantinople on the eve of festivals into the twelfth century, perhaps until 1204, and included the singing of a kontakion, if sometimes truncated. For the most part, new kontakia ceased to be composed after the ninth century, but the earlier texts provided ample material for the liturgical cycle. That is, Romanos's style of the self coexisted in ninth-century Byzantine liturgical life with Andrew's and Kassia's. Indeed, these subjectivities coalesced and reinforced each other.

The persistence and prominence of the kontakion means that while Andrew composed kanons for Morning Prayer in the late seventh or early eighth century, Romanos was almost certainly still chanted during the Night Vigil. Perhaps we should imagine that Andrew, a deacon during his years in Constantinople, himself chanted them at night before rising the next morning to sing one of his kanons. Or perhaps he chanted all night through, beginning Morning Prayer at dawn. In any case, Romanos would have cast a long shadow over any aspiring hymnographer. Evidence for direct influence is slight but telling. In a few places, Andrew's *Great Kanon* seems to echo Romanos.[84] Two stanzas in Ode 4 recall the prelude to Romanos's hymn *On the Crucifixion*, also called *On the Powers of Hell*. Andrew writes, "The end draws near, O soul; it draws near and you neither take thought nor prepare [Ἐγγίζει ψυχὴ τὸ τέλος, ἐγγίζει καὶ οὐ φροντίζεις, οὐχ ἑτοιμάζῃ]" (4.2), possibly rephrasing Romanos:

> O my soul, my soul, wake up! Why do you sleep?
> The end draws near and you will be troubled
> [Ψυχή μου, ψυχή μου, ἀνάστα· τί καθεύδεις;
> Τὸ τέλος ἐγγίζει καὶ μέλλεις θορυβεῖσθαι]. (Romanos, *Hymns* 21 prelude [SC 37])

The phrase "the end draws near" may seem a commonplace, but Romanos continues, "Come to your senses [ἀνάνηψον] so that Christ the God might spare you." And in his following stanza, Andrew rebukes himself, "Come to your senses, O my soul! [Ἀνάνηψον ὦ ψυχή μου]" (4.3).[85] This is just the sort of echoing in sequence that one might expect if Andrew knew his Romanos intimately. There is also some evidence in his treatment of the Harlot that Andrew was dependent on Romanos's poem about her. After the Lukan Harlot wipes Jesus' feet with her tears in the passage quoted above, Andrew introduces an image from a different biblical text, Colossians 2:14, where the Pauline author describes forgiveness as the blotting out of a handwritten accusation, or *cheirographon*.[86] In Andrew's words, the Lord "tore up for her the hand-written document with the ancient accusations [τῶν ἀρχαίων ἐγκλημάτων, τὸ χειρόγραφον ῥηγνύοντος αὐτῇ]" (9.18). The intercutting of the *cheirographon* and the story of the Harlot also occurs in the final stanza of Romanos's hymn *On the Harlot*, where Jesus addresses both the Harlot and Simon the Pharisee. He forgives them both:

> Depart. You have both been released from the rest of your debts.
> Go. You are exempt from every obligation.
> You have been freed. Do not be subjected again.
> The handwritten documentation [of your debts] has been torn up
>   [τοῦ χειρογράφου σχισθέντος]. Do not incur another. (10.18;
>   trans. Lash, 84)

Only the *cheirographon* is common to both hymns, but the linking of the *cheirographon* to Luke's Sinful Woman may indicate how Romanos shaped Andrew's conception.[87]

Andrew's new presentation of the self arose in a context where Romanos's approach still operated, but where creative energies were shifting from the narrative exegesis of the kontakion to the interior reflection of the kanon. In later centuries, the occasions for singing the kontakia of Romanos became less frequent. Monks truncated these hymns to one or two stanzas to insert them between the sixth and seventh odes of the kanon at Morning Prayer. These stanzas were generally the ones where Romanos speaks in his own voice, either introspectively or on behalf of the congregation. That is, these are the stanzas most like Andrew's *Kanon*. Middle Byzantine liturgical aesthetics apparently preferred the *Kanon*. As the tenth-century liturgical manuscript at St. Catherine's Monastery in the Sinai, Sinai graecus 734–735, attests, the *Great Kanon* was so popular and important that it moved at some point from the Morning Prayer liturgy to the Vespers service of the fifth Thursday of Lent, perhaps to provide sufficient time for the long work.[88] Andrew's use of the Bible in the shaping of a common personal religion would long outlive him, displaying an icon of the style of Orthodox self that the church encouraged, particularly during Lent.

*   *   *

Prayer scripts the self. The recitation of set prayers conforms the speaker to a particular model of self-understanding and self-expression. In praying, one becomes the subject of the prayer, both in the sense of becoming the persona the text talks about and in the sense that one is acted upon, is under the creative power of the prayer to produce a particular self. In its emotionally charged performance, the *Great Kanon* both expresses and produces contrition. Its use of biblical models renders exegesis an instrument of subjectivation, a reading of the Bible to make the self and make it known. Andrew is dogged in applying biblical stories for the recognition of sin, imposing an interpretive unity on the self. The self that emerges is remarkably consistent in its construction. In the course of nine odes, Andrew shapes an interior life that became a Byzantine model for interiority. The hymn, then, provides evidence not precisely for the religion of individuals, but for established and institutional images or imaginings of individual interior life.

The *Great Kanon* sheds light on the technologies by which the institutional apparatus of the church shaped individual subjectivities. If we imagine Andrew, the bishop, chanting his kanon before congregants in his large three-aisled basilica at Gortyna, we can reflect on the effects of his remarkable liturgical self-abasement. Among listeners, the Christian self promulgated by the *Great Kanon* forms not through identity with biblical figures directly, but rather with the poem's "I." The hearer is to identify with the singer or singers, and with his or their performance of lamentation and self-reproach. The poem works by forming the interior life of each Christian person in the image of the cantor or choir. In contrast to Romanos, whose encounters with the biblical narratives afford increasingly textured and nuanced access to and insights into a biblical reality, Andrew's Bible points in a single direction, toward the self. The effect of the poem is to apply a master pattern for the subject upon congregants. Watching the singers perform the anguish encouraged a recognition of the self as sinner in need of divine assistance. Andrew implicitly called all to see themselves through the penitential lens of scripture. The entirety of biblical history results in the convicted conscience, and this is his instruction to his flock.

CHAPTER 6

The Voice of the Sinner in First-Person
Hymns of the Lenten Triodion

Early in the ninth century, at the recently reestablished Monastery of Saint John the Forerunner at Stoudios (ἐν τοῖς Στουδίου) in Constantinople, the abbot Theodore the Stoudite (759–826) and his brother Joseph (762–832) assembled a new hymnal for the season of Lent.[1] Known as the Triodion, this service book assigned the propers, or variable components, to the Sundays and weekdays of the great penitential fast and the weeks of preparation that preceded it, most especially the hymns keyed to each day's lections.[2] The manual's conception and execution ranks among the greatest achievements of the Stoudite liturgical reforms and resulted in a cycle of chants especially responsive to the liturgical moment.[3] Theodore and his followers envisioned a catechetical liturgy instrumental in the shaping of the monastic self.[4] In this endeavor they inherited expressions of the self from the Psalter, and from the works of earlier hymnographers, including Romanos and Andrew of Crete. Focused especially on the office of Morning Prayer, or Orthros, most of the Triodion was devoted to kanons, a genre of hymnody that first emerged in the late seventh or early eighth century to supplement or replace the chanting of the biblical canticles. In a brief lecture, included among his *Small Catecheses*, delivered at Orthros on Meatfare Sunday, or Apokreas, the Sunday for putting aside meat, Theodore bid his monks to concern themselves, "to consider the Gospel we are going to listen to, thinking [about it], while the canon is being chanted."[5] A fitting kanon thus previewed the themes to be drawn from the lection during the Divine Liturgy. In their representations of interiority, the hymns of the Triodion provide invaluable insight into the formation of subjectivity early in the cultural revival of the middle Byzantine centuries.

The project of creating the Triodion involved collecting, collating, and composing a repertory of liturgical hymns.[6] In their effort, the Stoudites gathered the works of older hymnographers and wrote a number of new works, filling out the calendar in response to the lectionary cycle.[7] The format that Theodore and Joseph initiated remained flexible and open. Subsequent generations of authors continued to compose for the Triodion, so that by the time of our earliest manuscript witness, Sinai graecus 734–735, copied in the tenth century (and which also provides one of the earliest witnesses to Andrew's *Great Kanon* and Kassia's hymn *On the Sinful Woman*), the Triodion functioned as an anthology, with multiple hymns available for each day, arranged roughly chronologically with respect to period of composition.[8] A cornerstone of the Stoudite liturgical reforms, the service book disseminated rapidly among monastic communities, both male and, apparently, female, and not long after came into use in lay cathedrals and parishes as well.[9]

The Stoudite construction of the penitential subject features most prominently in a series of kanons composed in the ninth century and assigned to the three weeks leading up to Lent itself. Here the cantor or choir sings in the first person singular on three successive Sundays, preparing the congregation for the coming fast, enacting lively portraits of the Christian self. Writing for the weeks preceding Lent, the Stoudite poets of the Triodion endeavored to elicit compunction and sorrowful regret through a performative display of fear, grief, self-accusation, and lament. They thus framed Lent not only as a period appropriate for introspection but for a specific range of affective states. A poem *On the Prodigal Son*, written for the ninth Sunday before Easter, and signed in an acrostic by a certain Joseph, most probably Theodore's brother, opens with a request to Jesus for salvation that invokes the precedent of the biblical wastrel's repentance:

> Jesus my God, now accept me too as I repent like the Prodigal Son.
> All my life I have lived in carelessness and provoked you to anger.[10]

The following Sunday, Apokreas or Meatfare, the eighth before Easter, in a poem on the Last Judgment attributed to Theodore himself, the poet inserts himself directly into the eschatological drama, ritualizing anxiety in the face of the final reckoning.

> I tremble with fear when I ponder and foresee the dreadful day of
> your ineffable coming

on which you will sit judging the living and the dead, O my God all
    powerful.
When you will come, O God, with thousands and ten thousands of
    the heavenly powers of angels,
count also me in my wretchedness worthy to meet you, O Christ, on
    the clouds [1 Thess 4:16–17].[11]

And on the next Sunday, Cheesefare, the last day before the beginning of the
forty-day fast, a hymn attributed to an otherwise unknown Christopher reflects on the fall of Adam by identifying with the torment of the first created
human and taking it on as his own:

Come my wretched soul, weep today over your deeds,
remembering how once you were stripped naked in Eden,
cast out from delight and unending joy.[12]

In each of these poems, the poet employs the rhetorical technique of ethopoeia (ἠθοποιία) or speech-in-character, plumbing the affective imaginary to dramatize the remorse, anguish, and terror fitting to Christian
repentance.

The inculcation of pre-Lenten self-regard among those assembled for
Morning Prayer benefited from the mode of performance itself. Although the
precise practice at the times these hymns were composed or when they were
included in the Triodion cannot be established with complete certainty, there
is strong evidence that the kanon was chanted in monasteries by the entire
choir. This contrasts with the performance of the kontakion at the Night Vigil,
which alternated a long strophe sung by a cantor with a short refrain chanted
by the choir or congregation. The pre-Stoudite typikon, or monastic rule, of a
monastery on the island of Pantelleria (southwest of Sicily), probably dating
from the late eighth century, assumes that all the monks will sing the kanon,
and specifies that "worshippers sing the odes [i.e., the biblical canticles]," if at
all possible in the entirety of their verses, "and then start singing the *troparia*
[i.e., the stanzas of the kanon hymn]." This practice predates the assembling
of the Triodion. The monks knew their psalms and canticles from memory,
but the kanon varied and required a kanonarch, literally the one in charge of
the singing of the kanon, or precentor, to recite the text to be sung before each
verse or sense unit: "When you are [standing] in church for the hymnody,
listen to what the precentor says and sing [exactly] as he is prescribing."[13] This

allowed both for choral singing, and for a single written copy of the kanon in the hands of the choir leader.

Practice at the Stoudios Monastery was likely similar: one recension of its mid-ninth century typikon provides directions for Morning Prayer on the Sunday after Easter and on the following morning, that indicate communal singing of the kanon, and this was almost certainly the common practice throughout the year.[14] Although this typikon postdates the initial compilation of the Triodion, the evidence strongly suggests that each monk sang the words of these first-person singular pre-Lenten kanons as part of the ensemble, taking on the voice of the poem and its attendant subjectivity for himself. Theodore himself registered concern for the quality of singing in his monastery and the attention to the text required in the performance of the liturgy. One day in the early 820s after Morning Prayer, he chastised his monks: "Ever since yesterday I have been annoyed at you on account of the psalmody; I ask and beseech you to sing the psalms in an orderly manner and according to the rules, and not simply haphazardly or confusedly."[15] In another lecture he warned against asceticism so rigorous that it made one unable to "sing clearly during the psalmody."[16] Conveying the meaning and sense of the text through chant was critical to the discipline and formation of the monastic self.

The Triodion lacks a critical edition, largely because it represents an open tradition without a fixed text. Lamentably, uncertainties about attribution and dating of even its earliest stratum of poetry have largely postponed serious scholarly consideration of these works. After addressing the expansion of Lent and the history of the Triodion, this chapter will treat the relationship between exegesis and subjectivity in these three pre-Lenten poems to explore the Christian rhetoric of the self in the Stoudite liturgical reform. In the hands of the Stoudite poets, Lent provided an occasion to mediate styles of penitent self-recognition. Engaging with the biblical past and the apocalyptic future, these hymns strive to render such affects or emotions normative.

The history of the emotions in Byzantium deserves further investigation, although excellent work has considered compunction and its attendant tears in some detail.[17] The emotions expressed in Byzantine writing were embedded in broader Byzantine Christian social and religious contexts. Their portrayal relied on specific emotional vocabularies and expressive repertoires that provided the parameters for communicating and understanding them.[18] The Byzantine Church constituted a community of affective habits, instilled, at least in part, through liturgical expression of interior mental states. Monastic literature abounds in the analysis of problematic emotions, whether termed *pathoi* or *logismoi*, including gluttony, lust, greed, sorrow for things that cannot be changed, anger, boredom, vainglory, and pride.[19] But other emotional states such as patience, love, compunction, contrition, and even joy, received encouragement. As Martin Hinterberger has written, "emotions were understood mostly as a problem for the relationship between humans and God and, at times, as a prerequisite for the functioning of this relationship."[20] Liturgy encouraged these valued emotions and dispositions. Through choral performance and expression, the first-person hymns of the Triodion represented and conveyed a range of clerically encouraged emotions.[21] The singers took on the roles of the poems' "I"s, instantiating penitential personae, and they conveyed their compunction and distress to other listeners. The kanons' performative gestures of fear and remorse did not originate in the reforms associated with Theodore and the Stoudios Monastery; rather, the singers enacted modes of rhetoric, liturgical formulas, and exegetical patterns familiar from earlier hymnography, from set prayers, and from biblical passages further elaborated in sermons. However, the ninth-century reform of the Lenten cycle crystallized earlier traditions and transmitted them and their attendant emotional ranges in new liturgical settings.

Lent and the Triodion

In the wake of the council of Nicaea in 325, Lent was increasingly standardized as a period of fasting that preceded Pascha, or Easter, and lasted 40 days, although the calculation of these days varied by region and depended in part on whether one included Saturdays and Sundays or counted the fasting during Great and Holy Week. Before the end of the fourth century Jerusalem and Constantinople, together with Antioch, had apparently adopted a six-week Lenten fast, beginning seven weeks before Easter and ending before Palm Sunday and Great Week.[22] In the seventh century, the emperor Heraclius (610–641) extended the period of abstinence from meat by an additional week, beginning the week before formal Lent. In time, the eighth Sunday before Easter would be identified as Apokreas, or Meatfare Sunday, in effect an equivalent for Western Christian Carnival, but without the bawdy pomp, and on a Sunday, not a Tuesday. During the following week, known as Cheesefare Week, meat was forbidden, but milk products and eggs were still permitted. The following Sunday, the last Sunday before Lent and its strict fast, came to be known as Cheesefare Sunday. Jerusalem maintained this eight-week observance, with two pre-Lenten Sundays, followed by the five Sundays of Lent, Palm Sunday, and Easter.

In the middle Byzantine period, Constantinople would add two additional Sundays to the sequence. In the ninth century, probably coinciding with the initial creation of the Triodion, the ninth Sunday before Easter came to be known as "the Sunday of the Prodigal," with the assignment of Luke 15:11–32 as the Gospel lection. Some early manuscripts of the Triodion, including Sinai graecus 734–735, begin with this Sunday, and the tenth-century *Typikon of the Great Church*, which lists the lectionary readings for Constantinople, begins the movable cycle of the Lenten season with this "Sunday before Apokreas/Meatfare." [23] The eleventh century saw the assimilation of the last Sunday after Pentecost (that is, the last Sunday of the fixed cycle), which already had as its lectionary assignment the parable of the Tax Collector and the Pharisee (Luke 18:10–14) and its theme of repentance, to the Lenten cycle. The result was a ten-week sequence of four pre-Lenten Sundays, five Sundays in Lent, followed by Palm Sunday leading up to Easter, a structure reflected in all later complete manuscripts of the Triodion.[24]

The Triodion reflects the Stoudites' attempts to define and codify the character of Lent, especially for the office of Morning Prayer, the part of Byzantine liturgy most adaptable to the shifting emphases of the calendar. Although the name "Triodion" suggests that the hymnal contains works consisting of three odes, or sections, many of the compositions include the full range of eight or nine odes constituting a kanon, especially for Sundays. Indeed, while in later practice kanons chanted outside of Lent itself lack a second ode, the early Sinai manuscript preserves second odes for both *On the Prodigal Son* and *On the Second Coming*.[25] In this fullest form, the nine-ode kanon adorned and expanded the series of nine biblical canticles. As the Pantelleria typikon makes clear, some monastic leaders preferred that the canticles continued to be sung "if at all possible . . . in their entirety" along with the kanon odes, although the decision was reserved "to the authority of the elders." This was apparently due to constraints of time, especially in the winter months, when the daylight was short, but perhaps also when the kanon was particularly long.[26] Additional hymns would interrupt the kanon after the third and the sixth odes, usually a sessional, or seated, hymn (κάθισμα) after the third ode, and a truncated kontakion after the sixth. In its entirety, as is well documented for later practice, the kanon performance would usually alternate the canticles, the kanon odes, and the interpolated hymns.[27] Or at least we can say that such a performance, regularly enjoined in the sources, was regarded as desirable, whether conducted in its entirety or not.[28]

Despite the complexity of the performance, the kanon was conceived as a literary unit with compositional integrity. Kanons appear in the early manuscripts in full, without interruption by performance indicators or the interpolation of the hymns that would—or might—be sung with them in the liturgy. That is, the poems appear as works in themselves, often with their ascription to authors. In the kanon, in contrast to the usual and invariable psalmody and canticles of the morning office, lay the opportunity to include hymns that would key worship to the assigned readings of the lectionary and other traditional observances of the year. Starting with the hymnographers of the late seventh and early eighth centuries, the authors of these kanons usually set their poetry to existing chants. The manuscripts provide the modes, or tonal systems (akin to keys), for each kanon, together with the truncated text of the model melody, or *irmos* (εἱρμός), for each ode. The mode could determine the character or shading of the tune, while the irmos indicated that the ode was to be sung to the tune and stress pattern already established, either for verses of the biblical canticle, a text based on the canticle, or a preexisting kanon ode that the new ode supplemented (or replaced).[29] Mostly likely, at a minimum, the precentor led the choir in the singing of the familiar irmos, and then supplied the words of each sense unit of the appointed kanon as the choir then sang these words to the tune of the irmos. Each ode within the kanon had a different melody, although usually each irmos within the kanon was in a single mode. An effective performance could convey or greatly enhance the emotional content of the text as each singer took the words for his own.

The Triodion as a service book passed through a number of stages of development.[30] Some early manuscripts of the Triodion list Theodore the Stoudite and his brother Joseph, later the archbishop of Thessalonike, in their main titles, indicating their primary responsibility for first assembling the compendium.[31] In fact, Theodore and Joseph wrote only some of the poems in the collection, probably fewer than are attributed to them, and many poems in the collection remain anonymous. We might rather think of Theodore and Joseph as contributing editors. In assembling older works they drew on Palestinian poets associated with the Monastery of Mar Saba, including John of Damascus (c. 680–c. 749) and Kosmas of Maiouma (c. 685–c. 750), as well as their contemporary Andrew of Crete (c. 680–c. 740), who began his career in Jerusalem but spent most of his life in Constantinople and on that Aegean island.[32] Theodore and his companions had brought their distinctive ascetic and liturgical practices to Constantinople from the Sakkoudion Monastery in

Bithynia in 799, a form of work and prayer already influenced by the influx of Palestinian monastic styles in the wake of the rise of Islam.[33] Part of their work involved canonizing and extending the Sabaite hymnographic tradition in the capital, although many of the earlier poems they selected likely already circulated there. Much of this effort must have been complete by the death of Theodore in 826.[34]

Later in the ninth century, the collection expanded as additional extant poems were introduced and other Constantinopolitan poets wrote for the collection, including Klement and another Joseph, known as Joseph the Hymnographer, who lived from the second decade of the ninth century (between 812 and 818) until 886, and who composed some 385 kanons for the celebration of the saints. This Joseph was largely responsible for the creation of the Menaia, the service books for the cycle of fixed observances in the liturgical calendar.[35] It was most likely in this period that Kassia's sticheron *On the Sinful Woman* was added to the corpus. Three of the earliest manuscripts of the Triodion, including Sinai graecus 734–735, reflect the next stage in the history of the tradition, although they contain different elements.[36] The provenance of the Sinai manuscript remains unclear, although it resembles other manuscripts associated with the Stoudios Monastery itself.[37] In any event, the manuscript bears evidence of the development of the Triodion in Constantinople after its initial conception: In addition to the works ascribed to the early Stoudites and their monastic successors, the manuscript includes works of two emperors: Leo the Wise (886–911) and Constantine Porphyrogenitos (913–959).[38] This manuscript presents the Triodion as a compendium, offering various choices for many observances. For example, the hymn *On the Prodigal Son* by Joseph appears as the first of three options for the ninth Sunday before Easter.[39] The manuscripts of the Triodion as a whole reveal a rather wide range of different kanons assigned to particular days, probably reflecting the selection of different hymns in a variety of locations and under pressure from differing lectionary traditions.[40] In some instances, multiple hymns in a single manuscript may indicate that in some performances all of the hymns ascribed for a given day were chanted in sequence.

The explosion of new materials continued through the eleventh century, although much of this later composition would subsequently disappear.[41] The last phase of the development of the Triodion, from the twelfth century onward, from which the vast majority of surviving manuscripts derive, need not concern us here, except to observe that over time the tradition winnowed down toward fixed selections and the preservation of materials that later copyists and patrons regarded as early, thus preserving each of the three pre-Lenten kanons in question. The first printed edition of the Triodion, on which all subsequent printed editions were based, appeared in Venice in 1522, thus establishing what we may regard as the received tradition, best exemplified by the 1879 Vatican edition.[42]

The Stoudite hymns, composed for the hymnal itself, give witness, perhaps more than the earlier materials they collated, to a Stoudite vision of Lent and of Lenten preparation, where hymnography guided Christians toward the penitent self, a self constructed in correspondence with and in meditation on biblical lections and eschatological teachings. As a repository of penitential hymnody, the Triodion offered the Constantinopolitan monastic liturgy something new, an extensive template for the representation and performance of a confessing and anguished self, deemed appropriate to Lent. The Triodion was quickly and broadly disseminated in the Byzantine world and among Byzantine Orthodox monks beyond the empire's border. As it traveled, the rubrics maintained a marked flexibility. Later poets continued to write additional selections; copyists made substitutions. This vision of the Lenten subject, however, did not reside exclusively in the monastery. One result of the Stoudite monastic reform and the charisma and reputation of Theodore himself was the progressive monasticization of the so-called cathedral liturgy attended by lay Christians.[43] The Stoudite liturgical reform already combined elements of the Palestinian monastic rite with the liturgy of the Great Church.[44] Moreover, Andrew of Crete's long tenure as metropolitan of Gortyna suggests that the kanon had already become a feature of Morning Prayer in some cathedral contexts. The *Typikon of the Anastasis* (Jerusalem Stavrou 43), copied in 1122, shows that the rite of Jerusalem itself had come to absorb some Stoudite hymnody. How quickly the kanons of the Triodion were heard in lay congregations in Constantinople is unclear. The tenth-century *Typikon of the Great Church* does not assign kanons at Hagia Sophia, although one manuscript (Jerusalem Stavrou 40) may assume the chanting of kanons, including the *Great Kanon* of Andrew of Crete in the course of Lent.[45] In time, however, by the thirteenth century, the Orthros services of the Triodion would be celebrated beyond the monastery throughout the Orthodox world to become the common ritual practice of the Byzantine Church. And thus the Triodion's subjectivities would inform monks and laity alike.

Identifying with the Prodigal Son

Consideration of kanons in their entirety reveals the Christian voice responding to scripture. The kanon *On the Prodigal Son* invokes the parable in Luke
15:11–32, of a debauched son's return to his father, as a type for the salvation
of sinners. The poet seeks a recapitulation of the father's reception of his er-
rant and repentant son in his own longed-for return to God. As such, the
poet models the self on the example of the Prodigal, expressing a Christian
subjectivity in correspondence to the biblical narrative. The individual odes
largely lack any reference to the biblical canticles. Instead, over the course of
the poem, the poem's "I" sustains a penitential prayer, expressed in the first-
person singular, to "Jesus My God [Ἰησοῦ ὁ Θεός]" and maintains a focus
on the example of the Prodigal. In the earliest manuscript tradition, represented by Sinai graecus 734, the kanon consists of nine odes.[46] The first eight
odes have three stanzas, or troparia, followed by a theotokion, a prayer for
the intercession of the Virgin Mary.[47] The ninth ode has four stanzas plus a
theotokion; the initial letters of these five stanzas spell out in an acrostic the
name of the author, Joseph [ΙΩΣΗΦ]. This Joseph is mostly likely Theodore's
brother and fellow Stoudite, although it is also possible that the hymn is the
work of Joseph the Hymnographer.[48] In any event, the poem can be securely
dated to the ninth century, as can its assignment to the Triodion. If the kanon
is the work of Joseph the Stoudite, it is certainly possible that this assignment
reflects the original conception of the Stoudite Triodion.[49]

In the Gospel of Luke, Jesus narrates the story of a man who divided his
wealth between his two sons. While the elder one remained with his father,
the younger "gathered all he had and traveled to a distant [μακρὰν] country, and there he squandered [διεσκόπισεν] his property in dissolute living
[ζῶν ἀσώτως]" (Lk 15:13). The adjective "asōtos," here used as an adverb, derives from the verb sōzō [σῴζω], to save, and describes a profligate or spend-
thrift, someone who does not save, hence the "Prodigal." But the term carries
heavier connotations of sin: In the Septuagint it describes the prostitute of
Proverbs 7:11 as "excited and debauched [ἄσωτος]," whose "feet cannot stay at
home." In the New Testament epistles "asōtia" [ἀσωτία] conveys debauchery
in drunkenness (Eph 5:18), offers a contrast to chaste marriage (Tit 1:6), or
serves as a catchall combining "licentiousness, passions, drunkenness, revels,
carousing, and lawless idolatry" (1 Pet 4:4). Proverbs 28:7 provided perhaps
the inspiration for Luke's parable: "An intelligent son keeps the law, but he

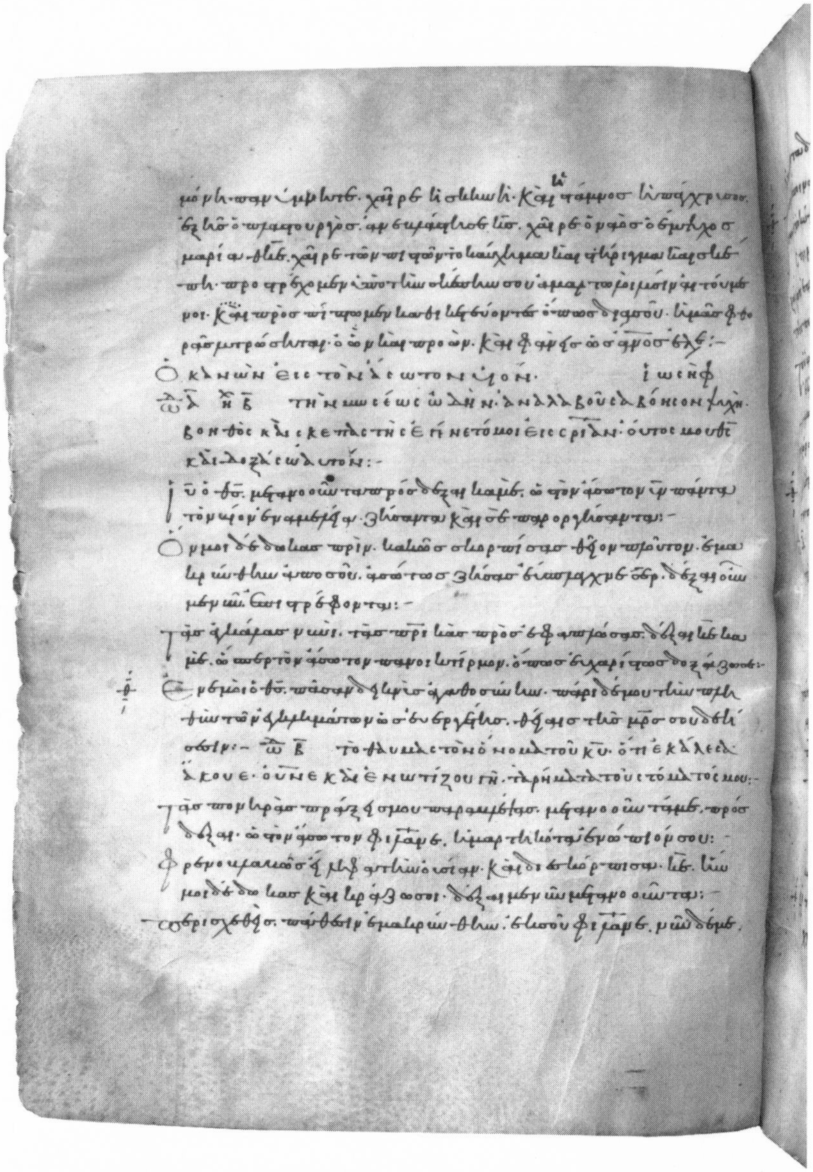

Figure 15. Page from the manuscript Sinai graecus 734, a Triodion of the tenth century with a Stoudite-type hand and mostly likely penned in Constantinople, containing the first and second odes of Joseph's kanon *On the Prodigal Son*. The seventh line gives the hymn's title and, at the *right*, the poet's name. The first ode begins on the eighth line (marked Ode 1 [alpha] in the second mode [beta]) and ends with its theotokion (marked in the left margin with a symbol that includes the letter theta). Sinai graecus 734, f. 3v. Photo by permission of Saint Catherine's Monastery, Sinai, Egypt.

who feeds debauchery [ποιμαίνει ἀσωτίαν] disgraces his father." In Luke, the older son reminds his father that his younger brother has "devoured [his father's] property with prostitutes" (Lk 15:30).

The kanon's Byzantine poet employs the Prodigal as a typological exemplar of wayward life. Yet the poet dramatizes not the story of the Prodigal Son, but rather an appropriate Christian response to the parable. In self-identification with the Prodigal, the "I" forms his authorial voice by applying the outlines of the biblical narrative. He renders his confession by modeling himself on some of the narrative details of the Lukan text.

> The divine wealth that you once gave me I have squandered wickedly [κακῶς ἐσκόρπισα]. I have gone far from you [ἐμακρύνθην ἀπὸ σοῦ] and lived like the Prodigal [ἀσώτως ζήσας], compassionate Father. And so accept me too as I return. (1.2)

In calling on God's acceptance, the poet's voice hews closely to the shape and language of the biblical text, calling attention to the moment when the father does not chastise his son, but welcomes him home by putting his arms around him (Lk 15:20). However, whereas the Prodigal's father orders the slaughter of the fatted calf and calls on everyone to "eat," "celebrate," and "rejoice" [Lk 15:23: φαγόντες εὐφρανθῶμεν; Lk 15:32: εὐφρανθῆναι δὲ καὶ χαρῆναι]," the poet supplies a more explicitly Christian ritual vocabulary of the Eucharist and of doxology.

> Spread wide your fatherly embrace now and accept me too like the Prodigal, compassionate Lord, that with thanksgiving I may glorify you [ὅπως εὐχαρίστως δοξάζω σε]." (1.3)

The idea of glorifying God recalls the first of the canticles, the Song of Moses from Exodus 15: "This is my God, and I will glorify him, my father's God and I will exalt him" (Ex 15:2), but the real interest lies with the celebratory receiving of the Prodigal. The liturgical theme recurs in the kanon's final ode, underscoring the application of the model of the parable to the conception of the hymnographic self and the hope for its redemption:

> The joy that you once wrought at the voluntary return of the Prodigal, O Good One, now create once again because of me, wretch though I

am. Open wide your holy arms to me, that saved I may sing hymns of
your profound condescension. (9.4)

In addition to the banquet of the Eucharist, the poet connects his hope for
salvation to his performance of hymnody: he longs to celebrate God's work of
redemption in song, if only God would embrace him.

Our poet Joseph's treatment of the story of the Prodigal Son as a narrative
of sin and redemption through which to fashion the Christian self, while not
novel, was also not inevitable. Consideration of the treatment of the parable
in earlier hymnographic works offers some perspective. In his sixth-century
kontakion *On the Prodigal Son*, Romanos the Melodist focuses attention on
the father's mercy in laying on a banquet.[50] "Let us contemplate a supper mag-
nificently spread" (1.1). Treating the parable as an allegory of divine provision,
Romanos's primary interest lies with the father, "or rather the Father of hu-
mankind" (1.3). The feast is immediately identified as the Eucharist, and the
fatted calf figures as Christ. Romanos exhorts his listeners, "So let us hasten
and share in the supper" (2.1). Throughout much of the poem, God the Father
speaks, explaining his rationale in receiving the sinner with a celebration (5–
9). In his own voice, the Father rehearses the events of the parable and emphasizes his compassion, which is never in doubt. Romanos's other interest
lies with the Good Son, who, as in the biblical narrative, voices his resentment
with indignation.

> For so long I have been a slave to your will
> and have always served your commandments,
> and not a single commandment of yours have I transgressed at all.
>   (16.2–4)

Romanos does nothing to contradict this assertion. Hearing him out, the Father addresses the obedient son "with mildness [σὺν πραότητι]," explaining
his actions, reminding the Good Son of his love and that he too inherits his
portion. The Prodigal himself never speaks.[51]

Romanos would seem more interested in addressing the apparent unfair-
ness of the Father's actions, either calling on his audience to identify with the
moral conflict of the elder son, or perhaps assuming that most of the congregation shares the Good Son's concerns. This focus is possibly surprising,
given Romanos's interest elsewhere in inviting his listeners to identify with
a variety of biblical sinners. And indeed Romanos does use his final strophe

to address a collective prayer on behalf of those assembled in response to the story.

> O Son and Word of God, Creator of all things,
> we your unworthy servants ask and implore you:
> have mercy on all who call upon you.
> As you did the Prodigal, spare those who have sinned.
> Accept and save through compassion
> those who in repentance [ἐν μετανοίᾳ] run to you, O King, crying
>   "We have sinned." (22.1–6)

It is significant that this invocation of the Prodigal works collectively, in the first person plural; Romanos does not represent an individual conscience responding to the parable. Moreover, Romanos's interest remains in shaping the experience of the Eucharist: "Make us partakers of your supper, as you did the Prodigal" (22.11).[52] The original liturgical placement of Romanos's hymn is unclear. The Patmos manuscript of the eleventh century assigns it to the second Sunday of Lent, probably influenced by the Jerusalem lectionary, which never adopted the practice of reading the Parable of the Prodigal Son in the weeks prior to Lent, but maintained the older Hagiopolite tradition of reading the story on the second Sunday of the fast itself. The Athos manuscript makes no assignment. At the very least, we can say that the poem is not distinctly Lenten in its concerns and scope.

The eighth-century hymnographer Andrew of Crete's interest in the Prodigal is also surprisingly limited. Despite his invocation of a large cast of biblical characters and his profound interest in models of repentance, he does not mention the Prodigal Son in the eighth or ninth odes of the *Great Kanon*, where he surveys the New Testament.[53] He alludes to him only in passing in the first ode:

> Although I also have sinned, O Savior, yet I know you are a lover of humanity: your chastisement is merciful, and fervent your compassion: you see tears and hasten, as the Father calling the Prodigal. (1.12)

As with Romanos, Andrew's interest lies with the father of the Prodigal Son, who serves as a type for God in his mercy.[54] Both Romanos and Andrew, with whose work the Stoudite compilers of the Triodion were deeply familiar, wrote before the assimilation of the parable to the extended preparation for Lent.[55]

If Joseph's *On the Prodigal Son* placed a new emphasis on the Prodigal's self, it did so in a typical fashion. The poet extended the portraits of penitential interiority familiar from the opening and closing strophes of many of Romanos's hymns and from Andrew's *Great Kanon*, although perhaps with a healthier concern for demonic temptations. As the kanon assigned to the Sunday of the Prodigal progresses, the poem articulates a typical Byzantine theory of the sinful self, in which the deviation from proper behavior figures as a sort of madness within the self. This departure from the true self subsequently leads to an enslavement to demonic forces: "Wholly beside myself, I attached myself in madness to the inventors of the passions [τοῖς παθῶν ἐφευρέταις]" (3.1; cf. 7.1). Allegorizing the element in the biblical story where the Prodigal hires himself out to the "citizens of that country" where he had squandered all his money (Lk 15:15), our Joseph declares himself "enslaved to citizens of a foreign country [ξένοις πολίταις δουλούμενος]" (4.1). Possessed by the demons, the poem's "I" has become "enslaved to every evil and, wretchedly bowed down to the creators of the passions [τοῖς παθῶν δημιουργοῖς] (4.2). He declares, "Through negligence I have lost possession of myself" (4.2). The movement toward evil thus begins within the subject, with a departure from rationality that is nonetheless willed. This initial deviation leads to a subjection to evil forces beyond the control of the subject himself. No longer a self-determining agent, the self has become the subject of the demiurgic passions, the evil thoughts that take control and determine the subject's intentions.[56]

With autonomy but not responsibility compromised, the self in bondage requires rescue. The poem clarifies that the sinner has deviated from divine law, "in foolishness I alone have angered you, rejecting your ordinances [προστάγματα]" (7.2); "Distancing myself from your commandments [Ἀπὸ τῶν σῶν ἐντολῶν], in utter wretchedness I became enslaved to the deceiver" (8.3). Recalling the Good Son's assertion that he "never disobeyed [his father's] command [ἐντολή]' (Lk 15:29), the "I" indentifies himself with the opposite. The moral theology conveyed in the poem was hardly novel; rather, the poet Joseph uses the context of liturgical performance to reinforce this etiology of the sinful self for each member of the assembled choir. All share this etiology of their own sin.

In fact, the poem rehearses a narrow repertoire of penitential self-expression, repeating the central confession, "I have sinned [ἥμαρτον]," derived directly from the biblical lection. The word appears twice in the Lukan parable, first as the son's interior speech while toiling in the distant country—"When he came to himself [εἰς ἑαυτὸν δὲ ἐλθὼν]," he thought, "I will get up and go to my father, and I will say to him, 'Father I have sinned [ἥμαρτον] against heaven and before you'" (Lk 15:17–18)—and second as he verbalizes this speech to his father upon his return. The kanon's singers repeat this simple confession seven times and explicitly ground their own speech in the Prodigal's precedent: "Imitating the words of the Prodigal, I cry aloud, "I have sinned, Father" (3.2); "But now I cry out with the voice of the Prodigal, 'I have sinned, O Christ'" (7.1). Moreover, each speaker provides a description of his interior motivations in voicing his confession, "Now I as I return I cry aloud in compunction [ἐκβοῶ κατανύξει], 'I have sinned against you. Receive me King of all'" (4.3).[57] The performance of a first-person voice thus reflects the successful production of a penitent interior disposition, melding the speaker with the content of his speech by repeating the words of the biblical model.

Even so, Joseph alters a critical element of the biblical parable, setting the stage for the long Lenten season of repentance and entreaty. In the biblical account the son does not speak his confession to his father until his father has already embraced him: "But while he was still far off, his father saw him and was filled with compassion [ἐσπλαγχνίσθη]; he ran and put his arms around him and kissed him" (Lk 15:30). This detail might provide license to imagine that confession always already takes place in a context of acceptance and forgiveness. But whereas one might counsel such a comfort to another, to be convicted of such certainty in the self would count as arrogance. Instead, the proper interior disposition exhibits doubt. In the fifth ode the speaker's sense of how God might react to him is uncertain. On the one hand, he predicates his confession on "knowing [God's] compassion"; on the other, he calls on God,

> Open to me now your fatherly compassion [τὰ πατρῷά σου σπλάγχνα]
> as I return from evils; in your surpassing mercy do not reject me. (5.2)

He thus not only offers the Prodigal Son as a model for his own action, but bids the Heavenly Father to imitate the biblical precedent of the parable's father. If the sinner can follow the shape of the biblical narrative, perhaps so can God.

In the ninth and final ode, the poet expands the cast of biblical penitents to include two additional figures unique to the Gospel of Luke, the Thief who was crucified next to Christ, whom Christ promised would be with him in

Paradise, and the Tax Collector from Jesus' parable of the Tax Collector and the Pharisee, who identified himself as a sinner and called on God for mercy. Here again, the biblical figures provide the lines for the penitent singer to vocalize, and even the physical actions to express remorse.

> Like the Thief I cry to you, "Remember me" [Lk 23:42]. Like the Tax Collector, with downcast eyes, I now beat my breast and say, "Be merciful [Lk 18:13]." (9.2)

This short chain of additional penitential types recalls the strophe in the *Great Kanon* of Andrew of Crete, where amid his compendious cataloguing of biblical exemplars of sin and confession, he groups five New Testament figures, both men and women: the Thief, Peter, the Tax Collector, the Harlot, and the Canaanite Woman (*Great Kanon* 8.14). Yet the composer of the kanon *On the Prodigal Son* takes fewer liberties with the biblical text itself, quoting rather than paraphrasing the scriptural speech or even, in the case of Andrew's words for the Tax Collector, supplying different words entirely. The comparison reveals an author either less creative or more disciplined. Likely familiar with Andrew's monumental composition, Joseph may be even more eager to adhere to the textual example. Theodore the Stoudite uses a similar list of biblical exemplars to encourage repentance in one of the *Small Catecheses*: " '[Christ] is expiation for our sins [1 Jn 2:2],' and he has not shut the doors against us, he has not turned away from someone who turns back, but he lets them approach like the Harlot, the Prodigal, and the Thief."[58] In the world of the Stoudios and the Triodion, the Prodigal Son had taken his place among the ideal types of the penitent self.

The Trembling Self and the Day of Judgment

Both the earliest manuscript and the received tradition of the Triodion assign the kanon *On the Second Coming*, with its fear and trembling at "the dreadful day [τὴν ἡμέραν τὴν φρικτήν]," to the Sunday of Apokreas, or Meatfare, the eighth Sunday before Easter. Sinai graecus 734 provides it as the first of two kanons for "The Sunday of Apokreas on the Second Coming of the Lord" (f. 20v), without attribution to an author.[59] Another early manuscript, Vaticanus graecus 771, copied at the Grottaferrata Monastery in Italy in the eleventh century, introduces the hymn as the "Kanon of the Second Coming [δευτέρας παρουσιας], sung on the Sunday of Apokreas," and ascribes the composition to Theodore the Stoudite (f. 14r), who is credited with its authorship throughout the later tradition.[60] Both manuscripts preserve substantially the same hymn, although their version lacks some stanzas included in the received tradition, and both manuscripts preserve the second ode.[61] The kanon may well be the work of Theodore himself, but the following discussion does not depend on it. In any case, the hymn reflects a characterization of the individual conscience in the face of impending judgment also found in Theodore's sermons. In its themes and language, the kanon resembles the thirteenth-century Latin hymn *Dies Irae* (*Day of Wrath*), whose speaker declares, "How much fear will there be when the judge will come investigating everything with severity!"[62] With its strongly affective response to frightening predictions of the eschaton, the Stoudite kanon instills terror as Lent and the Last Judgment both approach. Most significantly, the poet has utilized the same irmoi as those used in the *Great Kanon* of Andrew of Crete, their metrical patterns and melodies.[63] Any singer or listener would likely assimilate the penitential content of the hymn for Apokreas and its familiar tunes and meters with Andrew's anguished catalogue of faults.

The tenth-century Constantinopolitan lectionary assigns Matthew 25:31–46, an expansion of Mark's apocalyptic discourse, as the Gospel reading for the eighth Sunday before Easter. This practice, certainly established already in the early ninth century, does not appear in the Jerusalem lectionary tradition, and probably originated in Constantinople.[64] In Matthew, Jesus predicts the coming of the Son of Man and the Great Judgment. He describes the gathering of all peoples before the judge and the separation of the sheep and the goats. The lection concludes with Jesus' moral exhortation to care for the hungry, the stranger, the poor, the sick, and the imprisoned. "Then he [the Son of Man] will answer them, 'Truly I tell you, just as you did not do it to one of the least of these, you did not do it to me.' And these will go away into eternal punishment, but the righteous into eternal life" (Mt 25:45–46). Those responsible for the lectionary assignment sought to prepare people for repentance during Lent by reminding them of the judgment to come.

Our kanon's author has responded to the lection with vigor. Six quotations and echoes of Matthew's pericope in the course of the kanon (1.5; 3.5; 4.5; 6.5; 8.4; 9.5) confirm that the poet wanted to prepare listeners for the Gospel to be read later that day. But the poet also employs other common eschatological passages, including 1 Thessalonians 4:17 on the elect rising to meet Christ on the cloud (1.2); Matthew 22:13 on the man not properly robed for the wedding (1.4); and Matthew 25:10 about the foolish virgins encountering a shut door at the wedding banquet (3.5; 9.5). Indeed, the kanon offers a pastiche of standard tropes regarding judgment at the end of time. Already in the first ode, the illustration of damnation calls on a number of tropes of eternal punishment drawn from the Old and New Testaments: the singer is amazed and frightened by "the unquenchable fire [Mk 9:43] of Gehenna, the bitter worm [Is 14:11; 66.24] and the gnashing of teeth [Mt 8:12]" (1.4). This cluster of images recurs at three other points in the poem (7.4, 8.2, 9.4) as the singer's anxiety fixes on biblical warnings of torment and suffering in the end times. In combining these elements, the poet follows biblical precedent. The fire and the worm appear together in the Wisdom of Sirach (Ecclesiasticus) 7:17: "Humble your soul greatly, for the punishment of the impious is fire and worm"; and in Isaiah 66:24, "And they shall go forth and see the corpses of the people who have transgressed against me; for their worm shall not die and their fire shall not be quenched." The fear of punishment expressed in the poem thus reflects attention to biblical teachings beyond the lectionary assignment itself, calling to mind a range of biblical images associated with the eschaton.

The kanonist was not the first to bring these images together in Byzantine hymnody. In fact, the poet may also have in mind the prelude and first strophe of Romanos's hymn *On the Second Coming*, with its rather more vivid use of many of these images: "A river of fire flows before the seat of judgment. . . . Deliver me from the unquenchable fire" (prelude). "Loudly will the fire of Gehenna crackle, while sinners will gnash their teeth" (1.7).[65] Romanos's hymn, which begins, "When you come upon the earth, O God, in glory," was likely still in use at the Cathedral Vigil the previous evening.[66] We know for certain that subsequent hearers continued to associate the Triodion's kanon with Romanos's treatment: the Sinai manuscript includes the prelude of Romanos's hymn among the hymns for the day (f. 20v). Although its placement in the service is unclear, since the manuscript is arranged by the genres of hymns rather than their order of performance, by a later date we can be certain that Romanos's prelude and first strophe were inserted between the kanon's sixth and seventh odes, where they remain to this day.[67] A careful listener would hear a description of the end with complex intertextual associations.

Cast as more than a catalogue of terrifying threats, the ninth-century kanon *On the Second Coming* emphasizes the interior disposition of a well-churched Christian who fears what he has learned may be in store for him. In choral performance, this disposition would be shared among the members of the congregation. The hymn maintains the focus on the self quavering at the prospect of eternal punishment.

> When I think, Lord, about our meeting at your fearful second coming,
> I tremble at your threat, I fear your anger. In that hour, I cry out, save
> me forever. (8.1)

Each singer alternates his address to God with an address to himself. As in Andrew of Crete's *Great Kanon*, the subject is not unified, but divides in two, as the singer admonishes his soul. Thinking of the hour when God shall appear before him and judge him, the hymn's "I" calls to his soul,

> Wail and lament to be found pure at the hour of trial. (1.3)
> . . . .
> Groan and weep, soul, before the judge comes.
> You hear the trumpet [Mt 24:31; 1 Cor 15:52; 1 Thess 4:16] and the
>   boiling fire[68]; what will you do, O my soul?" (2.4–5).

Unable to maintain a discourse of inwardly directed exhortation, the speaker's voice quickly shifts to prayer. Kneeling and prostrating himself before God, he calls out, "Lord, Lord. . . . Save me in that hour!" (2.6). Employing juridical diction, he pleads with God, "Do not enter into judgment with me, bringing before me the things I should have done, investigating my words and examining my impulses. But in your mercy, overlook my sins [τὰ δεινά]" (1.6). Elsewhere, the kanon's voice calls himself to repentance: "Turn back and lament, O wretched soul, before the festival [πανήγυρις] of life comes to an end, before the Lord shuts the door of the bridal chamber [Mt 25:10]" (3.5). He confesses, surely exaggerating, "O Lord, I have sinned as no other person has before" (3.6).

As the hymn progresses, the descriptions of the punishments of hell meld with the singer's dread of them: he imagines them as if they are already happening. "Trembling and fear indescribable are there" (5.1). "The fiery river troubles me, melts me; the gnashing of teeth grinds me down; the darkness of the abyss!" (5.2). These thoughts are too horrible, and he breaks off the enumeration of his suffering to exclaim in despair, "And how or what should I do to propitiate God [καὶ πῶς; ἢ τί πεπραχώς, Θεὸν ἐξιλεώσω]?" (5.2). He dreads especially the "bitter tormenters," "relentless angels" (5.3).[69]

But despite his terror at the prospect of "soul-destroying hell," he does not come to true compunction (7.4). In his alternating address, varying strategies, and multiple motives, the poet characterizes the anxiety of an unquiet mind, searching desperately for rescue in the face of doom. In enacting this persona in liturgical performance, the chanters assume this anxiety and transmit it to each other and any assembled audience, using emotive speech to create a congregation of subjects prepared for Lent.

While couched largely in the first person singular, the later odes offer advice to the collective. With pastoral exhortation, the poetic voice reveals the broader purpose of his characterization of such a self: "Let us fall down and lament in expectation [προκλαύσωμεν], O faithful ones, before that [day of] judgment, when the heavens shall be destroyed, the stars fall, and the whole earth be shaken" (7.1). Elsewhere the hymn reminds its singers and listeners that "everyone who breathes" (8.3; cf. 2.1) will be held to account, "together kings and princes, rich and poor" (4.1), "monastic and worldly [μοναςταὶ καὶ μιγάδες]" (2.2). "Each in his own order, monk and hierarch, old and young, slave and master, will be examined. Widow and virgin shall be corrected" (4.2). But this concern with the whole of humanity standing before God turns again toward the self: "When at the judgment of the world you will divide the sinners from the righteous, reckon me as one of your sheep and separate me from the goats" (4.5). Referring to the parable of the Rich Man and Lazarus in Luke 16, a standard prooftext for establishing that the punishment of the wicked after death already occurs in the current era, even before the end of time, the singer declares that he already hears the "reasonable lamentation [θρηνολογία] of the Rich Man in the flames of torment" (4.7).[70] Thus, even as he cites biblical passages about the general judgment, the "I" of the poem's concern lies with personal or individual eschatology. The "I" trembles with fear at the prospect of judgment; and the "I" seeks his own salvation, wishing to meet Jesus on the cloud. As he prays on his own behalf, he seeks to avoid the fate of the Rich Man consigned to torment in the life beyond. In warning the group, he encourages them to be similarly self-focused.

Whether it is the work of Theodore the Stoudite or not, the kanon *On the Second Coming* reflects broader concern within the traditions of the Stoudios Monastery with individual eschatology and repentance. Its outward expression of self-directed grief enacts a disposition frequently prescribed in Theodore's *Small Catecheses*. Reflecting on the judgment to come, Theodore taught that the soul that knows its own sinfulness remains "manifestly tormented and in a state of distress," but "tears and compunction are very powerful," together with participation in the sacraments.[71] Theodore placed self-accusation and repentance in a sequence that leads to reconciliation and perhaps even union with God. In another sermon, he encouraged his monks to contemplate their own death, explaining, "For it is obvious that wherever there is the thought of death, there is self-awareness [συναίσθησις], compunction, tears, sweetness, enlightenment, and desire for better and supermundane things."[72] Thus the fear of judgment at the Second Coming marks a stage in a progression that the Triodion's hymn inhabits.

Like earlier Christian authors such as John Chrysostom and Romanos, the kanonist conceives of a court proceeding built on damning evidence. Invoking the scenes of judgment at the end of time in Daniel 7:10 and Revelation 20:12, the kanon's subject laments that when the books "recording all our acts are opened" his soul will have no answer (4.6; see also 6.1). In the heavenly tribunal, the usual methods for prevailing in legal cases will be of no use: "There, nothing can help you, since God is the judge, neither eagerness, nor skill, nor fame, nor friendship," only the record of your own deeds (6.2). Nothing can be gained with bribes (7.4). He tells his soul that it should think of the "fearful examination [λογοθέσιον]" before the judge, and "trembling" it should prepare its defense to avoid the condemnation of eternal bondage (6.4). Praying for forgiveness is the only option. Recalling liturgical prayers for forgiveness, the speaker models proper penitence: "Pardon, remit, Lord, and forgive [me]—I have sinned so greatly against you—and do not point [μὴ δείξῃς] me there, face to face with the angels, to the punishment of fire, unending shame" (5.5).[73] The formula "pardon, remit, forgive" quotes a prayer for forgiveness likely part of the Sabaite heritage at Stoudios.[74] Salvation requires absolution, but proper worship may in fact counter one's offenses, or in any case constitutes the sinner's appropriate recourse. At the end of the hymn, each singer prays, "Grant me before the end to worship you [λατρεῦσαι] acceptably and gain your kingdom" (9.3). For salvation is in fact possible: "The fire is prepared, the worm; [but also] ready is the glory of rejoicing, the rest, the light without evening, the joy of the righteous" (9.4). Each prays to escape the former and be assigned the latter.

As in the kanon *On the Prodigal Son*, the ninth and final ode broadens the typological base, calling upon Old Testament exemplars who feared before the Lord, although this invocation hardly offers encouragement to those the poet has instructed to "tremble and lament, and call to mind that day when [God will] uncover humans' unseen and hidden [deeds]" (9.1; cf. 2.1). "Terrified and shaking," the hymn explains, Moses saw the hind parts of God: "How then shall I in my sorry state withstand to see your face when you come from heaven?" (9.2). Addressing God again and singing in the first person, the hymn transposes Moses' emotions from the scene of the breaking of the tablets of the law in Deuteronomy 9:19 to the theophany before the burning bush (Ex 33:20–23), where the Bible describes no reaction. In doing so, the author presumably follows the book of Hebrews, whose diction he adopts: "So terrifying was the sight that Moses said 'I am terrified and shaking [ἔκφοβός εἰμι καὶ ἔντρομος]'" (Heb 12:21). The prophet Daniel also provides an opportunity for the singers to contrast themselves with a biblical hero. In the scene of judgment, with the Ancient One upon his throne, attended by thousands and thousands of angels, and with fire flowing from the throne, Daniel saw the vision of the coming of the Son of Man (Dan 7:9–14). Daniel relates, "my spirit trembled within me, and the visions of my head terrified me" (Dan 7:15).[75] The poet writes, "Daniel was seized with fear at the hour of trial. What's to become of me [τί πάθω], unhappy as I am, Lord, when I come upon that terrible day?" (9.3). Far from providing comfort, the typology serves here to magnify the terror appropriate before the prospect of the end times.

Enacting Adam

In the kanons *On the Prodigal Son* and *On the Second Coming*, the singers play a typical Christian, living in the Byzantine present, situating himself with respect to biblical teachings. To the extent that these poems engage in ethopoeia they enact a character different from a biblical personage. The kanon for the following Sunday morning enacts a more complex persona. Both the tenth-century Sinai manuscript and the eleventh-century Vatican manuscript from Grottaferrata supply only one kanon for Cheesefare Sunday, the last day before Lent, with the title "Kanon on the Transgression of Adam."[76] This assignment persists in the received tradition. Opening with an address to the self, "Come, my wretched soul [Δεῦρο, ψυχή μου ἀθλία]" the hymn explores the mind of the first-created human, or protoplast, testing the boundaries between imagining the interiority of a biblical character and assuming it for oneself.

Relying through most of the kanon on the first person singular, the poet creates an extended speech-in-character that plays on ambiguities of voice. Who is it that is speaking? What role are the singers playing? They sing, "Long ago the crafty serpent envied my honor and whispered deceit in Eve's ear" (3.1, cf. 7.1); "Rashly I stretched out my hand and tasted from the tree of knowledge" (3.2). Does each sing as Adam, who in turn is a type for humanity? Or is each some version of himself, already molded into the type Adam represents? In the theotokia, the final stanzas of each ode addressing a prayer to the Virgin, the choir sings of Adam in the third person, as someone other than themselves whose salvation has already been accomplished by the incarnation. "O holy [Virgin], who alone long ago covered the nakedness of fallen Adam, by your childbearing, O pure one, clothe me anew with incorruption" (3.4); "Holy Lady, who has opened up for all the faithful the gates of Paradise that Adam closed long ago by [his] transgression, open for me the gates of mercy" (4.5). But does this mean that in each ode the theotokion initiates a shift in voice from Adam to the self of the chanters or poet? Or has the singer always been other than Adam, or another Adam, an iteration of the first human? In the ninth ode, even before the theotokion, the poet refers to Adam in the third person as he praises God who "opened for those who worship you the gates of Paradise that were once closed to Adam" (9.4). The poet thus engages a typological construction of the self that melds the subject with the biblical model, such that the voices become only imperfectly distinct.

The identity of the poet is uncertain. Later manuscripts of the Triodion and the received tradition assign the poem to "Christopher the Protasekretes," that is, the chief of the imperial chancery, suggesting that author held an influential post on the emperor's staff. This might raise questions about whether the poem was written by a layman or whether the author wrote after entering the monastic life. Perhaps this is to be identified with Christopher, a protospatharios and protasekretes who lived in the third quarter of the ninth century and was the addressee of a letter from the patriarch Photios.[77] Given the tenth-century date of the Sinai manuscript and the poem's style, this Christopher is certainly not Christopher of Mitylene, a high-ranking official and composer of epigrams in a learned register who lived in the first half of the eleventh century in Constantinople.[78] But the Sinai Triodion assigns the poem to "Christopher" without an epithet, and only in the margin in what may or may not be the same hand as the main text, whereas most authors, where they are indicated, are named in the running text. In the Vatican manuscript, the poem lacks an attribution. Given its appearance and exclusive assignment to this Sunday in the earliest witnesses, it is most likely that the poem derives from the early phases of the development of the Triodion. Perhaps this is the work of Christopher, a monk of the Stoudios Monastery, mentioned in two letters of Theodore the Stoudite written between 809 and 811.[79] In any case, it is unclear whether the poem was written during the initial assembly of the Triodion in the early ninth century or during the subsequent decades. Neither early manuscript witness contains a second ode, but we cannot know whether the kanon was composed this way or whether an original second ode fell out of the tradition very early on.

Unlike the kanons for the two previous Sundays, *On the Transgression of Adam* does not respond to the day's lectionary passages. For Cheesefare Sunday [τῆς τυροφάγου], the tenth-century Constantinopolitan typikon assigns Matthew 6:14–21 to the Divine Liturgy. That passage stresses themes of fasting and forgiveness, appropriate to the beginning of the Lenten Fast on the following day.[80] Later tradition would refer to the observance as the Sunday of Forgiveness. The sequential reading of Genesis does not begin until Vespers on the first Monday of Lent, in effect, that very Sunday evening, since the liturgical day begins at sunset. But the story of the fall of Adam and Eve does not occur until Vespers for Friday of that week, the only time it was read in the middle Byzantine lectionary system in the course of the liturgical year.[81] It remains unclear whether consideration of the fall of Adam had long been traditional on the threshold of Lent, or whether this assignment began with the creation of the Triodion. The kontakaria, manuscripts assigning the kontakia to be chanted on each day, begin to appear in the eleventh century.[82] These are universal in assigning a late fifth- or early sixth-century anonymous composition *On the Lament of Adam*, quoted in Chapter 1, to the last Sunday before Lent, but whether this reflects a fitting of preexisting material to a new liturgical arrangement or preserves an ancient practice cannot be known with certainty. The same poem appears in shortened form in the earliest manuscripts of the Triodion.[83] It is most tantalizing that the treatment of Adam in the kontakaria begins a series of hymns dedicated to Old Testament patriarchs to be chanted during the course of Lent, many of these the works of Romanos. The Prophetologion, the lectionary of Old Testament readings, was assembled in the later eighth century, but likely reflects earlier Constantinopolitan practices.[84] It assigns the continuous reading of Genesis at Vespers throughout Lent. Thus it is quite possible that meditation on the fall of Adam was already established as part of a Lenten sequence of observance of Old Testament narratives going back perhaps even to the sixth century.[85]

Although he does not follow the lectionary, the poet recreates a liturgical moment in the life of Adam. In reflecting on the protoplast's fall from grace, the kanon contrasts liturgies in exile with the liturgies of heaven. The hymn opens with the speaker bidding himself to lament his casting out from Eden. Then the address shifts to God, who in "abundant compassion and mercy" "gave [him] life from the dust" and commanded him to sing hymns to God along with the angels (1.2). The hymn presents liturgical song as a response to divine command, even as other human deeds constitute disobedience. Yet while the "I" of the poem remains a singer, his repertoire has quite obviously changed: "I have cut myself off from the choir of your angels" (6.3). Now, "taken captive from the glory of Paradise" (6.4; cf. 7.3), he sings laments and prayers of entreaty, both to the Virgin and to God. The emotional character and genre of his music fit the unhappy situation.

With great pathos, the poem conveys a painful longing for the original placement of humanity where God "planted . . . in Eden the delight of Paradise," and urged him to enjoy "the fair and pleasant fruits that never pass away" (1.3).[86] The address shifts back to reflexive chastisement and interrogation: "Woe to you, my wretched soul!" He had been charged with enjoying the pleasures of Eden and commanded "not to eat the fruit of knowledge." Now he asks, "Why did you transgress the law of God?" (1.4) In the theotokion, which addresses the Virgin and conceiver of God [θεοκυήτορ] as a "daughter of Adam by descent, but the mother of God by the grace of Christ," the chanters sing, "I am an exile from Eden; now call me back" (1.5). Calling out for sympathy in an elaborate apostrophe, the singer asks "the ranks of angels, the beauties of Paradise, and comeliness of the plantings there" to lament on his behalf (4.2). Invoking the flowery register of more literary laments he calls out, "O blessed meadow, O greenery planted by God [φυτὰ θεόφυτα], O pleasantness of Paradise, let tears drip on my behalf from [your] leaves as if from eyes" (4.3). In this, the plants of Paradise should mimic the speaker: "I lament and mourn my soul, and from my eyes I wish to add an abundance of tears when I regard and consider for myself the nakedness that I have acquired through transgression" (5.2). Here the poet echoes the kontakion *On the Lament of Adam*, which the manuscripts also assign for this day and which contains a similar appeal. In that earlier work, Adam bids Paradise to "implore the creator with the sound of your leaves" (3), and to "bend down your trees like living beings and fall before / him who holds the key, that thus you may remain open" (4), imitating the postures of human supplication. Cast out of Paradise and subject to death, each of the ninth-century singers playing Adam bewails that he has "exchanged Eden for hell" (5.3). Now he reproaches his soul, deceived as it was by the hissing of the serpent (8.1), asking, "Why have you listened to bitter counsel and disobeyed the divine decree?" (8.2)

Unlike the kontakion, the genre of the kanon did not lend itself to narrative development. The poet does not progress through the details of the story in Genesis 3. Instead, the kanon repeats and recasts the anguish of one in the mold of Adam, latching onto various elements of the story. In the first ode the speaker is already cast out of Eden and recalls his creation and God's command not to eat from the tree of knowledge. The serpent shows up in the third and eighth odes. The eating itself, the salient crime, recurs both as an action and as a memory in the third and ninth odes. Although in the ninth ode the speaker identifies his sin, somewhat generically, as "lack of self-control [ἀκρασία]," the poem does not enact a progression of psychological insight. It presents neither the investigation nor revelation of sin; instead the speaker understands the problem from the start. If the singer sings in his own voice, the problem is his complete identity with Adam and his fall. If not, he plays Adam as a character in the ritual drama. The performance illustrates anguish itself in the psychological portrait of a troubled mind fixated, circling back to various elements of the story in unreasoned threnody, rehearsing the trauma. One can imagine a very affecting performance, evoking pity and fear in the congregation. Each member of the choir sings his own staging and direction:

> I wail, I groan, I lament bitterly [θρηνῶ, στενάζω, καὶ ἀποδύρομαι] as
> I behold the cherubim with the flaming sword arrayed to guard Eden's
> entrance against all transgressors. Alas! (9.3)

The voice, at once Adam and the Byzantine Christian, displays awareness of its own performativity, its theatricality or staginess. Although the original melodic shape cannot be known with certainty, three eleventh-century heirmologia indicate that the model melody for this kanon includes an emotionally affecting melisma on the word *thrēnō*, "I wail."[87]

The story of Adam, of course, had long been iconic for Christian self-conception. And we have seen Andrew of Crete's interest in comparing the disobedient self with the first transgressor. Such an understanding of Adam continued to develop within the Stoudite tradition. Theodore himself invoked the elements of Adam's narrative to encourage fortitude and the rejection of the passions during Lent in one of the *Small Catecheses*.

I beseech you, my brother, should not we also, since we have the same aim and seek the same Pascha, bravely and courageously bear our present condition, not falling, not succumbing to despondency, but rather roused with greater fervour watching for the wicked serpent who works to deceive us by the passions, transforming himself into an angel of light [2 Cor 11:14], and altering things from what they are; show dark as light, bitter as sweet. This was how he ensnared our forefather, bewitching his sight and depicting as beautiful what was not, and as a result through food casting him out of Paradise. But let us, who have learned by experience what a deceiver he is, not leave the paradise of God's commandments, nor, when he indicates to us that the fruit is beautiful, let the eye of soul or body be directed there, otherwise we are being caught in the snare. But let us flee by every means from looking.[88]

Here, Adam becomes a source for exhortation, an example not to be followed and from whom the Christian remains distinct, or from whom he should try to remain distinct. By contrast, the kanon hymn accepts the ethos of Adam, melding the "I"'s identity with Adam's through the medium of performance.

The Rhetoric of Stoudite Hymnography

The character portraits in each of these poems—the voice of the Christian who recognizes his affinity with the Prodigal Son; the voice of the Christian terrified by the prospect of judgment and damnation; and the voice of the Christian so identified with Adam as to become Adam—raise questions about the rhetorical techniques at play in Stoudite liturgical poetry and the effects of Christian hymnography in middle Byzantium. These kanons for pre-Lenten Sundays demonstrate the desire to employ first-person speech to explore Christian interiorities and endorse specific patterns of self-regard. Moreover, they do so by conveying emotional states such as anguish, grief, and fear. Given multiple authors and the elongated process of edition, expansion, and winnowing, we cannot speak so much of the mind of the Triodion as of its dominant ethos and the degree to which a shared sensibility shaped a distinctly middle Byzantine penitential subjectivity. The authorial, editorial, and performance practices that depicted this pre-Lenten subject endorsed ethopoeia, or characterization, as a technique for conveying the self.

The Stoudites' relationship with formal rhetorical training as a tool in the formation of Christian selves is complex, as the following narrative attests. In the earliest biography of Theodore the Stoudite, Michael the Monk relates a story he claims to have heard firsthand about a miraculous appearance of the saint after his death. For a long time, a "Christ-loving and exceedingly pious man" in Sardinia had been singing the triodia [τὰ τριῴδια], or the kanon hymns, that Theodore had composed for Lent "according to the liturgical year [κατ' ἐνιαυτόν]" and "with fitting faith." Then some monks from Sicily visited him, disciples of Gregory the Archbishop of Syracuse, and stayed for a while. The Sardinian, who was most probably a monk although it is unclear in the narrative, tells it thus: "Then the time of holy Lent began. I made preparation in my place [according to] the prevailing order, for the glorification of God, proposing that the triodia of our saintly father be sung during Lent, just as it had been my custom from the previous years. But when they heard this, they were immediately upset and were astonished that the teaching and reputation of our blessed father had already reached us. And they began to criticize the saint, and denigrate [διακερτομεῖν] his poems as not composed according to the rules of learning [οὐ κατὰ λόγον παιδείας]."[89] The Sardinian confesses that his thoughts were corrupted by their judgment against the literary quality of the kanons, so that he no longer wanted to sing them during Lent. But Theodore appeared to him the following night, looking advanced in years, "wizened and pale, grizzled and balding," accompanied by men holding rods. The saint ordered them to beat the man forcefully and shouted at him, "Why do you despise my poems, faithless one?" He ordered the men to continue the punishment, "so that he will learn [παιδευθῇ] not to receive bad company [ὁμιλίας; also 'word' or 'teaching']." After a good flogging, the man awoke agitated and in pain. Chastised, he threw the Sicilian visitors out of his house. "And from that time on, until today, we have the venerable and preeminent poems of the saintly father, and we hold him to be as one of the apostles of Christ and a God-given doctor of the universal church."[90]

Written down after 868, some four decades after Theodore's death, and likely in circulation orally before that, this tale of posthumous appearance attests controversy over the rhetorical register and style of one of the early Stoudites' most significant accomplishments, namely the conception and execution of a service book of hymns proper to the season of Lent.[91] The narrative of the faithful if feckless Sardinian plays on the status of *paideia*, or classical learning, in liturgical texts. Punning on the "learning" embodied in the "rules" of poetic meter and versification and the "learning" conveyed in a sound beating, the story sets up a contrast between high literary culture and the language of the church. It even mocks the Sardinian for having taken instruction from the wrong sort of "homily," one with snooty ideas about the linguistic register appropriate to ritualized expressions of Christian prayer. But the story also gives us early evidence for the rapid dissemination of the Triodion and its Stoudite poems by the middle of the ninth century, even to the distant parts of the Byzantine Orthodox *oikoumene,* even as it records— and repeats—criticism of their relative lack of refinement. We might argue that it is unlikely that the Sardinian's service book contained Theodore's hymns alone; rather, he had developed a strong devotion to an early version of the Triodion. By the time the story was written down, the whole of the Triodion was regarded as "the triodia of Theodore." The tale also establishes a strange warning to learned critics, not so much conceding as justifying that the Triodion's poems are written in a lower, and therefore more accessible, literary style.[92]

Theodore himself had received an education appropriate for a son of an official of the imperial court, including the standard curriculum in grammar and rhetoric. In the later eighth century, Constantinople had no formal academies for higher education, and most scholars agree that his studies in philosophy and theology were most likely directed by tutors.[93] Theodore wrote in a variety of genres and pitched his language according to his various audiences. Nevertheless, modern judgment of his prose has been nearly as harsh as the Sicilians' criticism of his poetry. The great scholar of Byzantine humanism, Paul Lemerle, averred, "[Theodore] is not a great writer, although his forceful temperament saves him from banality. Neither is he erudite, unless you prefer to think that he voluntarily refrained from displaying his secular knowledge."[94] But this is to miss the mark. Theodore's use of simpler language in his catecheses, hymns, and epigrams reflects his success in recruiting less educated men to the Stoudios Monastery, where many came from modest backgrounds.[95] Moreover, such judgments discount the popularity of the Triodion as the hymns were received, sung, and heard in the subsequent decades and centuries. To be sure, when compared with the hymns of Romanos the Melodist or Andrew of Crete, the Stoudite hymns for the morning office in Lent are less inventive. One student of the Triodion has observed, "The triodia of Theodore are less rich in language, but show a greater openness to a theological view of Lent that takes into consideration its moral and spiritual aspects."[96] What then of this humbler but effective rhetoric?

Both the poems of the Triodion and more especially the manuscripts themselves are records of and indicators for live performance.[97] And these performances depended on common rhetorical devices for the transmission of affect. Probably the most widely disseminated rhetorical handbook in Byzantium was the *Progymnasmata*, or *Preliminary Exercises*, of Aphthonios the Sophist, a student of Libanios of Antioch who wrote in the late fourth or early fifth century. Following earlier rhetorical theorists, Aphthonios described ethopoeia as the "imitation of the character of a proposed speaker [μίμησις ἤθους ὑποκειμένου προσώπου]."[98] The task of the author was to invent the characterization. Aphthonios notes, "Some characterizations are pathetical [παθητικαί], some ethical [ἠθικαί], some mixed. Pathetical are those showing emotion [πάθος] in everything: for example, the words Hecuba might say when Troy was destroyed. Ethical are those that only introduce character; for example, what words a man from inland might say on first seeing the sea. Mixed are those having both character and pathos; for example, what words Achilles might say over the body of Patroclos when planning to continue war; for the plan shows character, the fallen friend pathos" (11). Successful rhetoric involved portraying the thoughts and emotions appropriate to the character and the moment. Such an approach was also favored in the middle Byzantine period. John of Sardis, perhaps to be identified as the recipient of two of Theodore the Stoudite's extant letters, composed a commentary on Aphthonios showing particular interest in the affective power of character speeches, pointing not just to the creation of a character, but to the effect of characterization on an audience. He stressed that ethopoeia "makes the language alive [ἔμψυχον γὰρ τὸν λόγον ποιεῖ, literally: makes the language ensouled] and moves the hearer to share the emotion [πρὸς συμπάθειαν] of the speaker by presenting his character."[99] This sympathy, or co-suffering, with the speaker involved the transmission of the emotion through affective and effective rhetoric, involving "vivid expression" and "creating pathos."[100]

The author of the kanon *On the Transgression of Adam* engages in just such an exercise, illustrating Adam's state of mind as he reflects on his expulsion from Eden; the poet encouraged his singers and his listeners to share in Adam's grief, to share it ultimately as their own. It remains a matter of debate, and perhaps irresolvable, whether there was continuity in the learned rhetorical tradition through the so-called Dark Ages of the late seventh and eighth centuries, or a whether this tradition was rediscovered in the ninth century.[101] But the hymnographic iteration of the technique of ethopoeia in the kanons of the Triodion need not have depended on higher education. By the ninth century, it was hardly necessary to receive formal rhetorical instruction in constructing ethopoeia in the classical curriculum either to compose or to understand such speeches-in-character. The idea of imagining, inhabiting, and identifying with a biblical personage was long assimilated to the hymnographic and performance practices of the Byzantine church. Moreover, hymnographers were not limited to imaging biblical characters. As the kanons *On the Prodigal Son* and *On the Second Coming* demonstrate, the ethos being created could simply be the ethos of an ideal Byzantine Christian, the character of one who had heard the story of the Prodigal and responded with introspection and self-accusation, or the ideal Christian terrified at the prospect of judgment. Indeed, within a Christian rhetoric, the ethopoeia constructed and enacted the liturgical subject.

*   *   *

The three poems for pre-Lenten Sundays considered here and the penitential characters performed and displayed within them attest both a Stoudite recasting of Lent and the enduring legacy of the Stoudites' efforts. Each hymn is present in the earliest manuscript, and each has continued to be transmitted as integral to the received tradition. Together, these hymns frame Lent by presenting ideal subjectivities, informed by the biblical narrative and profoundly penitent. Through ritual performance, these hymns standardized a liturgical portrait of the self. The Constantinopolitan poets and the monks who first received their works transmitted these subjectivities from the exegetical and rhetorical imagination to the texts, from the precentor to the choir, and thus to any other listeners. In this process, poets and singers gave voice to a Byzantine Christian interior life with its appropriate emotional range of anguish and remorse.

Early in the eleventh century, the Stoudites assimilated the Sunday of the Tax Collector and the Pharisee to the penitential sequence as the tenth Sunday before Lent. As we have seen, the Tax Collecter had already long played a part in the cast of repentant sinners. Responding to the parable in Luke that contrasts the mistaken self-confidence of a proud Pharisee on the steps of the temple with the humble confession of the Tax Collector who "was beating his breast and saying, 'God, be merciful to me, a sinner!'" (Lk 18:13), the Stoudites assigned a six-ode kanon by a certain George, who signed his name in the first letters of the kanon's theotokia. The hymn, which first appears in the manuscript Sinai graecus 736, dated 1027/28 or 1028/29, models the song of the penitent. It instructs each member of the congregation: "Imitate the good

deeds of the Tax Collector and hate the evil deeds of the Pharisee (1.2)."[102]
As if in response, the singers declare to God, "I groan as the Tax Collector,
and with lamentations that are never silent, O Lord, I now approach your
compassion" (1.4). Exhorting everyone to replicate the penitential type, the
singers call out, "Like the Tax Collector, let us also, beating upon our breast,
cry out with compunction [κατανύξει], 'God, be merciful to us sinners'" (3.3).
In collective performance, the first-person singular prayer becomes plural.
Response to the biblical text requires reflection on the assembly of several
similar selves.

> All pondering the parable of the Tax Collector in our mind, come let
> us emulate him with tears, offering God a crushed spirit seeking the
> remission of our sins. (5.4)

The new frame opening the season of Lent merely expanded opportunities to
engage the penitent subject.

CHAPTER 7

Liturgies of the Monastic Self in
Symeon the New Theologian

Hymns and prayers provided models for the self, offering access to interior lives, focusing introspection, and patterning affect. Byzantine liturgy provided a venue for the merging of speech and subjectivity, where Christians might immerse themselves in scripted performances, becoming themselves through the making or doing (τὸ ποιεῖν) of the self. The songs of the sinners conveyed identities that could be produced and inhabited through repetition. Implicit in such practices of chanting, singing, or prayer lay theories of how subjects formed. The Stoudite hymns rendered the personas of the lectionary as roles to be played. The monastery became a sort of Actors Studio to teach the poetics of the Byzantine Christian self through ritual. Ultimately the monastic program of self-fashioning pervaded consciousness, bringing the methods of the liturgy to all habits of mind and body.

Preaching at the Monastery of St. Mamas in the years between 980 and 998, Symeon the New Theologian provided interior monologues to shape his novices' self-reflection.[1] In the Twenty-Sixth Catechetical Discourse, Symeon lays out daily ascetic practices "as in a [monastic] rule [ὡς ἐν τύπῳ]" for his charges, "who have newly come from the world to enter, as it were, this school" (*Catechetical Discourses* 26.15–17). He instructs the monks about keeping to themselves, not entering the cells of other monks without the permission of their spiritual father, and observing silence and solitude (26.67–79). To encourage silence a monk should say to himself, "What good have I to say, who am altogether mud, and a fool? Besides, I am a stranger and unworthy to speak and listen and to be numbered among men" (26.97–99). Such internal prolixity counters the impulse to speak aloud with an introspective performance of humility. And to enforce solitude, Symeon provides a longer monologue of thoughts the monk should "think" and "say to himself." "Who am I rejected and worthless, base and poor, that I should enter anyone's cell? When he sees me, will he not turn away from me as from an abomination? Will he not say, 'Why did that wretch come to me to defile my cell?'" (26.101–3). Having scripted internal speech, Symeon provides further direction, "Set your sins before your eyes, and say this not by moving your lips, but from the depth of your soul" (26.105–7). Symeon understands that these lines do not necessarily yet reflect the monk's internal disposition; in fact, he regards these internal speeches as a having the potential to effect a new subjectivity.[2] He advises his monks, "Even though at the beginning you cannot say this from your soul, yet will you gradually come to this, as grace helps you" (26.107–9). The speeches that Symeon provides are thus the script for a role that a monk may not yet have come to inhabit. Only through rehearsal and with divine assistance will the monk become the subject of his own soliloquy.

Symeon, who lived from 949 to 1022, was arguably the most important religious thinker of the middle Byzantine period. The *Life of Symeon the New Theologian*, written by his some-time student, Niketas Stethatos, relates how he was born to a noble family in the region of Paphlagonia in Anatolia, and how he encountered the charismatic monastic teacher Symeon the Stoudite at age fourteen.[3] Although the younger Symeon remained a layman and served as a courtier to the emperors Basil II and Constantine VIII, the elder Symeon became his spiritual guide. At twenty-seven or twenty-eight he entered the Monastery of Stoudios, dedicating himself to asceticism and the contemplative life. Around three years later he was appointed abbot of the smaller Monastery of St. Mamas, where he served for about twenty-five years. This tenure was marked not only by a remarkable literary output that engaged the spiritual practices of the Stoudite reforms, but also by strife. In 998, possibly reacting to the rigors of the discipline imposed on them, his monks complained to the patriarch and revolted, only to repent and beg to have Symeon back as their superior. For reasons that remain unclear, he resigned his post in 1005. Conflicts with the archbishop Stephen of Nikomedia, ostensibly over Symeon's veneration of his now deceased teacher Symeon the Stoudite, but more likely over the extent of Symeon's considerable charismatic authority, led to Symeon the New Theologian's exile across the Bosporus in 1009, where he refounded a small monastery dedicated to Saint Marina. There he continued to write both theological treatises and mystical hymns. Although the discussion here focuses on Symeon's instructions while at St. Mamas, he continued to teach about the processes of monastic formation throughout his career.

Symeon's works allow us to interrogate not only the place of ritualization in the formation of the self, but the extent to which Byzantine religious leaders themselves saw such ritualization as a tool for successful subjectivation.

In his later works, Michel Foucault turned attention to the role of monasticism in the formation of Christian subjectivity. Focusing on the desert fathers of late antiquity, he highlighted the "technologies of the self" through which a monk came to understand himself as sinner and penitent, including obedience to a master, self-examination, and confession.[4] In the past three decades, scholars have elaborated Foucault's insights, rewriting the history of monasticism as a productive enterprise, effecting the self through regimen, discipline, liturgy, public and private prayer, and particularly through an abbot's exhortations, both in late antiquity and in the medieval West.[5] The importance of monastic practice and literature for the history of Byzantine subjectivity more generally cannot be underestimated: Through the dissemination of liturgical hymns, such as the *Great Kanon* of Andrew of Crete or the briefer kanons of the Stoudite Triodion, into cathedral and parish liturgies, for example, and through collective prayer, the church mediated monastic models for interiority to a broader lay public. At the same time, Byzantium's contributions to the history of the monastic self remain poorly integrated into larger discussions about the history of the subject in Christian cultures. Both the mechanisms and the indigenous Byzantine theories of the self embedded in Byzantine monastic life thus further our work of fleshing out a history of subjectivity in Byzantium—the history of how Byzantines came to be present to themselves.

Interior Speeches

While the abbot of St. Mamas, Symeon delivered his *Discourses* orally, most probably during Orthros, or Morning Prayer. It would seem likely that he himself then edited and published them as a collection before 998, when his monks rebelled.[6] As a group, the *Discourses* present the most complete and reasoned program for the formation of monks to survive from the middle Byzantine centuries, albeit an unsystematic one. In prescribing interior speech as a tool in the formation of a monk, Symeon encodes a Byzantine theory of subjectivity. He places confidence in the efficacy of repetition and ritualization as a technology for the formation of the monastic self, and thus reveals his sense of monasticism as a performed identity.

Symeon would seem to anticipate a theory of interpellation, through which authorities call their subjects into being through accusation and its acceptation. Mladen Dolar has augmented Althusser's conception of interpellation by stressing the degree to which the process materializing the subject takes place through ritual.[7] Symeon emphasizes the role of the abbot in instilling a model of the self, but also shows in his instruction how this name-calling becomes interiorized through repetition. Symeon gives his monks speeches through which to identify themselves, and which they in turn put into practice. In Symeon's instruction for maintaining solitude through internal self-abasement, the novice monk will in time interpellate himself as the subject of his self-accusing speech.

Symeon constructs similar speeches for mealtimes, especially to counter a monk's interest in whether others have received larger portions or have taken better seats. "Who am I, the worthless and unworthy one, that I should have become one who shares the seats and the table of these saints" (26.152–53). "Who am I?" The persistence of the question underscores the role of these patterned thoughts in the formation and recognition of the self. Symeon describes the interior self-assessment that accompanies this speech: "As you are saying these words within yourself [ἐν ἑαυτῷ], with your soul consider yourself alone to be a sinner [ἔχε μόνον ἀπὸ ψυχῆς σεαυτὸν ἁμαρτωλόν]" (26.153–55). In fact, self and soul would seem here separate entities, although interrelated, the self at once the agent of sin and a venue for a conversation about identity and subjectivity, and the soul an instrument capable of reflection on this dialogue. And the inner interrogation continues: "Under what pretense can I eat and drink and rejoice with the saints, when I have not yet repented and received full pardon from God, who loves mankind, like those who have never sinned, or who, when they have sinned, have received His pardon?" (26.174–77). In this manner, encounters with other monks throughout the day, near their cells, in the refectory, and throughout the monastery provide opportunities to reinforce a particular subjectivity, a humble self-regard that identifies the monk as sinful and insufficiently repentant. The self that matters is the sinful one, constituted discursively in language provided by the *hegoumenos*. Through this sort of discipline of interior dialogue, the monk can hope to become the subject of his own internal speech.

The Failure to Repent as the Archetypal Sin

Failure to acknowledge one's own sinfulness, to identify self as sinner, has archetypal significance, for it repeats Adam's fault in Eden. Throughout his writings, Symeon sees the reason for Adam's expulsion from the garden not in his disobedience—eating the fruit in defiance of God's command—but in Adam's failure to confess and repent. In the Fifth Discourse, Symeon uses this interpretation of Genesis to illustrate the centrality of penance in monastic life. In the retelling, the events in Eden provide another occasion for a superior to compose speeches for his subject:

> Listen to the divine Scripture as it speaks: "And God said to Adam (that is, after his Fall), 'Adam where are you?'" Why does the Maker of all things speak in this way? Surely it is because He wishes to make him conscious [of his guilt] and so call him to repent that he says, "Adam, where are you?" "Understand yourself, realize your nakedness. See of what a garment, of how great glory, you have deprived yourself." It is as though He spoke to encourage him, "Yes come to your senses, poor fellow, come out of your hiding place. Do you think that you are hidden from me? Just say, 'I have sinned.'" (*Catechetical Discourses* 5.173–82)

God coaxes Adam to identify himself—to interpellate himself—through confession, to acknowledge his sin, his nakedness, and the good things that he has forfeited.[8] Symeon stresses that God asked Adam twice, "giving him the opportunity of a second reply" (5.193–94). Eventually God composes for Adam the words that he should say, providing him with the appropriate speech: "It is as though [God] said, 'Do you really think that you can hide from Me? Do I not know what you have done? Will you not say, "I have sinned"? Say, O wretch, "Yes, it is true Master, I have transgressed Thy command, I have fallen by listening to the woman's counsel, I am greatly at fault for doing what she said and disobeying Thy word, have mercy on me [ἐλέησόν με]!'" (5.211–16). But Adam does not say these words; he does not repeat the script that his Lord has supplied. Eve also fails to repent. She too refuses to recite the words of confession that God scripts on her behalf. "He said, 'What is it that you have done [Gen 3:13]?' so that she at least might be able to say 'I have sinned'" (5.258–60). But instead she only blames the serpent for beguiling her. For

Symeon the message is clear: had they repented then and there, Adam and Eve would not have been expelled.

But Adam is not the only poor disciple. Adam may serve as a negative exemplar, but Symeon refuses to allow him to be an excuse. "As for those who make excuses for themselves, let them not say that we are totally under the influence of Adam's transgression and so dragged down to sin" (5.395–97). "Let no one of us accuse and blame Adam, but rather himself" (5.467–68). In a performance of his own humility, Symeon identifies himself with Adam. Observing that Adam does not say what God tells him to say: "I have sinned," Symeon interjects: "Or rather, it is I, miserable one, who do not say this, for I am in this position" (5.183–84). As Adam fails to ask for mercy—"he does not humble himself, he does not bend"—Symeon exclaims, "The neck of his heart is like a sinew of iron [cf. Is 48:4], as is mine, wretch that I am" (5.217–19). In accusing himself, Symeon identifies the core of Adam's fault: Adam refuses to accuse himself of being the sinner that God knows him to be, that God calls him to call himself. His sin lies in his resistance to God's interpellation. In Symeon's model, superiors—whether God or the abbot—provide their subjects the appropriate words, but the subject often fails to repeat them.

Symeon's own display of humility reveals to his new monks both a negative and a positive example in one. Symeon resists God, but in his public confession, he humiliates himself. He identifies himself as a disobedient sinner. Symeon performs the role of the failed subject, which by a paradoxical logic is the role of the successful subject. Such humility governs the authorial voice throughout the *Catechetical Discourses*. The series opens with Symeon's confession of inadequacy to instruct his monks. "It is my intention to speak to you about the things that pertain to the benefit of the soul. Yet, as Christ who is the truth bears witness, I feel shame before your charity, because I know my unworthiness. For this reason I would rather be silent forever, as the Lord knows, without even lifting up my eyes to look at any man's face, since my conscience condemns me. I was appointed to be the superior of you all, though I am wholly unworthy" (1.8–14). Symeon is aware of the performative qualities of such humble speech and the possibility that the speaker may be insincere or has not sufficiently conformed himself to the humility he expresses.[9] The ritualization inherent in performance, however, has the goal of shaping the speaker to the speech. Elsewhere Symeon explains, "Where there is unfeigned humiliation [ταπείνωσις ἀψευδής] there is also the depth of humility, and where there is humility there is also the enlightenment of the Spirit" (2.217–19). The seal of Christ and the illumination of the Spirit depend first and foremost on humiliation and second on "sorrow [πένθος] and the fountain of tears" (2.258–59).[10] Tears offer the marker of sincerity, in effect authenticating the reality of the self emergent and expressed.[11] Thus the performance of sorrow generates the truth of the self. Paraphrasing Isaiah 66:2, Symeon quotes God, "On whom will I look, but on him who is humble and contrite in spirit and trembles at my word?" (2.257–58). Thus Symeon ritualizes his own humility and sorrow as an example to his monks, even as he confesses his sin. And in this regard he scripts himself.

Models of Repentance

If Adam was obdurate, other figures from the biblical tradition and the communion of saints provide better models for the penitent self. Symeon's God reminds women (and indirectly the male novices to whom he preaches) of repentant holy women whose *vitae* they have heard read in churches: Pelagia "the former harlot," Mary of Egypt "the former prodigal/profligate [τῆς ἀσώτου ποτέ]," Theodora "the Adulterous, who became a Wonderworker," as well as Euphrosyne and Xena. "Why," God asks women absent from Symeon's audience, "have you not imitated those and similar women—you who were once prostitutes; you who were once prodigals; you who were married (αἱ δὲ ὕπανδροι) [why have you not imitated] the wives who were sinners, those who are virgins, the virgins like yourselves?" (5.559–72). God calls them to identify with women, most of them sexual sinners, and then imitate their conversion.[12] Together with the biblical figures, these saintly women dwell in the land of the exemplars, available to the Christian self both in the readings of the liturgy and in images on the walls of the church.

To men who are kings and rulers, by contrast, Symeon's God proffers David, who after he had sinned did not contradict the prophet Nathan's accusation, but "rose up from his throne and fell down on the ground before all the people and said, 'I have sinned against my Lord (1 Sam 12:13)' " (5.579). Day and night he wept and lamented. Symeon quotes psalm verses familiar to his monks to illustrate David's self-recognition and contrition. "Why," God asks these men, "have you not imitated him and those like him? Do you think that you are more glorious or more wealthy than he, and therefore unwilling to be humbled before me?" (5.593–96). "Why have you refused to be subject [ὑποταγῆναι] to Me your Maker and Master, and to serve Me with fear and trembling?" (5.602–4). With the echo of Psalm 2:11 ("Serve the Lord with fear, with trembling kiss his feet"), Symeon underscores the role of the Psalter in providing the monk with appropriately subjectivating speech. By praying the Psalms, the monk may imitate the penitent David.

In fact, David serves Symeon as the biblical penitent par excellence, despite the fact that he lived his life in the world. In a letter concerning repentance most likely composed to a lay Christian for whom Symeon served as a spiritual advisor, the New Theologian argues that a sinner's introspection and outward demeanor matters more than any ascetic deeds. "He [the sinner] must display repentance and penitence, not displayed by his words or through abstaining from food, drinking only water, having his pallet on the floor, and practices of this kind, but that which is created by the disposition in the soul [ἐν διαθέσει ψυχῆς], and which the blessed David demonstrated, encompassed as he was by the world and the cares of this life. For he always remembered and weighed up within himself how good and compassionate a Master he had provoked to anger, because he had been a transgressor of his commandments, and was revealed as unmindful of his many and countless gifts and graces and ungrateful."[13] In this letter, which shares many themes with the *Catechetical Discourses,* Symeon qualifies the centrality of some aspects of monastic praxis and suggests that David's words in the Psalms offer the more necessary model. David says that he "went mourning and with a sad countenance [Ps 34:14, 37:7]." Symeon elaborates, "he himself very greatly afflicted and humbled himself, 'roaring by reason of the lamentation of his heart [Ps 37:9],' and everything else as the psalms sung each day teach us" (*Letters* 2.20–25). The Psalter—and especially the Hexapsalmos, the invariable set of six psalms that open Morning Prayer—thus provides both the lines and the motivation for the proper performance.

The commands of Christ (*Catechetical Discourses* 5.497–558) produce a knowledge of sin and a conception of the self; the Psalms produce penitence and tears. The result is what the historical anthropologist Gavin Flood has termed "the entextualisation of the body," a ritualized formation of the self in accord with sacred texts.[14] But while the body is absorbed into the textual models, it is not passive in this labor. Bodily actions shape the formation of this prescribed interiority and the attendant penitent disposition.

The Formation of the Ritual Body

In his Thirtieth Discourse, Symeon provided his newly arrived monks a set of practices for private prayer at bedtime. Once they had retired to their cells for the evening, he instructed his spiritual charges to sit on their beds and engage in a solitary liturgy, first giving thanks to God for having sustained them through the day and providing food, drink, clothing, and the shelter of their cells. Then he commanded them to examine themselves, "calling to mind how much [they] ha[d] sinned against God" (*Catechetical Discourses* 30.112–13). This self-examination had its roots in early Christian practice, monastic and lay: Athanasios reports that Antony required his monks to keep diaries of their sins; John Chrysostom urged his lay parishioners to do the same, "For if you write them down, God blots them out. . . . If you omit writing them, God both inscribes them and exacts their penalty."[15] Drawing on the works of late antique monastic teachers such as John Klimax, the Stoudite movement renewed emphasis on practices of *exagoreusis;* Theodore encouraged his monks to report their thoughts regularly to their abbot or spiritual father.[16] Symeon had been formed in this tradition and sought to carry it forward in his own spiritual direction of his monastic charges.[17] Reviewing the failures of the day provided access to self-knowledge or self-recognition. By framing this confessional exercise with a litany of thanksgiving, Symeon ritualizes an epistemology of the self through prayer. Symeon regards this form of introspective prayer as normative: As soon as the monk wakes the following morning, he is to "rise at once and pray again in the aforesaid manner," persevering in private prayer and reading until the wooden gong sounds for the collective office of Morning Prayer (30.185–88).

Symeon however, does not limit this technology of the self to a novice's control of his internal reflexive speech. At this point, Symeon presents an additional and optional practice, one which will more quickly produce tears, especially in those "slow to mourn and without compunction" (30.123–26). Most dramatically, the New Theologian extends his disciplinary purview upon the entirety of the monk's body, prescribing a ritual of subjectivation with brutalizing force. Symeon knows that what follows will seem irregular and will need some defense: He pleads, "But do not let that which I am about to counsel appear as something strange and unfamiliar to the faithful without testing it!" (30.126–28). Thereupon he begins to introduce a ritual process, strange indeed, composed of set prayers, mental exercises, and bodily postures.[18] "Once

you have prepared for yourself the mat of your bed on which you are about
to lie, rise up and pray as one who is under condemnation [ὡς κατάκριτος]"
(30.145–47). With the subject positioned to receive punishment, the mind
engages in recollection and the mouth begins in supplication. The rite opens
with the Trisagion ("Holy Lord, Holy and Mighty, Holy Immortal, have mercy
on us"), followed by the Lord's Prayer. As they say the "Our Father," Symeon
tells his monks, "Remember who you are [μνήσθητι τίς ὤν] and whom you
call your Father" (30.147–49). Thus the service uses the words of set prayer to
form interiority, providing a prompt for the monk to be present to himself as
a supplicant for divine mercy.

These habits of mind reinforce themselves in the body, for the monk's act
of remembrance now calls on him to move his hands and attend to them.
The hands both express prayer and cue self-regard. With his hands now outstretched, the monk sees them not only in their gesture of supplication but
also as the instruments of sin. "When you come to say 'Lord have mercy'
and wish to stretch out your hands to the height of heaven look upwards
with your physical eyes and fix your sight on your hands. Concentrate your
thoughts and recall your wicked actions and how much you have sinned with
your hands" (30.149–54). This act of self-review hopes to forestall God's own
gaze, effectively replicating (or duplicating) divine surveillance within the
conscience. "Remember the foul deeds [your hands] may have committed
and with fear say within yourself [λέγων ἐν σεαυτῷ], 'Woe to me, unclean
and defiled as I am! May it not be that when God sees me stretching out my
hands to Him without shame He will remember my misdeeds I have committed with them, and so send fire on me to consume me!'" (30.154–59). Even
here, the monk questions his motivations, accusing himself of shamelessness
even in confession and supplication.

Shifting his stance, the monk then joins these same hands behind his
back, "as though being led off to death [ὡς ἐπὶ θάνατον ἀγόμενος]," a pose
accompanied by the following lines, to be recited with a sigh and "a pitiful
voice": "Have mercy on me a sinner [Lk 18:13; the words of the Tax Collec-
tor] who am not fit to live, but who am truly worthy of punishment." At this
point, the monk may add any other words that "the grace of God has given
[him] to utter" (30.161–64). Causing him to play the part of a prisoner convicted of a capital offense, Symeon scripts an imaginative and emotionally
compelling performance of the self, even permitting his agent to speak ad li-
bitum. In the privacy of the cell, one wonders who is watching this spectacle?
While the prayers are addressed to God, the one who needs to be convinced

by the performance is the self. The self needs to see himself represented to himself.[19]

There are perhaps peculiar parallels between this liturgy of memory and the anamnesis of the Divine Liturgy. The eucharistic service employs remembering to extol in thanksgiving all of the acts of God, while the monk's private litany performs a recollection of the self that both inspires and produces reproach. Both are liturgies of memory; both rites employ recollection and narrative in the hope of a divinely confected transformation.[20] Moreover, in between the postures of punishment, the monk assumes the postures of prayer, thus moving the body through the gestural formation of the prisoner and the penitent, using the body to form the self.[21]

And at this point, the monk's role shifts: having played the condemned criminal and the prosecutor, he now performs the role of enforcer. Now the hands have, again, a new task. As we have seen, compunction, *katanyxis* in Greek, is the metaphorical puncturing or wounding of the self. It is the pricking of the conscience that generates emotional pain and remorse, or *penthos*. As Symeon's monk recalls (ἀναμνημονεύων) his sinful acts and decries them, he externalizes this compunction—his wounded and wounding self—upon the surface of the body. He strikes himself "violently and unsparingly" (30.165). He disciplines and punishes himself for his failure to conform to God's will. After returning briefly to the stance with his hands behind his back and interrogating himself about his motives in committing each sin, he begins his self-pummeling anew. "Then beat your face, pluck at your hair and pull it, as though some terrible enemy had plotted against you, and say, 'Why did you commit such and such a sin?'" (30.167–70). His confessional interior speech has unleashed horrible reflexive violence. Recriminating himself, the monk subjects himself to ritualized self-battery.

In describing Symeon's work in rebuilding the monastery and reforming its monks, his biographer Niketas mentions how the New Theologian modeled austere practices and provides the most extreme with a biblical prooftext to explain them. "So, at the same time as he 'punished and enslaved [cf. 1 Cor 9:27]' himself, he presented himself to his disciples as a model of the 'most narrow and hard way [cf. Mt 7:14].'"[22] The echo of 1 Corinthians 9:27, "but I punish my body and enslave it, so that after proclaiming to others I myself should not be disqualified," serves to justify seemingly excessive practices as an imitation of the Apostle Paul. "While he acted and taught in this way, the heavenly gift of compunction developed in him through his extreme humility. . . . [H]e set aside for himself three times of the day for this labor [i.e., compunction], as has been mentioned: first thing in the morning after the hymns of matins, at the holy eucharistic prayer when the Son of God is slain, and in the evening after all the other hymn singing. For at these times he would stand by himself in prayer and would converse through his tears, one on one with God" (*Life of Symeon* 35). The hagiographer presents Symeon's tears both as a specific charism and as the result of great discipline and effort. The body becomes an instrument for the production of sentiment.

When, according to Symeon's instructions to his monks, this portion of the private liturgy has run its self-abusive course—when the monk has "flogged himself sufficiently [μαστίξας σεαυτὸν ἱκανῶς]"—Symeon directs the monk into a new pose and provides him with a new motivation: "Join your hands in front of you and stand with a joyful soul [ἐν ἱλαρᾷ τῇ ψυχῇ]." With this shift in disposition, the service proceeds with "two or three psalms" that the monk may choose, recited with attention, and as many prostrations (προσκυνήσεις) as the monk is able (*Catechetical Discourses* 30.170–73). Standing still again, Symeon commands the monk to reflect on what he has told them.[23]

The goals of this private service are tears and compunction, an interior disposition and its exteriorization, both of which may come through divine grace. If the tears come, the monk is not to retire until they have subsided. If they do not, Symeon counsels, "Do not be discouraged," and he scripts a final set of lines: "Say this to yourself: 'Compunction and tears belong to those who are worthy and are ready for them.'" Indeed, the lack of tears provides another opportunity for recrimination: "By what deeds have I prepared myself to receive [tears]? Is it not enough for me that I am still alive?" (30.177–81). The service closes with a prayer of thanksgiving and the making of the sign of the cross on the face, breast, and body, before the monk collapses upon his sleeping mat. Scripted and choreographed, this performance employs the body to reform the self.[24] Interior self-regard and reflection are somatized, embodied, inaugurating a new subjectivity, an expressly penitent self.

The Tears of Repentance

Tears pass over the boundaries of the body, from the inside to the outside. Tears thus express and externalize interior mental states. They signify the successful subjection of the monk. Elsewhere in the *Discourses*, Symeon expounds a common Byzantine emphasis on the necessity of tears in monastic formation, explaining, "There is no weeping without repentance, there are no tears apart from weeping." (*Catechetical Discourses* 4.12). Perhaps counterintuitively, Symeon argues that the shedding of tears is as necessary for the soul as taking in food and drink are for the body. "He who does not daily weep—I hesitate to say every hour for fear of seeming to exaggerate—will destroy his soul and cause it to perish from hunger" (29.230–34).[25] In thus weeping the monk is "continually penitent at all times and mindful of his own failures" (29.245–46). Indeed, it is only in vision blurred by tears that one can see God (29.250–53).[26]

Hannah Hunt, in her book *Joy Bearing Grief*, has explored the theme of tears of contrition in the Byzantine tradition, connecting Symeon's conception of *penthos* with the patristic tradition and especially the seventh chapter of John Klimax's *Ladder*, where mournful sorrow regarding one's misdeeds provides an opportunity for spiritual growth.[27] She has perhaps underestimated the degree to which Symeon connects weeping with other bodily disciplines. The nightly rites of the Thirtieth Discourse inform also the fourth of Symeon's *Erotes*, the hymns on divine love.[28] According to the introductory note that Symeon's designated editor Niketas Stethatos appended to the hymn, Symeon directed this chant also at monks beginning the ascetic life.

> Always sigh from the depths of your heart
> and wash your face only with tears.
> . . .
> Also keep your hands together;
> may you not shamelessly hold them out to God,
> these hands, which you have often stretched toward sin. (*Hymns*
>   4.10–11, 14–16)

Modeling an appropriate prayer, Symeon sings,

> Cleanse the filth [ῥύπον] of my soul,
> and grant to me tears of repentance,
> tears of yearning, tears of salvation,
> tears that cleanse the gloom of my mind,
> and in the end make me radiant from on high,
> desiring to see You the light of the world. (4.84–89)

Ritual weeping—and rituals to provoke weeping—produce contrition, purification, and the vision of God. Embodied and theatrical, penance generates its sincerity by being rehearsed.[29]

Symeon expects that his monks will weep during the Divine Liturgy, both underscoring an understanding of the Eucharist as a penitential rite and endorsing a theory of ritual efficacy in which the texts and chants of the liturgy cultivate compunction. He writes in the Fourth Discourse: "Do you wish, then, never to take communion without tears [μὴ κοινωνῆσαί ποτε δίχα δακρύων]? Practice what you daily sing and read out, and then you will be able to continually [or: without ceasing] achieve this" (*Catechetical Discourses* 4.517–20). Once again, ritual repetition produces both interior disposition and bodily expression. Over time, the tears of compunction effect the transformation of the self. "When your soul is pricked by compunction and gradually changed, it becomes a fountain flowing with rivers of tears and compunction" (4.653–55). But Symeon also warns that tears should not be reserved for the Liturgy alone; rather weeping during the Liturgy should set a pattern for the whole of monastic life. "If any one of you ever happens to take communion with tears, whether you weep before the Liturgy or in the course of the Divine Liturgy, or at the very time that you receive the divine Gifts, and does not desire to do this for the rest of his days and nights, it will avail him nothing to have wept merely once." (4.659–63). Symeon invokes David's example in Psalm 6:7: "Every night I wash my bed, with my tears I will drench my couch" (4.650–51). In the monastic ideal, crying becomes incessant, the outward sign of the constant affect of contrition.

In the letter on repentance quoted earlier, Symeon appeals to a range of biblical exemplars to illustrate the efficacy of tears. Having invoked David, he now mentions Manasseh, whose prayer for forgiveness was included among the Canticles, and was likely chanted at the late evening office of Apodeipnon, or Compline.[30] "And what of those of a later date?" he asks, referring to a standard repertoire of New Testament penitents, long familiar in the works of Romanos and Andrew of Crete, and, to some extent, in Stoudite hymnography.

I mean Peter the chief of the apostles, the tax-collector, the thief, the prostitute, and—why speak at length—the prodigal son who squandered his father's property with prostitutes and tax collectors. By what kind of works did these people gain pardon for their wrongdoings? Consider! Was it by fasting, keeping vigil, sleeping on the floor, ridding themselves of their possessions to benefit the needy, or by some other laborious activity which is performed by means of the body? Certainly not, but it was simply by repentance, and heart-felt tears, and being condemned by their conscience. For each of them having come to a perception of their own sins, and having condemned themselves and lamented with all their heart, they gained pardon for their faults, and now too this is effected in all of us who genuinely and fervently come, by means of repentance and tears, to Christ our Master. (Letter 2.25–39)

Thus biblical figures exhibit repentance and tears independently of the monastic tradition, even as Symeon regards monasticism as a form of life conducive to the production of tears and contrition.[31] In Hymn 17, Symeon looks to Thief, the Harlot, and the Prodigal as models for turning toward God.

> [The Thief] alone confessed
> that I was both God
> and King and immortal,
> he cried aloud from his heart.
> . . .
> What words would show
> the yearning of the Harlot?
> That desire she bore
> in her heart as she approached
> Me as God and Master.
> . . .
> And likewise the Prodigal,
> having turned around from the depths of his heart,
> he sincerely repented. (*Hymns* 17.685–88, 691–95, 715–17)

Such New Testament sinners once again offer precedents. And they answer questions that Symeon poses in his own voice about proper comportment, both interior and exterior.

> How shall I dare to speak,
> how shall I ask forgiveness
> for my immeasurable stumbling,
> for my many trespasses? (*Hymns* 17.14–17)

But these figures also offer points of identification, as Symeon reveals in Hymn 20: "me the sinner, the Prodigal, the Tax Collector, / the Thief" (*Hymns*

20.67–68). Symeon is each of the biblical characters on the cusp of their confession of sin and of faithfulness.

Penitent Liturgies and the Production of the Subject

The sincerity of one's contrition, it would seem, increases with repetition.
Symeon subscribes to an indigenous, Byzantine Christian theory of the formation of the self in which rehearsing the scripted thoughts and physical postures produces an authentic subject. Such a theory of subjectivity undergirds
the work of Byzantine liturgical agents throughout the long period considered in this study, and is reflected in works of the crafters of prayers and
hymns for the Byzantine Orthodox church. Symeon's focus on interior formation, in continuity with earlier efforts at monastic instruction, brings such
a theory of ritual efficacy to the making of monks. Through the practices, the
monk becomes the subject of his own thoughts; he becomes the subjunctive
self: no longer "as if," but now "as is."[32] Scripted, he becomes the character
whose lines he speaks. He identifies as the speaker of the self-reproach. While
Symeon acknowledges an initial gap between a new monk's self and the target
self, Symeon's monastic program achieves the monastic subject through ritual
performance. Collective and individual rites converge to produce a proper
interiority, a way of regarding the self as sinful and redeemed, condemned
and pardoned.

Having described his private nightly ritual in the cell in the Thirtieth
Discourse, Symeon extends his discussion of penitence and ritual life to the
common liturgical offices of the monastery, particularly Orthros, or Morning
Prayer. Rather than emphasizing aspects of collective prayer, Symeon charges
the monk to pay attention to himself alone and to call to mind the prayer
that he had offered in his cell the night before. The private rite thus frames
the monk's performance of the public rites. Participation in the liturgy also,
therefore, provides a technology of the self, an opportunity for self-expression
through tears. For the liturgy to work to form the monk, however, the tears
must become constant. In producing tears and contrition, the monk has
achieved the object of his desire, a penitent self. As the concern with weeping
both during and after the Eucharist demonstrates, public collective ritual and
private rites both can generate a monk present to himself in his own weeping. To the extent that Symeon advocates tearful penitence as normative for
the monastic self, various monastic practices converge to produce this ideal.

In the end, Symeon sees continuity between private and public ritual practice as technologies of the monastic self. In suggesting the option of nightly violence, Symeon not only offers a method for the process of monastic subjectivation, but reveals his confidence in ritualization as a tool or method. The production of the appropriate self is greatly aided—indeed is provided with a certain and effective shortcut—by the careful use of self-directed corporal and corporeal punishment. This is not merely a Byzantine analogue of the psychoanalytic superego. The monk intentionally inflicts tearful punishments upon his body to achieve the monastic body. In doing so he incorporates other aspects of the monastic regulatory structure. Symeon offers his instructions for the production of contrition "as in a rule." And it is worth pondering that certain forms of corporal punishment, in particular beatings with a whip, had been banned by the Typikon of the Stoudios Monastery in the ninth century.[33] Symeon trained and trusted his monks to punish themselves.

In *People and Power in Byzantium*, Alexander Kazhdan saw in the works of Symeon the New Theologian a shift in monastic sensibilities toward concern with "individual salvation."[34] Yet, if all monks are to conform themselves to this rule for the formation of the self, these individuals become strikingly similar. Furthermore, salvation, it would seem, is never really in question. Indeed, a final aspect of Symeon's instruction reveals the performative qualities of his optional rite, one that underscores what it might mean to ritualize "as if" a prisoner condemned to death. Symeon assures his monks that if they "persevere in these practices," God will not hesitate to show them mercy. "Only practice these things without hesitation of heart, without double-mindedness [διψυχία]" (30.221–27). In fact the abbot, confessing his own rashness, offers his own soul to the fire as a guarantee of God's compassion and love of humanity. Quoting verbatim, without attribution, a sixth-century letter of the monastic teachers Barsanouphios and John, Symeon explains that this "hesitation of heart" consists in doubting whether God will have mercy or not. "This 'not' belongs to unbelief [ἀπιστία]," and Symeon reminds the monk that the entire supplication of God is predicated on believing that "God is even more willing to have mercy on you than you hope for." The "double-mindedness" lies in "not giving oneself over complete, even to the point of death, for the kingdom of heaven, but being anxious, however little, for the life of one's flesh."[35] Thus, Symeon once again connects repentance to the life and work of the body: indeed, the only limit for the one "strenuously repenting [ὁ ἐμπόνως μετανοῶν]" is that he does not kill himself, "such as by casting himself down from a precipice or hanging himself or by committing

some other crime" (30.228–40). Although Symeon reveals this only after prescribing the brutal rite, the assurance of forgiveness and redemption reframes
the exercise. The supplications do not compel divine action on the monk's
behalf; indeed, given that the monk's performance effects no actual change
in God, Symeon removes self-interest in the monk's private production of
penance and preemptive punishment. The ritual effects not redemption but
subjectivity. The accusation of the soul and the pummeling of the flesh produce the identity of the sinner redeemed.

A Communion of Savable Sinners

At the turn of the thirteenth century, Nikolaos Mesarites, an aristocratic sacristan of the churches of the Great Palace in Constantinople, composed a literary description, or ekphrasis, of the Church of the Holy Apostles, the burial place of Byzantine emperors since the time of Constantine.[1] He was struck in particular by the image of the Pantokrator, the Almighty, high above in the church's central dome, part of an elaborate decorative program probably dating from the later ninth century, when the middle Byzantine cross-in-square church plan began to take hold.[2] In a fashion typical for the middle Byzantine period, the dome depicted "in an image [εἰκονικῶς]" the bust of the God-Man Christ, "leaning out as though from the rim of heaven toward the floor of the church and everything in it" (14.1). Everyone under heaven was the subject of his gaze. There in the dome, "one can see him, to use the words of the Song of Songs [2:9], 'peering forth from windows' . . . like a vehement and uncontrollable lover [κατὰ τοὺς σφοδροὺς καὶ ἀκατασχέτους τῶν ἐραστῶν]" (14.2). God's desire for humanity, however, is double-edged. As Nikolaos explains, Christ appears differently to those in his purview, depending on their own interior reflection and moral development. "To those who possess an uncondemned conscience [ἀκατάγνωστος τὸ συνειδός], [Christ's] eyes are cheerful and friendly, instilling the sweetness of compunction in the souls of the 'pure in heart' and 'poor of spirit' [Mt 5:3, 8]." Nikolaos quotes Psalm 33 to explain God's vision: "the eyes of the Lord are upon the righteous [Ps 33:16 (34:15)]" (14.3).[3] Those of clear conscience are not those free of sin; indeed, there are none like that. Alluding to Matthew's Beatitudes, Nikolaos instead compares those blessed with God's cheerful expression to the pure in heart and poor of spirit—the contrite, those who have acknowledged their sin and purified themselves through repentance. For these viewers, "his gaze is gentle and wholly mild, looking neither to the left nor the right, but wholly at the same time toward all and toward each individual separately [πρὸς τὸν καθέκαστον μερικῶς]" (14.4).

In contrast to those of clean conscience, others looking into the dome of Holy Apostles see God's wrath. "To those condemned in their own judgment," the eyes are "angry, unapproachable, and boding of ill. The face is wild, terrifying, determined, and full of hardness." Nikolaos again explains God's aspect with an allusion to Psalm 33: "The face of the Lord has this manner against evildoers [Ps 33:17 (34:16)]" (14.5). Christ's face thus mirrors one's vision of the self. The dome of the church externalizes one's self-reproach. In fact, the conscience determines how one sees God—and how one sees God seeing the self. Inspiring "sweetness in compunction" or alternatively fear, the image elicits or demands an emotional response. Indeed, Nikolaos exhibits sensitivity both to Christ's affect and the viewers'.[4] The relationship between God and humanity is passionate.

While the image at Holy Apostles does not survive, other Byzantine churches offer images with similar effect, such as the late twelfth-century painting at the Church of the Panagia tou Arakou at Lagoudera on Cyprus (Figure 16). The representation of Christ Pantokrator in the dome of the eleventh-century church at Daphni, outside Athens, perhaps emphasizes the forbidding and chastising Christ (Figure 17).[5] The bivalent representation of Christ's face emerged even earlier, in the sixth century, as in the famous Sinai encaustic panel icon (Figure 1). What was it then, to imagine a God's-eye view of the self? And how did one learn to acquire such a view?

While icon veneration, as a theological and historical problem, has remained beyond the scope of this study, iconophiles' confidence that Christ was present in his image contributed to and reflected the development of interior pieties. Icons ultimately framed viewers' experience of themselves. Worshiping before and beneath images of Christ, Byzantines reinforced their view of themselves as subjects of the divine gaze. Visualizing God in images, as in prayers and hymns, Orthodox Christians imagined how God might see them. Such images looking down from the highest point, the dome of heaven, rendered the entire church, and indeed the whole of creation, as a panopticon, a disciplinary theater under divine surveillance.[6] It was in such spaces that from the ninth century Byzantine Christians prayed for forgiveness, listened to the lections, celebrated the festivals of Christ, partook of the Eucharist, heard and sang hymns. But they were not quite sinners in the dome of an angry God. As the kontakia, kanons, and prayers have demonstrated, confession and contrition always presumed an ultimately merciful God, even as the

Figure 16. Fresco of Christ Pantokrator in the dome of the Church of the Panagia tou Arakou, Lagoudera, Cyprus, from a painting phase dated by inscription to 1192. © Dumbarton Oaks, Image Collections and Fieldwork Archives, Washington, D.C.

liturgy positioned the Christian as falling grievously short of the mark. In Romanos the Melodist, Andrew of Crete, the Stoudites, Kassia, and Symeon the New Theologian, the assurance of amnesty made space for the troubled conscience to examine, convict, and even punish itself. In this way, Christian subjects participated in their own redemption.

The rites and offices of the church offered the forum where Byzantine Christians learned to apply a penitential Bible to themselves. The liturgy produced not only the body and blood of Christ, but also a Christian congregation—itself a body of Christ—situated in liturgical time, revisiting the life of Christ in the course of the liturgical calendar. Throughout the festal cycle, hymns and sermons inculcated certain dispositions to teach Christians who they were within the history of salvation. After the Iconoclasm, Byzantine churches depicted scenes from the life of Christ in the space below the dome and above the congregation. The Annunciation, Nativity, Baptism, and Transfiguration adorn the squinches supporting the dome at Daphni. The north and south bays of the naos depict the Entry into Jerusalem, Crucifixion, Resurrection, and Incredulity of Thomas. Together with hymns and sermons, the interior surfaces of the church surrounded Byzantine Christians with sacred narrative, situating them in the midst of the Gospel. This saturation occurred more consistently and more intensely than in Western Romanesque or Gothic churches. Within the space of Byzantine churches, Orthodox Christians learned the history of their own redemption. But they were more than spectators. Through the hymns of the church, Byzantine worshippers joined a large cast of biblical characters. They lamented with Adam; repented with David; approached Christ in supplication with the Harlot, the Leper, the Samaritan, and the Hemorrhaging Woman; awaited Christ's saving hand like Peter. Like Thomas, they longed to approach God's body in astonished recognition. Like the Thief they requested his remembrance: they longed to be with him in Paradise. In this respect, they did not imitate Christ, but figured themselves as minor characters in dialogue with him, not following after him so much as encountering him face to face.

By historicizing Byzantine Orthodox concepts of guilt, our inquiry has articulated the cultural construction of self-blame and penance as a method for resolving the potential effects and apparent consequences of sin. Byzantine Orthodox guilt looks different from Catholic guilt or, for that matter, modern conceptions of Jewish guilt. An introspective conscience emerged and flourished in Byzantium independent of Augustine or a doctrine of original sin. Moreover, it was embedded in distinctively Byzantine ways of narrating

Figure 17. Mosaic of Christ Pantokrator, Church of the Monastery at Daphni, Greece. Eleventh century. Josephine Powell Photograph, Courtesy of Special Collections, Fine Arts Library, Harvard University.

and interpreting salvation history. Guilt and sin emerge not as transhistorical constants but as cultural products.[7] By focusing on performances of the self, this study has offered a history of neither sin itself, nor fear of damnation. Rather, by focusing on the self's construction, this volume has illustrated the history and the constitution of a "negative self-image" in Byzantium.[8] Liturgy acknowledged sin in the formative apprehension of the self. The conception of the sinful self took shape in Byzantium through scriptural exegesis and theological speculation and was mediated in ritual practice by means of hymnography and prayer. Liturgical authors and clerical leaders supplied models for self-recognition and self-knowledge. Their hymns and prayers showed persons constituted in their defects and redeemed by divine grace and the practice of virtues.

At the same time, the Byzantine liturgy taught that God would not be angry forever. Christ always remained open to persuasion by multiple supplicants. In the decoration of middle Byzantine Churches, Mary regularly stands at the left side of the bema, the wall dividing the naos, or nave, where the congregation stands, from the sanctuary and its altar. Across the space of the golden doors she intercedes with Christ on behalf of humanity. In some twelfth-century churches on Cyprus, Mary holds a scroll inscribed with twelve-syllable verse, a dialogue between her and her son about the fate of humanity. The poem dates from at least the eleventh century; the version at the Church of the Virgin Phorbiotissa at Asinou reads:

[Mary:] "Receive the entreaty of the one who bore you, O Logos."
[Jesus:] "What is it you seek, mother?" [Mary:] "The salvation of
    mortals."
[Jesus:] "They have angered me." [Mary:] "Have compassion my
    son."
[Jesus:] "But they do not repent [ἐπιστρέφουσιν]" [Mary:] "And save
    them [out of your] charity [σῶσον χάριν]."
[Jesus:] They shall be redeemed." [Mary:] "I thank you, O Logos."[9]

Further studies into Byzantine subjectivities may explore the role of Mary's intercession in appealing to Christ's mercy for conceptions of the self. While admitting humans' utter failure, both in their sinning and in their failure to repent, the poem reminds the viewer of Christ's ultimate love. In constructing a Christ finally willing and eager to save humanity, Christ himself also figures as a subject of liturgy, not merely as the addressee of petitionary prayer but as a character in a dynamic narrative.[10] While ultimately the penitent Christian subject is destined for entry into the divine life, becoming God though *theōsis*, here the liturgy situates God in the moment before consummation when God and salvation both remain objects of human longing.

The liturgy provided scripts for a savable self. In the course of this study, we have explored Byzantine practices of subjectivation through liturgy, prayer, and interior monologue between the sixth and the eleventh centuries. The hymns did not merely teach penance but ritualized the worshipper's self-expression as penitent. The rhetoric of compunction transmitted a range of sentiments, some of them quite acute. They constituted the Christian self as a repertoire of emotions. Far from exhibiting a "sense of personal order," Byzantine liturgists preferred performances of a *disordered* self, wracked with remorse, bewailing its past, overwrought with inwardly directed grief.[11] Such subjectivities were not stable but dynamic, and thus poised, perhaps, for moral growth and transformation. Communal liturgy identified worshippers with these loud and troubled voices. Byzantine religious experts and professionals understood that repetition formed interior religious dispositions. They presented the Eucharist as largely a penitential rite. Liturgical hymnography, especially that composed for the extended season of Lent, offered Byzantine Christians models for knowledge of the self as sinner. Ritual repetition inculcated patterns of self-accusation and self-formation, as participants became the subjects of liturgy. As the hymnographic tradition taught by example, and Symeon taught explicitly, saying such words with the lips would tend to produce appropriate dispositions in the soul. Thus Christians gained access to themselves through penitential rhetoric. Repentant speech provided a mechanism through which to understand themselves. Confidence in the ability of the speaker to inhabit the role lay at the heart of Byzantine ritual theory and undergirded Byzantine ritual practice. Anguished first-person performances of compunction effected the formation of the self. In a moment before their amnesty, the liturgy called selves into being with interpellative force. It produced a communion of liturgical subjects poised between self-recognition and salvation.

NOTES

Chapter 1. Shaping Liturgical Selves

1. Taft, *Precommunion Rites*, 307–13; Taft, *Great Entrance*, 54, 68–70, 487–88; and Schattauer, "Koinonicon," 109–10. The event occurred in either 565 or 577. Eutychios held the patriarchal throne in 552–565 and 577–582. On the impact of this and other liturgical changes, see Krueger, "Christian Piety and Practice."

2. John of Ephesus, *Historiae ecclesiasticae: pars tertia*, ed. Brooks, 107–8; trans., 78. Taft, *Precommunion Rites*, 305–6, 310. Writing in the twelfth century, George Kedrenos reported that Justin II introduced the troparion *At Your Mystical Supper* into the celebrations of Holy Thursday in 573/4, but there is no reason to prefer his account to that of John of Ephesus. Kedrenos, *Historiarum Compendium*, ed. Bekker, 1:684–85. Schattauer, "Koinonicon," 101–3.

3. Although John of Ephesus depicts the emperor as prevailing against Eutychios, later evidence suggests otherwise. Liturgical historian Robert Taft believes that the troparion was promptly accepted into the liturgy in the years following Justin II's death in 578, and its place remained secure. Indeed, it remains an integral part of the *Liturgy of St. John Chrysostom* used regularly in Orthodox churches today. *Liturgies Eastern and Western*, ed. Brightman, 1:394; Taft, *Great Entrance*, 85–86, 98–112.

4. Anastasios of Sinai, *Questions and Answers* q.46 (ed. Richard and Munitiz); trans. Munitiz, 158. For the themes of repentance in monastic life, see Torrance, *Repentance in Late Antiquity*.

5. Anastasios of Sinai, *Questions and Answers* q.10; trans. Munitiz, 62 (modified).

6. Taft, *Through Their Own Eyes*.

7. For those seeking studies of Byzantine history in the relevant periods, see Shepard, ed., *Cambridge History of the Byzantine Empire*, with further bibliography; Maas, ed., *Cambridge Companion to the Age of Justinian*; Haldon, *Byzantium in the Seventh Century*; Brubaker and Haldon, *Byzantium in the Iconoclast Era: A History*; *Le monde byzantin*, vol. 1, *L'empire romain d'orient: 330–641*, ed. Morrisson et al.; vol. 2, *L'empire byzantin: 641–1204*, ed. Cheynet et al.

8. For accessible histories of the Byzantine Liturgy, see Taft, "Liturgy," in *Oxford Handbook of Byzantine Studies*, ed. Jeffreys, Haldon, and Cormack, 599–610; Taft, *Byzantine Rite*. For more detailed analysis, the definitive work is Taft's multivolume *History of the Liturgy of St. John Chrysostom*.

9. Taft, "Cathedral vs. Monastic Liturgy"; Parenti, "Cathedral Rite of Constantinople"; Mateos, "Quelques problèmes de l'orthros byzantin"; Parpulov, "Psalters and Personal Piety."

10. Taft, "Cathedral vs. Monastic Liturgy," 188–97; Frøyshov, "La réticence à l'hymnographie."

11. The cathedral and urban-monastic rites continued to be distinguished, among other things, by their service books. See Taft, "Cathedral vs. Monastic Liturgy," 206–16; Velkovska, "Byzantine Liturgical Books."

12. On the history of the kontakion after the sixth century, see Lingas, "Liturgical Place of the Kontakion"; Grosdidier de Matons, *Romanos et les origines de la poésie religieuse à Byzance*, 48–65.

13. Parenti, "Cathedral Rite of Constantinople," 455–56.

14. Taft, "Baumstark's Comparative Liturgy Revisited," 225.

15. On the history of singers as professionals in late antique Christian communities and for singing as a responsibility of deacons and lectors, see Page, *Christian West and Its Singers*, 89–115, 155–71.

16. See now the outstanding work of Papaioannou, "Gregory and the Constraint of Sameness"; idem, *Michael Psellos*.

17. P. Miller, "Strategies of Representation," 221n5.

18. See Cameron, *Christianity and the Rhetoric of Empire*; Clark, "The Lady Vanishes"; eadem, *Reading Renunciation*.

19. On Romanos and the formation of subjectivity, see also Frank, "Dialogue and Deliberation," 174–75.

20. Foucault, "Technologies of the Self," 40. See also Foucault, "About the Beginning of the Hermeneutics of the Self," 171–74.

21. For a critique of this model, see Brakke, "Making Public the Monastic Life," 222–33.

22. Meyendorff, *Byzantine Theology*, 195–96. Jugie, *Theologia dogmatica*, 331–89.

23. *On Adam's Lament* 9–11 (ed. Maas), trans. Lash at http://www.anastasis.org.uk/adam's_lament.htm.

24. Greenblatt, *Renaissance Self-Fashioning*, 1. The problem of locating ancient religious selves is handled particularly well in the introduction to Brakke, ed., *Religion and the Self*, 1–11. For a more recent genealogy of modern selfhood, see Morgan, *On Becoming God*, 60–82.

25. Krueger, *Writing and Holiness*, 2–3, 97–104.

26. Foucault, *Discipline and Punish*, 141–49; Carrette, *Foucault and Religion*, 118–20; Landry, "Confession, Obedience, and Subjectivity." For a more contextualized approach, see Delumeau, *Sin and Fear*, 188–211.

27. Asad, *Genealogies of Religion*, 141.

28. Ibid., 131.

29. Such a model was common to Eastern and Western Christianities, of course, and endured well into modernity. See Frei, *Eclipse of Biblical Narrative*.

30. For another author stressing context over a general theory, see Flood, *Ascetic Self*.

31. Morris, *Discovery of the Individual*; idem, "Individualism in Twelfth-Century Religion"; Benton, "Consciousness of Self." For important qualifications, see Constable, *Reformation of the Twelfth Century*, 257–95. On problems in the search for a Byzantine self, see Papaioannou, "Byzantine Mirrors." For the broader pre-Christian and Patristic background see Chadwick, "Gewissen." Chadwick traces the conscience from late antiquity into the Western Middle Ages, but, typically and regretably, abandons Eastern Christian materials after John of Damascus.

32. Stendahl, "Paul and the Introspective Conscience."

33. Stowers, *Rereading Romans*, 1–4, 258–73; idem, "Romans 7:7–25 as a Speech-in-Character"; Harrill, "Paul and the Slave Self."

34. I thank Peter Brown for stressing this point.

35. Harrill, "Paul and the Slave Self," 52. See Fredriksen, "Paul and Augustine"; eadem, "Beyond the Body/Soul Dichotomy"; TeSelle, "Exploring the Inner Conflict"; BeDuhn, *Augustine's Manichaean Dilemma: 2*, 192–238; Mitchell, *Heavenly Trumpet*, 411–23. For Paul's debt to Plato, see Betz, "Concept of the 'Inner Human Being.'"

36. Stendahl, "Paul and the Introspective Conscience," 205.

37. Taylor, *Sources of the Self*, 139.

38. On the constructed, rhetorical character of the selves presented in the *Confessions*, see BeDuhn, *Augustine's Manichaean Dilemma: 1*, 9, 197–204, 238–40, 294–95; idem, *Augustine's Manichaean Dilemma: 2*, 314–68; Clark, "Rewriting Early Christian History"; O'Connell, *Images of Conversion*; Courcelle, *Recherches sur les Confessions*.

39. Athanasios, *Life of Antony* 55; John Chrysostom, *Homilies on Matthew* 41.6 (PG 57:540).

40. See Stelzenberger, "Conscientia."

41. John Chrysostom, *On Lazarus* 1.11 (PG 48.979); trans. Roth, *St. John Chrysostom: On Wealth and Poverty*, 34–35.

42. Rousseau, "Knowing Theodoret," 285.

43. For a standard interpretation see Dunn, *Theology of Paul*, 156–59, 472–77.

44. I thank Stratis Papaioannou for sharing his thoughts on the Byzantine vocabulary of selfhood.

45. Athanasios, *Letter to Markellinos* 11; trans. Gregg, *Life of Antony*, 109–10. See also Kolbet, "Athanasius, the Psalms"; Ernest, *Bible in Athanasius*, 332–36; Brakke, *Athanasius and Asceticism*, 194–96. For Christian psalmody in late antiquity, see Smith, *Music in Ancient Judaism and Early Christianity*, 198–206, 208–16.

46. Athanasios, *Letter to Markellinos* 12; trans. Gregg, 111. On affect and ancient rhetoric, see Webb, "Imagination and the Arousal of Emotions"; Agosti, "L'etopea nella poesia greca tardoantica," and Ventrella, "L'etopea nella definizione degli antichi retori." I have found Brennan, *Transmission of Affect* useful for thinking of broader implications.

47. Athanasios, *Letter to Markellinos* 11; trans, Gregg, 109.

48. Athanasios, *Letter to Markellinos* 12; trans. Gregg, 111.

49. Brakke, "Making Public the Monastic Life," 231.

50. For the classic description, see Stanislavsky, *An Actor Prepares*.

51. See Athanasios, *Letter to Markellinos* 14.

52. Athanasios, *Letter to Markellinos* 12; trans. Gregg, 111.

53. Krueger, "Old Testament in Monasticism," 217–19. On psalmody in the cathedral rite, see Taft, *Liturgy of the Hours in East and West*, 31–56, 165–90, 273–91.

54. Talbot, "Women's Space"; eadem, "Devotional Life of Laywomen." Dubowchik, "Singing with the Angels."

55. Taft, "Women at Church"; idem, "Women at Worship"; Gerstel, "Layperson in Church." Karras, "Liturgical Function of Consecrated Women." Evidence for laywomen's choirs in Byzantium

is considerably thinner than in the Syriac East; for a review of the Byzantine evidence, see Harvey, "Performance as Exegesis," 51–53.

56. See, for example, Gregory of Nyssa, *Life of Makrina* 3, 22, 34 (ed. Maraval); Gerontios, *Life of Melania the Younger* 26, 42 (ed. Gorce).

57. For reflection on the problems of extracting information about real people or historical subjects from literary accounts see Kraemer, *Unreliable Witnesses*. While Kraemer focuses on women, the problems apply also to men, and to Byzantium as much as to earlier periods. For examples of gendered figures as symbols see Harvey, "Bride of Blood."

58. Eve provides an example of a female figure instructive to both men and women. See Harrison, "Eve in Greek Patristic and Byzantine Theology"; Harvey, "Encountering Eve."

59. Getcha, *Typikon Decoded*, 15–21; Strunk, "Byzantine Office at Hagia Sophia"; Mateos, *La célébration de la parole*, 7–26; Parenti, "Cathedral Rite of Constantinople," 451–54.

60. Basil of Caesarea, *Longer Rules* 37 (trans. Wagner, 309), assigns the recitation to the third hour. Taft, *Liturgy of the Hours*, 40–41, 79, 87, 277–78. In monastic communities, Psalm 40 originally opened the morning office, although as the service assimilated elements from the night office, it was preceded by additional psalmody. Mateos, "Quelques problèmes de l'orthros byzantin," 216. Getcha, *Typikon Decoded*, 70, 75. For the recitation of Psalm 50 in the tradition of the Stoudios Monastery, see *BMFD*, 99 (even at Easter), 103.

61. Getcha, *Typikon Decoded*, 71–72. Taft, *Liturgy of the Hours*, 199. This is a different scheme from the Seven Penitential Psalms identified by Cassiodorus in the sixth century and used in the Roman Catholic tradition, especially during Lent, despite some overlap: Psalms 6, 31 [32], 37 [38], 50 [51], 101 [102], 129 [130], and 142 [143].

62. I thank Georgia Frank for stressing this point with me.

63. For practice at the Stoudios Monastery, see *BMFD* 102, 105, 113. For the omission in the week after Easter, see *BMFD* 99.

64. *BMFD* 102, version A; although in version B (attested in a ninth- or tenth-century manuscript) this instruction is in the passive: "the Six Psalms are begun."

65. See for example Sinai gr. 1094 (12th century), ff. 3v–4r, 71r., and Sin gr. 1096 (dated 1214), f. 157v. Trans. in Getcha, *Typikon Decoded*, 72. Getcha cites Losky, *Le typicon byzantin*, which I was unable to consult.

66. Trans. in Getcha, *Typikon Decoded*, 72.

67. Theodoret of Cyrrhus, *Commentary on the Psalms*, PG 80:901; trans. Hill, 1:74.

68. For Augustine's doctrine of original sin, see *City of God* 13.4, 14 (text and trans. Levine, 144–49, 180–81); *On Nature and Grace* (trans. in *Four Anti-Pelagian Writings*, trans. Mourant and Collinge, 22–90); and *On the Grace of Christ and On Original Sin* (trans. in Oates, *Basic Writings of Saint Augustine*, 582–654). Augustine's teaching depended in part on the Latin version of Romans 5:12. The Greek reads, "As sin came into the world though one human, and through sin, death, so death spread to all humans because all have sinned." But the Latin translation has rendered the text, "so death spread to all humans *in whom* [i.e. Adam] all humans have sinned." See Meyendorff, "*Ἐφ' ᾧ* (Rom. 5,12)"; Bonner, "Augustine on Romans 5,12"; Burns, "Interpretation of Romans." For an accessible general account, see Pagels, *Adam, Eve, and the Serpent*, 108–11, 143; and for the trajectory

in the Latin tradition, Wiley, *Original Sin*. For a contextual study of the impact and expression of Western theories of sin, see Delumeau, *Sin and Fear*, 245–81.

69. For an excellent overview, see Meyendorff, *Byzantine Theology*, 143–46. Maximos the Confessor (*Asketikon* 44; PG 90:956) did argue that Christians "were freed by holy baptism from ancestral sin," but without a theory for the transmission of this sin; see Pelikan, *Christian Tradition*. 2:182–83; Daley, "Making a Human Will Divine"; Thunberg, *Microcosm and Mediator*, 160–61, 226–30.

70. Andrew of Crete, *Great Kanon* 1.16–18, 24–25. The phrase echoes Deuteronomy 28:48, although the meaning is quite different.

71. John Klimax, *Ladder of Paradise* 7; PG 88:809; trans. Luibheid and Russell, 141.

72. Ibid.; PG 88:801; trans. 136 (modified).

73. Symeon the New Theologian, *Catechetical Discourses* 5.160–275 (ed. Krivocheine). See Chapter 7.

74. Althusser, "Ideology and State Apparatuses"; Butler, *The Psychic Life of Power*, 106–31. See also eadem, *Excitable Speech*, 24.

75. For the history and character of the liturgical calendar, see Velkovska, "Liturgical Year in the East"; and Bradshaw and Johnson, *Origins of Feasts*, which substantially revises the views of Talley, *Origins of the Liturgical Calendar*.

76. Mateos, *La célébration de la parole*, 127–47.

77. Christmas: GL lection 30; Mateos, *Typicon*, 1:159. Theophany: GL lection 114; Mateos, *Typicon*, 1:187.

78. GL lections 686, 690, 694, 698; Mateos, *Typicon*, 2:81.

79. English translations of AL and GL in a convenient schema are available at http://www. bombaxo.com/lectionaries.html. For descriptions and discussion, see Baldovin, *Urban Character*, 64–80.

80. Mateos, *Typicon*, 1:x–xix; Baldovin, *Urban Character*, 190–97; Getcha, *Typikon Decoded*, 40–42.

81. Mateos, *Typicon*, 2:129. Psalm 46 [47] had been associated with Ascension in Jerusalem since the fourth century; Frank, "Sensing Ascension," 299–303.

82. GL lections 13–23, 722–35; Mateos, *Typicon*, 1:149–55, 2:85–91. Bertonière, *Historical Development of the Easter Vigil*.

83. Chatzidakis, "Encaustic Icon," 4; Belting, *Likeness and Presence*, 133; Büchsel, *Die Entstehung des Christusporträts*, 45–50. On the history of the representation of Christ's face, see also *Il volto di Cristo*, ed. Morello and Wolf.

Chapter 2. Romanos the Melodist and the Christian Self

1. In addition to Romanos, *Hymns*, and Grosdidier de Matons, ed., *Romanos le Mélode: Hymnes*, the poems appear with emendations in Maisano, ed. *Cantici di Romano il Melodo*. Where possible I have employed the fine translations of Lash, *On the Life of Christ: Kontakia*, occasionally modified. Translations of other hymns are my own, although I have consulted Schork, trans.,

Sacred Song from the Byzantine Pulpit, and Carpenter, trans., *Kontakia of Romanos*. Especially useful is the German translation and commentary of Koder, *Romanos Melodos: Die Hymnen*.

2. On the dialogic qualities of the hymns see Dubrov, "Dialogue with Death"; Frank, "Dialogue and Deliberation."

3. Louth in Lash, *On the Life of Christ*, xvi.

4. Frank, "Romanos and the Night Vigil."

5. In some cases, a hymn survives with different preludes in different manuscripts, and it can be hard to tell which reflects the original composition or whether Romanos composed new preludes for some of his hymns at a later date. The cantor sings in the first person in the first or final strophes of *Hymns* 3, 5, 6, 9, 10, 12, 21, 29, 30, 31, 34, 37, 40, 41, 44, 47, 48, 49, 52, 54, 55, 56, 57; in addition to these, we find the first person singular in the preludes of 7, 21, 50, 51. See also Barkhuizen, "Analysis of the Form and Content."

6. Barkhuizen, "Romanos and the Composition of His Hymns," 62–77. See also Grosdidier de Matons, "Liturgie et hymnographie."

7. For a summary of what little we know of the music and the performance practice, see Koder, "Imperial Propaganda," 286–90; Raasted, "Zum Melodie." On the emergence of accentual metrics in the kontakion, see Lauxtermann, *Spring of Rhythm*, 55–61.

8. On the form and meter of the hymns, see Grosdidier de Matons, *Romanos et les origines*, 3–37. On the refrains see Koder, "Romanos Melodos und sein Publikum," 63–69; idem, "Imperial Propaganda," 288–90.

9. Lingas, "Liturgical Place of the Kontakion"; Grosdidier de Matons, "Liturgie et hymnographie"; idem, "Aux origines de l'hymnographie byzantine"; Krueger, *Writing and Holiness*, 166–69; Frank, "Romanos and the Night Vigil." Some hymns may have been composed for occasions other than the Night Vigil. Some possible exceptions include the *Prayer of Romanos* (56) and *On Earthquakes and Fires* (54). However, Koder, "Imperial Propaganda," 280–82, has read *On Earthquakes and Fires* as a Lenten hymn.

10. For a review of the evidence, see Taft, "Women at Worship," 275–79; idem, *Liturgy of the Hours in East and West*, 165–87; idem, "Women at Church," 72–74. For men and women at vigils in the Syrian Christian world, see Harvey, "Liturgy and Ethics," 302.

11. *Life of Matrona of Perge* 2–3; text: *Acta Sanctorum Novembris*, 3:791, 794; trans. Featherstone, 20.

12. See, for example, *Miracles of Artemios* 10, 12, 34, 44, and 45. For the chanting of Romanos, see 18.

13. Romanos, *Hymns* 47.31 (SC 31). The manuscript tradition preserves multiple versions of the hymn *On the Ten Virgins I*. The first strophe appears in all manuscripts, and the final strophe is secure even in variant forms of the hymn. See Grosdidier de Matons, *Romanos le Mélode: Hymnes*, 3:303–23.

14. Mateos, *Typicon*, 2:68–71; GL 615. Cf. AL 36, and see Renoux's discussion in AL, 1:118–22. Morozowich, "Jerusalem Celebration of Great Week," 105–6. Maisano, *Cantici*, 1:99–102, provides a useful table indicating the place of each poem within the liturgical cycle according to the assignments in the manuscripts, the earliest of which date from the tenth and eleventh centuries. Koder, *Romanos Melodos: Die Hymnen*, reorders the hymns to reflect the course of a middle Byzantine liturgical year as ascribed in the manuscripts.

15. Cameron, *Christianity and the Rhetoric of Empire*, 57.

16. For the discussion of the sources for Romanos's biography, see Grosdidier de Matons, *Romanos le Mélode et les origines*, 159–98. See also Schork, *Sacred Song*, 3–6; Lash, *On the Life of Christ*, xxvi–xviii; Maisano, *Cantici*, 1:9–11, 33–38; Koder, "Romanos Melodos und sein Publikum," 63–69; idem, *Romanos Melodos: Die Hymnen*, 1:9–14, 25–33; Hunger, "Romanos Melodos, Dichter, Prediger, Rhetor," 16; Krueger, *Writing and Holiness*, 166–69.

17. See, for example, Koder, "Justinians Sieg über Salomon"; idem, "Imperial Propaganda," 275–92; Scott, "Justinian's New Age."

18. See Krueger, *Writing and Holiness*, 169–74 (on Romanos's acrostics) and 94–109 (on authorial performances of humility).

19. On the impact of hearing such literary texts in Byzantium, see Bourbouhakis, "Rhetoric and Performance."

20. Mateos, *Typicon*, 2:2–3; TR, 34–41. See Chapter 6.

21. Writing in the mid-sixth century, Dorotheos of Gaza explained the addition of two weeks to Lent, making for an eight-week period leading up to Easter, which would include this Sunday; *Discourses* 15.159–60 (ed. Regnault and de Préville, 446–49; trans., Wheeler, 215–16). Theophanes the Confessor includes the curious report that in 546, Justinian delayed the abstinence from meat in a year when there was confusion about the dating of Easter, effectively declaring an eight-week period, instead of nine (*Chronography*, ed. de Boor, 225; trans. Mango and Scott, 326–27). In any case, Romanos would have known a period of abstinence beginning with the eighth Sunday before Easter, that is, from Meatfare Sunday. On the other hand, the Jerusalem lectionary (GL 283–89) does not assign particularly apocalyptic passages. See also Bertonière, *Sundays of Lent*, 30, 46–47, for divergence in the lectionary assignments.

22. Romanos, *Hymns* 34.1 (SC 50); trans. Lash, 221. Scott ("Justinian's New Age") and Verghese ("Kaiserkritik in Two Kontakia"), have seen this poem as part of a larger theme of eschatological expectation within Romanos's corpus and have tied it to worries about the end of the world in light of the many disasters of the sixth century. On the one hand, this strain in Romanos's thought reflects the lectionary, where biblical passages about the coming of the End appeared at their appointed times and usually prompted worries about individual salvation. On the other, I suspect it was inevitable that some would hear this material as a harbinger of the eschaton. The discourse of divine punishment was not usually an eschatological discourse in itself. More research into these issues would be helpful.

23. Romanos, *Hymns* 56 (SC 55). See Barkhuizen, "Romanos, Kontakion 55SC." Grosdidier de Matons, *Hymnes*, 5:501–2.

24. Romanos, *Hymns* 41.1 (SC 3). Bertonière, *Sundays of Lent*, 57–61. The manuscript Patmos 213 (eleventh century) assigns a cycle of poems on Old Testament figures to the Sundays of Lent. Given that these assignments do not occur in other middle Byzantine kontakaria (the service books containing the kontakia assigned to various days), Bertonière (*Sundays of Lent*, 58) has argued, "there is a good chance that this manuscript has preserved for us a glimpse of the liturgical themes of these Sundays in an earlier age." See also Grosdidier de Matons, *Hymns*, 1:129–30. On kontakaria, see Grosdidier de Matons, *Romanos et les origines*, 67–118; Koder, *Romanos Melodos: Die Hymnen*, 1:35–36. It is unclear whether in the sixth century Constantinople already lacked Old Testament

readings during the Divine Liturgy, as was certainly the case in the ensuing centuries. For the place of the Old Testament in the Byzantine lectionary cycle, see J. Miller, "Prophetologion." Before the ninth century, Old Testament passages were largely relegated to vigils of the major festivals and Vespers services during Lent, precisely when it would seem Romanos's hymns were sung.

25. See Augustine, *Confessions* 7.8.

26. *On Joseph II*; Romanos, *Hymns* 44 (SC 6). For discussion of this poem, see Grosdidier de Matons, *Romanos le Mélode: Hymnes*, 1:247–50; Barkhuizen, "Romanos, On the Temptation of Joseph." For parallels in Jewish piyyutim, see Lieber, "The Play's the Thing."

27. Basil of Caesarea, *Hexaemeron* 7.5.29 (ed. Giet): Πάντα σκοπεύει ὁ ἀκοίμητος ὀφθαλμός. The "unsleeping eye" also appears in a number of homilies spuriously attributed to John Chrysostom that could either pre- or post-date Romanos.

28. For this reading, see Maisano, *Cantici* 1:90; 2:260.

29. For the forensic images in the poem see Barkhuizen, "Romanos, On the Temptation of Joseph," 12–14.

30. Romanos, *Hymns* 30.18 (SC 46); trans. Lash, 190–91.

31. Krueger, *Writing and Holiness*, 94–109.

32. Romanos, *Hymns* 17.5 (SC 33); trans. Lash, 117. On this poem, see the remarks of Barkhuizen, "Narrative Apostrophe"; Louth in Lash, *On the Life of Christ*, 21; Frank, "Romanos and the Night Vigil," 67–70.

33. Romanos, *Hymns* 17.15; trans. Lash, 121, modified.

34. GL indicates that in late antique Jerusalem, Matthew's account of Judas's betrayal (Mt 26:14–16, 47–50) was read in two parts, roughly when their events might fall in the course of the week's marking of these episodes: Mt 26:2–16 (GL 623; cf. AL 37bis and Renoux's discussion in AL 1:123–28) was read at Vespers on Wednesday of Holy Week (thus preceding the Vigil for Holy Thursday), while Mt 26:36–56 (GL 653; AL 40ter and 1:140–42) was read on Holy Thursday at Gethsemane. See also Morozowich, "Jerusalem Celebration of Great Week," 107, 111–12. Luke's and John's accounts were also read in the course of Holy Thursday in Jerusalem; GL 625, 640, 644, 647. This structure for readings is also attested in tenth-century Constantinople, where Matthew's account was read roughly when its events might fall in the course of the week's commemoration: For Vespers on Wednesday of Holy Week the lection was Mt 26:6–16, while Mt 26:40–27:2 was among the group of Gospel readings for the Divine Liturgy on Holy Thursday (Mateos, *Typicon* 2:70–77). If these were the lections in the sixth century, Romanos's poem would have fit perfectly at the Vigil for Holy Thursday, sung just after Wednesday Vespers. The account in John 18 was part of a long sequence of lections from John's passion at the vigil kept on Thursday night, the eve of Good Friday (Mateos, *Typicon*, 2:76–77).

35. Taft, *Precommunion Rites*, 307–13; Schattauer, "Koinonicon," 109–10; Krueger, "Christian Piety and Practice," 292–97.

36. Romanos, *Hymns* 10 (SC 21). Maas and Trypanis title the hymn *On the Sinful Woman*, but the manuscripts have *On the Harlot*. On other aspects of this hymn see Frank, "Dialogue and Deliberation," 169–71; and Harvey, "Spoken Words, Voiced Silence," 120–24; eadem, "Why the Perfume Mattered."

37. Maisano, "Romanos's Use of Greek Patristic Sources," 269. The tradition goes back as far as

Origen's *Homilies on Jeremiah* 15.5 (PG 13:436A). See also the early sixth-century catena on the Book of Mark: Lamb, *The* Catena in Marcum, 414–17.

38. Grosdidier de Matons, *Hymnes* 3:12–15. This was the assignment for Jerusalem in late antiquity: see AL 37bis (2:264–65); GL 623. In tenth-century Constantinople, the relevant pericope was heard both at Vespers on Holy Wednesday and at the Divine Liturgy on Holy Thursday; Mateos, *Typicon*, 2:70–71, 76–77

39. For consideration of this point with respect to hagiography, see P. Miller, "Strategies of Representation"; Krueger, *Writing and Holiness*, 17–27, 191–97.

40. This contrasts with Augustine's *Confessions*, a work that initially circulated only among other learned readers. For the perplexity of one early reader of the *Confessions*, see the letter by Consentius to Augustine (*Letter 12**, ed. Divjak, 70–80; trans. Eno, 99–108).

41. Kennedy, *Progymnasmata*; Agosti, "L'etopea nella poesia greca tardoantica"; Ventrella, "L'etopea nella definizione degli antichi retori."

42. For Romanos's proficiency in a variety of rhetorical techniques, see Gador-Whyte, *Theology and Poetry in Early Byzantium*.

43. Sellew ("Interior Monologue") has identified brief instances of interiority in the Gospel of Luke, where Jesus as a narrator has insight into the thoughts of characters in the stories he tells. These are not opportunities to present moral reflection of the sort we find in Romanos.

44. Romanos, *Hymns* 30.7.4–6 (SC 46); trans. Lash, 186. On other aspects of this hymn, see Krueger, *Writing and Holiness*, 178–81. On the assignment to the Sunday after Easter, see Grosdidier de Matons, *Hymnes* 5:13–15. Cf. AL 52bis (2:324–25); GL 746 (Jn 20:26–31); Mateos, *Typicon*, 108–9 (Jn 20:19–31).

45. He also engages to himself, in retrospect, in theological analogy, comparing Christ's appearance in the closed room to the Virgin birth: "Had I managed to learn that it was thus he had come, / I would not have doubted for I had only to think / of his entering and coming forth from Mary" (9.5–7).

46. Matthew 26:6–13 follows Mark 14:3–9 in placing the action in the house of Simon the Leper, but Luke 7:36–50 alters the venue to the house of a Pharisee. For the interiority of the Sinful Woman in the broader tradition, see Harvey, "Why the Perfume Mattered"; Hunt, *Joy-Bearing Grief*, 114–25.

47. Romanos, *Hymns* 9 (SC 19). The poem survives in a single manuscript where the text is both corrupted and damaged in places, making reconstruction of some passages difficult. Its original liturgical assignment is uncertain, although likely sometime after Easter. See Grosdidier de Matons, 2:323–24.

48. Reading Grosdidier de Matons's correction (*Hymnes*, 2:346): ἐν ἀνθρώπῳ rather than the manuscript's ἐν οὐρανῷ, which does not make sense or scan properly. See also Lash, 70n17.

49. Romanos invokes this verse elsewhere in his corpus. Joseph protests to Potiphar's Wife, "How can I deceive the examiner of hearts and kidneys" (*Hymns*, 44.17.9). See also, *On the Resurrection VI*, *Hymns* 29.10.1, when Mary Magdalene recognizes Christ, and *On Doubting Thomas*, *Hymns* 30.10.2–3.

50. PG 55:95. John Chrysostom, *Commentary on the Psalms*, trans. Hill, 1:131–32 (modified).

51. PG 80:912. Theodoret of Cyrrhus, *Commentary on the Psalms*, trans. Hill, 1:79.

52. The text is corrupt here. Grosdidier de Matons (2:332) supplies οἱ διψῶντες.

53. Grosdidier de Matons, *Hymns*, 2:323–25.

54. Romanos, *Hymns* 8, prelude (SC 20); trans. Lash, 51. On this hymn see also Krueger, *Writing and Holiness*, 174–78.

55. See Grosdidier de Matons, *Hymnes*, 2:364–65n1.

56. Romanos, *Hymns* 19 (SC 35). On healing and salvation with reference to *On Mary at the Cross*, see Krueger, "Healing and the Scope of Religion."

57. For the sinfulness of acts against nature identified with same-sex sexual activity in Romans 1:26–27 among patristic authors, see John Chrysostom, *Homilies on Romans* 4 (on Romans 1:26–27), PG 50:417–22; trans. NPNF 1.11:355–56; partial translation with notes in Boswell, *Christianity, Social Tolerance, and Homosexuality*, 359–62 (see also 109–12, 156–57); Martin, "Heterosexism and the Interpretation of Romans."

58. Rogers (*After the Spirit*, 98–104) addresses Romanos's usage of the phrase "against nature," including in *On the Leper*. An early sixth-century commentator, however, stresses that while the Leper's body was afflicted, his mind and heart were clean; Lamb, *The* Catena in Marcum, 239–40.

59. Romanos, *Hymns* 7.1–6; trans. Lash, 53–54. Romanos conflates the man at the pool of Bethesda in Jn 5:1–9 with the paralytic of Mt 9:2–7; see Lash, 245.

60. On the peculiarly hybrid oral and written nature of his supplication, see Krueger, *Writing and Holiness*, 175–76.

61. Romanos, *Hymns* 12.13.1 (SC 23); my trans. The poem survives only in Patmos 213, which assigns it to the Wednesday of the sixth week after Easter, that is, the eve of Ascension. But there is not much reason to be confident that this was the original ascription. Cf. Lamb, *The* Catena in Marcum, 288.

62. Grosdidier de Matons (*Hymnes*, 3:79–83) has seen the close relation between these two hymns.

63. Romanos puns on στολή, a stole, and επιστολή, an epistle.

64. Romanos also grants a glimpse of the Virgin Mary's interiority. See Harvey, "On Mary's Voice"; Arentzen, "Your Virginity Shines."

65. For an index of quotations of Paul in Romanos, see Maisano, *Cantici*, 2:634–37.

66. Romanos, *Hymns* 56.5.2–3 (SC 55).

67. GL attests a relatively sequential reading of Acts during the paschal season in the Holy Land at the end of the seventh century. AL attests this practice only for the octave of Easter. In both cases, Acts takes the place of the Old Testament lection, and is followed by the Epistle and Gospel reading. GL assigns Acts 9:1–22 to the second Thursday after Pascha.

68. Much later, the tenth-century *Typikon* for Hagia Sophia lacks a commemoration of the conversion of Paul on January 25 that would correspond with Western practice but does include observances for the Feast of Peter and Paul on June 29, as does GL for Jerusalem from around 700. Mateos, *Typicon*, 1:322–27; GL 1066.

69. Romanos, *Hymns* 23.20.3–6 (SC 39).

70. Romanos, *Hymns* 31.21 (SC 47).

71. Maisano, *Cantici*, 2:617–20.

72. Lampe, s. v., esp. III.

73. Kolbet, "Athanasius, the Psalms"; Ernest, *Bible in Athanasius*, 332–36; Brakke, *Athanasius*

and Asceticism, 194–96; Krueger, "Old Testament in Monasticism," 217–19; Frank, "Memory Palace of Marcellinus."

74. *Life of Mary of Egypt*, PG 87:3697–726; trans. Kouli in *Holy Women of Byzantium*, ed. Talbot, 65–93. Burrus, *Sex Lives of Saints*, 147–55; P. Miller, "Is There a Harlot in This Text?"; Krueger, "Mary at the Threshold."

75. Romanos, *Hymns* 52, prelude (SC 8A). The poem survives in only one manuscript and lacks Romanos's name in the acrostic, which has raised some questions about its authorship. However, Grosdidier de Matons (*Hymnes*, 1:405–8) and Koder (*Die Hymnen*, 1:409–10) have argued for its authenticity.

76. Romanos, *Hymns* 48.15 (SC 51); my trans. For discussion of this strophe, see Grosdidier de Matons, *Hymnes* 5:318–21.

77. Dorotheos, *Discourses* 3, 7.

78. Romanos, *Hymns* 55 (SC 53). The original occasion for the composition is unclear, and it may in fact not have been written for a Night Vigil. The manuscripts indicate that the hymn was later assigned to the Saturday of the pre-Lenten Cheesefare Week, where it encouraged enthusiasm for fasting. See Grosdidier de Matons, *Hymnes*, 5:373–74.

79. See Koder, "Romanos der Melode: Der Dichter"; idem, *Romanos Melodos: Die Hymnen*, 1:37.

80. Crisafulli and Nesbitt, *Miracles of St. Artemios*, 114–15. For speculation that the cantor in question is none other than the anonymous author of the miracle collection, see Efthymiadis, "A Day and Ten Months in the Life of a Lonely Bachelor." A quotation of the refrain of Romanos's hymn *On the Harlot* in the *Life of Mary of Egypt* attests the poem's liturgical use in Palestine in the seventh century. See *Life of Mary of Egypt* 23: "A salvific word touched the eyes of my heart, showing me that it was '*The filth of my deeds*' that was barring entrance [to the Church of the Anastasis in Jerusalem]."

81. Lingas, "Liturgical Place," 54–56.

82. *BMFD* 1:99A for the Stoudios Monastery in the ninth century. On the contents of the kontakaria, service books with the parts of these compositions to be chanted during the performance of the kanon hymn during Morning Prayer in medieval monasteries, see Grosdidier de Matons, *Romanos le Mélode et les origines*, 67–93, 98–118. See also Lingas, "Liturgical Place of the Kontakion," 56.

Chapter 3. Calendar and Community in the Sixth Century

1. Gonosová and Kondoleon, *Art of Late Rome and Byzantium*, 274–77, cat. no. 95. For a listing of other examples, see Richter-Siebles, *Die palästinensischen Weihrauchgefäße*, 1:13–39. For an especially refined treatment in Munich, see *Byzanz: Das Licht aus dem Osten*, 187–89. At the Princeton Art Museum, see Ćurčić and St. Clair, *Byzantium at Princeton*, 76–77, cat. no. 56. At Dumbarton Oaks, *Handbook of the Byzantine Collection*, 34–35, cat. no. 124; Vikan, *Early Byzantine Pilgrimage Art*, 66–68. At the Brooklyn Museum, *Late Egyptian and Coptic Art*, 19–20, pl. no. 34.

2. The Passover takes place at the full moon, the fourteenth of Nisan, according to the lunar Jewish calendar. Thus both the sun and the moon shine on that day, offering continuous lighting. See Daniélou, *Bible and Liturgy*, 297–301. The sun and the moon also appear in the crucifixion

scene in a manuscript folio now interleaved in the Rabbula Gospels, dated to 586 and produced near Apamea in Syria. Rouwhorst ("Liturgical Background of the Crucifixion and Resurrection Scene") has noted that the iconography for this page of the Rabbula Gospels bears a resemblance to the scene as described in fourth-century hymns of Ephrem the Syrian on the crucifixion that had become canonical for recitation in northern Mesopotamia in the sixth or seventh century.

3. Harvey, *Scenting Salvation*, 75–79, 134–48. Taft, *Liturgy of the Hours in East and West*, 39, 42–43, 51.

4. Pantanella, "Reliquary Box," in *Treasures of Heaven*, ed. Bagnoli et al., 36 (cat. no. 13); Bergman et al., *Vatican Treasures*, 30–33; Krueger, "Religion of Relics," 11; Reudenbach, "Reliquien von Orten"; Morey, "Painted Panel from the Sancta Sanctorum," 151–68. The current arrangement of rocks and wood inside the box is not original; see Krueger, "Liturgical Time and Holy Land Reliquaries," n. 3.

5. Egeria, *Travels*, trans. Wilkinson, 16–22, 34–35; Vikan, "Early Byzantine Pilgrimage *Devotionalia*"; idem, *Early Byzantine Pilgrimage Art*, 11–12, 37–39; Weitzmann, "*Loca Sancta* and Representational Arts." For consideration of the ways in which travel might be encapsulated within texts, see Johnson, "Apostolic Geography."

6. Elsner, "Replicating Palestine," 120; Krueger, "Liturgical Time and Holy Land Reliquaries." On the formation of the desire for pilgrimage, see Frank, *Memory of the Eyes*. For a classic treatment of place, space, and time, see Smith, *To Take Place*.

7. Vikan, *Early Byzantine Pilgrimage Art*, 66–68; Krueger, "Liturgical Time and Holy Land Reliquaries."

8. See for example, Orsi, *Between Heaven and Earth*, 67–68.

9. For Romanos's biography, see Grosdidier de Matons, *Romanos le Mélode et les origines*, 159–98; Koder, "Romanos Melodos und sein Publikum," 63–69; idem, *Romanos Melodos: Die Hymnen*, 1:9–14, 25–33; Hunger, "Romanos Melodos, Dichter, Prediger, Rhetor," 16; Krueger, *Writing and Holiness*, 166–69.

10. Text: *Leontii presbyteri Constantinopolitani: Homiliae*, ed. Datema and Allen; trans. and study: Leontius, Presbyter of Constantinople, *Fourteen Homilies*, trans. Allen and Datema. Allen, "Sixth-Century Greek Homily." For additional historical background, see Cunningham, "Homilies."

11. Allen and Datema in *Leontii presbyteri Constantinopolitani: Homiliae*, 54–58.

12. Elsner, "Iconoclasm as Discourse," 369. See also P. Miller, *Corporeal Imagination*, 148–78. For assessment of the theories elaborated in the course of the iconoclastic controversy, see Barber, *Figure and Likeness*.

13. Grabar, *L'empereur dans l'art byzantin*; Kartsonis, "Responding Icon." For shifts in attitudes toward and strategies for the representation of emperors, see Elsner, *Art and the Roman Viewer*, 157–89.

14. Freedberg, "Holy Images and Other Images."

15. For an overview of the calendar and its development, see Velkovska, "Liturgical Year," 157–76.

16. Barkhuizen, "Poetics of his Kontakion 'Resurrection of Christ,'" 18, characterizes Romanos as "a narrator of the *authorial* type, i.e., characterized by his omnipresence and his omniscience. As such he is no actor of the narrative, and is consequently a *non-dramatized informant*. But he may *dramatize* himself, becoming manifest in the narrative proper as well as in the non-narrative texts."

17. For a fuller treatment of this theme against the backdrop of sixth- and seventh-century Christian religious practice, see Krueger, "Liturgical Time and Holy Land Reliquaries."

18. Talley, *Origins of the Liturgical Year*. Taft, "Historicism Revisited."

19. Bradshaw and Johnson, *Origins of Feasts*, 89–90, emphasis in original. See, for example, a sermon on the festival of the Calends (that is, New Year's) of Asterios of Amasea (c. 375–405) emphasizing "recollection" and "rejoicing." Asterios of Amasea, *Sermon* 4.2: Ἀνάμνησίς ἐστιν καὶ εὐφροσύνη ἐνιαυτοῦ (ed. Datema, 39–43; trans. Anderson and Goodspeed, 111–29).

20. Bradshaw and Johnson, *Origins of Feasts*, 119. Stevenson (*Jerusalem Revisited*, 9) termed such liturgies "rememorative."

21. Gregory of Nazianzos, *Orations* 38.1; 39.14; 45.1 (ed. Moreschini). *Oration* 41 can be found in PG 36:625–64. See Harrison, in Gregory of Nazianzus, *Festal Orations*, 24–33; eadem, "Gregory Nazianzen's Festal Spirituality"; Tollefsen, "*Theosis* according to Gregory," 265.

22. Galavaris, *Illustrations of the Liturgical Homilies*, 6–17; Harrison, *Festal Orations*, 12, 191–92; Karavites, "Gregory of Nazianzinos and Byzantine Hymnography"; Noret, "Grégoire de Nazianze."

23. Proklos, *Homily 4: On the Birthday of the Lord*, ll. 75–85 (ed. Constas, *Proclus of Constantinople and the Cult of the Virgin*, 186–206); Proklos, *Homily 24: On the Nativity of the Lord* 1.1, 4.4, 7.3, 11.2–7, 12.4 (ed. Martin, "Un florilège grec," 40–48); Proklos, *Homily 29: On the Crucifixion*, 2.5.1–3 (ed. Leroy, *L'Homiletique de Proclus*, 204–12). On Proklos, see Barkhuizen, "Proclus of Constantinople"; and the introduction to *Proclus Bishop of Constantinople*, trans. Barkhuizen.

24. Jacob of Sarug, *On the Resurrection* [Homily 54], in Jacob of Sarug, *Homilies on the Resurrection*, ed. Kollamparampil, 6–33, esp. lines 1, 9, 15, 17, 19, 23, 25, 29. On Jacob's audience, see Harvey, "To Whom Did Jacob Preach?"

25. The best introduction to the early history of the major festivals is Bradshaw and Johnson, *Origins of Feasts*. For Christmas, see 123–30. Bradshaw and Johnson revised the work of Talley, *Origins of the Liturgical Calendar*.

26. Romanos, *Hymns* 1, prelude and 1 (SC 10); trans. Lash, 3 (modified). Compare Romanos's hymn *On the Nativity II* (*Hymns* 2 prelude [SC 11]). For an attempt to reconstruct the original melody from later manuscripts, see Raasted, "Zum Melodie des Kontakions Ἡ παρθένος σήμερον."

27. *New Oxford Book of Carols*, ed. Keyte et al., 238–43.

28. Grabar, *Ampoules de Terre Sainte*, 16–17, plate II (Monza 1; cf. Monza 3). Krueger, "Religion of Relics," 11.

29. Vikan, "Pilgrims in Magi's Clothing," 103–4 (emphasis in original). For additional examples of pilgrims' tokens see idem, *Early Byzantine Pilgrimage Art*, 32–33; Hahn, "Loca Sancta Souvenirs."

30. Romanos, *Hymns* 29.1.7–10 (SC 40); trans. Lash, 167–68. Of the six poems *On the Resurrection* in the Patmos manuscript, which contains complete kontakia, only this one is well represented in monastic kontakaria, service books indicating the excerpts from Romanos (usually the prelude and first strophe) to be sung during middle Byzantine monastic Morning Prayer. One Stoudite Pentakostarion, Vat. gr. 778, dated to 1170, gives six strophes of the hymn for Morning Prayer on Easter Sunday; Bertonière, *Historical Development of the Easter Vigil*, 205.

31. Grabar, *Ampoules de Terre Sainte*, 17; see also 18, 20, 21, 23. Compare the inscriptions on Monza 2, 3, 4 (where it encircles the Virgin and Child Flanked by Angels), 6 (where it encircles the Crucifixion).

32. AL 1, 2 (2:211, 217), see also 1:75–78. GL 3, 9. A sixth-century East Syrian lectionary confirms the use of these verses beyond Jerusalem. Burkitt, *Early Syriac Lectionary System*, 6 (where

both verses are assigned to Epiphany), see also 28, 31. Mt. 1:23 was assigned to both Christmas and Epiphany. Mateos, *Typicon*, 1:153, 2:183. See also Baldovin, *Urban Character of Christian Worship*, 190–92.

33. Leontios the Presbyter, *Homilies* 12.1 (ll. 4–7); trans. Allen and Datema, 172.

34. Leontios the Presbyter, *Homilies* 12.1 (ll. 16–17); trans. Allen and Datema, 172, and discussion 168. On the use of anaphora and other forms of repetition, see Allen, "Sixth-century Greek Homily," 212–13.

35. Leontios the Presbyter, *Homilies* 12.1 (ll. 18–19); trans. Allen and Datema, 172.

36. On Theophany/Epiphany in the late antique East, see Bradshaw and Johnson, *Origins of Feasts*, 131–51.

37. Romanos, *Hymns* 5, prelude (SC 16); trans. Lash, 39 (modified).

38. See also Krueger, *Writing and Holiness*, 182–84.

39. On baptism as clothing in Christ, see Hunt, *Clothed in the Body*, 143–48.

40. Bradshaw and Johnson, *Origins of Feasts*, 159, 210; Calabuig, "Liturgical Cult of Mary," 256. Van Esbroeck, "La lettre de l'empereur Justinien."

41. *Byzantium and Islam*, ed. Evans and Ratliff, 91; Buckton, *Byzantium: Treasures*, 114–15, cat. no. 130. Gerard et al., "Argiles et eulogies en forme de jetons," 9–24. For the broader corpus, see Sodini, "La terre de semelles." For Mary's work in textile production, see Constas, "Weaving the Body of God."

42. Romanos, *Hymns* 36.1.1–4 (SC 9); my trans. On other aspects of this hymn see Arentzen, "Your Virginity Shines."

43. Romanos, *Hymns* 1.5–10. On the obvious parallels with the fifth-century *Akathistos* hymn, see Grosdidier de Matons, *Hymnes*, 2:22.

44. *Sacrorum conciliorum nova et amplissima collectio*, ed. Mansi, 13:269BC; trans. Sahas, *Icon and Logos*, 98 (modified). For additional discussion, see Kartsonis, "Protection Against All Evil," 99; Brubaker and Haldon, *Byzantium in the Iconoclast Era: The Sources*, 236–37.

45. Romanos, *Hymns* 16.1.1–3 (SC 32); my trans.

46. Egeria, *Travels* 31. For Jerusalem, GL 584 and 594 assign Mk 11:1–10 to the processional liturgy on Palm Sunday and Mt 21:1–17 to an extended cycle of readings for the Eucharist. For the lection from Matthew, see also AL 34 and 1:110–13. For Constantinople, Mateos, *Typicon*, 2:182 (in a supplement reflecting Palestinian influence) assigns Mt 21.1–11, 15–17 to Morning Prayer; Baldovin, *Urban Character of Christian Worship*, 61, 98. For a complete discussion of the sources see Morozowich, "Palm Sunday Procession." For an eighth-century witness to two prayers to be recited over those processing on Palm Sunday, see Parenti and Velkovska, *L'Eucologio Barberini*, 204–5. For additional evidence, we can look to the ironic reversal of the Entry into Jerusalem in Leontios of Neapolis's *Life of Symeon the Fool*; see Krueger, *Symeon the Holy Fool*, 111–13.

47. Romanos, *Hymns* 16.16.9–10; on the textual and translation challenges of line 9, see Grosdidier de Matons, *Hymnes*, 4:53.

48. Mateos, *Typicon*, 2:66–67; Allen and Datema in Leontios the Presbyter, *Fourteen Homilies*, 31–34. The sermon was subsequently popular in at least two recensions, as attested in over seventy manuscripts; *Leontii presbyteri Constantinopolitani: Homiliae*, ed. Datema and Allen, 103–49.

49. Leontios the Presbyter, *Homilies* 3.1 (ll. 1–19); trans. Allen and Datema, 51.

50. Ibid. 3.18 (ll. 227–47); trans. Allen and Datema, 57.

51. Ibid. 2.2 (ll. 23–25); trans. Allen and Datema, 40.

52. On the olfactory world of early Byzantine Christianity, see Harvey, *Scenting Salvation*.

53. Codex purpureus rossanensis, 2. See Loerke in *Codex purpureus rossanensis*, 115, 123–26. The oldest surviving illustrated Greek Gospel book, its provenance is unclear, although northern Syria and Constantinople have both been proposed.

54. GL 585, 549. Cf. AL 34bis (2:259), which assigns Matthew 21 and Psalm 117:26. For Constantinople see Mateos, *Typicon*, 2:64–67. Romanos, *Hymns* 16.1 (Ps 117:26), 2, 10 (Zachariah 9:9).

55. Mateos, *Typicon* 2:66–67.

56. *Poetae Latini aevi Carolini*, ed. Duemmler, 1:558. Neale and Lawson, *Collected Hymns, Sequences, and Carols*, 17.

57. GL 695. Later Constantinopolitan practice assigns the passage to Vespers on the eve of Ascension; Mateos, *Typicon*, 126–27.

58. Leontios the Presbyter, *Homilies* 7.3 (ll. 29–33); trans. Allen and Datema, 87.

59. Romanos, *Hymns* 20 prelude and 1 (SC 36); trans. Schork, *Sacred Song from the Byzantine Pulpit*, 116 (modified).

60. Romanos, *Hymns* 20.2.1–3; trans. Schork, 117 (modified).

61. Romanos, *Hymns* 24 (SC 41) and 25 (SC 42).

62. Vikan, *Early Byzantine Pilgrimage Art*, 36–40; idem, Vikan, "Early Byzantine Pilgrimage Devotionalia"; Krueger, "Christian Piety and Practice," 303–4; idem, "Liturgical Time."

63. For the ways in which prior experience might condition the experience of pilgrimage, see Frank, *Memory of the Eyes*.

64. On the complex history of the Easter Vigil, see Bertonière, *Historical Development of the Easter Vigil*.

65. Romanos, *Hymns* 24, prelude (my trans.). On this hymn, see the detailed analysis of Barkhuizen, "On the Poetics of His Kontakion 'Resurrection of Christ,'" 17–28, 268–81. Grosdidier de Matons, *Hymnes* 4:423–29.

66. For the personification of Hell as a character in Christian hymns, including in Romanos, see Frank, "Death in the Flesh."

67. Romanos, *Hymns* 25, prelude (my trans.); for discussion see Grosdidier de Matons, *Hymnes* 4:453–56.

68. Allen and Datema in Leontios the Presbyter, *Fourteen Homilies*, 96, and *Homilies* 9.1. Cf. Mateos, *Typicon*, 2:95–96, where Ps 117 [118]:24 is indicated as the prokeimenon, or psalm refrain, preceding the reading of Acts 1:1–8. In late ancient Jerusalem, the verse preceded the first lection of the Easter Vigil; AL 44bis (2:298–99); GL 745.

69. Leontios the Presbyter, *Homilies* 8.3 (ll. 42–50); trans. Allen and Datema, 105 (modified).

70. Ibid. (ll. 53–60). For this passage, Leontios appears dependent on a sermon of Asterios the Sophist: see Datema and Allen in *Leontii presbyteri Constantinopolitani Homiliae*, 29–30.

71. Leontios the Presbyter, *Homilies* 8.4 (ll. 65–71); trans. Allen and Datema, 106.

72. Romanos, *Hymns* 32.1.6–8 (SC 48); trans. Lash, 195.

73. British Museum, 1983,0704.1. Tait, ed., *Seven Thousands Years of Jewellery*, no. 501; Entwistle, "Two Late-Antique Gold Pendants."

74. Krueger, "Liturgical Time." For the image of the Ascension in the Rabbula Gospels: Florence, Biblioteca Medicea Laurenziana, Plut. I, 56, f.13b. While the Syriac Gospel text was copied out in 586 near Apamea, Bernabò (*Il tetravangelo di Rabbula*, 10, 19–21, 105–10) has argued rather convincingly that folio 13 likely derived from a Greek Gospel book and was interleaved into the manuscript at a later date. He proposes a date in the second quarter of the sixth century, thus contemporary with the floruit of Romanos. For the Ascension on other flasks, see the example from the Cleveland Museum (1999.46) in *Treasures of Heaven*, ed. Bagnoli, 43 (no. 23); and additional examples from the treasury at Monza in Grabar, *Ampoules de Terre Sainte*, including 10 (plate XVII), 11 (plate XIX).

75. Romanos, *Hymns* 32.1.3–5; trans. Lash, 195 (modified). Frank, "Sensing Ascension." For further consideration of the relationship between viewing and contemplation see Elsner, *Art and the Roman Viewer*, 97–123. For the the engagement of the broader sensorium during church attendance, see Caseau, "Experiencing the Sacred."

76. Frank, "Sensing Ascension."

77. Romanos, *Hymns* 33.1.1–2 (SC 49); trans. Lash, 209.

78. On the disciples as unlearned and the ideal of Christian simplicity, see Krueger, *Writing and Holiness*, 45–46.

79. Allen and Datema in Leontios the Presbyter, *Fourteen Homilies*, 140; Cf. Mateos, *Typicon*, 2:138–39, which lists Acts 2:1–11 and John 7:37–53 and 8:12. But Leontios's congregation has apparently heard a lection that included Acts 2:15.

80. Leontios the Presbyter, *Homilies* 11.12 (ll. 172–76); trans. Allen and Datema, 148–49.

81. For this trope, see also Romanos, *On Pentecost, Hymns* 33.18; Krueger, *Writing and Holiness*, 45–46.

82. Leontios's Homily 13 survives in a single manuscript, where it is attributed to John Chrysostom. Datema and Allen (*Leontii presbyteri Constantinopolitani Homiliae*, 390–93) have demonstrated conclusively that the sermon is by Leontios.

83. Frank, "Sensing Ascension." For Ps 46:6 in fourth-century Jerusalem, see Cyril of Jerusalem, *Catechetical Homilies*, 14.24 (ed. Reischl and Rupp, *Cyrilli Hierosolymorum archiepiscopi opera*, 2:140). For Jerusalem in subsequent centuries: AL 57 (2:339); cf. variants for GL 856. Mateos, *Typicon* 2:126–29 assigns the entire psalm to the Feast of Ascension, both to the Vigil and the Divine Liturgy.

84. Leontios the Presbyter, *Homilies* 13.1 (ll. 6–7); trans. Allen and Datema, 158.

85. Ibid. (ll. 14–15); trans. Allen and Datema, 158.

86. Leontios merits more attention in the study of popular Christian anti-Judaism in the sixth century. See Datema and Allen in *Leontii presbyteri Constantinopolitani Homiliae*, 54.

87. Leontios the Presbyter, *Homilies* 13.14 (ll. 163–80); trans. Allen and Datema, 162.

88. On the penchant for paradox in sixth-century religious discourse, see Averil Cameron, *Christianity and the Rhetoric of Empire*, 155–88.

89. Kartsonis, 95–110, 116, figs. 25a, b; Bacci, "Croce pettorale con scene cristologiche," 242–45 (with fine color images); Biehl, "Die Staurothek von Vicopisano"; Tschilingirov, "Eine byzantinische Goldschmiedewerkstatt," 85 (figs. 13, 14). Other closely related objects include the Pliska Cross at the National Institute of Archaeology and Museum in Sofia (inv. no. 4882) and the Fieschi-Morgan

Reliquary of the True Cross at the Metropolitan Museum of Art; *Treasures of Heaven*, ed. Bagnoli, 49 (cat. no. 32) and 81–82 (cat. no. 37). Klein, *Byzanz, der Westen und das "wahre" Kreuz*, 159. For the broader context of historiated reliquary crosses see Pitarakis, *Les croix-reliquaires pectorales*, 55–68; see also the example in bronze, 251 (cat. no. 206). Pitarakis's caption assigns the Vicopisano cross to the tenth century, although her reasons are unclear (63, 65, fig. 40).

90. Bradshaw and Johnson, *Origins of the Feasts*, 211. The original date, was February 13, forty days after Epiphany, but this was later moved (except by the Armenians) to February 2, forty days after Christmas. Stephenson, "Origin and Development of Candlemas"; *ODB* s.v. Hypapante.

91. Kartsonis, "Protection Against All Evil," 95. Pitarakis, "Objects of Devotion and Protection."

92. Nikephoros, *Antirrhetikos* 3.36 (PG 100:433); trans. Kartsonis, "Protection Against All Evil," 84 (modified). On the text, see Brubaker and Haldon, *Byzantium in the Iconoclast Era: Sources*, 256–57.

93. Nikephoros, *Antirrhetikos* 3.35 (PG 100:432); trans. in Mondzain, *Image, Icon, Economy*, 244 (modified).

Chapter 4. Eucharistic Prayers: Compunction and the History of Salvation

1. Justinian, *Novels* 137.6; ed. Kroll and Schöll, *Corpus iuris civilis*, 3:695–99; trans. Taft, "Was the Anaphora Recited Aloud?" 38.

2. Taft, "Was the Anaphora Recited Aloud?" 39.

3. Eustratios, *Life of Eutychios* 78, 94 (ed. Laga); trans. in Taft, "Decline of Communion," 32 (modified).

4. Taft, "Was the Anaphora Recited Aloud?" 37–38, cites Ps.-Narsai *Homily* 17 and Jacob of Sarug, although the evidence is far from decisive. For late sixth- and early seventh-century eucharistic miracle stories that depend on an audible anaphora but also justify shifting to a silent one, see Krueger, "Unbounded Body."

5. Butler, *Excitable Speech*, 24, augmenting Althusser, "Ideology and Ideological State Apparatuses."

6. Thus the result of a search of the TLG online. See also Mayr, *Vocabularium codicis Iustiniani*, vol. 2, *Pars graeca*. On the earlier and Latin context for *paenitentia* and *pudor*, see Kaster, *Emotion, Restraint, and Community*. On the Christianization of shame, see Burrus, *Saving Shame*.

7. Romanos, *Hymns* 27.20.8–10 (SC 45). The sole manuscript witness assigns the hymn to the third Sunday after Easter.

8. Romanos, *Hymns* 10, prelude 2.1 (SC 21); 12, prelude 4 (SC 23). For *On the Prodigal Son II* (which Maas and Trypanis regarded as spurious), see Grosdidier de Matons, *Hymnes*, 3:269.

9. Romanos, *Hymns* 31.1.1–3 (SC 47).

10. Romanos, *Hymns* 34.23.8 (SC 50).

11. Romanos, *Hymns* 47 prelude 3 (SC 31 prelude 6). On tears and compunction see also 56.2.3–4 (SC 55).

12. Romanos, *Hymns* 52.3.7–10 (SC 8A).

13. Taft, "Interpolation of the Sanctus"; Spinks, *Sanctus in the Eucharistic Prayer*; Winkler, *Das Sanctus*; Johnson, "Origins of the Anaphoral Sanctus."

14. For the history of the Cherubic Hymn, see Taft, *Great Entrance*, 53–118. Kedrenos, *Historiarum Compendium*, ad annum 573/4 (PG 121.748). The hymn *Let All Mortal Flesh Keep Silence* was considerably later. It likely emerged in the Levant as a hymn for the transfer of gifts, probably by the ninth century. Near the turn of the twelfth century, it entered Constantinopolitan practice as a hymn for the dedication of churches, also sung on December 23, the anniversary of the dedication of Hagia Sophia. Manuscripts provide evidence for its use on Holy Saturday from the late Byzantine period. Parenti, "Nota sull'impiego e l'origine dell'inno ΣΙΓΗΣΑΤΩ ΠΑΣΑ ΣΑΡΞ ΒΡΟΤΕΙΑ."

15. Anastasios of Sinai, *Hexaemeron* 7.7.2 (ll. 470–72); ed. and trans. Kuehn and Baggarly, 228–29.

16. Anastasios of Sinai, *Questions and Answers* q.6 a.3 (ed. Richard and Munitiz); trans. Munitiz, Anastasios of Sinai, *Questions and Answers*, 58.

17. Romanos, *Hymns* 34.12.7 (SC 50); trans. Lash, 226. See Lash's commentary, 260. For Romanos's dependence on Greek Ephrem, *On the Second Coming, the End of the World, and the Coming of the Antichrist*, see Grosdidier de Matons, *Hymnes*, 5:254; Wehofer, "Untersuchungen zum Lied des Romanos."

18. Parenti and Velkovska, *L'Eucologio Barberini gr. 336*, 57–71. For a reconstruction of the Greek text based on both manuscripts, see Brightman, *Liturgies Eastern and Western*, 1:309–44, which follows the Grottaferrata manuscript for 327–36.

19. For a study of the Roman Rite from the perspective of contemporary ritual and performance studies, see McCall, *Do This*. For overviews of the history of the liturgy in late antiquity and early Byzantium, see Taft, *Through Their Own Eyes*; idem, *Byzantine Rite*; Parenti, "Eucharistic Liturgy in the East"; Caseau, "L'eucharistie au centre de la vie religieuse"; Wybrew, *Orthodox Liturgy*.

20. M. Mango, *Silver from Early Byzantium*, 165–70. See also Nelson and Collins, eds., *Holy Image, Hallowed Ground*, 216–17, no. 37; Toynbee and Painter, "Silver Picture Plates," 57–58, no. 80; Caillet, *L'art du Moyen Age*, 43, fig. 35; Durand, *L'art byzantin*, 53, fig. 47. For a similar object in the Istanbul Archaeological Museum, see Mango, *Silver from Early Byzantium*, 20–25, 159–64.

21. The Eastern-influenced Gallican Rite (used in France until around 800) does include a brief recounting of the Creation and Fall in its *contestatio*; Gallican Liturgy 16–19; ed. Mone, in *Prex eucharistica*, 1:467–68. For a description of the rite, see De Clerck, "Les prières eucharistiques gallicanes," in *Prex eucharistica*, 3:203–23. Such a narrative of salvation history is lacking in the *Ordo Romanus Primus* (Roman Liturgy), in *Prex eucharistica*, 1:424–47.

22. Jasper and Cuming, *Prayers of the Eucharist*, collects, translates, and comments on most of the extant early eucharistic prayers. The major texts appear in the original Greek where extant and in Latin translations of other languages—Syriac, Coptic, and Armenian—in *Prex eucharistica*, vol. 1, ed. Hänggi and Pahl. Shepherd, "Formation and Influence of the Antiochene Liturgy" remains a useful and cautious overview of the early formation of Antiochene liturgical traditions.

23. *L'Eucologio Barberini gr. 336* 15.2 (ed. Parenti and Velkovska, 65); trans. in Jasper and Cuming, *Prayers of the Eucharist*, 117 (modified). This translation has been reprinted in Ray, *Tasting Heaven on Earth*, 93–99.

24. *L'Eucologio Barberini gr. 336* 15.2.

25. Ibid.

26. Ibid., 15.1.

27. For late antique claims, see Leontios of Byzantium, *Contra Nestorianos et Eutychianos* (PG

86.1368C) (c. 546 C.E.); *Canons of the Council in Trullo* 32 (692 C.E.) (NPNF 2.14:380); Fenwick, *Fourth-Century Anaphoral Construction*, 6; Parenti and Velkovska, *L'Eucologio Barberini*, 57.

28. Bouley, *From Freedom to Formula*; Hanson, "Liberty of the Bishop"; Taft, "Was the Anaphora Recited Aloud?" 27–32.

29. Justin Martyr, *First Apology* 65, 67.

30. *Apostolic Tradition* 9 (ed. Botte); trans. Bouley, *From Freedom to Formula*, 123. The prayer is given in *Apostolic Tradition* 4. Bradshaw et al., *The Apostolic Tradition*, 44–48. Metzger, "La Prière eucharistique," in *Prex eucharistica*, 3:263–80.

31. Taft, "Was the Anaphora Recited Aloud?" 31.

32. Ibid. 34; idem, "Epiclesis Question," 212, 235–36. Lampe, s.v. ἐπίκλησις, B4.

33. A great number of these forms are collected in *Prex eucharistica*, vol. 1., ed. Hänggi and Pahl and translated in Jasper and Cuming, *Prayers of the Eucharist*.

34. John Moschos, *Spiritual Meadow* 25 (PG 87.3:2870–72), 196 (PG 87.3:3080–84); trans. Wortley, 17, 172–74; Krueger, "Unbounded Body"; Taft, "Was the Anaphora Recited Aloud?" 35; Déroche, "Représentations de l'eucharistie." For another version of the story about the monk, see Antony of Choziba, *Miracles of the Mother of God at Choziba* 5 (ed. Houze); trans. Vivian and Athanassakis in Antony of Choziba, *Life of Saint George of Choziba*, 95–105.

35. On the *Liturgy of James*, see Fenwick, *Fourth-Century Anaphoral Construction*, 11–16; Jasper and Cuming, *Prayers of the Eucharist*, 88–99; Tarby, *La prière eucharistique*. In the earliest surviving Greek manuscript, Vat. gr. 2282, penned in or near Damascus in the ninth century, the text of the *Liturgy of James* already shows some influence from the traditions of the *Liturgy of Basil*. This version includes mention of the creation, fall, law, and prophets in the post-Sanctus of the anaphora. For this text, see *Prex eucharistica*, 1:244–61. The text in Brightman, *Liturgies Eastern and Western*, 31–68, is based on a fourteenth-century manuscript. Study of the *Liturgy of James* has been greatly advanced by the publication of the Georgian version (including a Greek retroversion by Stéphane Verhelst), based on late ninth- to eleventh-century manuscript witnesses, including from the New Finds at St. Catherine's Monastery at Sinai: *Liturgia Ibero-graeca Sancti Iacobi*, ed. Khevsuriani et al. The received Syriac text (see Brightman, *Liturgies Eastern and Western*, 69–110 and *Prex eucharistica*, 1:269–75) includes a shorter version of this encapsulation of salvation history. The *Narration of the Abbots John and Sophronios* suggests that Moschos and his companion were familiar with the *Liturgy of James*, although in their extensive travels they surely encountered a variety of eucharistic liturgies; see Taft, "The βηματίκιον."

36. Taft, "Decline of Communion," 40–45. Egypt may provide important exceptions: see Bolman, "Veiling Sanctity," 73–104.

37. See *Thresholds of the Sacred*, ed. Gerstel; C. Mango, "History of the *Templon*." On church architecture and the liturgy, see Mathews, *Early Churches of Constantinople*; Ousterhout, "Holy Space"; Marinis, "Defining Liturgical Space." The Eucharist contained important tactile dimensions as well: communicants still received the host in their hands in this period. See Caseau, "L'abandon de la communion dans la main." On the acoustics of Hagia Sophia and it effects, see Pentcheva, *Sensual Icon*, 45–56.

38. Taft, *Beyond East and West*, 87–110; idem, "Decline of Communion in Byzantium."

39. Maxwell, *Christianization and Communication*, 94–95; Taft, *Through their Own Eyes*, 76–77; Taft, "Was the Anaphora Recited Aloud?" 38–39.

40. Taft, *Through Their Own Eyes*, 77–78, cites Anastasios of Sinai, *Oratio de sacra synaxi* (PG 89:830–32) (c. 700 C.E.), a text that merits further study. For more perspective on early Byzantine preachers and their audiences, see Harvey, "To Whom Did Jacob Preach?"

41. Bibliotheca Rahmani Codex Syr. 303 (eighth or ninth century): text in Rahmani, "Ritus receptionis episcopi," fasc. 3, 1–22 and 1–4 (Syriac numerals). For translation and discussion, see Taft, *Through Their Own Eyes*, 40–41, 64–67; idem, "The βηματίκιον"; idem, *Great Entrance*, 40–42; and idem, "Worship on Sinai," 157–61.

42. *Narration of the Abbots John and Sophronios* (ed. Longo); discussion in Taft, "The βηματίκιον"; idem, "Worship on Sinai," 152–55.

43. Barberini Euchologion 16.1–2. Justin Martyr, *First Apology* 65, 67.

44. The style of the Byzantine Liturgy of Basil corresponds to the "middle style" identified by Ševčenko, "Levels of Style." For perspectives on the linguistic levels of popular Christian works in the period, see Horrocks, *Greek: A History of the Language*, 164–65, 185–88.

45. Budde, *Die ägyptische Basilios-Anaphora*, 67–73. For earlier studies see Engberding, *Das eucharistische Hochgebet*; L. Mitchell, "Alexandrian Anaphora of St. Basil." Budde's Greek text depends principally on the manuscripts dating from the late thirteenth and fourteenth centuries, thus the critical importance of the Coptic witnesses. A discussion of other witnesses to the Basilian family is beyond the scope of this chapter, but the relevant elements of the prayer are confirmed in the trajectory of Armenian versions as well: Winkler, *Die Basilius-anaphora*. For the earliest witness to the Egyptian form, see Zheltov, "Anaphora and the Thanksgiving Prayer."

46. Budde, *Die ägyptische Basilios-Anaphora*, 95–96; Doresse and Lanne, *Un témoin archaïque de la liturgie copte*. See also Fenwick, *Fourth-Century Anaphoral Construction*, 6–10.

47. Budde, *Die ägyptische Basilios-Anaphora*, 144–45, 248–50; Jasper and Cuming, *Prayers of the Eucharist*, 70.

48. Budde, *Die ägyptische Basilios-Anaphora*, 146–47, 260–62. For the broader history of this section of the prayer, see Winkler, *Die Basilius-anaphora*, 490–525.

49. Budde, *Die ägyptische Basilios-Anaphora*, 146–47, 280–82; Jasper and Cuming, *Prayers of the Eucharist*, 70.

50. Budde, *Die ägyptische Basilios-Anaphora*, 148–49, 282–83. Compare an Armenian fragment from the second half of the fifth century: Winkler, *Die Basilius-anaphora*, 72–75; see also 566–75.

51. On the expansion of liturgies over time, see Taft, *Beyond East and West*, 203–32.

52. *Apostolic Constitutions* 8.12.4–51 (ed. Marcel Metzger); trans. Jasper and Cuming, *Prayers of the Eucharist*, 104–14. See Pitt, "Anamnesis and Institution Narrative"; Metzger, *Les constitutions apostoliques*, 2:81–84.

53. I leave aside the debates about possibly semi-Arian Christological formulas in the text, except to say that the liturgy would fit comfortably in Apollinarian contexts. Turner, "Notes on the Apostolic Constitutions"; but see Metzger, *Les constitutions apostoliques*, 2:10–18.

54. *Apostolic Constitutions* 8.12.7–26.

55. Bouyer, *Eucharist*, 250–51. See Metzger, *Les constitutions apostoliques*, 3:179n12.

56. On Marcionites and Jews in northwest Syria into the fifth century and the assertion of Christian use of the Old Testament, see Krueger, *Writing and Holiness*, 23–24. Jews, of course,

would have claimed the history of Israel as their own, while Marcionites regarded the Old Testament as, at best, irrelevant.

57. Bousset, "Eine jüdische Gebetssammlung"; Ligier, "Autour du sacrifice eucharistique"; Metzger, *Les constitutions apostoliques*, 1:20–23.

58. On salvation history in the *Apostolic Constitutions*, see Metzger, *Les constitutions apostoliques*, 2.19–23. See also Saxer, "L'usage de la Bible"; Dalmais, "Biblical Themes in Greek Eucharistic Anaphoras."

59. *Apostolic Constitutions* 8.12.8–17.

60. Greek text in Kelly, *Early Christian Creeds*, 297 after Dossetti; my trans.

61. Theodore Lector, *Ecclesiastical History* 4.501 (ed. Hansen); trans. and discussion in Taft, *Great Entrance*, 398–99. Taft warns that the text introduced was likely not identical to the Chalcedonian text of the "Nicene Creed." See also Kelly, *Early Christian Creeds*, 348–51.

62. Maximos the Confessor, *Mystagogy* 18; trans. Berthold, *Maximus Confessor: Selected Writings*, 202.

63. Taft, *Great Entrance*, 404–5 adds that the addition of the creed to the liturgy was "superfluous" since "the eucharistic prayer itself, with its account of salvation history and its repletion of the banquet of the New Covenant, is an entirely sufficient profession of faith." This raises the question whether the effect of the introduction of the creed at a time when the anaphora was beginning to be said silently meant that the creed came to fill the need for an audible liturgical recitation of the broad narrative of Christian faith.

64. Thus Taft, "Was the Anaphora Recited Aloud?" 41.

65. In treating the history of Israel as the history of the church, the prayers engage in what Soulen (*God of Israel*, 27–33) dubs "economic supersessionism."

66. *L'Eucologio Barberini gr. 336* 15.2.

67. Parenti and Velkovska, *L'Eucologio Barberini*, 66–67 identifies forty quotations and echoes of scripture in the post-Sanctus of the anaphora with its recounting of salvation history. The text of the Barberini manuscript breaks off just before the words of institution.

68. Grottaferrata Γβ VII, trans. Jasper and Cuming, *Prayers of the Eucharist*, 119. Greek text in Brightman, *Liturgies Eastern and Western*, 329.

69. Budde, *Die ägyptische Basilios-Anaphora*, 158–61, and see the discussion, 397–430; Winkler, *Die Basilius-anaphora*, 775–92. Trans. in Jasper and Cuming, *Prayers of the Eucharist*, 71 (modified).

70. For an overview see Bell, *Ritual*.

71. McCall, *Do This;* Bell (*Ritual Theory, Ritual Practice*) and Bourdieu (*Logic of Practice*) have also observed that ritualization often occurs independent of specific narrative contexts, particularly in the routine activities and quotidian habits that make up much of culture.

72. John Chrysostom, *Homilies on Ephesians* 3.4; PG 62:28–29; trans. NPNF 1.13:63 (modified). See discussion in Taft, "The Decline of Communion," 30–32.

73. John Chrysostom, *Homilies on Ephesians* 3.4; PG 62:28–29; trans. NPNF 1.13:63 (modified).

74. On these prayers, see Taft, "Byzantine Communion Rites II," 296–99; Alexopoulos and van den Hoek, "Endicott Scroll," 163–67.

75. Cyril of Scythopolis, *Life of Euthymios* 29 (ed. Schwartz); trans. Price and Binns in Cyril of

Scythopolis, *The Lives of the Monks of Palestine*, 43. Krueger, "Unbounded Body," 277; Taft, "Decline of Communion," 33.

76. Anastasios of Sinai, *Questions and Answers*, q.41 a.1; trans. Munitiz, 147.

77. Barsanouphios and John, *Letters* 170 (ed. Neyt and de Angelis-Noah); trans. Chyrssavgis, 1:185.

78. Text and translation according to the twelfth-/thirteenth-century Endicott Scroll in the Museum of Fine Arts in Boston, Alexopoulos and van den Hoek, "Endicott Scroll," 148–49. The text also appears in the eleventh-century scroll, Byzantine Museum of Athens 127; see Alexopoulos and van den Hoek, 180–81.

Chapter 5. The Penitential Bible and the *Great Kanon* of Andrew of Crete

1. Andrew of Crete's *Great Kanon* lacks a critical edition, which poses a number of problems regarding our confidence in some words and phrases in the text and questions about the genuineness and order of some of the stanzas. The text of the seventeenth-century Dominican François Combefis reproduced in PG 97:1329–85 interpolates a number of other prayers and liturgical directions that reflect the use of Andrew's hymn in later Orthodox practice. A similar text appears in the Lenten service book of the Orthodox Church, TR, 463–91. A much-shortened text appears in von Christ and Paranikas, *Anthologia Graeca Carminum Christianorum*, 147–61, which is of little use. In her study and partial edition of later Byzantine commentaries on Andrew's *Great Kanon*, Giannouli (*Die beiden byzantinischen Kommentare*, 182–224) has reconstructed the text of the *Kanon* as it was available to the thirteenth-century scholar Akakios Sabaites. While Akakios's text of the *Kanon* contains some obvious errors and questionable emendations, it often presents useful variant readings, and sometimes produces an order of the stanzas that makes better chronological sense. Whether this reflects Andrew's own ordering or the corrective reordering by subsequent scribes is unclear. Translations are my own, although I have consulted the two serviceable English translations, the first more literal, the second more liturgically elegant: *Great Canon of St. Andrew* trans. Katherine and Thecla, 35–77; and Mary and Ware, *Lenten Triodion*, 378–415. Both translations include later Byzantine prayers, hymns, and refrains interspersed with Andrew's composition.

2. The fourteenth-century ecclesiastical historian Nikephoros Kallistos Xanthopoulos handed down a tradition that Andrew originally composed the *Kanon* late in life as an expression of personal repentance, but this piece of biographical criticism, while perhaps romantic, hardly accounts for the overwhelming generic force of the performed confession and the utter lack of specific autobiographical details in the poem. This tradition is rehearsed most recently by Getcha, *Typikon Decoded*, 174–75. Andrew's *Great Kanon* is no more a self-portrait than Romanos's preludes, and the work, while long, conforms in its structure and meters to the liturgical kanon becoming prevalent in Andrew's lifetime for Morning Prayer.

3. See Lukashevich, "Velikij Kanon"; Diakovskij, *Posledovanie časov i izobrazitel'nyx*, 167–69. I thank Dr. Sr. Vassa Larin for the references and Sergey Minov for translation from the Russian. According to Lukashevich, Sinai gr. 734–735 of the tenth century is the earliest witness to the practice of chanting the *Great Kanon* at Vespers (*hesperinos*) on Thursday of the fifth week of Lent. Andrew's composition appears in Sinai gr. 735, from f. 69r to 83v, without refrains. The division of the poem

into sections to be chanted on separate days occurred later. Vat. gr. 771 of the eleventh century divides the poem and assigns it in parts to various days during the fifth week of Lent. The *Kanon* is linked with readings from the *Life of Mary of Egypt* only after the eleventh century, and then not consistently. The practice of reading the *Kanon* in parts during Compline is later still. For the current practice, see *Lenten Triodion*, 199–209, 218–28, 237–47, 255–66, and 378–415. It would be fair to say that the *Great Kanon* dominates the Lenten liturgy and continues to guide Orthodox spiritual practice. For its continuing popular importance see, for example, Mathewes-Green, *First Fruits of Prayer*; and Glaros, *Theia Paidagogia*.

4. The remarkable wealth of late antique treatments of the story can be seen in Glenthøj, *Cain and Abel*.

5. A hagiographical *Life of Andrew of Crete* (ed. Papadopoulos-Kerameus) was composed by an otherwise unknown Niketas, mostly likely in the tenth century. Its historical reliability has been contested and debated. For critical studies of Andrew's life, see Vailhé, "Saint André de Crète"; the less cautious Auzépy, "La carrière d'André de Crète"; and the usefully skeptical Kazhdan, *History of Byzantine Literature*, 37–41. See also Giannouli, *Die beiden byzantinischen Kommentare*, 28–31.

6. Most of the works of Andrew appear in PG 97:805–1304. For English translations of four sermons on the Nativity and one on the Annunciation, see Cunningham, *Wider than Heaven*, 71–138, 197–219; for three sermons on the Dormition of Mary, see Daley, *On the Dormition of Mary*, 103–52.

7. A new critical history of the kanon would be very useful. The classic treatment of the kanon remains Wellesz, *History of Byzantine Music*, 198–239. For an overview of the emergence of the kanon, see Grosdidier de Matons, "Liturgie et hymnographie"; Louth, "Christian Hymnography," 195–206. For an attempt to situate Andrew's literary output within the context of his early formation in and around Jerusalem, see Peristeris, "Literary and Scribal Activities at the Monastery of St. Sabas," 174. Hannick ("Hymnographie et hymnographes sabaïtes," 217–28) considers the history of the composition of kanons by Andrew, Kosmas of Maiouma, and John of Damascus, although his placement of all these authors in the context of Mar Saba is speculative and problematic.

8. On John of Damascus and Kosmas of Maiouma, see Louth, *St. John Damascene*, 13–15, 256–57.

9. See Wellesz, *History of Byzantine Music*, 206; Louth, *St. John Damascene*, 254–58; Cunningham, "Reception of Romanos."

10. Taft, *Liturgy of the Hours in East and West*, 198–99, 273–83.

11. Kazhdan (*A History of Byzantine Literature*, 38–42) briefly considers Andrew's life and works in the contexts of the monothelete controversy, the rise of iconoclasm, and military victories in 678 or 718. In any case, the poem's broad dissemination throughout the empire in subsequent centuries indicates that it was known in the capital.

12. Giannouli, "Die Tränen der Zerknirschung," 150–52. For later compositions as a genre, see Giannouli, "*Catanyctic* Religious Poetry."

13. I am especially grateful to Mary Cunningham for generously thinking through these ideas with me. Clearly these issues need more study.

14. On the self in Romanos, see Chapter 2; Frank, "Dialogue and Deliberation."

15. Perrone, "Aus Gehorsam zum Vater"; Hevelone-Harper, *Disciples of the Desert*, 79–105; Torrance, *Repentance in Late Antiquity*, 118–56.

16. For the most comprehensive survey, see Kazhdan, *History of Byzantine Literature*.

17. The classic study is Hausherr, *Penthos*. For more recent treatments, see Carruthers, *Craft of Thought*, 101–5; Müller, *Der Weg des Weinens*; Hunt, *Joy-bearing Grief*; Fernández, "Byzantine Tears."

18. Foucault, "Technologies of the Self," 40.

19. Ibid., 41. See also Foucault, "Beginning of the Hermeneutics of the Self," 170–71.

20. Wellesz, *History of Byzantine Music*, 204.

21. See Dörries, "Place of Confession"; Guy, "Aveu thérapeutique et aveu pédagogique," 25–40; Déroche, "Quand l'ascèse devient péché"; Bitton-Ashkelony and Kofsky, *Monastic School of Gaza*, 145–56.

22. The most significant example is John the Monk's *Kanonarion*, later elaborated by a certain Basil the Monk. See Arranz, *I Penitenziali bizantini*; Raes, "Les formulaires grecs"; Erickson, "Penitential Discipline."

23. See Hausherr, *Penthos*, 3–10.

24. For useful perspective, see Rapp, "Spiritual Guarantors."

25. *L'Eucologio Barberini gr. 336*, 194–95 (nos. 201–2). For an earlier edition and discussion of these prayers and their continued development into the eleventh century, see Arranz, "Les prières pénitentielles."

26. Phenix and Horn, "Prayer and Penance."

27. Ibid., 229–45. See also Arranz, "Les prières pénitentielles," 87–89.

28. *L'Eucologio Barberini gr. 336*, 194; trans. Phenix and Horn, "Prayer and Penance," 230–31.

29. Phenix and Horn, "Prayer and Penance," 232–33; Arranz, "Les prières pénitentielles," 91. Rahlfs's edition of the LXX includes the Prayer of Manasseh as Ode 12. Its liturgical use in the late eighth century is unclear.

30. *L'Eucologio Barberini gr. 336*, 195; trans. Phenix and Horn, "Prayer and Penance," 235 (modified).

31. Phenix and Horn, "Prayer and Penance," 238–42.

32. For example, Peter appears in Ode 2.4 and 6.13; the Harlot in Ode 2.5 and 2.22; the Tax Collector in 2.24 and 4.24; the Prodigal Son in 1.13; the Thief in 6. 18.

33. In the *Life of Mary of Egypt* 13, the Prodigal and the Harlot also appear in the heroine's penitential prayers.

34. The verb βεβορβόρωμαι is derived from the noun βόρβορος, "filth." Especially with its reduplication, the word has fecal overtones or recalls intestinal burbling. As a noun, the word appears in Romanos the Melodist's hymn *On the Harlot*. The poem's refrain is τοῦ βορβόρου τῶν ἔργων μου "of [or in] the filth of my deeds." Romanos, *Hymns* 10 (SC 21). As we shall see below, Andrew quite likely knew this hymn, which is also quoted in the *Life of Mary of Egypt* 23.

35. I thank Alexandru Prelipcean for alerting me to two studies in Romanian, despite their French titles: Durlea, "*Metanoia*"; Prelipcean, "Le concept de *metanoia*."

36. I am grateful to Antonia Giannouli for sharing this suggestion in private correspondence.

37. Harris, "The 'Kanon' and the Heirmologion," 185–87.

38. See Reed, "Job as Jobab." A variant tradition that identified Job's friend Eliphaz (Job 4.1) with Eliphaz, the son of Esau (Genesis 36:10), and identified Job with Jobab, King of Edom, was

known to Eusebios of Caesarea (*Praeparatio Evangelica* 9.25.1–3 [ed. Mras]). Eusebios cites a lost work *Concerning the Jews* by the first-century B.C.E. scholar Aristeas the Exegete. The third-century chronographer, Julius Africanus, regarded Job as Esau's grandson, a tradition also found in the ninth-century Byzantine chronographer George the Monk. *Iulius Africanus Chronographiae: The Extant Fragments*, ed. Wallraft and trans. Adler, 68–69, fragment F 31, quoted in the mid-eleventh-century chronography of George Kedrenos, *Compendium historiarum*, ed. Bekker, 1:76–77. George the Monk, *Chronicon*, ed. de Boor and Wirth, 1:108–9. I thank Roger Scott for discussing this with me. The pseudepigraphical *Testament of Job* (first century B.C.E. to first century C.E.) makes a similar if slightly different claim; see Reed, "Job as Jobab," 51–53.

39. Despite Wellesz, *History of Byzantine Music*, 204, and von Christ and Paranikas, *Anthologia Graeca*, xlii, the number of stanzas does not correspond to the number of verses in the nine biblical canticles. The *Great Kanon* has approximately 250 stanzas. According to conventional numbering, the canticles taken together have 196 verses. Nor does Andrew write longer or shorter odes to correspond with the longer or shorter canticles. The canticles vary from 8 to 43 verses. Andrew's odes vary from 20 to 41 stanzas. The sixth biblical canticle is the shortest (8 verses); the sixth ode has 33 stanzas in two separate irmoi. The shortest ode is the eighth, and replaces the eighth canticle, which at 32 verses is the second longest.

40. Cf. Septuagint, ed. Rahlfs 2:164–88; Wellesz, *History of Byzantine Music*, 38–39.

41. Taft, *Liturgy of the Hours in East and West*, 198–99; 277–83. *Narration of the Abbots John and Sophronios*, ed. Longo, 251–52. See also Woolfenden, *Daily Liturgical Prayer*, 63–65. We may think of Andrew's *Kanon* as very long, but it is worth noting that the chanting of the Nine Canticles would have been lengthy as well.

42. The introduction of the hymn *At Your Mystical Supper* to the liturgy for Holy Thursday in Constantinople in either 565 or 577 provides another example of alterations to the liturgy to fit the liturgical season. See Krueger, "Christian Piety and Practice," 292–97.

43. The most accessible overview is J. Miller, "Prophetologion." The lectionary cycle in current use in the Greek Orthodox Church is substantially similar to that transmitted in middle Byzantine service books. Therefore, the lectionary printed in *The Orthodox Study Bible*, 1767–74, can serve as a handy reference, if used cautiously and checked against the Byzantine sources. A schematic representation of this lectionary is available in electronic form at http://www.bombaxo.com/greek.html.

44. The critical text is *Prophetologium*, ed. Høeg, Zuntz, and Engberg. On the contents, see J. Miller, "Prophetologion," 66–72. For an overview, see Engberg, "Prophetologion Manuscripts."

45. J. Miller, "Prophetologion," 66, esp. n. 29.

46. Engberg, "*Prophetologion* and the Triple-Lection Theory," makes a reasonable case that there was never a triple-lection tradition in Constantinople. But this has been strongly refuted by Taft, "Were There Once Old Testament Readings?"

47. For the Armenian lectionary in use in Jerusalem in the first half of the fifth century, see AL. For the Georgian lectionary in use in Jerusalem around 700, see GL. The Georgian lectionary may reflect liturgical usage familiar to Andrew himself during his youth and training in Jerusalem before 685, although it is uncertain whether the identical cycle of readings was in use by Greek speakers in the same city or even sharing space at the Church of the Anastasis. The five sixth-century hymns of Romanos on stories from Genesis are assigned in the manuscript tradition to Lent and

Holy Week: Noah, Abraham and Isaac, and Jacob and Esau to the Vigils of the third, fourth and fifth Sundays of Lent; the two hymns on Joseph to the Tuesday of Holy Week; his hymns on Elijah and on the Three Children are assigned to their commemorations on 20 July and 17 December (or a Sunday during Advent) respectively. This arrangement, occurring as it does in middle Byzantine *kontakaria*, or service books with the hymns for various feasts, may reflect later usage rather than the original occasions for Romanos's compositions.

48. See J. Miller, "Prophetologion," 67–68.

49. Rahlfs, *Die altestamentlichen Lektionen*, 168–71; Engberg, "*Prophetologion* and the Triple-Lection Theory," 70–87; J. Miller, "Prophetologion," 71–72. A fragmentary sixth-century East Syrian lectionary also reflects a practice of extensive and sequential readings from Genesis on weekdays during Lent. See Burkitt, *Early Syriac Lectionary System*, 7.

50. *Prophetologium*, ed. Høeg, Zuntz, and Engberg, 602–3 (vol. 1, fasc. 6 [1970]).

51. On this text, see Adler, "Palaea Historica." The critical edition is found in *Anecdota graeco-byzantina: Pars prior*, ed. Vassiliev, 188–299.

52. See Giannouli, *Die beiden byzantinischen Kommentare*. Akakios included in his lengthy commentary an older, shorter one, falsely attributed to John of Damascus, written perhaps in the twelfth century.

53. For a reading of Andrew's approach to the Fall within the contexts of the Byzantine theological tradition, see Costache, "Byzantine Insights into Genesis."

54. See the tables in *Prophetologium*, ed. Høeg, Zuntz, and Engberg, 1:106 and 601. This assignment is not reflected in AL or GL. GL 13 (1:10) assigns Genesis 1–3 to the Vigil of the Feast of the Nativity at Bethlehem.

55. See Brock in Ephrem the Syrian, *Hymns on Paradise*, 66–72; Brock, "Clothing Metaphors"; idem, *Luminous Eye*, 85–97.

56. Anderson, *Genesis of Perfection*, 117–34.

57. For an interesting treatment of Adam and Eve's evasive confessions, see John Chrysostom, *Homilies on Genesis* 17.17–24; trans. Hill, 1:230–35. For the serpent as the weaver of the clothing after the Fall, see also Romanos the Melodist's hymn *On the Nativity II*; Romanos, *Hymns* 2.8.9 [SC 11]: "the rags that I carry that the serpent wove for me."

58. For other places where Andrew discusses theōria, see 5.10 (with Moses before the burning bush), 6.3. For the distinction between "action" (πράξις) and "thought" or "word" (usually λόγος) already in the third century in the works of Origen, see Perrone, "Christianity as 'Practice'", 303n33.

59. Basil of Caesarea, *Letter* 2 to Gregory of Nazianzos (ed. Deferrari and Maguire). See also Taft, *Liturgy of the Hours in East and West*, 41–42, 204, 212–13, 277–82; and Taft, "Liturgy of the Hours in the East," 29–30. The other option was Psalm 63.

60. Andrew's use of the verb ἐλέγχω recalls the context of the courtroom, where deeds are "exposed" or subject to "cross-examination." His term for painting, συγγράφω, also carries associations with the drafting of legal documents.

61. Romanos also locates models for himself as a writer in various biblical characters. See Krueger, *Writing and Holiness*, 159–88.

62. Ὡς ὁ Λῃστὴς ἐκβοῶ σοι· Μνήσθητι, ὡς Πέτρος κλαίω πικρῶς. Ἄνες μοι Σωτήρ, κράζω ὡς ὁ Τελώνης, δακρύω ὡς ἡ Πόρνη, δέξαι μου τὸν θρῆνον, καθὼς ποτὲ τῆς Χαναναίας (8.2).

63. Both assign the passage to a processional liturgy that began on the Mount of Olives and descended to Gethsemane before entering the city. The story of Jesus' appearance before Caiaphas and Peter's denial was read in the courtyard of the house of Caiaphas. AL, 1:45, 133, 146–48; 2:277. GL 656 (1:2.95). A church of St. Peter had been built on the spot by 530. See also Baldovin, *Urban Character of Christian Worship*, 53, 68, 81.

64. AL, 1:149–55; 2:291. GL 694 (1:2.103).

65. Mateos, *Typicon*, 2:76–77, 80–81. See also Baldovin, *Urban Character of Christian Worship*, 190–92. Although these witnesses date from the ninth and tenth centuries, the lectionary assignments for Holy Week in particular seem to have been very conservative, and thus it seems likely that these readings were used in Constantinople and also on Crete in Andrew's day.

66. Mateos, *Typicon*, 2:167. For a comparison of lectionary indications for Lenten Sundays in Jerusalem and Constantinople, see Bertonière, *Sundays of Lent*, 45–50. For the development of liturgies for the pre-Lenten Sundays, see the following chapter.

67. For example, the Thief is a main character in Romanos's hymn *On the Adoration of the Cross* (Romanos, *Hymns* 23 [SC 39]). This hymn is assigned variously in the manuscripts to Friday of the fourth week of Lent and to the Feast of the Elevation of the Cross on 14 September, although the latter must be a later usage, since the Feast of the Elevation was introduced in Constantinople in the early seventh century (in or after 614). The Thief is also mentioned in *On the Victory of the Cross* (*Hymns* 22 [SC 38]), assigned to Wednesday of the fourth week of Lent. Peter receives extensive reflection in *On Peter's Denial* (*Hymns* 18 [SC 38]), assigned variously to Good Friday and Holy Thursday, as does the Harlot in *On the Harlot*, (*Hymns* 10 [SC 21]). Tax collectors appear with harlots in *On the Man Possessed by Demons* (11.18 [SC 22]), and the Harlot and the Tax Collector appear in the final stanza of *On the Prodigal Son* (49.22 [SC 28]), indicating that their pairing as model penitents and recipients of grace may have been commonplace. The Canaanite woman is mentioned in *On the Crucifixion* (also called *On the Powers of Hell*; 21.16 [SC 37]), a hymn later paired with the *Great Kanon* in the Vespers service for Thursday in the fifth week of Lent; in *On Earthquakes and Fires* (54.5 [SC 54]); and (unless he means the woman of Zarephath (III Kgds 17 [1 Kgs 17]) in *On the Harlot* (10.3 [SC 21]). On the pairing of *On the Crucifixion* and the *Great Kanon*, see Grosdidier de Matons, ed., *Romanos le Mélode: Hymnes*, 4:233–35.

68. Harvey, "Why the Perfume Mattered"; Frank, "Dialogue and Deliberation," 169–71.

69. Romanos, *On the Harlot* (*Hymns* 10), trans. Lash, 78.

70. Τὸ τῶν δακρύων, Σωτὴρ ἀλάβαστρον, ὡς μύρον κατακενῶν, ἐπὶ κεφαλῆς, κράζω σοι ὡς ἡ Πόρνη, τὸν ἔλεον ζητοῦσα, δέησιν προσάγω, καὶ ἄφεσιν αἰτῶ λαβεῖν με (8.17).

71. Τὴν Πόρνην, ὦ τάλαινα ψυχή μου, οὐκ ἐζήλωσας, ἥτις λαβοῦσα, μύρου τὸ ἀλάβαστρον, σὺν δάκρυσιν ἤλειψε, τοὺς πόδας τοῦ Κυρίου, ἐξέμαξε δὲ ταῖς θριξί (9.18).

72. See Chapter 2.

73. My analysis of the poem depends heavily on the fine work of Riehle, "Authorship and Gender (and) Identity"; Tsironis, "Body and the Senses," 139–57. The Greek text appears in TR, 644–45. I have employed the translation of Dyck, "On Cassia, Κύριε ἡ ἐν πολλαῖς. . . ," with some modification. Other studies include Topping, "The Psalmist, St. Luke and Kassia"; Kazhdan, *History of Byzantine Literature*, 317–20. Musical notation in later manuscripts allows the sensible reconstruction

of Kassia's original melody, which provides insights into proper versification: see Raasted, "Voice and Verse."

74. For more general studies of Kassia, see Lauxtermann, "Three Biographical Notes," 391–97, which has the most cautious and plausible reconstruction of her biography; idem, *Byzantine Poetry*, 241–70, on her epigrams; Rochow, *Studien zu der Dichterin Kassia*; Silvas, "Kassia the Nun," including translations of Theodore's letters; Simić, "Kassia's Hymnography." The entire corpus of poetry appears in Tripolitis, *Kassia*.

75. See Tsironis, "Body and the Senses," 142. The hymn probably predates the creation of the women's liturgical choir known as the myrrhbearers that sang at Easter services in later Byzantine times, on which see Karras, "Liturgical Function of Consecrated Women," 109–14.

76. Sinai. gr. 735, f. 159r-v. See Quinlan, *Sin. Gr. 734–735*, 51, although Quinlan does not identify this as Kassia's poem. This manuscript was originally a single volume and is now bound in two codices. Although Rochow, *Studien zu der Dichterin Kassia*, 40–42, 222n296, lists many manuscripts containing the poem, dating as early as the twelfth century, she was apparently unaware of these earlier, unattributed witnesses.

77. Vat. gr. 771, f. 162v. On the manuscript, its eleventh-century dating, production at Grottaferrata, and scribe, see Malatesta Zilembo, "Gli amanuensi di Grottaferrata," 26–27.

78. Cunningham, "Reception of Romanos," 257.

79. Louth, *St. John Damascene*, 258–82.

80. See, for example, the massive *piyyut Az be-'En Kol [When all was not]*, dated to the sixth to eighth centuries in *Avodah*, ed. and trans. Swartz and Yahalom, 95–210. On the need for comparative study of Jewish and Christian liturgical hymns from late antiquity, see Münz-Manor, "Liturgical Poetry."

81. See Frank, "Romanos and the Night Vigil."

82. *Miracles of Artemios* 18; ed. and trans. Crisafulli and Nesbitt, 114–15.

83. Lingas, "Liturgical Place of the Kontakion." See also Louth, "Christian Hymnography," 199–200; Cunningham, "Reception of Romanos," 251–52. I return to monastic reuse of the kontakion below.

84. What follows is surely incomplete. A thorough study of echoes and quotations of Romanos in Andrew of Crete would be very helpful.

85. See Grosdidier de Matons, ed., *Romanos le Mélode: Hymnes*, 4:233–35 and 242n1. Also Krumbacher, *Geschichte der byzantinischen Litteratur*, 667; Cunningham, "Reception of Romanos," 257.

86. Col 2:13–14: "He forgave us all our trespasses, erasing the record that stood against us with its legal demands [ἐξαλείψας τὸ καθ' ἡμῶν χειρόγραφον τοῖς δόγμασιν ὃ ἦν ὑπεναντίον ἡμῖν]."

87. The only other pairing of these passages that I have found is in the *Sacra Parallela* of John of Damascus, Andrew's rough contemporary: Ἡ πόρνη φιλήσασα τοὺς πόδας τοῦ Ἰησοῦ, τὴν ψυχὴν ἀνεκαλέσατο, τὸ χειρόγραφον τῶν ἁμαρτιῶν διέρρηξεν (PG 96:149). This may well also be dependent on Romanos.

88. For the subsequent history of the *Great Kanon*, see Lukashevich, "Velikij Kanon."

Chapter 6. The Voice of the Sinner in First-Person Hymns of the Lenten Triodion

1. On Theodore the Stoudite see *PMBZ* 1.4:429–33. For a study of Theodore's life in its ecclesiastical and political contexts, see Pratsch, *Theodoros Studites*; for a study of Theodore's theological

views and the best biographical overview available in English, see Cholij, *Theodore the Stoudite*. For a broader view of the time period, see Brubaker and Haldon, *Byzantium in the Iconoclast Era: A History*, 290–91, 372–92, 650–63. On Joseph of Stoudios, later archbishop of Thessalonike, see *PMBZ* 1.2:400–402. See also Pratsch, *Theodoros Studites*, 50–51; Cholij, *Theodore the Stoudite*, 17, 48–53. Some early manuscripts of the Triodion list Theodore and Joseph in their main titles, indicating their primary responsibility for first assembling the compendium, even though these manuscripts contain later compositions. See Sinai gr. 733 (11th century), Sinai gr. 736 (1027/28 or 1028/9), and Sinai gr. 741 (1099 and copied at the Monastery of Mar Sabas in Palestine). Bertonière, *Sundays of Lent*, 97–98.

2. In the absence of a critical edition, I have employed the Rome edition (TR) of 1879, which best represents the received tradition. As indicated in subsequent notes, I have also consulted earlier printed editions and two early manuscripts. Anglophone Orthodox Christians will be most familiar with the versions in *The Lenten Triodion*, although I have employed other translations here for greater precision. On the Triodion, see Getcha, *Typikon Decoded*, 35–39, 141–232. For general introductions reflecting modern and contemporary practice, see Wybrew, *Orthodox Lent*; Schmemann, *Great Lent*.

3. For an overview see Pott, *Byzantine Liturgical Reform*, 115–51; idem, "Réforme monastique." The critical work was undertaken by Leroy, "La réforme studite"; idem, *Studitisches Mönchtum*. Taft, "Liturgy"; Getcha, *Typikon Decoded*, 42–44. For a history of the Stoudios Monastery, see Delouis, *Saint-Jean-Baptiste de Stoudios*.

4. Pott, *Byzantine Liturgical Reform*, 142–49.

5. *Small Catecheses* 50; ed. Auvray, 182. On the preaching of the catecheses and their context in Theodore's career see also Leroy, *Études sur les Grandes catéchèses*, 25–37. Wolfram, "Der Beitrag des Theodoros Studites."

6. See Pott, *Byzantine Liturgical Reform*, 137–40.

7. Simon Harris ("The 'Kanon' and the Heirmologion," 187) observes in the attribution of various hymns that Theodore seems to have taken on the task of composing hymns for the six weeks of Lent proper and for the eight weeks from Easter until the week after Pentecost, while Joseph wrote for the week preceding Lent, that is, Cheesefare Week.

8. Quinlan, *Sin. Gr. 734–735*. This manuscript was originally a single volume now bound in two codices. In Sinai gr. 734, the Triodion begins with a title page on f. 3r. The first two pages contain additional stichera for the Sunday of Apokreas. See Quinlan, *Sin. Gr. 734–735*, 7. Apparently the scribe has included these additional hymns without interleaving them in the text of his archetype.

9. The early dissemination of the Triodion merits further study. See my discussion below. For the period after iconoclasm, scholars have generally assumed that nuns and monks participated in the same sort of common worship, although the evidence in monastic typika is generally later. See Dubowchik, "Singing with the Angels," 282–89.

10. Joseph [the Stoudite?], *On the Prodigal Son* 1.1; TR, 12. I have numbered the stanzas, or troparia, by ode number and stanza number. English translation by Ephrem Lash at http://www.anastasis.org.uk/ProdigalE.htm, slightly modified (including "prodigal" for "profligate"). For an English translation in rhymed couplets of troparia from Odes 6 and 8, see Neale, *Hymns of the Eastern Church*, 203–5.

11. Theodore the Stoudite, *On the Second Coming* 1.1–2; TR, 34. My trans. Neale, *Hymns of the Eastern Church*, 179–88 translates Odes 1, 3, 4 and 9.

12. Christopher, *On the Transgression of Adam* 1.1; TR, 102; my trans.

13. *Typikon of the Monastery of St. John the Forerunner on Pantelleria* 8–10 (ed. Mansvetov, *Tserkovnii ustav*, 441–45; trans. *BMFD*, 63–64). On the kanonarch and related officials, see also Leroy, *Studitisches Mönchtum*, 60–66; Dubowchik, "Singing with the Angels," 285–89. For later performance practice, see Troelsgård, "Kanon Performance in the Eleventh Century"; idem, "What Kind of Chant Books?" 565.

14. "On the Sunday of Renovation we begin the Six Psalms. We also sing the 'God is Lord' [Ps 117 (118): 27] . . . and the *troparion* 'When the tomb was sealed' and immediately the canon." *Typikon of the Monastery of St. John Stoudios in Constantinople* 3A, 4A; ed. Dmitrievsky, *Opisanie liturgicheskikh rykopisei*, 1:1.224–38; trans. *BMFD*, 102.

15. Theodore the Stoudite, *Small Catecheses* 99 (ed. Auvray); trans. Cholij, *Theodore the Stoudite*, 85. See also Cholij, *Theodore the Stoudite*, 34–35, 65–67, on the text and dating of the *Small Catecheses* and the context for delivering them.

16. Theodore the Stoudite, *Small Catecheses* 55 (ed. Auvray, 200); Pott, *Byzantine Liturgical Reform*, 136.

17. Giannouli, "Die Tränen der Zerknirschung"; eadem, "*Catanyctic* Religious Poetry"; Lauxtermann, *Spring of Rhythm*, 31–35; Hinterberger, "Emotions in Byzantium"; idem, "Tränen in der byzantinischen Literatur"; Müller, *Der Weg des Weinens*; Hunt, *Joy-Bearing Grief*.

18. See Rosenwein, *Emotional Communities*, 1–2. I have also found helpful McNamer, *Affective Meditation*. For consideration of the place of emotions in religious experience more generally see Ebersole, "Function of Ritual Weeping." See also the essays collected in Corrigan, ed., *Religion and Emotion*. Even so, Byzantium and indeed subsequent Orthodoxy have been neglected in broader narratives about Christianity and the emotions; see, for example, Tallon, "Christianity."

19. The literature on Evagrios of Pontus's theory of the passions and its afterlife is now vast. See Stewart, "Evagrius Ponticus and the Eastern Monastic Tradition"; idem, "Evagrius Ponticus and the 'Eight Generic Logismoi'"; Brakke, *Demons and the Making of the Monk*. For a more modern perspective, see Roberts, *Spiritual Emotions*.

20. Hinterberger, "Emotions in Byzantium," 126.

21. For a broader theoretical context, see Brennan, *Transmission of Affect*; and for an excellent consideration of aspects of performance with respect to medieval Spanish discourses, see Swift, "Penitent Prepares." Swift's comparisons with Stanislavsky's Method acting are tantalizing.

22. The best survey of the early evidence is Bradshaw and Johnson, *Origins of Feasts*, 89–113; see also Talley, *Origins of the Liturgical Year*, 27–31, 214–22.

23. Mateos, *Typicon*, 2:2–3. Another manuscript also representing the earliest surviving stages of the tradition, Vat. gr. 771, copied in South Italy at Grottaferrata in the eleventh century, first gathers hymns for each of the Sundays of Lent properly speaking and then begins the pre-Lenten cycle with the Sunday of the Prodigal Son (f. 8v), here designated "the second Sunday before Apokreas." See *Codices vaticani graeci, III*, ed. Devreesse, 286–87. Sinai gr. 734–735 and Vat. gr. 771, which is even more anthological, do not derive from a common source, and thus the material they share, which is substantial, derives from an earlier period, perhaps from the second half of the ninth century.

Quinlan, *Sin. Gr. 734–735*, 37, following Karabinov, *Postnaia Triod'*, 205–16. The third manuscript that Quinlan ("Triodia Manuscripts," 145–48) groups in the earliest surviving stage of the Triodion, Grottaferrata Δβ I of the eleventh to twelfth century and of uncertain Italo-Greek provenance, begins with the Sunday of Apokreas, suggesting that among some Byzantine Rite Christians in eleventh-century South Italy the pre-Lenten period began with Meatfare Sunday. Bertonière, *Sundays of Lent*, 155–56, 158–59. Even before the ninth century, Constantinopolitan lectionary practice assigned a relatively continuous sequence of readings from the Gospel of Luke, beginning with the seventeenth Sunday after Pentecost, in September, and ending with Luke 18, just on the cusp of Lent. See Getcha, "Le système des lectures bibliques," 25–56; Getcha, *Typikon Decoded*, 146. But it is worth noting that in this schema, Luke 15 would have fallen earlier in the sequence of the fixed cycle, some six weeks before Meatfare Sunday. Thus the assignment of the parable of the Prodigal Son to this pre-Lenten slot reflects a deliberate choice to assimilate its narrative to the moveable calendar. The lectionary system of Constantinople may already have assigned the reading of the parable of the Prodigal Son to this Sunday before it was assimilated to the Lenten service book's schema, but it is also possible that addition of this pre-Lenten Sunday occurred early in the ninth century, at the same time as the conception of the Triodion. The ninth- or tenth-century New Testament lectionary Vat. gr. 1067 (Gregory-Aland ℓ 36) has one preparatory Sunday for Lent called "The Sunday before Apokreas." Bertonière (*Sundays of Lent*, 32) posits a "gradual attraction of the last Sundays of Pentecost" into the Lenten cycle, "because of the appropriateness of their Gospel readings to the general theme of Lent." Mateos, *Typicon*, 2:157–67. Thus the Stoudites themselves may have been instrumental in this expansion of Lent to include a Sunday dedicated to the Prodigal.

24. On the expansion of the Lenten fast in the early and middle Byzantine periods, see Bertonière, *Sundays of Lent*, 29–32. Getcha, *Typikon Decoded*, 145–46. Sinai gr. 736, dated to 1028/29, opens with the Sunday "of the Pharisee and the Tax Collector."

25. Quinlan (*Sin. Gr. 734–735*, 62) has transcribed the text of the second ode of *On the Prodigal Son*. The disappearance of the second ode in later centuries deserves further consideration; Bernhard ("Der Ausfall der 2. Ode") provides an unsatisfactory explanation. Alexander Lingas helpfully summarized for me the conclusions of Krivko, "K istorii vtoroi pesni." See also Frøyshov, "Georgian Witness to the Jerusalem Liturgy," 262–63. There is some evidence for the eighth and ninth centuries that hymnographers writing in Palestine such as John of Damascus and Kosmas of Maiouma preferred eight-ode canons, while those writing in the Constantinople or its orbit, such as Andrew of Crete, Patriarch Germanos, and the early Stoudites preferred nine odes. See Harris, "The 'Kanon' and the Heirmologion," 175–97.

26. *Typikon of the Monastery of St. John the Forerunner on Pantelleria* 9; BMFD, 63–64.

27. Velimirović, "Byzantine Heirmos and Heirmologion." Getcha, *Typikon Decoded*, 75–82. For contemporary Athonite practice, see Lash, "Matins for Weekdays," http://www.anastasis.org.uk/Matheb.pdf, esp. 26–27.

28. Harris ("The 'Kanon' and the Heirmologion," 196–97) shows that the canticles were already being discarded in some contexts in the eleventh century, effectively rendering the kanon a freestanding hymn.

29. Velimirović, "Byzantine Heirmos and Heirmologion," 192–244. Simon Harris, "The 'Kanon' and the Heirmologion."

30. Quinlan, *Sin. Gr. 734–735*, 20–21; Quinlan, "Triodia Manuscripts," which revises the classic but confusing work of Karabinov, *Postnaia triod'*.

31. See Sinai gr. 733 (eleventh century), 736 (1027/28 or 1028/9), and 741 (1099 and copied at the Monastery of Mar Sabas in Palestine). See Bertonière, *Sundays of Lent*, 97–98.

32. For assessment of each of these hymnographers, see Kazhdan, *History of Byzantine Literature*, 46–52, 87–90, 111–26.

33. Griffith, "What Has Constantinople to Do with Jerusalem?" On the move to the Stoudios, see Hatlie, *Monks and Monasteries of Constantinople*, 338–43.

34. Bertonière, *Sundays of Lent*, 24.

35. Ševčenko, "Canon and Calendar." Spanos, *Codex* Lesbiacus Leimonos *11*, 76–81. Kazhdan, *History of Byzantine Literature*, 261–79.

36. The others are Vaticanus graecus 771 (eleventh century) and Grottaferrata Δβ I (eleventh-twelfth century). See Quinlan, "Triodia Manuscripts," 148; Bertonière, *Sundays of Lent*, 155, 158–59.

37. Quinlan (*Sin. Gr. 734–735*, 30–31) found that the scribal hand responsible for most of manuscript bears some resemblance to a manuscript tentatively assigned to the Stoudios Monastery and dated 1018, namely Vat. gr. 1675. See Follieri, *Codices graeci*, table 24. A second hand can be found at Sinai gr. 735, ff. 116r–118r. Quinlan associates this hand with one attributed to a tenth-century deacon at Stoudios named Dorotheos in Vat. gr. 1671; Follieri, *Codices graeci*, table 15.

38. Quinlan, *Sin. Gr. 734–735*, 22–23, 30.

39. The second option is attributed to a certain Peter, and the third is attributed in an acrostic made up the initial letters of its theotokia to Theophanes, probably Theophanes Graptos, "the Branded," (775–845), originally a Sabaite monk, later persecuted in Constantinople in 815 during the Second Iconoclasm, and thus a contemporary of the early Stoudites.

40. See, for example, the variety of kanons assigned to the second Sunday of Lent in the manuscripts: Bertonière, *Sundays of Lent*, 79–87.

41. Quinlan, *Sin. Gr. 734–735*, 23–25.

42. *Triodion*, ed. Cunadi (Venice, 1522); TR.

43. Pott, *Byzantine Liturgical Reform*, 166–69; Taft, "Liturgy," 603–6; idem, "A Tale of Two Cities," 22–23.

44. Quinlan, *Sin. Gr. 734–735*, 22–23. Quinlan writes (22), "The work of the early Stoudites provides a good starting point in the examination of [the historical forces shaping the later tradition], as it both transmitted the previous developments in the Triodion and eventually determined its most characteristic features."

45. Mateos, *Typicon*, 2:10–11. This may reflect practice in Jerusalem rather than Constantinople. I am indebted to Alexander Lingas for discussing the evidence for the dissemination of Stoudite hymnography.

46. The hymn appears in Sinai gr. 734, ff. 3v–6r. In the received tradition, exemplified by TR, 12–16, the kanon lacks its second ode. Quinlan (*Sin. Gr. 734–735*, 63) has transcribed the second ode.

47. The first of the theotokia bids God to accept the prayers of his mother on the speaker's behalf, while rest address the Virgin herself. The theotokia at the end of each ode are part of the convention for the genre of the kanon; in this case they afford an alternation in the recipient of the

speaker's entreaties. On the development of the theotokion appended to the end of the odes of the kanon, see Kazhdan, *History of Byzantine Literature*, 88–90, 263. Initially the theotokion was not present in all kanons: The odes of John of Damascus's *Golden Kanon* for Easter Sunday and his kanon for Pentecost both lack theotokia. Similarly, theotokia are rare in the works of Kosmas of Maiouma, and where they do appear they may have been added later (Kazhdan, 112). I thank Mary Cunningham for sharing her insights.

48. But Tomadakis, Ἰωσὴφ ὁ Ὑμνογράφος, does not list the work in his catalogue of genuine works (107–225), and lists relatively few compositions for the Triodion (200–1). Joseph the Hymnographer's output began in the 830s or 840s. On the problem of distinguishing the works of Joseph the Stoudite from those of Joseph the Hymnographer, see Steirnon, "La vie et l'œuvre de S. Joseph l'Hymnographe," 244, 264.

49. A later Triodion, Sinai gr. 733, of the eleventh century, assigns the kanon to the second Sunday of Lent, reflecting the lectionary traditions of Jerusalem. See Bertonière, *Sundays of Lent*, 47–46. The calendar of Jerusalem did not extend the Lenten cycle to include Constantinople's two preparatory Sundays, but assigned the parable of the Prodigal Son to the second Sunday of Lent. GL 399 (1:66 [text]; 1:57 [trans.]). The liturgy at Sinai itself followed the Hagiopolite lectionary system; see Taft, "Worship on Sinai."

50. Romanos, *Hymns*, 420–29 (49; SC 28); trans. Lash, 101–11.

51. Romanos follows closely a sermon on the Prodigal Son wrongly attributed to John Chrysostom that maintains similar themes. The homily, however, does reflect at some length on the Prodigal Son's interior thought. PG 59:515–522. See Lash's comments in Romanos, *On the Life of Christ*, 247–49; Brock, "Fragments of a Ps-John Chrysostom Homily."

52. Romanos also bids God to provide the congregation with the tears of the Harlot and calls on God to grant them pity, "as you did the Tax Collector" (22.7–9). The two manuscripts preserving the poem have different preludes. The proemion in the Patmos manuscript (Patmiacus 213, eleventh century),which assigns the hymn to the second Sunday of Lent, compares the poet and the Prodigal in the first person: "I have rivaled the Prodigal by my senseless deeds / and like him I fall down before you and seek forgiveness" (prelude 1). In the Athos manuscript (Athous Vatopedinus 1041, tenth-eleventh century), however, the proemion emphasizes the Eucharist, "Of our mystical table, O Immortal, count me worthy, who have been corrupted by living as a prodigal." Here the poem lacks an assignment to a particular Sunday. See Grosdidier de Matons, *Hymnes* 3:227–30, 234–35.

53. PG 97:1329–1385; my trans.

54. Andrew may have included one additional, if oblique reference to the Prodigal, although in the absence of a critical edition, this is uncertain. In the PG and TR texts of verse 1.21, Andrew refers to himself as having "squandered the substance of my soul in prodigalities [καταναλώσας ταῖς ἀσωτίαις]" (PG 97:1333; TR, 464; see also *Lenten Triodion*, 380), a reading supported by the Slavic versions. But other texts of the Triodion have "squandered the substance of my soul in sin [καταναλώσας τῇ ἁμαρτίᾳ], a reading reflected in the thirteenth-century commentary of Akakios Sabaites; see Giannouli, *Die beiden byzantinischen Kommentare*, 185. Neither the verb καταναλίσκω nor its participles appear in the Lukan account.

55. Sinai gr. 734 does not give a kontakion for the Sunday of the Prodigal Son. The proemion

and single strophe for the kontakion given in the received tradition represented by TR (14–15) are not the hymn by Romanos.

56. Brakke, "Making Public the Monastic Life"; Stewart, "Evagrius Ponticus and the 'Eight Generic Logismoi.'"

57. See also 4.1, 5.1, 5.3, 7.1, 7.2.

58. Theodore the Stoudite, *Small Catecheses* 103; trans. Lash at http://www.anastasis.org.uk/catechesis_103.htm. See also *Small Catecheses* 35.

59. Sinai gr. 734, ff. 22r–25v; TR 34–41. The Greek text can also be found, with some errors, at http://www.christopherklitou.com/triodion_meatfare_sunday_greek.htm. There is an English translation in *Lenten Triodion*, 153–63, but I have supplied my own translation here. For ease of reference, I refer to the stanzas within each ode by their order in TR even though some of these stanzas are absent or transposed in the early manuscript version.

60. Vat. gr. 771 ff. 14r–17v. *Codices vaticani graeci, III*, 286–87. Émereau, "Hymnographi byzantini," 179. On the manuscript, see Malatesta Zilembo, "Gli amanuensi di Grottaferrata," 26–27. See also Buonocore, *Bibliografia dei fondi manoscritti*, 852; Maisano, "Un inno inedito di S. Andrea di Creta," 519. On the scriptorium at Grottaferrata, see Lucà, "Scritture e libri," 1:319–89 plus plates. The monastery copied a number of Stoudite texts, including multiple copies of the Theodore's *Small Catecheses*. For the reception of Theodore in Southern Italy, see also *Codici greci dell'Italia meridionale* [exh. cat.], ed. Canart and Lucà, 71–72, 79–80.

61. The second ode appears in the appendix to an early printed edition, *Triōdion sun Theōi agiōi periechon tēn prepousan autō akolouthian* ([Rome: n.p.], 1738), χvς' (=656).

62. "Quantus tremor est futurus / Quando iudex est venturus / Cuncta stricte discusurrus!" *Roman Missal*, 117.

63. Harris, "The 'Kanon' and the Heirmologion," 186–87. In Sinai. gr. 73, f. 22r, the irmos is indicated with the same second plagal mode and words as those Andrew uses from Exodus 15:2: Βοηθός και σκεπαστής.

64. Mateos, *Typicon* 2:2–3; Bertonière, *Sundays of Lent*, 46–47. For Jerusalem, GL (lection 286) assigns Mt 6:34–7:21, part of the Sermon on the Mount, which ends with the verse "Not everyone who says to me 'Lord, Lord,' will enter the kingdom of heaven, but only the one who does the will of my Father in heaven." See also Getcha, *Typikon Decoded*, 150–51.

65. Romanos, *Hymns*, 266–67 (34; SC 50); trans. Lash, *On the Life of Christ: Kontakia*, 221.

66. Lingas, "Liturgical Place of the Kontakion."

67. See TR, 38–39; *Lenten Triodion*, 159. The practice of inserting additional hymnographic material after the third and sixth biblical canticles is attested in Palestinian monastic contexts already in the sixth century. *Narration of John and Sophronios* 1.21–23 (ed. Longo). Velimirović, "Byzantine Heirmos and Heirmologion," 196–97.

68. Ἀναβράζοντος πυρός. Possibly a reference to the lake of fire in Revelation 20:15.

69. This verse poses textual problems both as it stands in TR and in the manuscripts.

70. A search of the TLG suggests that this is the earliest instance of θρηνολογία, a rare locution in Byzantine Greek. To some extent it is an oxymoron, since lament (*thrēnos*) was regarded as inherently illogical, characterized by a lack of control. It is unclear whether the poet means that

it would be reasonable for the Rich Man to lament, or whether he understands lament itself as a discourse or logos with parameters and conventions. For broader perspective, see Alexiou, *Ritual Lament in the Greek Tradition*, 62–71. The sixth and seventh stanzas of Ode 4 in TR appear in reverse order in both Sinai gr. 734 and Vat. gr. 771, which likely preserve their original arrangement.

71. Theodore the Stoudite, *Small Catecheses*, 107.13–14, 38–39; my trans. This sermon was apparently composed for a time outside of Lent.

72. Theodore the Stoudite, *Small Catecheses*, 115.9–12; my trans.

73. Stanzas 5.4 and 5.6 of the Rome edition (TR) are lacking in the early manuscripts.

74. Wade, "La prière ἄνες, ἄφες, συγχώρησον." I thank Alex Lingas for the reference. See also the similar form in the prayer of propitiation at the conclusion of the Liturgy of Saint James in some versions: "Forgive, remit, pardon, O God, our offenses, voluntary and involuntary, committed knowingly or in ignorance, by transgression or through omission." Hammond, *Ancient Liturgies*, 54; trans. MacDonald, ANF 7:550. This placement may be later, or may have been assimilated from elsewhere in the Euchologion. The prayer does not appear in the earliest forms of the Liturgy of Saint James as witnessed in the Georgian translation; see *Liturgia ibero-graeca Sancti Iacobi*, ed. Khevsuriani et al. See also Arranz, "Les prières pénitentielles," 102–9 (at line 10), where the phrase occurs in a prayer for general absolution dated to the tenth century from outside Constantinople, for use in the service of the Typika, chanted after the ninth hour. Arranz noted similarities to Yom Kippur formulae and suggested a Syriac medium for the phrase's entry into Greek liturgy, as have Phenix and Horn, "Prayer and Penance," 237.

75. According to the version of the Theodotion translation of Daniel, which would have been in general use. See NETS, 991–92.

76. TR, 102–7; Sinai gr. 734, ff. 46v–49r; Vat. gr. 771, ff. 30r–32r. The Greek text can also be found, with some errors, at http://www.christopherklitou.com/triodion_cheesefare_sunday_greek .htm. I have provided my translation, but there is also an English translation in *Lenten Triodion*, 171–77. Vat. gr. 771, f. 30r titles the poem Κανὼν εἰς τὴν παράβασιν τοῦ Ἀδάμ. Sinai gr. 734, f. 46v, which is difficult to read at this point, abbreviates the title. Although Quinlan (*Sin. Gr. 734–735*, 88) was able to decipher less, the title here can be reconstructed as Ὁ κανὼν εἰς τὴν παρά[βασιν] τοῦ Ἀδάμ. Getcha, *Typikon Decoded*, 160–61.

77. PMBZ 1.1:372 (#1143). Photios, *Letters* 129 and 187 (ed. Laourdas-Westerink, 1:168 and 2:77–87). For two other poems attributed to Christopher the Protasekretes, see Ciccolella, "Basil I and the Jews." Ciccolella writes (69), "All attempts to identify this poet have failed." See also Lauxtermann, *Byzantine Poetry*, 281.

78. Christopher of Mitylene, *Poems*, ed. Kurtz, xviii; Beck, *Kirche und theologische Literatur*, 605; Cresci, "Διὰ βραχέων ἐπέων (K 83.2)."

79. PMBZ 1.1:336 (#1118). Theodore the Stoudite, *Letters* 40, 41 (ed. Fatouros).

80. Mateos, *Typicon*, 2:8–11; Getcha, *The Typikon Decoded*, 64.

81. Mateos, *Typicon*, 2:18–19. The lectionary cycle of Jerusalem in late antiquity read the first three chapters of Genesis at the Easter Vigil, and, according to the Armenian version, at Christmas and Epiphany as well. See GL 1.1:138, 1.2:110; AL 1.1:87–89; 114–15; 2.1:47, 123, 161; 2.2:211, 261, 299. Bertonière, *Historical Development of the Easter Vigil*, chart A.

82. The earliest is Patmos 213. See Bertonière, *Sundays of Lent,* 58–59.

83. For a critical edition of the anonymous kontakion based on a large number of kontakarion manuscripts, see Maas, *Frühbyzantinische Kirchenpoesie,* 16–20. Grosdidier de Matons, *Romanos le Mélode et les origines,* 28–31. Sinai gr. 734, f. 45r includes the proemion and, remarkably, the first ten strophes of the hymn, rather than the usual truncation to the proemion and a single strophe for other kontakia at Orthros, suggesting its importance for framing the last Sunday before Lent. (Strophes 9 and 5 are transposed in the Sinai Triodion.) A translation by Lash can be found at http://www.anastasis.org.uk/adam's_lament.htm.

84. J. Miller, "Prophetologion."

85. Grosdidier de Matons, *Romanos le Mélode: Hymnes,* 5:214–17.

86. The phrase "the delight of paradise" echoes the first strophe of the early anonymous kontakion *On Adam's Lament.* The phrase may ultimately derive from the anaphora, or prayer of eucharistic offering, in the *Liturgy of Basil,* where God made humanity "taking dust from the earth" and "placed him in a paradise of delight," although this prayer would have been recited only silently by the priest at the time the kanon was written. For the earliest surviving form of the text of the anaphora of the *Liturgy of Basil,* see *L'Euchologio Barberini gr. 336,* 65.

87. *Hirmologium Athoum: Codex Monasterii Hiberorum 470,* ed. Høeg, 99r; *Hirmologium Cryptense: Codex Cryptensis EPSILON.gamma.II,* ed. Tardo, 163v; *Hirmologium Sabbaiticum: Codex Monasterii S. Sabbae 83,* ed. Raasted, 145r. I am indebted to Alex Lingas for bringing these to my attention.

88. Theodore the Stoudite, *Small Catecheses* 66.34–48; trans. Lash, http://www.anastasis.org .uk/ths66–67.htm.

89. Michael the Monk, *Life of Theodore the Stoudite (Vita B)* 56 (PG 99:312–14). See Cholij, *Theodore the Stoudite,* 21–22; Taft, "Cathedral vs. Monastic Liturgy," 204–5.

90. Michael the Monk, *Life of Theodore the Stoudite (Vita B)* 56 (PG 99:314).

91. The *Vita B* was written after 868, since it assumes the death of the Stoudite monk Nikolaos who died in that year. See Cholij, *Theodore the Stoudite,* 7n23.

92. For broader background on the distinction between high literary style and the ecclesiastical "middle style," see Ševčenko, "Levels of Style." Michael the Monk apparently registers no irony about the discipline of the Sardinian's sound beating, both dreamed and palpable, despite the terrible history of corporal punishment for Theodore and other Stoudites as they opposed both imperial and ecclesiastical authorities. Theodore had been flogged in 797 for opposing the Emperor Constantine VI's second marriage to his mistress on the grounds that it violated canon law. Theodore held that the divorce of his first wife was invalid, since it was not grounded on adultery. Theophanes, *Chronographia,* 470–71 (ed. de Boor). On the so-called Moechian, or "adulterous," Controversy, see Pratsch, *Theodoros Studites,* 83–114; Cholij, *Theodore the Stoudite,* 38–45; Efthymiadis, *Life of the Patriarch Tarasios,* 23–24. Later, during the iconoclastic persecutions in 815 under Leo V, some of Theodore's companions received severe lashings for their support of icon veneration. It is unclear how many monks were actually subject to physical persecution and martyrdom during the Second Iconoclasm. For a useful reassessment of the period, see Pratsch, *Theodoros Studites,* 203–61; see also Hatlie, *Monks and Monasteries,* 383–88. Michael himself relates (*Life of Theodore* 42–43 [PG 99:296A-297C]) that Theodore was sentenced in 819 to one hundred strokes of the lash for sending letters while in exile. His wounds

festered so badly that he nearly died. See Cholij, *Theodore the Stoudite*, 57–58. If in Stoudite ideology, these travails constituted martyrdom, the Sardinian's flogging asserted the criteria for judging liturgical composition. Theodore himself, an "apostle of Christ," would guarantee their positive reception; it would be akin to heresy to think otherwise.

93. Cholij, *Theodore the Stoudite*, 19–21; Moffett, "Schooling in the Iconoclast Centuries"; Lemerle, *Byzantine Humanism*, 112–20, 139–44.

94. Lemerle, *Byzantine Humanism*, 140.

95. On the varied social classes of monks at the Stoudios, see Hatlie, *Monks and Monasteries*, 270–79. On literary culture and production, see Karlin-Hayter, "Où l'abeille butine."

96. Quinlan, *Sin. Gr. 734–735*, 43.

97. See Alexiou, *After Antiquity*, 53.

98. Aphthonios, *Progymnasmata* 11 (ed. Rabe); trans. Kennedy, *Progymnasmata*, 89–127. For more perspective, see Agosti, "L'etopea nella poesia greca tardoantica" and Ventrella, "L'etopea nella definizione degli antichi retori." For consideration of late ancient and medieval Western examples, see Woods and Copeland, "Classroom and Confession," and Woods, "Weeping for Dido." See Alpers, *Untersuchungen zu Johannes Sardianos*.

99. John of Sardis, *Commentary on the* Progymnasmata *of Aphthonios* 11; ed. Rabe, 194; trans. Kennedy, *Progymnasmata*, 213. Efthymiadis, "John of Sardis"; idem, "Notes on the Correspondence of Theodore," 157. Others have proposed a tenth-century date for the treatise. See the discussion in Alpers, *Untersuchungen zu Johannes*, 16–20.

100. John of Sardis, *Commentary on the* Progymnasmata *of Aphthonios* 11, ed. Rabe 195; trans. Kennedy, *Progymnasmata*, 214.

101. For overviews, see Kennedy, *Classical Rhetoric*, 183–95; Jeffreys, "Rhetoric."

102. Sinai gr. 736, ff. 2r–3v. The text is in TR, 2–5; my trans. I thank Father Justin Sinaites for providing photographs of the manuscript. The hymn lacks a second ode.

Chapter 7. Liturgies of the Monastic Self in Symeon the New Theologian

1. For interpretations of Symeon's biography and writings, see Golitzin, *St. Symeon the New Theologian*; Krivocheine, *In the Light of Christ*; H. Turner, *St. Symeon and Spiritual Fatherhood*; Alfeyev, *St. Symeon and the Orthodox Tradition*; Keselopoulos, *Man and the Environment*; Hunt, *Joy-Bearing Grief*, 171–209. The text of the *Catechetical Discourses* is ed. Krivocheine; the excellent English translation employed here is by de Cantanzaro, occasionally modified.

2. For critical perspective on the mechanisms of subjectivity formation in religious contexts, see Furey, "Body, Society, and Subjectivity"; Valantasis, *Making of the Self*; Flood, *Ascetic Self*.

3. Niketas Stethatos, *Life of Saint Symeon the New Theologian*, ed. and trans. Greenfield, xi–xv. The following paragraph follows Greenfield's admirable caution.

4. Foucault, "Technologies of the Self"; idem, "About the Beginning of the Hermeneutics of the Self," 171–74.

5. The contributions in this endeavor have been vast and have included Brown, *Body and Society*; Brakke, *Athanasius and Asceticism*; idem, *Demons and the Making of the Monk*; Shaw, *Burden*

of the Flesh; Clark, *Reading Renunciation*; Schroeder, *Monastic Bodies*; Burrus, *Sex Lives of Saints*; eadem, *Saving Shame*. For important nuance, see Brakke, "Making Public the Monastic Life."

6. Maloney in the introduction to Symeon the New Theologian, *Discourses*, trans. deCantazaro, 15. See also Krausmüller, "Monastic Communities of Stoudios and St Mamas."

7. Althusser, "Ideology and Ideological State Apparatuses"; Butler, *Psychic Life of Power*, 106–31; Dolar, "Beyond Interpellation."

8. On the voicing of such accepted self-recognitions, see Butler, *Psychic Life of Power*, 106–7.

9. On the performance of authorial humility, see Krueger, *Writing and Holiness*, 94–109.

10. On the intimate connection between *penthos* and tears in Symeon, see Hunt, *Joy-Bearing Grief*, 211–23.

11. For the problematic of assessing sincerity in religious practice see Seligman et al., *Ritual and Its Consequences*; Bell, "Performance," 204–24.

12. For the *Life of Pelagia*, see Ward, *Harlots of the Desert*, 57–66. For the *Life of Mary of Egypt*, see Talbot, ed., *Holy Women of Byzantium*, 63–93. Vitae of Theodora of Alexandria are listed in BHG, nos. 1727–30; of Eusebia/Xena of Mylasa, as Eusebia, BHG, nos. 633–634. Euphrosyne joined a monastery as a male novice. See *Catholic Encyclopedia*, s. vv. Eusebia and Euphrosyne. I thank Alice-Mary Talbot for her assistance in sorting these names out. For studies, see Patlagean, "L'histoire de la femme déguisée en moine"; Hunt, *Clothed in the Body*, 63–77; Burrus, *Sex Lives of Saints*, 128–59; Davis, "Crossed Texts, Crossed Sex"; Miller, "Is There a Harlot in This Text?"

13. Symeon the New Theologian, *Letters* 2.10–18; Symeon, *Epistles*, ed. and trans. Turner, 70–71. See also *Letters* 1.284–88 (trans. Turner, 50–1; ll. 333–38). Preaching to his monks at St. Mamas, Symeon taught, "As holy David tells us, 'I therefore, as you see, did not fast, I did not keep vigil, nor did I sleep on the ground, yet "I humbled myself" ' " (*Catechetical Discourses* 22.8–10), despite the text of Psalm 35:13: "I would humble myself with fasting."

14. Flood, *Ascetic Self*, 221.

15. Athanasios, *Life of Antony* 55 (ed. Bartelink); John Chrysostom, *Homilies on Matthew* 41.6 (PG 57:540). Krueger, *Writing and Holiness*, 1–2.

16. Cholij, *Theodore the Stoudite*, 35, 174–82. Stewart, "Radical Honesty"; Zecher, "Angelic Life in Desert and *Ladder*."

17. H. Turner, *St. Symeon and Spiritual Fatherhood*, 70–73, 135–43.

18. For the importance of gesture in monastic formation, see Schmitt, *La raison des gestes*, 173–205. Flagellation in monastic formation merits more study. On flagellation in the West see Flood, *Ascetic Self*, 187–90; Largier, *In Praise of the Whip*, 35–100. See also de Bruyn, "Flogging a Son"; Chin, *Grammar and Christianity*, 110–38; Dickson, "Flagellation"; idem, "Flagellants of 1260"; Bulst, "Flagellanten."

19. In this Symeon reflects trends in earlier Neoplatonic thought. See Hadot, "Les niveaux de conscience."

20. On memory and liturgy in Byzantine hagiography, see Krueger, *Writing and Holiness*, 110–32.

21. For the self as the audience in Western monastic rites, see Asad, *Genealogies of Religion*, 141: "The program is performed primarily not for the sake of an audience but for the sake of the performers."

22. Niketas Stethatos, *Life of Symeon the New Theologian* 35 (ed. Greenfield; trans. modified).

23. For a private service of repentance prescribed possibly for a layman, see *Letters* 2.75–95 (ed. Turner, 74–77).

24. On the place of the performative in Byzantium, see Mullett, "Rhetoric, Theory," 151–70.

25. On tears, see Maloney, in *Symeon the New Theologian: The Discourses*, 30–31; Hinterberger, "Tränen in der byzantinischen Literatur"; Müller, *Der Weg des Weinens*, 112–31. On the range of the meaning of tears for Latin patristic authors, see Dulaey, "Les larmes."

26. On Symeon's theories of vision and visuality, see Barber, "Icons, Prayer, and Vision"; idem, *Contesting the Logic of Painting*, 23–59.

27. Hunt, *Joy-bearing Grief*, 199–209.

28. Symeon the New Theologian, *Hymns*; text: ed. Koder; trans.: Griggs. Symeon may well have written both texts around the same time; see Niketas, *Life of Symeon the New Theologian* 81. For an appreciation of the theological dimensions of the corpus, see McGuckin, "Symeon's Hymns of Divine Eros."

29. For excellent insight into the theatrical aspects of tears in later medieval Spain, see Swift, "A Penitent Prepares."

30. The Prayer of Manasseh is Ode 12 in Rahlfs's edition of the Septuagint. For the account of Manasseh, see 2 Ch 33:1–13. On Compline, see Getcha, *Typikon Decoded*, 92–97. For the earlier literature on the origins of Great Compline see Diakovskij, *Posledovanie časov i izobrazitel'nyx*, 167ff.; Skaballanovič, *Tolkovyj Tipikon*, 1:331–32, 423–30. The earliest manuscript evidence for the Prayer of Manasseh as part of Great Compline dates from the twelfth and thirteenth centuries. I thank Sister Vassa Larin for her generous assistance with the Russian scholarship.

31. The parable of the Prodigal Son figures prominently in Symeon's conception of God's loving acceptance and divinization of monks. See Krueger, "Homoerotic Spectacle."

32. Seligman et al. (*Ritual and Its Consequences*, 24) see in the work of ritual a gap between the outer self and inner beliefs. But Symeon sees the goal of ritual formation in the conformity of the outer self and the understanding of the inner self.

33. *Rule of the Monastery of St. John Stoudios* 25 (*BMFD*, 108).

34. Kazhdan and Constable, *People and Power in Byzantium*, 62. See also Bitton-Ashkelony, "Personal Experience."

35. *Catechetical Discourse* 30.229–35 reproduces Barsanouphios and John, *Letters* 846 (ed. de Angelis-Noah and Neyt). The passage explicates vocabulary in Mt 14:31, 28:17, and Jas 1:8, 4:8.

Conclusion

1. For the text, see Nikolaos Mesarites, *Description of Holy Apostles*, ed. Downey. I have supplied my own translation. James and Webb, "To Understand Ultimate Things."

2. Wharton Epstein, "Rebuilding and Decoration of Holy Apostles"; Maguire, "Cycle of Images in the Church."

3. In the thirteenth-century Church of Hagia Sophia at Trebizond, Christ Pantokrator is surrounded by verses from Psalm 101 [102]: 21–22: "The Lord from heaven looked down at the earth to hear the groaning of the prisoners, to set free the sons of those put to death, to declare the name of the Lord in Sion, and his praise in Jerusalem." Eastmond, *Art and Identity*, 100.

4. James and Webb, "To Understand Ultimate Things," 11–12.

5. Cormack, "Rediscovering the Christ Pantokrator." The image has undergone a series of restorations.

6. Maguire, "Cycle of Images in the Church," 136–38.

7. For the historicization of guilt in another context, see Delumeau, *Sin and Fear.*

8. Peculiarly, Delumeau (*Sin and Fear*, 3) glosses "the history of sin" as "the history of a negative self-image."

9. Translation and discussion, Ševčenko, "Metrical Inscriptions," 86–87; for the text and its history see Rhoby, *Byzantinische Epigramme*, 329–41. Lauxtermann, *Byzantine Poetry from Pisides to Geometres*, 166–70.

10. With reference to modern and postmodern philosophical debate, Hemming ("The Liturgical Subject") stresses the sublimation of the self in the presence of God.

11. For the "sense of personal order" as constitutive of the self, see Greenblatt, *Renaissance Self-Fashioning*, 1.

BIBLIOGRAPHY

Manuscripts

Athens, Byzantine Museum
    Athens, Byz. Museum 127 (11th century)
Athos, Vatopedi Monastery
    Athous Vatopedinus 1041 (10th/11th century)
Boston, Museum of Fine Arts
    Endicott Scroll (12th/13th century)
Florence, Biblioteca Medicea Laurenziana
    Plut. I, 56 (dated 586)
Grottaferrata, La Badia Greca
    Grottaferrata Γβ VII (10th century)
    Grottaferrata Δβ I (11th/12th century)
Patmos, Monastery of St. John
    Patmos 213 (11th century)
Rossano, Museo dell'Arcivescovada
    Rossano Gospels (6th century)
Sharfeh, Patriarchal Library
    Rahmani Codex Syr. 303 (8th or 9th century)
Sinai, Monastery of St. Catherine
    Sinai gr. 733 (11th century)
    Sinai gr. 734–735 (10th century)
    Sinai gr. 736 (dated 1027/28 or 1028/9)
    Sinai gr. 741 (dated 1099)
    Sinai gr. 1094 (12th century)
    Sinai gr. 1096 (dated 1214)
Vatican, Biblioteca Apostolica Vaticana
    Barberini gr. 336 (late 8th century)
    Vat. gr. 771 (11th century)
    Vat. gr. 778 (dated 1170)
    Vat. gr. 1067 (9th-10th century)
    Vat. gr. 1671 (10th century)
    Vat. gr. 1675 (dated 1018)
    Vat. gr. 2282 (9th century)

Primary Sources

Translations are cited below text editions. Preferred editions and translations appear first.

Andrew of Crete. *Great Kanon.* PG 97:1329–85.

———. *The Great Canon of St. Andrew and the Life of St. Mary of Egypt.* Trans. Mother Katherine and Mother Thecla. Toronto: Peregrina, 1997.

Antony of Choziba. *Life of George of Choziba and the Miracles of the Mother of God at Choziba.* Ed. C. Houze. *Analecta Bollandiana* 7 (1888): 3–368.

———. *The Life of Saint George of Choziba and the Miracles of the Most Holy Mother of God at Choziba.* Trans. Tim Vivian and Apostolos N. Athanassakis. San Francisco: Catholic Scholars Press, 1994.

Anastasios of Sinai. *Hexaemeron.* Ed. and trans. Clement A. Kuehn and John D. Baggarly. OCA 278. Rome: Pontificio Istituto Orientale, 2007.

———. *Oratio de sacra synaxi.* PG 89:825–49.

———. *Questions and Answers. Quaestiones et responsiones.* Ed. Marcel Richard and Joseph A. Munitiz. CCSG 59. Turnhout: Brepols, 2006.

———. *Questions and Answers.* Trans. Joseph A. Munitiz. Corpus Christianorum in Translation 7. Turnhout: Brepols, 2011.

Aphthonios. *Progymnasmata. Aphthonii Progymnasmata.* Ed. Hugo Rabe. Rhetores Graeci 10. Leipzig: Teubner, 1926.

Apostolic Constitutions. Les constitutions apostoliques. Ed. Marcel Metzger. 3 vols. SC 320, 329, 336. Paris: Cerf, 1985–87.

Asterios of Amasea. *Homilies. Asterius of Amasea: Homilies I–XVII.* Ed. Cornelis Datema. Leiden: Brill, 1970.

———. *Ancient Sermons for Modern Times.* Trans. Galusha Anderson and Edgar J. Goodspeed. New York: Pilgrim Press, 1904.

Athanasios of Alexandria. *Life of Antony. Vie d'Antoine.* Ed. G. J. M. Bartelink. SC 400. Paris: Cerf, 1994.

———. *The Life of Antony and the Letter to Marcellinus.* Trans. Robert C. Gregg. New York: Paulist, 1980.

Augustine. *Basic Writings of Saint Augustine.* Vol. 1. Trans. Whitney J. Oates. New York: Random House, 1948.

———. *The City of God Against the Pagans.* Vol. 4. Trans. Philip Levine. LCL. Cambridge, Mass.: Harvard University Press, 1966.

———. *Confessions.* Ed. James Joseph O'Donnell. Oxford: Clarendon, 1992.

———. *Four Anti-Pelagian Writings.* Trans. John Mourant and William J. Collinge. FOTC 86. Washington, D.C.: Catholic University of America Press, 1992.

———. *Epistolae ex duobus codidibus nuper in lucem prolatae.* Ed. Johannes Divjak CSEL 88. Vienna: Hoelder-Pichler-Tempsky, 1981.

———. *Letters: Volume VI (1*–29*).* Trans. Robert B. Eno. Washington, D.C.: Catholic University of America Press, 1989.

Avodah: An Anthology of Ancient Poetry for Yom Kippur. Ed. and trans. Michael D. Swartz and Joseph Yahalom. University Park: Pennsylvania State University Press, 2005.

Barsanouphios and John. *Letters. Barsanuphe et Jean de Gaza: Correspondance.* Ed. François Neyt and Paula de Angelis-Noah with French trans. Lucien Regnault. 5 vols. SC 426–27, 450–51, 468. Paris: Cerf, 1997–2002.

———. *Letters.* Trans. John Chryssavgis. 2 vols. FOTC 113–14. Washington, D.C.: Catholic University of America Press, 2006.

Basil of Caesarea. *Hexaemeron. Basile de Césarée: Homélies sur l'hexaéméron.* Ed. Stanislas Giet. 2nd ed. SC 26bis. Paris: Cerf, 1968.

———. *Letters.* Ed. Roy J. Deferrari and Martin R. P. Maguire. 4 vols. LCL. London: Heinemann, 1961–62.

———. *Longer Rules.* PG 31:901–1305.

———. *Longer Rules.* In *Ascetical Works*, trans. M. Monica Wagner. FOTC 9. Washington, D.C.: Catholic University of America Press, 1950.

Byzantine Monastic Foundation Documents: A Complete Translation of the Surviving Founders' Typika and Testaments. Ed. John Thomas and Angela Constantinides Hero. 5 vols. Washington, D.C.: Dumbarton Oaks, 2000.

Canons of the Council in Trullo. NPNF 2.14:369–408.

Christopher [?]. *On the Transgression of Adam.* TR, 102–7.

Christopher of Mitylene. *Poems. Die Gedichte des Christophoros Mitylenaios.* Ed. Eduard Kurtz. Leipzig: Neumann, 1903.

Cunningham, Mary B. *Wider than Heaven: Eighth-Century Homilies on the Mother of God.* Crestwood, N.Y.: St. Vladimir's Seminary Press, 2008.

Cyril of Jerusalem. *Catechetical Homilies. Cyrilli Hierosolymorum archiepiscopi opera quae supersunt onmia.* Ed. W. K. Reischl and J. Rupp. Munich: Lentner, 1860. Reprint, Hildesheim: Olms, 1967.

Cyril of Scythopolis. *Life of Euthymios.* Ed. Eduard Schwartz. In *Kyrillos von Skythopolis*, ed. Eduard Schwartz. *Texte und Untersuchungen* 49, 2 (1939): 3–85.

———. *The Lives of the Monks of Palestine.* Trans. R. M. Price and John Binns. Cistercian Studies 114. Kalamazoo, Mich.: Cistercian, 1991.

Daley, Brian E. *On the Dormition of Mary: Early Patristic Homilies.* Crestwood, N.Y.: St. Vladimir's Seminary Press, 1998.

Dmitrievsky, Aleksei. *Opisanie liturgicheskikh rykopisei.* Vol. 1, *Typika.* Kiev, 1895.

Dorotheos of Gaza. *Discourses. Dorothée de Gaza. Œuvres spirituelles.* Ed. Lucien Regnault and Jacques de Préville. SC 92. Paris: Cerf, 1963.

———. *Discourses and Sayings.* Trans. Eric P. Wheeler. Cistercian Studies 33. Kalamazoo, Mich.: Cistercian, 1977.

Egeria. *Travels.* Trans. John Wilkinson, *Egeria's Travels.* 3rd ed. Warminster: Aris & Phillips, 1999.

Ephrem the Syrian. *Hymns on Paradise.* Trans. Sebastian Brock. Crestwood, N.Y.: St. Vladimir's Seminary Press, 1990.

L'Eucologio Barberini gr. 336. Ed. Stefano Parenti and Elena Velkovska. 2nd ed. Rome: Edizioni Liturgiche, 2000.

Eusebios of Caesarea. *Praeparatio Evangelica.* Ed. K. Mras. Berlin: Akademie Verlag, 1954–56.

Eustratios. *Life of Eutychios. Eustratii presbyteri vita Eutychii patriarchae Constantinopolitani.* Ed. Carl Laga. CCSG 25. Turnhout: Brepols, 1992.

George the Monk. *Chronicon.* Ed. Carl de Boor and Peter Wirth. 2 vols. 1904. Reprint, Stuttgart: Teubner, 1978.

Gerontios. *Life of Melania the Younger. La vie de Sainte Mélanie.* Ed. Denys Gorce. SC 90. Paris: Cerf, 1962.

———. *The Life of Melania the Younger: Introduction, Translation, and Commentary.* Ed. and trans. Elizabeth A. Clark. New York: Edwin Mellen, 1984.

Gregory of Nazianzos. *Festal Orations. Grégoire de Nazianze: Discours 38–41.* Ed. Claudia Moreschini. SC 358. Paris: Cerf, 1990.

———. *Festal Orations.* Trans. Nonna Verna Harrison. Crestwood, N.Y.: St. Vladimir's Seminary Press, 2008.

Gregory of Nyssa. *Life of Makrina. Grégoire de Nysse: Vie de Sainte Macrine.* Ed. Pierre Maraval. SC 178. Paris: Cerf, 1971.

Hammond, C. E. *Ancient Liturgies.* Oxford: Clarendon, 1878.

Hippolytus of Rome. *Apostolic Tradition. Hippolyte de Rome: La tradition apostolique.* Ed. Bernard Botte. 2nd ed. SC 11bis. Paris: Cerf, 1968.

Hirmologium Athoum: Codex Monasterii Hiberorum 470. Ed. Carsten Høeg. Monumenta Musicae Byzantinae, Série Principale (Facsimilés) 2. Copenhagen: Munksgaard, 1938.

Hirmologium Cryptense: Codex Cryptensis EPSILON.gamma.II. Ed. Laurentius Tardo. Monumenta musicae Byzantinae, Série principale (Facsimilés) 3. Rome: Libreria dello Stato, 1951.

Hirmologium Sabbaiticum: Codex Monasterii S. Sabbae 83. Ed. Jørgen Raasted. Monumenta Musicae Byzantinae, Série Principale (Facsimilés) 8. Copenhagen: Munksgaard, 1969–70.

Kennedy, George A. *Progymnasmata: Greek Textbooks of Prose Composition and Rhetoric.* Atlanta: Society of Biblical Literature, 2003.

Jacob of Sarug. *Homilies on the Resurrection.* Ed. and trans. Thomas Kollamparampil. Metrical Homilies of Mar Jacob of Sarug 5. Piscataway, N.J.: Gorgias Press, 2008.

Jasper, R. C. D., and Geoffrey Cuming. *Prayers of the Eucharist: Early and Reformed.* 3rd. ed. Collegeville, Minn.: Liturgical Press, 1990.

John Chrysostom. *Commentary on the Psalms.* PG 55:39–498.

———. *Commentary on the Psalms.* Trans. Robert Charles Hill. 2 vols. Brookline, Mass.: Holy Cross Orthodox Press, 1998.

———. *Homilies on Ephesians.* PG 62:9–176; trans. NPNF 1.13:46–172.

———. *Homilies on Genesis.* PG 53:21–54:580.

———. *Homilies on Genesis.* Trans. Robert C. Hill. 3 vols. FOTC 74, 82, 87. Washington, D.C.: Catholic University of America Press, 1986–92.

———. *Homilies on Matthew.* PG 57:13–58:794; NPNF 1.10:1–334.

———. *On Lazarus.* PG 48.963–1054.

———. *On Wealth and Poverty.* Trans. Catherine P. Roth. Crestwood, N.Y.: St. Vladimir's Seminary Press, 1984.

John Klimax. *The Ladder of Paradise.* PG 88:631–1161.

———. *The Ladder of Divine Ascent.* Trans. Colm Luibheid and Norman Russell. New York: Paulist, 1982.

John Moschos. *Spiritual Meadow.* PG 87.3:2851–3112.

————. *The Spiritual Meadow*. Trans. John Wortley. Kalamazoo, Mich.: Cistercian, 1992.

John of Ephesus. *Historiae ecclesiasticae: pars tertia*. Ed. E. W. Brooks. CSCO 105–6; Scriptores Syri 54–55. 1935–36. Reprint, Louvain: Durbecq, 1952.

John of Sardis. *Commentary on the* Progymnasmata *of Aphthonios. Ioannes Sardianus: Commentarium in Aphthonium*. Ed. Hugo Rabe. Rhetores Graeci 15. Leipzig: Teubner, 1928.

Joseph [the Stoudite?]. *On the Prodigal Son*. TR, 12–16.

————. *On the Profligate Son*. Trans. Ephrem Lash. http://www.anastasis.org.uk/ProdigalE.htm.

Julius Africanus. *Chronography. Iulius Africanus Chronographiae: The Extant Fragments*. Ed. Martin Wallraff, trans. William Adler. Berlin: de Gruyter, 2007.

Justinian. *Novels. Corpus iuris civilis*. Ed. Wilhelm Kroll and Rudolf Schöll. Vol. 3. 1895. Reprint, Berlin: Weidmann, 1954.

Justin Martyr. *Apologies. Die ältesten Apologeten*. Ed. E. J. Goodspeed. 1915. Reprint, Göttingen: Vandenhoeck & Ruprecht, 1984.

Kedrenos, George. *Synopsis historion [Historiarum Compendium]*. PG 121:23–1166.

————. *Compendium historiarum*. Ed. Immanuel Bekker. 2 vols. Bonn: Weber, 1838–39.

Lectionaries Old and New. http://www.bombaxo.com/lectionaries.html.

The Lenten Triodion. Trans. Mother Mary and Kallistos Ware. London: Faber & Faber, 1978. Reprint, South Canaan, Pa.: St. Tikhon's Seminary Press, 2002.

Leontios of Byzantium. *Contra Nestorianos et Eutychianos*. PG 86:1268–1396.

Leontios the Presbyter. *Homilies. Leontii presbyteri Constantinopolitani: Homiliae*. Ed. Cornelis Datema and Pauline Allen. CCSG 17. Turnhout: Brepols: 1987.

————. *Homilies*. Leontius, Presbyter of Constantinople. *Fourteen Homilies*. Trans. Pauline Allen and Cornelis Datema. Byzantina Australiensia 9. Brisbane: Australian Association for Byzantine Studies, 1991.

Life of Andrew of Crete. Ed. Athanasios Papadopoulos-Kerameus. In *Analekta Hierosolymitikes Stachyologias*, 5:169–79. 1888. Reprint, Brussels: Culture et Civilisation, 1963.

Life of Matrona of Perge. In *Acta sanctorum Novembris*, vol. 3, 790–813. Brussels: Société des Bollandistes, 1910.

Life of Matrona of Perge. Trans. Jeffrey Featherstone. In *Holy Women of Byzantium: Ten Saints' Lives in English Translation*, ed. Alice-Mary Talbot, 18–64. Byzantine Saints' Lives in Translation 1. Washington, D.C.: Dumbarton Oaks, 1996.

Life of Mary of Egypt. PG 87:3697–726.

Life of Mary of Egypt. Trans. Maria Kouli. In *Holy Women of Byzantium: Ten Saints' Lives in English Translation*, ed. Alice-Mary Talbot, 65–93. Byzantine Saints Lives in Translation 1. Washington, D.C.: Dumbarton Oaks, 1996.

Liturgia Ibero-graeca Sancti Iacobi. Ed. Lili Khevsuriani et al. Münster: Aschendorff, 2011.

Liturgies Eastern and Western. Ed. F. E. Brightman. 1896. Reprint, Oxford: Clarendon, 1965.

Maas, Paul. *Frühbyzantinische Kirchenpoesie: I. Anonyme Hymnen des V–VI Jahrhunderts*. 2nd ed. Berlin: De Gruyter, 1931.

Mansvetov, Ivan D. *Tserkovnii ustav (tipik) ego obrazovanie i sudba v grečeskoi i russkoi tserkvi*. Moscow, 1885.

Maximos the Confessor. *Asketikon*. PG 90:912–56.

————. *Maximus Confessor: Selected Writings*. Trans. George Berthold. New York: Paulist, 1985.

Michael the Monk. *Life of Theodore the Stoudite (Vita B)*. PG 99:233–328.

The Miracles of St. Artemios. Ed. and trans.Virgil Crisafulli and John Nesbitt. Leiden: Brill, 1997.

Narration of the Abbots John and Sophronios. In Augusta Longo, "Il testo integrale della *Narrazione degli abati Giovanni e Sofronio* attraverso le *Hermêneiai* di Nicone," *Rivista di studi bizantini e neoellenici* 12–13 (1965–1966): 223–67.

Neale, John Mason. *Hymns of the Eastern Church*. London: Hayes, 1876.

The New Oxford Book of Carols. Ed. Hugh Keyte et al. Oxford: Oxford University Press, 1998.

Nikephoros I, Patriarch of Constantinople. *Antirrhetikos*. PG 100:206–573.

Niketas Stethatos. *The Life of Saint Symeon the New Theologian*. Trans. Richard P. H. Greenfield. Dumbarton Oaks Medieval Library. Cambridge, Mass.: Harvard University Press, 2013.

Nikolaos Mesarites. *Description of the Church of the Holy Apostles*. Ed. and trans. Glanville Downey. "Nikolaos Mesarites: Description of the Church of the Holy Apostles at Constantinople." *Transactions of the American Philosophical Society* n.s. 47 (1957): 857–924.

On Adam's Lament. In Paul Maas, ed., *Frühbyzantinische Kirchenpoesie: I. Anonyme Hymnen des V–VI Jahrhunderts*, 2nd ed., 16–20. Berlin: De Gruyter, 1931.

————. Trans. Ephrem Lash. http://www.anastasis.org.uk/adam's_lament.htm.

Origen of Alexandria. *Homilies on Jeremiah*. PG 13:256–525.

The Orthodox Study Bible. Nashville, Tenn.: Nelson, 2008.

Palaea Historica. In *Anecdota graeco-byzantina: Pars prior*. Ed. Afanasii Vassiliev, 188–299. Moscow: Universitas Caesarea, 1893.

————. Trans. William Adler. "Palaea Historica: Introduction and Translation." In *More Old Testament Pseudepigrapha*, ed. James Davila and Richard Bauckham, 585–672. Grand Rapids, Mich.: Eerdmans, 2013.

Photios. *Letters. Photii Patriarchae Constantinopolitani Epistulae et Amphilochia*. Ed. Vasileios Laourdas and Leendert Gerrit Westerink. 6 vols. Leipzig: Teubner, 1983–88.

Poetae Latini aevi Carolini. Ed. Ernest Duemmler. 4 vols. Berlin: Weidmann, 1881–1923.

Prex eucharistica: Textus e variis liturgiis antiquioribus selecti. Ed. Anton Hänggi et al. Fribourg: Éditions Universitaires, 1968–2005.

Proklos, Patriarch of Constantinople. *Homilies*. Ed. Nicholas P. Constas. *Proclus of Constantinople and the Cult of the Virgin in Late Antiquity: Homilies 1–5, Texts and Translations*. Leiden: Brill, 2003.

————. *Proclus Bishop of Constantinople: Homilies on the Life of Christ*. Trans. Jan Harm Barkhuizen. Brisbane: Australian Catholic University, Centre for Early Christian Studies, 2001.

————. *On the Crucifixion. L'Homiletique de Proclus de Constantinople: Tradition manuscrite, inédits, études connexes*. Ed. François Joseph Leroy. Studi e Testi 247. Vatican City: Biblioteca Apostolica Vaticana, 1967.

————. *On the Nativity of the Lord*. Ed. Ch. Martin. "Un florilège grec: Homélies christologiques des IVᵉ et Vᵉ siècles sur la Nativité." *Le Muséon* 54 (1941): 40–48.

Prophetologion. Prophetologium. Ed. Carsten Høeg, Günther Zuntz, and [Sysse] Gudrun Engberg. Monumenta Musicae Byzantinae: Lectionaria 1. Copenhagen: Munksgaard, 1939–81.

Ps.-Narsai. *The Liturgical Homilies of Narsai.* Trans. R. H. Connolly. Texts and Studies 8.1. Cambridge: Cambridge University Press, 1909.

Rahmani, Ignatius Ephrem. "Ritus receptionis episcopi et celebrationis liturgiae catechumenorum." In *Studia Syriaca: Seu, collectio documentorum hactenus ineditorum ex codicibus Syriacis,* fasc. 3, 1–22 and 1–4 (Syriac numerals). Monte Libano: Seminarium Scharfensi, 1908.

Renoux, Athanase. *Le codex arménien Jérusalem 121.* 2 vols. Patrologia Orientalis 163, 168. Turnhout: Brepols, 1969–71.

Roman Missal. Missale romanum: Ex decreto ss. concilii tridentini restitutum. Rome: Editio Typica, 1962.

Romanos the Melodist. *Hymns.* Ed. Paul Maas and C. A. Trypanis. *Sancti Romani Melodi Cantica: Cantica Genuina.* Oxford: Clarendon, 1963.

———. *Hymns.* Ed. and French trans. José Grosdidier de Matons. *Romanos le Mélode: Hymnes.* 5 vols. SC 99, 110, 114, 128, 283. Paris: Cerf, 1965–81.

———. *Hymns.* Ed. and Italian trans. Riccardo Maisano. *Cantici di Romano il Melodo.* 2 vols. Turin: UTET, 2002.

———. *On the Life of Christ: Kontakia.* Trans. Ephrem Lash. San Francisco: HarperCollins, 1995.

———. *Sacred Song from the Byzantine Pulpit: Romanos the Melodist.* Trans. R. J. Schork. Gainesville: University Press of Florida, 1995.

———. *Kontakia of Romanos, Byzantine Melodist.* Trans. Marjorie Carpenter. 2 vols. Columbia: University of Missouri Press, 1970–73.

———. *Romanos Melodos: Die Hymnen.* German trans. with commentary by Johannes Koder. 2 vols. Bibliothek der griechischen Literatur 62. Stuttgart: Hiersemann, 2005.

Sacrorum conciliorum nova et amplissima collectio. Ed. G. D. Mansi. 53 vols. Florence, 1759– . Reprint, Paris: Weller, 1901–27; Graz: Akademische Druck-und Verlagsanstalt, 1960.

Septuagint. Ed. Alfred Rahlfs. Stuttgart: Deutsche Bibelgesellschaft, 1979.

———. *A New English Translation of the Septuagint.* Ed. Albert Pietersma and Benjamin G. Wright. New York: Oxford University Press, 2007.

Spanos, Apostolos. *Codex* Lesbiacus Leimonos *11: Annotated Critical Edition of an Unpublished Byzantine* Menaion *for June.* Berlin: De Gruyter, 2010.

Symeon the New Theologian. *Catechetical Discourses. Catéchèse: Syméon le Nouveau Théologien.* Ed. Basil Krivocheine; French trans. Joseph Paramelle. 3 vols. SC 96, 104, 113. Paris: Cerf, 1963–65.

———. *The Discourses.* Trans. C. J. deCantanzaro, with an introduction by George Maloney. New York: Paulist, 1980.

———. *Hymns. Syméon le nouveau théologien: Hymnes.* Ed. Johannes Koder. 3 vols. SC 156, 174, 196. Paris: Cerf, 1969–73.

———. *Hymns. Divine Eros: Hymns of Saint Symeon the New Theologian.* Trans. Daniel K. Griggs. Crestwood, N.Y.: St. Vladimir's Seminary Press, 2010.

———. *Letters. The Epistles of St. Symeon the New Theologian.* Ed. and trans. H. J. M. Turner. Oxford: Oxford University Press, 2009.

Tarchnischvili, Michel. *Le grand lectionnaire de l'église de Jérusalem (V^e–VIIIe siécle).* 4 vols, CSCO 188, 189, 204, 205; Scriptores Iberici 9, 10, 13, 14. Louvain: Secrétariat du CorpusSCO, 1959–60.

Theodore Lector. *Ecclesiastical History. Theodoros Anagnostes: Kirchengeschichte.* Ed. G. C. Hansen. 2nd ed. Die griechischen christlichen Schriftsteller der ersten Jahrhunderte, New Series 3. Berlin: Akademie Verlag, 1995.

Theodore the Stoudite. *Letters. Theodori Studitae Epistulae.* Ed. Georgios Fatouros. Corpus Fontium Historiae Byzantinae 31. Berlin: de Gruyter, 1992.

———. *Small Catecheses. Tou hosiou patros hēmōn kai homologētou Theodōrou hēgoumenou tōn Stoudiou Mikra katēchēsis = Sancti patris nostri et confessoris Theodori studitis praepositi Parva catechesis.* Ed. Emmanuel Auvray. Paris: Lecoffre, 1891.

———. *Small Catecheses* (selections). Trans. Ephrem Lash. *Catecheses to His Monks.* http://www. anastasis.org.uk/theodore.htm.

[Theodore the Stoudite?]. *On the Second Coming.* TR 34–41.

Theodoret of Cyrrhus. *Commentary on the Psalms.* PG 80:857–1997.

———. *Commentary on the Psalms.* Trans. Robert C. Hill. 2 vols. Washington, D.C.: Catholic University of America Press, 2000.

Theophanes the Confessor. *Chronographia. Theophanis Chronographia.* Ed. Carolus de Boor. Leipzig: Teubner, 1893.

———. *The Chronicle of Theophanes Confessor: Byzantine and Near Eastern History A.D. 284–813.* Trans. Cyril Mango and Roger Scott. Oxford: Clarendon, 1997.

Triōdion katanyktikon: Periechon apasan tēn anēkousan autō akolouthian tēs hagias kai megalēs tessarakostēs [Τριῴδιον κατανυκτικόν, περιέχον ἅπασαν τὴν ἀνήκουσαν αὐτῷ ἀκολουθίαν τῆς ἁγίας καὶ μεγάλης Τεσσαρακοστῆς]. Rome: [n.p.], 1879.

Triōdion sun Theōi agiōi periechon tēn prepousan autō akolouthian. Rome: [n.p.], 1738.

Triodion. The Orthodox Pages: Τὸ Τριῴδιον. http://www.christopherklitou.com/triodion_greek_ index.htm.

Triodion. Ed. Andrea Cunadi. Venice: de Sabio, 1522.

Le typicon de la Grande Église. Ed. Juan Mateos. 2 vols. OCA 165, 166. Rome: Pontificium Institutum Orientalium Studiorum, 1962–63.

von Christ, Wilhelm, and Matthaios Paranikas. *Anthologia Graeca Carminum Christianorum.* Leipzig: Teubner, 1871.

Secondary Sources

Agosti, Gianfranco. "L'etopea nella poesia greca tardoantica." In *ΗΘΟΠΟΙΙΑ: La représentation de caractères entre fiction scolaire et réalité vivante à l'époque impériale et tardive,* ed. Eugenio Amato and Jacques Schamp, 24–60. Salerno: Helios, 2005.

Alexiou, Margaret. *After Antiquity: Greek Language, Myth, and Metaphor.* Ithaca, N.Y.: Cornell University Press, 2002.

———. *The Ritual Lament in the Greek Tradition.* Cambridge: Cambridge University Press, 1974.

Alexopoulos, Stefanos, and Annewies van den Hoek. "The Endicott Scroll and Its Place in the History of Private Communion Prayers." *DOP* 60 (2006): 165–88.

Alfeyev, Ilarion. *St. Symeon the New Theologian and the Orthodox Tradition.* New York: Oxford University Press, 2000.

Allen, Pauline. "The Sixth-Century Greek Homily: A Re-assessment." In *Preacher and Audience: Studies in Early Christian and Byzantine Homiletics*, ed. Mary Cunningham and Pauline Allen, 201–25. A New History of the Sermon 1. Leiden: Brill, 1998.

Alpers, Klaus. *Untersuchungen zu Johannes Sardianos und seinem Kommentar zu den Progymnasmata des Aphthonios*. Braunschweig: Cramer, 2009.

Althusser, Louis. "Ideology and Ideological State Apparatuses (Notes Toward an Investigation)." In *Lenin and Philosophy and Other Essays*, trans. Ben Brewster, 170–77. New York: Monthly Review Press, 1971.

Amato, Eugenio, and Jacques Schamp. *ΉΘΟΠΟΙΙΑ: La représentation de caractères entre fiction scolaire et réalité vivante à l'époque impériale et tardive*. Salerno: Helios, 2005.

Anderson, Gary A. *The Genesis of Perfection: Adam and Eve in Jewish and Christian Imagination*. Lousiville, Ky.: Westminster John Knox, 2001.

Arentzen, Thomas. "'Your Virginity Shines': The Attraction of the Virgin in the Annunciation Hymn by Romanos the Melodist." *Studia Patristica* 68 (2013): 125–32.

Arranz, Miguel. "Les prières pénitentielles de la tradition byzantine: Les sacrements de la restauration de l'ancien Euchologie Constantinopolitain." *OCP* 57 (1991): 87–143.

———. *I Penitenziali bizantini: Il Protokanonarion o Kanonarion primitivo di Giovanni monaco e diacono e il Deuterokanonarion o "Secondo Kanonarion" di Basilio monaco*. Kanonika 3. Rome: Pontificio Istituto Orientale, 1993.

Asad, Talal. *Genealogies of Religion: Discipline and Reasons of Power in Christianity and Islam*. Baltimore: Johns Hopkins University Press, 1993.

Auzépy, Marie-France. "La carrière d'André de Crète." *Byzantinische Zeitschrift* 88 (1995): 1–12.

Bacci, Michele. "Croce pettorale con scene cristologiche." In *Mandylion: Intorno al Sacro Volto, da Bisanzio a Genova*, ed. Gerhard Wolf, Colette Bozzo Dufour, and Anna Rosa Calderoni Masetti, 242–45. Milan: Skira, 2004.

Baldovin, John F. *The Urban Character of Christian Worship: The Origins, Development, and Meaning of Stational Liturgy*. Rome: Pontificium Institutum Studiorum Orientalium, 1987.

Barber, Charles. *Contesting the Logic of Painting: Art and Understanding in Eleventh-Century Byzantium*. Leiden: Brill, 2007.

———. *Figure and Likeness: On the Limits of Representation in Byzantine Iconoclasm*. Princeton, N.J.: Princeton University Press, 2002.

———. "Icons, Prayer, and Vision in the Eleventh Century." In *Byzantine Christianity*, ed. Derek Krueger, 149–63. A People's History of Christianity 3. Minneapolis: Fortress, 2006.

Barkhuizen, J. H. "Analysis of the Form and Content of Prayer as Liturgical Component in the Hymns of Romanos the Melodist." *Ekklesiastikos Pharos* 75 (1991): 91–102.

———. "Narrative Apostrophe in the Kontakia of Romanos the Melodist with Special Reference to His Hymn on Judas." *L'Antichité Classique* 29 (1986): 19–27.

———. "Proclus of Constantinople: A Popular Preacher in Fifth-Century Constantinople." In *Preacher and Audience: Studies in Early Christian and Byzantine Homiletics*, ed. Mary Cunningham and Pauline Allen, 179–200. A New History of the Sermon 1. Leiden: Brill, 1998.

———. "Romanos Melodos: Essay on the Poetics of his Kontakion 'Resurrection of Christ,' (Maas-Trypanis 24)." *BZ* 79 (1986): 17–28, 268–81.

———. "Romanos Melodos, On the Temptation of Joseph: A Study on His Use of Imagery." *Acta Patristica et Byzantina* 1 (1990): 1–31.

———. "Romanos the Melodist and the Composition of His Hymns: Prooimion and Final Strophe." *Hellenika* 40 (1989): 62–77.

———. "Romanos the Melodist, Kontakion 55SC: A Prayer of Penitence." *Ekklesiastikos Pharos* 74 (1992): 107–21.

Beck, Hans-Georg. *Kirche und theologische Literatur.* Munich: Beck, 1959.

BeDuhn, Jason David. *Augustine's Manichaean Dilemma 1: Conversion and Apostasy, 373–388 C.E.* Philadelphia: University of Pennsylvania Press, 2009.

———. *Augustine's Manichaean Dilemma 2: Making a "Catholic" Self, 388–401 C.E.* Philadelphia: University of Pennsylvania Press, 2013.

Bell, Catherine. "Performance." In *Critical Terms for Religious Studies*, ed. Mark C. Taylor, 204–24. Chicago: University of Chicago Press, 1998.

———. *Ritual: Perspectives and Dimensions.* New York: Oxford University Press, 1997.

———. *Ritual Theory, Ritual Practice.* New York: Oxford University Press, 1992.

Belting, Hans. *Likeness and Presence: A History of the Image Before the Era of Art.* Trans. Edmund Jephcott. Chicago: University of Chicago Press, 1994; original German ed., 1990.

Benton, John F. "Consciousness of Self and Perceptions of Individuality." In *Renaissance and Renewal in the Twelfth Century*, ed. Robert L. Benson and Giles Constable, 263–95. Cambridge, Mass.: Harvard University Press, 1982.

Bergman, Robert P., et al. *Vatican Treasures: Early Christian, Renaissance, and Baroque Art from the Papal Collections: An Exhibition in Honor of the Sesquicentenary of the Diocese of Cleveland.* Cleveland: Cleveland Museum of Art, 1998

Bernabò, Massimo. *Il tetravangelo di Rabbula. Firenze, Biblioteca Medicea Laurenziana, Plut 1, 56: L'illustrazione del Nuovo Testamento nella Siria del VI secolo.* Rome: Storia e Letteratura, 2008.

Bernhard, Ludger. "Der Ausfall der 2. Ode im byzantinischen Neunodenkanon." In *Heuresis: Festschrift für Andreas Rohracher, 25 Jahre Erzbischof von Salzburg*, ed. Thomas Michaels, 90–101. Salzburg: Müller, 1969.

Bertonière, Gabriel. *The Historical Development of the Easter Vigil and Related Services in the Greek Church.* OCA 193. Rome: Pontificium Institutum Studiorum Orientalium, 1972.

———. *The Sundays of Lent in the Triodion: The Sundays Without a Commemoration.* OCA 253. Rome: Pontificio Istitito Orientale, 1997.

Betz, Hans Dieter. "The Concept of the 'Inner Human Being' (*ho esō anthrōpos*) in the Anthropology of Paul." *New Testament Studies* 46 (2000): 315–413.

Bibliotheca hagiographica graeca. Ed. François Halkin. 3rd ed. 3 vols. Subsidia Hagiographica 8a. 1957. Reprinted, Brussels: Société des Bollandistes, 1986.

Biehl, Walter. "Die Staurothek von Vicopisano." *Mitteilungen des Kunsthistorischen Instituts in Florenz* 3, 4 (1930): 183–85.

Bitton-Ashkelony, Brouria. "Personal Experience and Self-Exposure in Eastern Christianity: From Pseudo-Macarius to Symeon the New Theologian." In *Between Personal and Institutional Religion: Self, Doctrine, and Practice in Late Antique Eastern Christianity*, ed. Brouria

Bitton-Ashkelony and Lorenzo Perrone. Cultural Encounters in Late Antiquity and the Middle Ages 15, 99–128. Turnhout: Brepols, 2014

Bitton-Ashkelony, Brouria, and Aryeh Kofsky. *The Monastic School of Gaza*. Leiden: Brill, 2006.

Bolman, Elizabeth. "Veiling Sanctity in Christian Egypt: Visual and Spatial Solutions." In *Thresholds of the Sacred: Architectural, Art Historical, Liturgical, and Theological Perspectives on Religious Screens, East and West*, ed. Sharon E. J. Gerstel, 73–104. Washington, D.C.: Dumbarton Oaks, 2006.

Bonner, Gerald. "Augustine on Romans 5,12." *Studia Evangelica* 2 (1968): 242–47.

Boswell, John. *Christianity, Social Tolerance, and Homosexuality: Gay People in Western Europe from the Beginning of the Christian Era to the Fourteenth Century*. Chicago: University of Chicago Press, 1980.

Bouley, Allen. *From Freedom to Formula: The Evolution of the Eucharistic Prayer from Oral Improvisation to Written Texts*. Washington, D.C.: Catholic University of America Press, 1981.

Bourbouhakis, Emmanuel C. "Rhetoric and Performance." In *The Byzantine World*, ed. Paul Stephenson, 175–87. London: Routledge, 2010.

Bourdieu, Pierre. *The Logic of Practice*. Trans. Richard Nice. Stanford, Calif.: Stanford University Press, 1990; original French ed., 1980.

Bousset, Wilhelm. "Eine jüdische Gebetssammlung im siebenten Buch der apost. Konst." *Nachrichten von der königl. Gesellschaft der Wissenschaften zu Göttingen* (1915): 435–89. Reprinted in Bousset, *Religionsgeschichtliche Studien*, ed. A. F. Verheule (Leiden: Brill, 1979), 231–86 .

Bouyer, Louis. *Eucharist: Theology and Spirituality of the Eucharistic Prayer*. Trans. Charles Underhill Quinn. Notre Dame, Ind.: University of Notre Dame Press, 1970; original French ed., 1966.

Bradshaw, Paul F. et al. *The Apostolic Tradition: A Commentary*. Minneapolis: Fortress, 2002.

Bradshaw, Paul F., and Maxwell E. Johnson. *The Origins of Feasts, Fasts, and Seasons in Early Christianity*. Collegeville, Minn.: Liturgical Press, 2011.

Brakke, David. *Athanasius and the Politics of Asceticism*. Oxford: Oxford University Press, 1995.

———. *Demons and the Making of the Monk: Spiritual Combat in Early Christianity*. Cambridge, Mass.: Harvard University Press, 2008.

———. "Making Public the Monastic Life: Reading the Self in Evagrius Ponticus' Talking Back." In *Religion and the Self in Antiquity*, ed. David Brakke, Michael L. Satlow, and Steven Weitzman, 222–33. Bloomington: Indiana University Press, 2005.

Brennan, Teresa. *The Transmission of Affect*. Ithaca, N.Y.: Cornell University Press, 2004.

Brock, Sebastian. "Clothing Metaphors as a Means of Theological Expression in Syriac Tradition." In *Typos, Symbol, Allegorie bei den östlichen Vätern und ihren Parallelen im Mittelalter*, ed. Margot Schmidt and Carl-Friedrich Geyer, 11–40. Regensburg: Pustet, 1982.

———. "Fragments of a Ps-John Chrysostom Homily on the Prodigal Son in Christian Palestinian Aramaic." *Le Muséon* 112 (1999): 335–62.

———. *The Luminous Eye: The Spiritual World Vision of St. Ephrem*. Kalamazoo, Mich.: Cistercian, 1990.

Brown, Peter. *The Body and Society: Men, Women, and Sexual Renunciation in Early Christianity*. New York: Columbia University Press, 1988.

Brubaker, Leslie, and John F. Haldon. *Byzantium in the Iconoclast Era (c. 680–850): A History*. Cambridge: Cambridge University Press, 2011.

———. *Byzantium in the Iconoclast Era (ca. 680–850): The Sources*. Birmingham Byzantine and Ottoman Monographs 7. Aldershot: Ashgate, 2001.

Büchsel, Martin. *Die Entstehung des Christusporträts: Bildarchäologie statt Bildhypnose*. Mainz: von Zabern, 2003.

Buckton, David. *Byzantium: Treasures of Byzantine Art and Culture*. London: British Museum, 1994.

Budde, Achim. *Die ägyptische Basilios-Anaphora: Text, Kommentar, Geschichte*. Münster: Aschendorff, 2004.

Bulst, Neithard. "Flagellanten." In *Lexikon des Mittelalters*, s. v. Munich: Artemis-Verlag, 1980–99.

Buonocore, Marco. *Bibliografia dei fondi manoscritti della Biblioteca vaticana (1968–1980)*. 2 vols. Vatican City: Biblioteca Apostolica Vaticana, 1986.

Burkitt, F. C. *The Early Syriac Lectionary System*. 1923. Piscataway, N.J.: Gorgias, 2007.

Burns, J. Patout. "The Interpretation of Romans in the Pelagian Controversy." *Augustinian Studies* 10 (1979): 43–54.

Burrus, Virginia. *Saving Shame: Martyrs, Saints, and Other Abject Subjects*. Philadelphia: University of Pennsylvania Press, 2008.

———. *The Sex Lives of Saints: An Erotics of Ancient Hagiography*. Philadelphia: University of Pennsylvania Press, 2004.

Butler, Judith. *Excitable Speech: A Politics of the Performative*. New York: Routledge, 1997.

———. *The Psychic Life of Power: Theories in Subjection*. Stanford, Calif.: Stanford University Press, 1997.

Byzantium and Islam: Age of Transition, 7th–9th Century. Ed. Helen C. Evans with Brandie Ratliff. New York: Metropolitan Museum of Art, 2012.

Byzanz: Das Licht aus dem Osten: Kult und Alltag im Byzantinischen Reich von 4. bis 15. Jahrhundert. Ed. Christoph Stiegemann. Mainz: Zabern, 2001.

Caillet, Jean-Pierre. *L'art du Moyen Âge: Occident, Byzance, Islam*. Collection Manuels d'histoire de l'art. Paris: Gallimard, 1995.

Calabuig, Ignazio M. "The Liturgical Cult of Mary in the East and West." In *Handbook for Liturgical Studies*, vol. 5, *Liturgical Time and Space*, ed. Anscar Chupungco, 219–98. Collegeville, Minn.: Liturgical Press, 2000.

Cameron, Averil. *Christianity and the Rhetoric of Empire: The Development of Christian Discourse*. Berkeley: University of California Press, 1991.

Carrette, Jeremy. *Foucault and Religion: Spiritual Corporeality and Political Spirituality*. London: Routledge, 2000.

Carruthers, Mary. *The Craft of Thought: Meditation, Rhetoric, and the Making of Images 400–1200*. Cambridge: Cambridge University Press, 1998.

Caseau, Béatrice. "L'abandon de la communion dans la main (IVe–XIIe siècles)." *Travaux et Mémoires* 14 (2002): 79–94.

———. "Experiencing the Sacred." In *Experiencing Byzantium: Papers from the 44th Spring Symposium of Byzantine Studies, Newcastle and Durham, April 2011*, ed. Claire Nesbitt and Mark Jackson, 59–77. Farnham: Ashgate, 2013.

———. "L'eucharistie au centre de la vie religieuse des communautés chrétiennes (fin du ive au xe siècle)." In *Eucharistia: Encyclopédie de l'eucharistie*, ed. Maurice Brouard, 125–44. Paris: Cerf, 2004.

Chadwick, Henry. "Gewissen." Trans. Heinzgerd Brachmann. *Reallexikon für Antike und Christentum*.

Chatzidakis, Manolis. "An Encaustic Icon of Christ at Sinai." Trans. Gerry Walters. *Art Bulletin* 49 (1967): 197–208.

Chin, Catherine M. *Grammar and Christianity in the Late Roman World*. Philadelphia: University of Pennsylvania Press, 2008.

Cholij, Roman. *Theodore the Stoudite: The Ordering of Holiness*. Oxford: Oxford University Press, 2002.

Ciccolella, Federica. "Basil I and the Jews: Two Poems of the Ninth Century." *Medioevo greco: Rivista di storia e filologia bizantina"* no. 0 (2000): 69–94.

Clark, Elizabeth A. "The Lady Vanishes: Dilemmas of a Feminist Historian After the 'Linguistic Turn.'" *Church History* 67 (1998): 1–31.

———. *Reading Renunciation: Asceticism and Scripture in Early Christianity*. Princeton, N.J.: Princeton University Press, 1999.

———. "Rewriting Early Christian History: Augustine's Representation of Monica." In *Portraits of Spiritual Authority: Religious Power in Early Christianity, Byzantium and the Christian Orient*, ed. Jan Willem Drijvers and John W. Watt, 3–23. Leiden: Brill, 1999.

Codex purpureus rossanensis: Museo dell'Arcivescovado, Rossano Calabro: Commentarium. Ed. Guglielmo Cavallo. Rome: Salerno, 1987.

Codices vaticani graeci, III: Codices 604–866. Ed. Robert Devreesse. Rome: Bibliotheca Vaticana, 1950.

Codici greci dell'Italia meridionale. Ed. Paul Canart and Santo Lucà. Rome: Retablo, 2000.

Constable, Giles. *The Reformation of the Twelfth Century*. Cambridge: Cambridge University Press, 1996.

Constas, Nicholas P. *Proclus of Constantinople and the Cult of the Virgin in Late Antiquity: Homilies 1–5, Texts and Translations*. Leiden: Brill, 2003.

———. "Weaving the Body of God: Proclus of Constantinople, the Theotokos, and the Loom of the Flesh." *JECS* 3 (1995): 169–94.

Cormack, Robin. "Rediscovering the Christ Pantokrator at Daphni." *Journal of the Warburg and Courtauld Institutes* 71 (2008): 55–74.

Corrigan, John, ed. *Religion and Emotion: Approaches and Interpretations*. New York: Oxford University Press, 2004.

Costache, Doru. "Byzantine Insights into Genesis 1–3: St Andrew of Crete's Great Canon." *Phronema* 24 (2009): 35–50.

Courcelle, Pierre. *Recherches sur les Confessions de Saint Augustin*. 2nd ed. Paris: de Boccard, 1968.

Cresci, Lia Raffaella. "Διὰ βραχέων ἐπέων (K 83.2): Stratégies de composition dans les calendriers métriques de Christophore Mitylenaios." In *Poetry and Its Contexts in Eleventh-Century Byzantium*, ed. Floris Bernard and Kristoffel Demoen, 151–31. Farnham: Ashgate, 2012.

Cunningham, Mary. "Homilies." In *The Oxford Handbook of Byzantine Studies*, ed. Elizabeth Jeffreys, John F. Haldon, and Robin Cormack, 872–81. Oxford: Oxford University Press, 2008.

———. "The Reception of Romanos in Middle Byzantine Homiletics and Hymnography." *DOP* 62 (2008): 251–60.

Ćurčić, Slobodan, and Archer St. Clair. *Byzantium at Princeton: Byzantine Art and Archaeology at Princeton University*. Princeton, N.J.: Princeton University Press, 1986.

Daley, Brian E. "Making a Human Will Divine: Augustine and Maximus on Christ and Human Salvation." In *Orthodox Readings of Augustine*, ed. George E. Demacopoulos and Aristotle Papanikolaou, 101–26. New York: St. Vladimir's Seminary Press, 2008.

Dalmais, Irénée-Henri. "Biblical Themes in Greek Eucharistic Anaphoras." In *The Bible in Greek Christian Antiquity*, ed. and trans. Paul M. Blowers, 329–41. Notre Dame, Ind.: University of Notre Dame Press, 1997; original French ed., 1984.

Daniélou, Jean. *The Bible and the Liturgy*. Notre Dame, Ind.: University of Notre Dame Press, 1956; original French ed., 1951.

Davis, Stephen J. "Crossed Texts, Crossed Sex: Intertextuality and Gender in Christian Legends of Holy Women Disguised as Men." *JECS* 10 (2002): 1–31.

de Bruyn, Theodore S. "Flogging a Son: The Emergence of the Pater Flagellans in Latin Christian Discourse." *JECS* 7 (1999): 249–90.

De Clerck, Paul. "Les prières eucharistiques gallicanes." In *Prex eucharistica*, vol. 3, *Studia: Pars prima: Ecclesia antiqua et occidentalis*, ed. Albert Gerhards et al., 203–23. Spicilegium Friburgense 42. Fribourg: Academic Press, 2005.

Delouis, Olivier. "Saint-Jean-Baptiste de Stoudios à Constantinople: La contribution d'un monastère à l'histoire de l'empire byzantin (v. 454–1204)." Ph.D. dissertation, Université Paris I-Panthéon Sorbonne, 2005.

Delumeau, Jean. *Sin and Fear: The Emergence of a Western Guilt Culture, 13th–18th Centuries*. Trans. Eric Nicholson. New York: St. Martin's 1990; original French ed., 1983.

Déroche, Vincent. "Quand l'ascèse devient péché: Les excès dans le monachisme byzantin d'après les témoignages contemporains." *Kentron: Revue du Monde Antique et de Psychologie Historique* 23 (2007): 167–78.

———. "Représentations de l'eucharistie dans la haute époque byzantine." *Travaux et Mémoires* 14 (2002): 167–80.

Dickson, Gary. "Flagellation." In *Encyclopedia of the Middle Ages*, s.v. Cambridge: Clark, 2001.

———. "The Flagellants of 1260 and the Crusades." *Journal of Medieval History* 15 (1989): 227–67.

Diakovskij, E. P. *Posledovanie časov i izobraziteľnyx: Istoričeskoe issledovanie [The Rite of the Hours and the "Typika": An Historical Inquiry]*. Kiev: Mejnander, 1913.

Dolar, Mladen. "Beyond Interpellation." *Qui Parle* 6 (1993): 73–96.

Doresse, Jean, and Emmanuel Lanne. *Un témoin archaïque de la liturgie copte de saint Basile*. Louvain: Publications Universitaires, 1960.

Dörries, Hermann. "The Place of Confession in Ancient Monasticism." *Studia Patristica* 5 (1962): 284–308.

Dubowchik, Rosemary. "Singing with the Angels: Foundation Documents as Evidence for Musical Life in Monasteries of the Byzantine Empire." *DOP* 56 (2002): 277–96.

Dubrov, Gregory W. "A Dialogue with Death: Ritual Lament and the *Threnos Theotokou* of Romanos the Melodos." *GRBS* (1994): 385–405.

Dulaey, Martine. "Les larmes dans les premiers siècles chrétiens: Ambroise et l'Occident latin." *Adamantius* 16 (2010): 320–37.

Dunn, James D. G. *The Theology of Paul the Apostle.* Grand Rapids, Mich.: Eerdmans, 1998.

Durand, Jannic. *L'art byzantin.* Paris: Terrail, 1999.

Durlea, Ionel. "'*Metanoia*' dans le Canon Grand de André de Crète." *Anuarul Facultăţii de Teologie Ortodoxă din Bucureşti* 1 (2001): 569–77.

Dyck, Andrew R. "On Cassia, Κύριε ἡ ἐν πολλαῖς. . . ." *Byzantion* 56 (1986): 63–76.

Eastmond, Anthony. *Art and Identity in Thirteenth-Century Byzantium: Hagia Sophia and the Empire of Trebizond.* Aldershot: Ashgate, 2004.

Ebersole, Gary L. "The Function of Ritual Weeping Revisited: Affective Expression and Moral Discourse." *History of Religions* 39 (2000): 211–46.

Efthymiadis, Stephanos. "A Day and Ten Months in the Life of a Lonely Bachelor: The Other Byzantium in *Miracula S. Artemii* 18 and 22." *DOP* 58 (2004): 1–26.

———. "John of Sardis and the *Metaphrasis* of the *Passio* of St. Nikephoros the Martyr *(BHG* 1334)." *Rivista di studi bizantini e neoellenici.* n.s. 28 (1991): 23–44.

———. *The Life of the Patriarch Tarasios by Ignatios the Deacon.* Aldershot: Ashgate, 1998.

———. "Notes on the Correspondence of Theodore the Studite." Revue des études byzantines 53 (1995): 141–63.

Elsner, Jaś. *Art and the Roman Viewer: The Transformation of Art from the Pagan World to Christianity.* Cambridge: Cambridge University Press, 1995.

———. "Iconoclasm as Discourse: From Antiquity to Byzantium." *Art Bulletin* 94 (2012): 368–94.

———. "Replicating Palestine and Reversing the Reformation: Pilgrimage and Collecting at Bobbio, Monza, and Walsingham." *Journal of the History of Collections* 1 (1997): 117–30.

Émereau, Casimir. "Hymnographi byzantini." *Echos d'Orient* 21 (1922): 258–79; 22 (1923): 11–25, 420–39; 23 (1924): 196–200, 276–85, 408–14; 24 (1925): 164–79; 25 (1926): 178–84.

Engberding, Hieronymus. *Das eucharistische Hochgebet der Basileiosliturgie: Textgeschichtliche Untersuchungen und kritische Ausgabe.* Münster: Aschendorff, 1931.

Engberg, Sysse Gudrun. "The *Prophetologion* and the Triple-Lection Theory: The Genesis of a Liturgical Book." *BBGG* 3rd. ser. 3 (2006): 67–91.

———. "Prophetologion Manuscripts in the 'New Finds' of St. Catherine's at Sinai." *Scriptorium* 57 (2003): 94–109.

Entwistle, Chris. "Some Notes on Two Late-Antique Gold Pendants in the British Museum." In *Image, Craft and the Classical World: Essays in Honour of Donald Bailey and Catherine Johns,* ed. Nina Crummy, 267–75. Montagnac: Éditions Monique Mergoil, 2005.

Erickson, John H. "Penitential Discipline in the Orthodox Canonical Tradition." *St. Vladimir's Theological Quarterly* 21 (1977): 191–206.

Ernest, James D. *The Bible in Athanasius of Alexandria.* Leiden: Brill, 2004.

Fenwick, John. *Fourth-Century Anaphoral Construction Techniques.* Nottingham: Grove, 1986.

Fernández, Tomás. "Byzantine Tears: A Pseudo-Chrysostomic Fragment on Weeping in the *Florilegium Coislinianum.*" In *Encyclopedic Trends in Byzantium?: Proceedings of the International Conference Held in Leuven, 6–8 May 2009,* ed. Peter van Deun and Caroline Macé, 125–42. Orientalia Lovaniensia Analecta 212. Leuven: Peeters, 2011.

Flood, Gavin. *The Ascetic Self: Subjectivity, Memory, and Tradition*. Cambridge: Cambridge University Press, 2004.

Follieri, Enrica. *Codices graeci Bibliotheca Vaticana selecti*. Rome: Bibliotheca Apostolica Vaticana, 1969.

Foucault, Michel. "About the Beginning of the Hermeneutics of the Self." In *Religion and Culture*, ed. Jeremy Carrette, 158–81. New York: Routledge, 1999.

———. *Discipline and Punish: The Birth of the Prison*. Trans. Alan Sheridan. New York: Vintage, 1979; original French ed., 1975.

———. "Technologies of the Self." In *Technologies of the Self: A Seminar with Michel Foucault*, ed. Luther Martin, Huck Gutman, and Patrick H. Hutton, 16–49. Amherst: University of Massachusetts Press, 1988.

Frank, Georgia. "Death in the Flesh: Picturing Death's Body and Abode in Late Antiquity." In *Looking Beyond: Visions, Dreams and Insights in Medieval Art and History*, ed. Colum Hourihane, 58–74. Occasional Papers from the Index of Christian Art 11. University Park: Pennsylvania State University Press, 2010.

———. "Dialogue and Deliberation: The Sensory Self in the Hymns of Romanos the Melodist." In *Religion and the Self in Antiquity*, ed. David Brakke, Michael L. Satlow, and Steven Weitzman, 163–79. Bloomington: Indiana University Press, 2005.

———. *The Memory of the Eyes: Pilgrims to Living Saints in Christian Late Antiquity*. Berkeley: University of California Press, 2000.

———. "The Memory Palace of Marcellinus: Athanasius and the Mirror of the Psalms." In *Ascetic Culture: Essays in Honor of Philip Rousseau*, ed. Blake Leyerle and Robin Darling Young. Notre Dame, Ind.: University of Notre Dame Press, 94–124.

———. "Romanos and the Night Vigil in the Sixth Century." In *Byzantine Christianity*, ed. Derek Krueger, 59–78. A People's History of Christianity 3. Minneapolis: Fortress, 2006.

———. "Sensing Ascension in Early Byzantium." In *Experiencing Byzantium: Papers from the 30th Spring Symposium of Byzantine Studies*, ed. Claire Nesbitt and Mark P. C. Jackson, 293–310. Farnham: Ashgate, 2013.

Fredriksen, Paula. "Beyond the Body/Soul Dichotomy: Augustine on Paul Against the Manichees and the Pelagians." *Recherches Augustiniennes* 23 (1988): 87–114.

———. "Paul and Augustine: Conversion Narratives, Orthodox Traditions, and the Redemptive Self." *JThS* n.s. 37 (1986): 3–34.

Freedberg, David. "Holy Images and Other Images." In *The Art of Interpreting*, ed. Susan C. Scott, 68–87. University Park: Pennsylvania State University Press, 1996.

Frei, Hans W. *The Eclipse of Biblical Narrative: A Study in Eighteenth and Nineteenth Century Hermeneutics*. New Haven, Conn.: Yale University Press, 1980.

Frøyshov, Stig Simeon. "The Georgian Witness to the Jerusalem Liturgy: New Sources and Studies." In *Inquiries into Eastern Christian Worship: Selected Papers of the Second International Congress of the Society of Oriental Liturgies, Rome, 17–21 September 2008*, ed. Bert Groen, Steven Hawkes-Teeples, and Stefanos Alexopoulos, 227–67. Eastern Christian Studies 12. Leuven: Peeters, 2012.

———. "La réticence à l'hymnographie chez des anachorètes de l'Égypte et du Sinaï du 6ᵉ au 8ᵉ siècles." In *L'hymnographie: Conférences Saint-Serge*, ed. Achille M. Triacca and Alessandro Pistoia, 229–45. Rome: Edizioni Liturgiche, 2000.

Furey, Constance. "Body, Society, and Subjectivity in Religious Studies." *Journal of the American Academy of Religion* 80 (2012): 7–33.

Gador-Whyte, Sarah. *Theology and Poetry in Early Byzantium: The Kontakia of Romanos the Melodist*. Cambridge: Cambridge University Press, forthcoming.

Galavaris, George. *The Illustrations of the Liturgical Homilies of Gregory Nazianzenus*. Princeton, N.J.: Princeton University Press, 1969.

Gerard, Martine, Catherine Metzger, Alain Person, and Jean-Pierre Sodini. "Argiles et eulogies en forme de jetons: Qal'at Sem'an en est-il une source possible?" In *Materials Analysis of Byzantine Pottery*, ed. Henry Maguire. 9–24. Washington, D.C.: Dumbarton Oaks, 1997.

Gerstel, Sharon E. J. "The Layperson in Church." In *Byzantine Christianity*, ed. Derek Krueger, 102–23. A People's History of Christianity 3. Minneapolis: Fortress, 2006.

———, ed. *Thresholds of the Sacred: Architectural, Art Historical, Liturgical, and Theological Perspectives on Religious Screens, East and West*. Washington, D.C.: Dumbarton Oaks, 2006.

Getcha, Job. "Le système des lectures bibliques du rite byzantin." In *La liturgie, interprète de l'écriture. I. Les lectures bibliques pour les dimanches et fêtes*, ed. Achille Maria Triacca and Alessandro Pistoia, 25–56. Rome: Edizione Liturgiche, 2002.

———. *The Typikon Decoded: An Explanation of Byzantine Liturgical Practice*. Trans. Paul Meyendorff. New York: St. Vladimir's Seminary Press, 2012; original French ed., 2009.

Giannouli, Antonia. "*Catanyctic* Religious Poetry: A Survey." In *Theologica Minora: The Minor Genres of Byzantine Theological Literatures*, ed. Antonio Rigo, 8.86–109. Byzantinos: Studies in Byzantine History and Civilization 8.86–109. Turnhout: Brepols, 2013.

———. *Die beiden byzantinischen Kommentare zum Großen Kanon des Andreas von Kreta: Eine quellenkritische und literarhistorische Studie*. Vienna: Österreichischen Akademie der Wissenschaften, 2007.

———. "Die Tränen der Zerknirschung: Zur *katanyktischen* Kirchendichtung als Heilmittel." In *"Doux remède...": Poésie et poétique à Byzance: Actes du IVe colloque international philologique, Paris, 23–24–25 février 2006*, ed. Paolo Odorico, Panagiotis A. Agapitos, and Martin Hinterberger, 141–55. Paris: Centre d'études byzantines, néo-helléniques et sud-est européennes, 2009.

Glaros, Athanasios V. *Theia Paidagogia: Paidagogika stoicheia sto Magalo Kanona tou Andrea Kretes: Didaktorike diatrive*. Nea Smyrne: Ekdoseis Akritas, 2000.

Glenthøj, Johannes Bartholdy. *Cain and Abel in Syriac and Greek Writers (4th–6th centuries)*. Louvain: Peeters, 1997.

Golitzin, Alexander. *St. Symeon the New Theologian: On the Mystical Life: The Ethical Discourses*, vol. 3, *Life, Times, and Theology*. Crestwood, N.Y.: St. Vladimir's Seminary Press, 1997.

Gonosová, Anna, and Christine Kondoleon. *Art of Late Rome and Byzantium in the Virginia Museum of Fine Arts*. Richmond, Va.: The Museum, 1994.

Grabar, André. *Ampoules de Terre Sainte (Monza-Bobbio)*. Paris: Klincksieck, 1958.

———. *L'empereur dans l'art byzantin*. Paris: Belles Lettres, 1936.

Greenblatt, Stephen. *Renaissance Self-Fashioning: From More to Shakespeare*. Chicago: University of Chicago Press, 1980.

Griffith, Sidney. "What Has Constantinople To Do with Jerusalem? Palestine in the Ninth Century: Byzantine Orthodoxy in the World of Islam." In *Byzantium in the Ninth Century: Dead or Alive?*, ed. Leslie Brubaker, 181–94. Aldershot: Ashgate, 1998.

Grosdidier de Matons, José. "Aux origines de l'hymnographie byzantine: Romanos le Mélode et le kontakion." In *Liturgie und Dichtung: Ein interdisziplinäres Kompendium I: Historische Präsentation*, ed. Hansjakob Becker and Reiner Kaczynski, 435–63. St. Ottilien: EOS-Verlag, 1983.

———. "Liturgie et hymnographie: Kontakion et canon." *DOP* 34/35 (1980–81): 31–43.

———. *Romanos le Mélode et les origines de la poésie religieuse à Byzance*. Paris: Beauchesne, 1977.

Guy, Jean-Claude. "Aveu thérapeutique et aveu pédagogique dans l'ascèse des pères du désert (IVᵉ–Vᵉ s.)." In *Pratiques de la confession: Des pères du désert à Vatican II*, 25–40. Paris: Cerf, 1983.

·Hadot, Pierre. "Les niveaux de conscience dans les états mystiques selon Plotin." *Journal de psychologie normale et pathologique* 2 (1980): 243–66.

Hahn, Cynthia. "Loca Sancta Souvenirs: Sealing the Pilgrim's Experience." In *The Blessings of Pilgrimage*, ed. Robert Ousterhout, 85–96. Urbana: University of Illinois Press, 1990.

Haldon, John F. *Byzantium in the Seventh Century: The Transformation of a Culture*. Cambridge: Cambridge University Press, 1990.

Handbook of the Byzantine Collection. Washington, D.C.: Dumbarton Oaks, 1967.

Hannick, Christian. "Hymnographie et hymnographes sabaites." In *The Sabaite Heritage in the Orthodox Church from the Fifth Century to the Present*, ed. Joseph Patrich, 217–28. Orientalia Lovaniensia Analecta 98. Leuven: Peeters, 2001.

Hanson, R. P. C. "The Liberty of the Bishop to Improvise Prayer in the Eucharist." *Vigiliae Christianae* 15 (1961): 173–76.

Harrill, J. Albert. "Paul and the Slave Self." In *Religion and the Self in Antiquity*, ed. David Brakke, Michael L. Satlow, and Steven Weitzman, 51–64. Bloomington: Indiana University Press, 2005.

Harris, Simon. "The 'Kanon' and the Heirmologion." *Music and Letters* 85 (2004): 175–97.

Harrison, Nonna Verna. "Eve in Greek Patristic and Byzantine Theology." In *Prayer and Spirituality in the Early Church*, ed. Bronwen Neil, vol. 3, *Liturgy and Life*, ed. Geoffrey Dunn and Lawrence Cross, 293–314. Strathfield, NSW: St. Pauls Publications, 2003.

———. "Gregory Nazianzen's Festal Spirituality: Anamnesis and Mimesis." *Philosophy and Theology* 18 (2006): 27–51.

Harvey, Susan Ashbrook. "Bride of Blood, Bride of Light: Biblical Women as Images of Church in Jacob of Serug." In *Malphono w-Rabo d-Malphone: Studies in Honor of Sebastian P. Brock*, ed. George A. Kiraz, 177–204. Piscataway, N.J.: Gorgias, 2008.

———. "Encountering Eve in the Syriac Liturgy." In *Syriac Encounters: Papers from the Sixth North American Syriac Symposium, Duke University, June 26–29, 2011*, ed. Maria Doerfler, Emanuel Fiano, and Kyle Smith, forthcoming.

———. "Liturgy and Ethics in Ancient Syriac Christianity: Two Paradigms." *Studies in Christian Ethics* 26 (2013): 300–16.

———. "On Mary's Voice: Gendered Words in Syriac Marian Tradition." In *The Cultural Turn in Late Ancient Studies: Gender, Asceticism, and Historiography*, ed. Dale Martin and Patricia Cox Miller, 63–86. Durham, N.C.: Duke University Press, 2005.

———. "Performance as Exegesis: Women's Liturgical Choirs in Syriac Tradition." In *Inquiries into*

Eastern Christian Worship: Selected Papers of the Second International Congress of the Society of Oriental Liturgies, Rome, 17–21 September 2008, ed. Bert Groen, Steven Hawkes-Teeples, and Stefanos Alexopoulos, 47–64. Eastern Christian Studies 12. Leuven: Peeters, 2012.

———. *"Scenting Salvation: Ancient Christianity and the Olfactory Imagination*. Berkeley: University of California Press, 2006.

———. "Spoken Words, Voiced Silence: Biblical Women in the Syriac Tradition." *JECS* 9 (2001): 105–31.

———. "To Whom Did Jacob Preach?" In *Jacob of Serugh and His Times: Studies in Sixth-Century Syriac Christianity*, ed. George A. Kiraz, 115–31. Piscataway, N.J.: Gorgias Press, 2010.

———. "Why the Perfume Mattered: The Sinful Woman in Syriac Exegetical Tradition." In *In Dominico Eloquio/In Lordly Eloquence: Essays on Patristic Exegesis in Honor of Robert Louis Wilken*, ed. Paul M. Blowers et al., 69–89. Grand Rapids, Mich.: Eerdmans, 2002.

Hatlie, Peter. *The Monks and Monasteries of Constantinople, ca. 350–850*. Cambridge: Cambridge University Press, 2007.

Hausherr, Irénée. *Penthos: The Doctrine of Compunction in the Christian East*. Trans. Anselm Hufstader. Kalamazoo, Mich.: Cistercian, 1982; original French ed., 1944.

Hemming, Laurence Paul. "The Liturgical Subject: Introductory Essay." In *The Liturgical Subject: Subject, Subjectivity, and the Human Person in Contemporary Liturgical Discussion and Critique*, ed. James G. Leachman, 1–16. Notre Dame, Ind.: University of Notre Dame Press, 2009.

Hevelone-Harper, Jennifer L. *Disciples of the Desert: Monks, Laity, and Spiritual Authority in Sixth-Century Gaza*. Baltimore: Johns Hopkins University Press, 2005.

Hinterberger, Martin. "Emotions in Byzantium." In *A Companion to Byzantium*, ed. Liz James, 123–34. Oxford: Wiley-Blackwell, 2010.

———. "Tränen in der byzantinischen Literatur: Ein Beitrag zur Geschichte der Emotion" *JÖB* 56 (2006): 27–51.

Horrocks, Geoffrey. *Greek: A History of the Language and Its Speakers*. London: Longman, 1997.

Hunger, Herbert. "Romanos Melodos, Dichter, Prediger, Rhetor—und sein Publikum." *JÖB* 34 (1984): 15–42.

Hunt, Hannah. *Clothed in the Body: Asceticism, the Body and the Spiritual in the Late Antique Era*. Farnham: Ashgate, 2012.

———. *Joy-Bearing Grief: Tears of Contrition in the Writings of the Early Syrian and Byzantine Fathers*. The Medieval Mediterranean 57. Leiden: Brill, 2004.

James, Liz, and Ruth Webb. "'To Understand Ultimate Things and Enter Secret Places': Ekphrasis and Art in Byzantium." *Art History* 14 (1991): 1–17.

Jeffreys, Elizabeth. "Rhetoric." In *The Oxford Handbook of Byzantine Studies*, ed. Elizabeth Jeffreys, John F. Haldon, and Robin Cormack, 827–37. Oxford: Oxford University Press, 2008.

Johnson, Maxwell E. "The Origins of the Anaphoral Sanctus and Epiclesis Revisited: The Contribution of Gabriele Winkler and Its Implications." In *Crossroads of Cultures: Studies in Liturgy and Patristics in Honor of Gabriele Winkler*, ed. Hans-Jürgen Feulner, Elena Velkovska, and Robert F. Taft. OCA 260, 405–42. Rome: Pontificio Istituto Orientale, 2000.

Johnson, Scott Fitzgerald. "Apostolic Geography: The Origins and Continuity of a Hagiographic Habit." *DOP* 64 (2010): 5–25.

Jugie, Martin. *Theologia dogmatica christianorum orientalium ab Ecclesia catholica dissidentium.* Vol. 3, *Theologiae dogmaticae Graeco-Russorum expositio de sacramentis.* Paris: Letouzey et Ané, 1930.

Karabinov, I. *Postnaia Triod': Istoricheskii obzor.* St. Petersburg: Smirnova, 1910.

Karavites, Peter. "Gregory Nazianzinos and Byzantine Hymnography." *Journal of Hellenic Studies* 113 (1993): 81–98.

Karlin-Hayter, Patricia. "Où l'abeille butine: La culture littéraire monastique à Byzance aux VIIIe et IXe siècles." *Revue Bénédictine* 103 (1993): 90–116.

Karras, Valerie A. "The Liturgical Function of Consecrated Women in the Byzantine Church." *Theological Studies* 66 (2005): 96–116.

Kartsonis, Anna. *Anastasis: The Making of an Image.* Princeton, N.J.: Princeton University Press, 1986.

———. "Protection against All Evil: Function, Use and Operation of Byzantine Historiated Phylacteries." *Byzantinische Forschungen* 20 (1994): 73–102.

———. "The Responding Icon." In *Heaven on Earth: Art and the Church in Byzantium,* ed. Linda Safran, 58–80. University Park: Pennsylvania State University Press, 1998.

Kaster, Robert A. *Emotion, Restraint, and Community in Ancient Rome.* New York: Oxford University Press, 2005.

Kazhdan, Alexander, and Giles Constable. *People and Power in Byzantium: An Introduction to Modern Byzantine Studies.* Washington, D.C.: Dumbarton Oaks, 1982.

Kazhdan, Alexander, with Lee F. Sherry and Christine Angelidi. *A History of Byzantine Literature (650–850).* Athens: National Hellenic Research Foundation, 1999.

Kelly, J. N. D. *Early Christian Creeds.* 3rd ed. New York: Continuum, 2006.

Kennedy, George A. *Classical Rhetoric and Its Christian and Secular Tradition from Ancient to Modern Times.* 2nd ed. Chapel Hill: University of North Carolina Press, 1999.

———. *Progymnasmata: Greek Textbooks of Prose Composition and Rhetoric.* Atlanta: Society of Biblical Literature, 2003.

Keselopoulos, Anestes. *Man and the Environment: A Study of Symeon the New Theologian.* Trans. Elizabeth Theokritoff. Crestwood, N.Y.: St. Vladimir's Seminary Press, 2001.

Klein, Holger A. *Byzanz, der Westen und das "wahre" Kreuz: Die Geschichte einer Reliquie und ihrer künstlerischen Fassung in Byzanz und im Abendland.* Wiesbaden: Reichert, 2004.

Kolbet, Paul R. "Athanasius, the Psalms, and the Reformation of the Self." *Harvard Theological Review* 99 (2006): 85–101.

Koder, Johannes. "Imperial Propaganda in the Kontakia of Romanos the Melode." *DOP* 62 (2008): 275–91.

———. "Justinians Sieg über Salomon." In *Thumiama: Stē mnēmē tēs Laskarinas Mpoura,* ed. Maria Vassilaki et al., 135–42. Athens: Benaki Museum, 1994.

———. "Romanos der Melode: Der Dichter hymnischer Bibelpredigten in Dokumenten seiner Zeit." In *Ein Buch verändert die Welt: Älteste Zeugnisse der Heiligen Schrift aus der Zeit des frühen Christentums in Ägypten,* ed. Harald Froschauer, Christian Gastgeber, and Hermann Harrauer, 59–71. Vienna: Phoibos, 2003.

——. "Romanos Melodos und sein Publikum: Überlegungen zur Beeinflussung des kirchlichen Auditoriums durch das Kontakion." *Anzeiger der philos.-histor. Klasse* 134 (1997–99): 63–94.

Kraemer, Ross Shepard. *Unreliable Witnesses: Religion, Gender, and History in the Greco-Roman Mediterranean*. New York: Oxford University Press, 2011.

Krausmuller, Dirk. "The Monastic Communities of Stoudios and St Mamas in the Second Half of the Tenth Century." In *The Theotokos Evergetis and Eleventh-Century Monasticism*, ed. Margaret Mullett and Anthony Kirby, 67–75. Belfast Byzantine Texts and Translations 6.1. Belfast: Belfast Byzantine Enterprises, 1994.

Krivocheine, Basil. *In the Light of Christ: St. Symeon the New Theologian: Life, Spirituality, Doctrine*. Trans. Anthony P. Gythiel. Crestwood, N.Y.: St. Vladimir's Seminary Press, 1986.

Krivko, Roman. "K istorii vtoroi pesni gimnograficheskogo kanona: Utraty i interpoliatsii." In *Bibel, Liturgie und Frömmigkeit in der Slavia Byzantina: Festgabe für Hans Rothe zum 80. Geburtstag*, ed. Dagmar Christians, Dieter Stern, and V. S. Tomelleri, 229–42. Munich: Sagner, 2009.

Krueger, Derek. "Christian Piety and Practice in the Sixth Century." In *The Cambridge Companion to the Age of Justinian*, ed. Michael Maas, 291–315. New York: Cambridge University Press, 2005.

——. "Healing and the Scope of Religion in Byzantium: A Response to Miller and Crislip." In *Holistic Healing in Byzantium*, ed. John Chirban, 119–30. Brookline, Mass.: Holy Cross Orthodox Press, 2010.

——. "Homoerotic Spectacle and the Monastic Body in Symeon the New Theologian." In *Toward a Theology of Eros: Transfiguring Passion at the Limits of Discipline*, ed. Virginia Burrus and Catherine Keller, 99–118, 399–403. New York: Fordham University Press, 2006.

——. "Liturgical Time and Holy Land Reliquaries in Early Byzantium." In *Saints and Sacred Matter: The Cult of Relics in Byzantium and Beyond*, ed. Holger Klein and Cynthia Hahn. Washington, D.C.: Dumbarton Oaks, forthcoming.

——. "Mary at the Threshold: The Mother of God as Guardian in Seventh-Century Palestinian Miracle Accounts." In *The Cult of the Mother of God in Byzantium: Texts and Images*, ed. Leslie Brubaker and Mary Cunningham, 31–38. Aldershot: Ashgate, 2011.

——. "The Old Testament in Monasticism." In *The Old Testament in Byzantium*, ed. Paul Magdalino and Robert Nelson, 199–221. Washington, D.C.: Dumbarton Oaks, 2010.

——. "The Religion of Relics in Late Antiquity and Byzantium." In *Treasures of Heaven: Saints, Relics, and Devotion in Medieval Europe*, ed. Martina Bagnoli et al., 5–17. Baltimore: Walters Art Museum, 2010.

——. *Symeon the Holy Fool: Leontius's Life and the Late Antique City*. Transformation of the Classical Heritage 25. Berkeley: University of California Press, 1996.

——. "The Unbounded Body in the Age of Liturgical Reproduction." *JECS* 17 (2009): 267–79.

——. *Writing and Holiness: The Practice of Authorship in the Early Christian East*. Philadelphia: University of Pennsylvania Press, 2004.

——, ed. *Byzantine Christianity*. People's History of Christianity 3. Minneapolis: Fortress, 2006.

Krumbacher, Karl. *Geschichte der byzantinischen Litteratur von Justinian bis zum Ende des oströmischen Reiches, 527–1453*. 2nd ed. Munich: Beck, 1897.

Lamb, William R. S. *The* Catena in Marcum: *A Byzantine Anthology of Early Commentary on Mark.* Leiden: Brill, 2012.

Lampe, G. W. H. *A Patristic Greek Lexicon.* Oxford: Clarendon, 1961.

Landry, Jean-Michel. "Confession, Obedience, and Subjectivity: Michel Foucault's Unpublished Lectures *On the Government of the Living*." *Telos* 146 (2009): 111–23.

Largier, Niklaus. *In Praise of the Whip: A Cultural History of Arousal.* New York: Zone, 2007.

Lash, Ephrem. "Matins for Weekdays." http://www.anastasis.org.uk/Matheb.pdf.

Late Egyptian and Coptic Art: An Introduction to the Collections in the Brooklyn Museum. Brooklyn, N.Y.: Brooklyn Institute of Arts and Sciences, 1943.

Lauxtermann, Marc Diederik. *Byzantine Poetry from Pisides to Geometres.* Vol. 1, *Texts and Context.* Wiener Byzantinische Studien 24. Vienna: Österreichischen Akademie der Wissenschaften, 2003.

———. *The Spring of Rhythm: An Essay on the Political Verse and Other Byzantine Metres.* Byzantina Vindobonensia 22. Vienna: Österreichischen Akademie der Wissenschaften, 1999.

———. "Three Biographical Notes." *BZ* 91 (1998): 391–405.

Lemerle, Paul. *Byzantine Humanism.* Trans. Helen Lindsay and Ann Moffatt. Canberra: Australian Association for Byzantine Studies, 1986; original French ed., 1971.

Leroy, Julien. *Études sur les* Grandes catéchèses *de S. Théodore Studite.* Ed. Olivier Delouis. Vatican City: Biblioteca Apostolica Vaticana, 2008.

———. "La réforme studite." In *Il monachesimo orientale,* ed. Convegno di studi orientali. Rome: Pontificium Institutum Orientalium Studiorum, 1958.

———. *Studitisches Mönchtum: Spiritualität und Lebensform.* Graz: Verlag Styria, 1969.

Lieber, Laura. "The Play's the Thing: The Theatricality of Jewish Aramaic Poetry from Late Antiquity." *Jewish Quarterly Review,* forthcoming.

Ligier, Louis. "Autour du sacrifice eucharistique: Anaphores orientales et anamnèse juive de Kippur." *Nouvelle revue theologique* 82 (1960): 40–55.

Lingas, Alexander. "The Liturgical Place of the Kontakion in Constantinople." In *Liturgy, Architecture, and Art in the Byzantine World: Papers of the XVIII International Byzantine Congress (Moscow, 8–15 August 1991) and Other Essays Dedicated to the Memory of Fr. John Meyendorff,* ed. Constantine C. Akentiev, 50–57. St. Petersburg: Publications of the St. Petersburg Society for Byzantine and Slavic Studies, 1995.

Losky, A. "Le Typicon byzantin: Édition d'une version grecque partiellement inéditée: Analyse de la partie liturgique." 2 vols. Th.D. dissertation, Strasbourg, 1987.

Louth, Andrew. "Christian Hymnography from Romanos the Melodist to John Damascene." *JECS* 57 (2005): 195–206.

———. *St. John Damascene: Tradition and Originality in Byzantine Theology.* Oxford: Oxford University Press, 2002.

Lucà, Santo. "Scritture e libri della 'scuola niliana.'" In *Scritture, libri e testi nelle aree provinciali di Bisanzio,* vol. 1, ed. Guglielmo Cavallo, Giuseppe De Gregorio, and Marilena Maniaci, 319–89. Spoleto: Centro Italiano di studi sull'alto Medioevo, 1991.

Lukashevich, A. "Velikij Kanon." *Pravoslavnaja Encyklopedia* 7:453–54.

Maas, Michael, ed. *The Cambridge Companion to the Age of Justinian.* Cambridge: Cambridge University Press, 2005.

Maguire, Henry. "The Cycle of Images in the Church." In *Heaven on Earth: Art and the Church in Byzantium*, ed. Linda Safran, 121–51. University Park: Pennsylvania State University Press, 1998.

Maisano, Riccardo. "Un inno inedito di S. Andrea di Creta per la domenica della palme." *Rivista di storia e letteratura religiosa* 6 (1970): 518–72.

———. "Romanos's Use of Greek Patristic Sources." *DOP* 62 (2008): 261–73.

Malatesta Zilembo, M. Giuseppina. "Gli amanuensi di Grottaferrata (continuazione)." *BBGG* 29 (1975): 3–53.

Mango, Cyril. "On the History of the *Templon* and the Martyrion of St. Artemios at Constantinople." *Zograf* 10 (1979): 40–48.

Mango, Maria Mundell. *Silver from Early Byzantium: The Kaper Koraon and Related Treasures.* Baltimore: Walters Art Gallery, 1986.

Marinis, Vasileios. "Defining Liturgical Space." In *The Byzantine World*, ed. Paul Stephenson, 284–302. London: Routledge, 2010.

Martin, Dale B. "Heterosexism and the Interpretation of Romans 1:18–32." *Biblical Interpretation* 3 (1995): 332–55. Reprinted in Martin, *Sex and the Single Savior: Gender and Sexuality in Biblical Interpretation* (Louisville, Ky.: Westminster John Knox, 2006).

Mateos, Juan. *La célébration de la parole dans la liturgie byzantine: Étude historique.* Rome: Pontificium Institutum Studiorum Orientalium, 1971.

———. "Quelques problèmes de l'orthros byzantin." *Proche Orient Chrétien* 11 (1961): 17–35, 201–20.

Mathews, Thomas. *The Early Churches of Constantinople: Architecture and Liturgy.* University Park: Pennsylvania State University Press, 1971.

Mathewes-Green, Frederica. *First Fruits of Prayer: A Forty-Day Journey Through the Canon of St. Andrew.* Brewster, Mass.: Paraclete, 2006.

Maxwell, Jaclyn. *Christianization and Communication in Late Antiquity: John Chrysostom and His Congregation in Antioch.* Cambridge: Cambridge University Press, 2006.

Mayr, Robert. *Vocabularium codicis Iustiniani.* Vol. 2, *Pars graeca.* Hildesheim: Olms, 1965.

McCall, Richard D. *Do This: Liturgy as Performance.* Notre Dame, Ind.: University of Notre Dame Press, 2007.

McGuckin, John. "Symeon the New Theologian's *Hymns of Divine Eros*: A Neglected Masterpiece of the Christian Mystical Tradition." *Spiritus* 5 (2005): 182–202.

McNamer, Sarah. *Affective Meditation and the Invention of Medieval Compassion.* Philadelphia: University of Pennsylvania Press, 2010.

Metzger, Marcel. "La prière eucharistique de la prétendue *Tradition apostolique*." *Prex eucharistica* 3:263–80.

Meyendorff, John. *Byzantine Theology: Historical Trends and Doctrinal Themes.* New York: Fordham University Press, 1974.

———. "Ἐφ' ᾧ (Rom. 5,12) chez Cyrille d'Alexandrie et Theodoret." *Studia Patristica* 4, *Texte und Untersuchungen* 79 (1961): 157–61.

Miller, James. "The Prophetologion: The Old Testament of Byzantine Christianity?" In *The Old Testament in Byzantium*, ed. Paul Magdalino and Robert Nelson, 55–76. Washington, D.C.: Dumbarton Oaks, 2010.

Miller, Patricia Cox. *The Corporeal Imagination: Signifying the Holy in Late Ancient Christianity.* Philadelphia: University of Pennsylvania Press, 2009.

———. "Is There a Harlot in This Text? Hagiography and the Grotesque." In *The Cultural Turn in Late Ancient Studies: Gender, Asceticism, and Historiography*, ed. Dale B. Martin and Patricia Cox Miller, 87–102. Durham, N.C.: Duke University Press, 2005.

———. "Strategies of Representation in Collective Biography: Constructing the Subject as Holy." In *Greek Biography and Panegyric in Late Antiquity*, ed. Thomas Hägg and Philip Rousseau, 209–54. Berkeley: University of California Press, 2000.

Mitchell, Leonel. "The Alexandrian Anaphora of St. Basil of Caesarea." *Anglican Theological Review* 58 (1976): 194–206.

Mitchell, Margaret M. *The Heavenly Trumpet: John Chrysostom and the Art of Pauline Interpretation.* Louisville, Ky.: Westminster John Knox, 2002.

Moffett, Ann. "Schooling in the Iconoclast Centuries." In *Iconoclasm: Papers Given at the Ninth Spring Symposium of Byzantine Studies, University of Birmingham, March 1975*, ed. Anthony Bryer and Judith Herrin, 85–92. Birmingham: Centre for Byzantine Studies, 1977.

Mondzain, Marie-José. *Image, Icon, Economy: The Byzantine Origins of the Contemporary Imaginary.* Trans. Rico Franses. Stanford, Calif.: Stanford University Press, 2005; original French ed., 1996.

Le monde byzantin. Vol. 1. *L'empire romain d'orient: 330–641.* Ed. Cécile Morrisson et al. Rev. ed. Paris: Presses Universitaires de France, 2012.

Le monde byzantin. Vol. 2. *L'empire byzantin: 641–1204.* Ed. Jean-Claude Cheynet et al. Paris: Presses Universitaires de France, 2006.

Morello, Giovanni, and Gerhard Wolf, eds. *Il volto di Cristo.* Milan: Electa: 2000.

Morey, C. R. "The Painted Panel from the Sancta Sanctorum." *Festschrift zum sechzigen Geburtstag von Paul Clemen.* Bonn: Cohen, 1926.

Morgan, Ben. *On Becoming God: Late Medieval Mysticism and the Modern Western Self.* New York: Fordham University Press, 2013.

Morozowich, Mark M. "Jerusalem Celebration of Great Week Evening Services from Monday to Wednesday in the First Millennium." *Studi sull'Oriente Cristiano* 14 (2010): 99–126.

———. "A Palm Sunday Procession in the Byzantine Tradition?: A Study of the Jerusalem and Constantinopolitan Evidence." *OCP* 75 (2009): 359–83.

Morris, Colin. *The Discovery of the Individual, 1050–1200.* London: Harper & Row, 1972.

———. "Individualism in Twelfth-Century Religion: Some Further Reflections." *Journal of Ecclesiastical History* 31 (1980): 195–206.

Müller, Barbara. *Der Weg des Weinens: Die Tradition des "Penthos" in den Apophthegmata Patrum.* Forschungen zur Kirchen- und Dogmengeschichte 77. Göttingen: Vandenhoeck and Ruprecht, 2000.

Mullett, Margaret. "Rhetoric, Theory, and Imperative of Performance: Byzantium and Now." In *Rhetoric in Byzantium*, ed. Elizabeth Jeffreys, 151–70. Farnham: Ashgate, 2003.

Münz-Manor, Ophir. "Liturgical Poetry in the Late Antique Near East: A Comparative Approach." *Journal of Ancient Judaism* 1 (2010): 336–61.

Nelson, Robert S., and Kristen M. Collins, eds. *Holy Image, Hallowed Ground: Icons from Sinai.* Los Angeles: J. Paul Getty Museum, 2006.

Noret, Jacques. "Grégoire de Nazianze, l'auteur le plus cité, après la Bible, dans la littérature ecclésiastique byzantine." In *Symposium Nazianzenum, Louvain-la-Neuve 25-28 août 1981*, ed. Justin Mossay, 259–66. Paderborn: Schöningh, 1983.

O'Connell, Robert J. *Images of Conversion in St. Augustine's Confessions*. New York: Fordham University Press, 1996.

Orsi, Robert A. *Between Heaven and Earth: The Religious Worlds People Make and the Scholars Who Study Them*. Princeton, N.J.: Princeton University Press, 2005.

Ousterhout, Robert. "Holy Space: Architecture and the Liturgy." In *Heaven on Earth: Art and the Church in Byzantium*, ed. Linda Safran, 81–120. University Park: Pennsylvania State University Press, 1988.

Page, Christopher. *The Christian West and Its Singers: The First Thousand Years*. New Haven, Conn.: Yale University Press, 2010.

Pagels, Elaine. *Adam, Eve, and the Serpent*. New York: Random House, 1988.

Pantanella, Cristina. "Reliquary Box with Stones from the Holy Land." In *Treasures of Heaven: Saints, Relics, and Devotion in Medieval Europe*, ed. Martina Bagnoli et al., 36. Baltimore: Walters Art Museum, 2010.

Papaioannou, Stratis. "Byzantine Mirrors: Self-Reflection in Medieval Greek Writing." *DOP* 64 (2010): 1–21.

———. "Gregory and the Constraint of Sameness." In *Gregory of Nazianzus: Images and Reflections*, ed. Jostein Børtnes and Tomas Hägg, 59–81. Copenhagen: Museum Tusculanum Press, 2006.

———. *Michael Psellos: Rhetoric and Authorship in Byzantium*. Cambridge: Cambridge University Press, 2013.

Parenti, Stephano. "The Cathedral Rite of Constantinople: Evolution of a Local Tradition." *OCP* 77 (2011): 449–69.

———. "The Eucharistic Liturgy in the East: The Various Orders of Celebration." In *Handbook for Liturgical Studies*, vol. 3, *The Eucharist*, ed. Anscar J. Chupungco, 61–75. Collegeville, Minn.: Liturgical Press, 1999.

———. "Nota sull'impiego e l'origine dell'inno ΣΙΓΗΣΑΤΩ ΠΑΣΑ ΣΑΡΞ ΒΡΟΤΕΙΑ." *Kypriakai Spoudai* 64–65 (2000–2001): 191–99.

Parpulov, Georgi. "Psalters and Personal Piety in Byzantium." In *The Old Testament in Byzantium*, ed. Paul Magdalino and Robert Nelson, 77–105. Washington, D.C.: Dumbarton Oaks, 2010.

Patlagean, Evelyne. "L'histoire de la femme déguisée en moine et l'évolution de la sainteté féminine à Byzance." *Studi Medievali* ser. 3, 17 (1976): 597–623.

Pelikan, Jaroslav. *The Christian Tradition: A History of the Development of Doctrine*, vol. 2, *The Spirit of Eastern Christendom*. Chicago: University of Chicago Press, 1977.

Pentcheva, Bissera. *The Sensual Icon: Space, Ritual, and the Senses in Byzantium*. University Park: Pennsylvania State University Press, 2010.

Peristeris, Aristarchos. "Literary and Scribal Activities at the Monastery of St. Sabas." In *The Sabaite Heritage in the Orthodox Church from the Fifth Century to the Present*, ed. Joseph Patrich, 171–77. Orientalia Lovaniensia Analecta 98. Leuven: Peeters, 2001.

Perrone, Lorenzo. "Aus Gehorsam zum Vater: Mönche und Laien in den Briefen von Barsanuphius und Johannes von Gaza." In *Foundations of Power and Conflicts of Authority in Late-Antique*

Monasticism, ed. Alberto Camplani and Giovanni Filaramo, 217–43. Orientalia Lovaniensia Analecta 157. Leuven: Peeters, 2007.

———. "Christianity as 'Practice' in Origen's *Contra Celsum*." In *Origeniana Nona: Origen and the Religious Practice of His Time*, ed. György Heidl and Róbert Somos, 293–317. Leuven: Peeters, 2009.

Phenix, Robert R., Jr., and Cornelia B. Horn. "Prayer and Penance in Early and Middle Byzantine Christianity: Some Trajectories from the Greek- and Syriac-Speaking Realms." In *Seeking the Favor of God*, vol. 3, *The Impact of Penitential Prayer Beyond Second Temple Judaism*, ed. Mark J. Boda, Daniel K. Falk, and Rodney A. Werline, 225–54. Atlanta: Society of Biblical Literature, 2008.

Pitarakis, Brigitte. *Les croix-reliquaires pectorales byzantines en bronze*. Paris: Picard, 2006.

———. "Objects of Devotion and Protection." In *Byzantine Christianity*, ed. Derek Krueger, 164–81. A People's History of Christianity 3. Minneapolis: Fortress, 2006.

Pitt, W. E. "The Anamnesis and Institution Narrative of the Liturgy of the Apostolic Constitutions Book VIII." *Journal of Ecclesiastical History* 9 (1958): 1–7.

Pott, Thomas. *Byzantine Liturgical Reform: A Study of Liturgical Change in the Byzantine Tradition*. Trans. Paul Meyendorff. Crestwood, N.Y.: St. Vladimir's Seminary Press, 2010; original French ed., 2000.

———. "Réforme monastique et évolution liturgique: La réforme stoudite." In *Crossroads of Cultures: Studies in Liturgy and Patristics in Honor of Gabriele Winkler*, ed. Hans-Jürgen Feulner, Elena Velkovska, and Robert F. Taft, OCA 260, 557–89. Rome: Pontificio Instituto Orientale, 2000.

Pratsch, Thomas. *Theodoros Studites (759–826): Zwischen Dogma und Pragma*. Berliner Byzantinistische Studien 4. Frankfurt: Peter Lang, 1998.

Prelipcean, Alexandru. "Le concept de *metanoia* dans le Canon de S. Andrė de Crète." *Anuarul Facultăţii de Teologie Ortodoxă din Bucureşti* 7 (2007): 641–63.

Prosopographie der mittelbyzantinischen Zeit. Conceived by F. Winkelmanns and ed. Ralph-Johannes von Lilie et al. 8 vols. Berlin: de Gruyter, 1998–2013.

Quinlan, Andrew John. *Sin. Gr. 734–735. Triodion*. Excerpta ex Dissertatione ad Doctorum. Newberry Springs, Calif.: [Pontificium institutum orientalium], 2004.

———. "Triodia Manuscripts: The Problem of Classification." *Byzantinische Forschungen* 23 (1997): 141–52.

Raasted, Jørgen. "Voice and Verse in a Troparion of Cassia." In *Studies in Eastern Chant, Vol. 3*, ed. Miloš Velimirović, 171–78. London: Oxford University Press, 1973.

———. "Zum Melodie des Kontakions Ἡ παρθένος σήμερον." *Cahiers de l'Institut du Moyen Âge Grec et Latin* 59 (1989): 233–46.

Raes, Alphonse. "Les formulaires grecs du rite de la pénitence." In *Mélanges en l'honneur de Monseigneur Michel Andrieu*, 365–72. Strasbourg: Palais Universitaire, 1956.

Rahlfs, Alfred. *Die altestamentlichen Lektionen der griechischen Kirche*. Berlin: Weidman, 1915.

Rapp, Claudia. "Spiritual Guarantors at Penance, Baptism, and Ordination in the Late Antique East." In *A New History of Penance*, ed. Abigail Frey, 121–48. Leiden: Brill, 2008.

Ray, Walter D. *Tasting Heaven on Earth: Worship in Sixth-Century Constantinople.* Grand Rapids, Mich.: Eerdmans, 2012.

Reed, Annette Yoshiko. "Job as Jobab: The Interpretation of Job in LXX Job 42:17b–e." *Journal of Biblical Literature* 120 (2001): 31–55.

Reudenbach, Bruno. "Reliquien von Orten: Ein frühchristliches Reliquar als Gedächtnisort." In *Reliquare im Mittelalter,* ed. Bruno Reudenbach and Gia Toussaint, 21–42. Berlin: Oldenbourg Akademieverlag, 2005.

Rhoby, Andreas. *Byzantinische Epigramme auf Fresken und Mosaiken.* Byzantinische Epigramme in inschriftlicher Überlieferung 1. Vienna: Verlag der Österreichischen Akademie der Wissenschaften, 2009.

Richter-Siebles, Ilse. *Die palästinensischen Weihrauchgefäße mit Reliefszenen aus dem Leben Christi.* 2 vols. Berlin: Zentrale Universitäts-Druckerei, 1990.

Riehle, Alexander. "Authorship and Gender (and) Identity: Women's Writing in the Middle Byzantine Period." In *The Author in Middle Byzantine Literature: Modes, Functions, and Identities,* ed. Aglae Pizzone. Byzantinisches Archiv. Berlin: DeGruyter, 2014.

Roberts, Robert C. *Spiritual Emotions: A Psychology of Christian Virtues.* Grand Rapids, Mich.: Eerdmans, 2007.

Rochow, Ilse. *Studien zu der Person, den Werken und dem Nachleben der Dichterin Kassia.* Berlin: Akademie-Verlag, 1967.

Rogers, Eugene F., Jr. *After the Spirit: A Constructive Pneumatology from Resources Outside the Modern West.* Grand Rapids, Mich.: Eerdmans, 2005.

Rosenwein, Barbara H. *Emotional Communities in the Early Middle Ages.* Ithaca, N.Y.: Cornell University Press, 2006.

Rousseau, Philip. "Knowing Theodoret: Text and Self." In *The Cultural Turn in Late Ancient Studies: Gender, Asceticism, and Historiography,* ed. Dale Martin and Patricia Cox Miller, 278–97. Durham, N.C.: Duke University Press, 2005.

Rouwhorst, Gerard. "The Liturgical Background of the Crucifixion and Resurrection Scene of the Syriac Gospel Codex of Rabbula: An Example of the Relatedness Between Liturgy and Iconography." In *Studies on the Liturgies of the Christian East: Selected Papers from the Third International Congress of the Society of Oriental Liturgy, Volos, May 26-30, 2010,* ed. Bert Groen, Steven Hawkes-Teeples, and Stefanos Alexopoulos, 225–38. Eastern Christian Studies 18. Leuven: Peeters, 2013.

Sahas, Daniel J. *Icon and Logos: Sources in Eighth-Century Iconoclasm.* Toronto: University of Toronto Press, 1986.

Saxer, Victor. "L'usage de la Bible et ses procédés dans quelques anaphores grecques anciennes: Le dialogue préparatoire, le sanctus et le récit de l'institution." In *Mens concordet voci pour Mgr A. G. Martimort,* 595–607. Paris: Declée de Brouwer, 1983.

Schattauer, Thomas H. "The Koinonicon of the Byzantine Liturgy: An Historical Study." *OCP* 49 (1983): 91–129.

Schmemann, Alexander. *Great Lent.* Crestwood, N.Y.: St. Vladimir's Seminary Press, 1974.

Schmitt, Jean-Claude. *La raison des gestes dans l'Occident médiéval.* Paris: Gallimard, 1990.

Schroeder, Caroline T. *Monastic Bodies: Discipline and Salvation in Shenoute of Atripe.* Philadelphia: University of Pennsylvania Press, 2007.

Scott, Roger. "Justinian's New Age and The Second Coming." In *Byzantine Chronicles and the Sixth Century.* Variorum Collected Studies Series CS 1004. Farnham: Ashgate, 2012.

Seligman, Adam B. et al. *Ritual and Its Consequences: An Essay on the Limits of Sincerity.* New York: Oxford University Press, 2008.

Sellew, Philip. "Interior Monologue as a Narrative Device in the Parables of Luke." *Journal of Biblical Literature* 111 (1992): 239–53.

Ševčenko, Ihor. "Levels of Style in Byzantine Prose." *JÖB* 31 (1981): 289–312.

Ševčenko, Nancy Patterson. "Canon and Calendar: The Role of a Ninth-Century Hymnographer in Shaping the Celebration of the Saints." In *Byzantium in the Ninth Century: Dead or Alive?*, ed. Leslie Brubaker, 101–14. Aldershot: Ashgate, 1998.

———. "The Metrical Inscriptions in the Murals of the Panagia Phorbiotissa." In *Asinou Across Time: Studies in the Architecture and Murals of the Panagia Phorbiotissa, Cyprus,* ed. Annemarie Weyl Carr and Andréas Nicolaïdès, 69–90. Washington, D.C.: Dumbarton Oaks, 2012.

Shaw, Teresa. *The Burden of the Flesh: Fasting, and Sexuality in Early Christianity.* Minneapolis: Fortress, 1998.

Shepard, Jonathan, ed. *The Cambridge History of the Byzantine Empire 500–1492.* Cambridge: Cambridge University Press, 2008.

Shepherd, Massey H. "The Formation and Influence of the Antiochene Liturgy." *DOP* 15 (1961): 23–44.

Silvas, Anna M. "Kassia the Nun c. 810–c.865: An Appreciation." In *Byzantine Women: Varieties of Experience 800–1200,* ed. Lynda Garland, 17–39. Aldershot: Ashgate, 2006.

Simić, Kosta. "Kassia's Hymnography in the Light of Patristic Sources and Earlier Hymnographical Works." *Recueil des Travaux de l'Institut d'Études Byzantines [Zbornik radova Vizantološkog Instituta]* 48 (2011): 7–37.

Skaballanovič, Michail. *Tolkovyj Tipikon [The Typikon Interpreted].* 3 vols. Kiev: Korčak-Novickij, 1910.

Smith, John Arthur. *Music in Ancient Judaism and Early Christianity.* Farnham: Ashgate, 2011.

Smith, Jonathan Z. *To Take Place: Toward Theory in Ritual.* Chicago: University of Chicago Press, 1987.

Sodini, Jean-Pierre. "La terre de semelles: Images pieuses ramenées par les pèlerins des Lieux saints (Terre sainte, Martyria d'Orient)." *Journal des Savants* (January–June 2011): 77–140.

Soulen, R. Kendal. *The God of Israel and Christian Theology.* Minneapolis: Fortress, 1996.

Spinks, Brian D. *The Sanctus in the Eucharistic Prayer.* New York: Cambridge University Press, 1991.

Stanislavsky, Constantin. *An Actor Prepares.* Trans. E. R. Hapgood. New York: Theatre Arts Books, 1961.

Steirnon, Daniel. "La vie et l'œuvre de S. Joseph l'Hymnographe: À propos d'une publication récente." *Revue des Études Byzantines* 31 (1973): 243–66.

Stelzenberger, Johannes. "Conscientia in der ost-westlichen Spannung der patristischen Theologie." *Tübinger Theologische Quartalschrift* 141 (1961): 174–205.

Stendahl, Krister. "The Apostle Paul and the Introspective Conscience of the West." *Harvard Theological Review* 56 (1963): 199–215.

Stevenson, Kenneth W. *Jerusalem Revisited: The Liturgical Meaning of Holy Week.* Washington, D.C.: Pastoral Press, 1988.

——. "The Origins and Development of Candlemas: A Struggle for Identity and Coherence?" *Ephemerides Liturgicae* 102 (1988): 316–46.

Stewart, Columba. "Evagrius Ponticus and the Eastern Monastic Tradition on the Intellect and the Passions." *Modern Theology* 27 (2011): 263–75.

——. "Evagrius Ponticus and the 'Eight Generic Logismoi.'" In *In the Garden of Evil: The Vices and Culture in the Middle Ages*, ed. Richard Newhauser, 5–16. Toronto: Pontifical Institute of Medieval Studies, 2005.

——. "Radical Honesty About the Self: The Practice of the Desert Fathers." *Sobornost* 12 (1990): 25–39.

Stowers, Stanley K. *A Rereading of Romans: Justice, Jews, and Gentiles.* New Haven, Conn.: Yale University Press, 1994.

——. "Romans 7:7–25 as a Speech-in-Character." In *Paul in His Hellenistic Context*, ed. Troels Engberg-Pedersen, 180–202. Edinburgh: T&T Clark, 1994.

Strunk, Otto. "The Byzantine Office at Hagia Sophia." *DOP* 9–10 (1955–56), 175–202.

Swift, Christopher. "A Penitent Prepares: Affect, Contrition and Tears." In *Crying in the Middle Ages: Tears of History*, ed. Elina Gertsman, 79–101. New York: Routledge, 2012.

Taft, Robert F. "Anton Baumstark's Comparative Liturgy Revisited." In *Acts of the International Congress: Comparative Liturgy Fifty Years After Anton Baumstark (1872–1948)*, ed. Robert F. Taft and Gabriele Winkler, 191–232. OCA 265. Rome: Edizioni Orientalia Christiana, 2001.

——. "The βηματίκιον in the 6/7th C. Narration of the Abbots John and Sophronius (BHGNA 1438w)." In *Crossroads of Cultures: Studies in Liturgy and Patristics in Honor of Gabriele Winkler*, ed. Hans-Jürgen Feulner, Elena Velkovska, and Robert F. Taft, 675–92. OCA 260. Rome: Pontificio Istituto Orientale, 2000. Reprinted in Robert F. Taft, *Divine Liturgies: Human Problems in Byzantium, Armenia, Syria and Palestine* (Aldershot: Ashgate, 2001).

——. *Beyond East and West: Problems in Liturgical Understanding.* 2nd ed. Rome: Orientalia Christiana, Pontifical Oriental Institute, 1997.

——. "Byzantine Communion Rites II: Later Formulas and Rubrics in the Ritual of Clergy Communion." *OCP* 67 (2001): 275–352.

——. *The Byzantine Rite: A Short History.* Collegeville, Minn.: Liturgical Press, 1992.

——. "Cathedral vs. Monastic Liturgy in the Christian East: Vindicating a Distinction." *BBGG* 2nd ser. 3 (2005): 173–219.

——. "The Decline of Communion in Byzantium and the Distancing of the Congregation from the Liturgical Action: Cause, Effect, or Neither?" In *Thresholds of the Sacred: Architectural, Art Historical, Liturgical, and Theological Perspectives on Religious Screens, East and West*, ed. Sharon E. J. Gerstel, 27–52. Washington, D.C.: Dumbarton Oaks, 2006.

——. *Divine Liturgies: Human Problems in Byzantium, Armenia, Syria and Palestine.* Aldershot: Ashgate, 2001.

——. "The Epiclesis Question in Light of the Orthodox and Catholic *lex orandi* Traditions." In *New Perspectives on Historical Theology: Essays in Memory of John Meyendorff*, ed. Bradley Nassif, 210–37. Grand Rapids, Mich.: Eerdmans, 1996.

——. *The Great Entrance: A History of the Transfer of Gifts and Other Preanaphoral Rites of the Liturgy of St. John Chrysostom.* 2nd ed. OCA 200. Rome: Pontificium Institutum Studiorum Orientalium, 1978.

——. "Historicism Revisited." In *Beyond East and West: Problems in Liturgical Understanding.* Washington, D.C.: Pastoral Press, 1984.

——. "The Interpolation of the Sanctus into the Anaphora: When and Where? A Review of the Dossier." *OCP* 57 (1991): 281–308; 58 (1992): 82–121. Reprinted in Robert F. Taft, *Liturgy in Byzantium and Beyond* (Aldershot: Variorum, 1995), IX, X.

——. "Liturgy." In *The Oxford Handbook of Byzantine Studies*, ed. Elizabeth Jeffreys, John F. Haldon, and Robin Cormack, 599–610. Oxford: Oxford University Press, 2008.

——. *Liturgy in Byzantium and Beyond.* Aldershot: Variorum, 1995.

——. *The Liturgy of the Hours in East and West: The Origins of the Divine Office and Its Meaning for Today.* 2nd ed. Collegeville, Minn.: Liturgical Press, 1993.

——. "The Liturgy of the Hours in the East." In *Handbook for Liturgical Studies*, Vol. 5, *Liturgical Time and Space.* Ed. Anscar J. Chupungco, 29–58. Collegeville, Minn.: Liturgical Press, 2000.

——. *The Precommunion Rites.* OCA 261. Rome: Pontificio Istituto Orientale, 2000.

——. "A Tale of Two Cities: The Byzantine Holy Week Triduum as a Paradigm of Liturgical History." In *Time and Community: In Honor of Thomas Julian Talley*, ed. J. Neil Alexander, 21–41. Washington, D.C.: Pastoral Press, 1990. Reprinted in Robert F. Taft, *Liturgy in Byzantium and Beyond* (Aldershot: Variorum, 1995), VI.

——. *Through Their Own Eyes: Liturgy as the Byzantines Saw It.* Berkeley, Calif.: InterOrthodox Press, 2006.

——. "Was the Eucharistic Anaphora Recited Secretly or Aloud? The Ancient Tradition and What Became of It." In *Worship Traditions in Armenia and the Neighboring Christian East*, ed. Roberta R. Ervine, 15–57. Crestwood, N.Y.: St. Vladimir's Seminary Press, 2006.

——. "Were There Once Old Testament Readings in the Byzantine Divine Liturgy? Apropos of an Article by Sysse Gudrun Engberg." *BBGG* 3rd ser. 8 (2011): 271–311.

——. "Women at Church in Byzantium: Where, When—and Why?" *DOP* 52 (1998): 89–103. Reprinted in Robert F. Taft, *Divine Liturgies: Human Problems in Byzantium, Armenia, Syria and Palestine* (Aldershot: Ashgate, 2001), I.

——. "Women at Worship in Byzantium: Glimpses of a Lost World." *BBGG* 3rd ser. 6 (2009): 255–86.

——. "Worship on Sinai in the First Christian Millenium." In *Approaching the Holy Mountain: Art and Liturgy at St Catherine's Monastery in the Sinai*, ed. Sharon E. J. Gerstel and Robert S. Nelson, 143–77. Turnhout: Brepols, 2010.

Tait, Hugh, ed. *Seven Thousands Years of Jewellery.* London: British Museum Press, 1986.

Talbot, Alice-Mary. "The Devotional Life of Laywomen." In *Byzantine Christianity*, ed. Derek Krueger, 201–20. A People's History of Christianity 3. Minneapolis: Fortress, 2006.

——. ed. *Holy Women of Byzantium: Ten Saints' Lives in English Translation.* Byzantine Saints' Lives in Translation 1. Washington, D.C.: Dumbarton Oaks, 1996.

——. "Women's Space in Byzantine Monasteries." *DOP* 52 (1998): 113–27.

Talley, Thomas J. *The Origins of the Liturgical Calendar*. 2nd ed. Collegeville, Minn.: Liturgical Press, 1991.

Tallon, Andrew. "Christianity." In *The Oxford Handbook of Religion and Emotion*, ed. John Corrigan, 111–24. New York: Oxford University Press, 2008.

Tarby, André. *La prière eucharistique de l'église de Jérusalem*. Paris: Beauchesne, 1972.

Taylor, Charles. *Sources of the Self: The Making of Modern Identity*. Cambridge, Mass.: Harvard University Press, 1989.

TeSelle, Eugene. "Exploring the Inner Conflict: Augustine's Sermons on Romans 7 and 8." In *Engaging Augustine on Romans: Self, Context, and Theology in Interpretation*, ed. Eugene TeSelle and Daniel Patte, 111–46. Harrisburg, Pa.: T&T Clark, 2002.

Thunberg, Lars. *Microcosm and Mediator: The Theological Anthropology of Maximus the Confessor*. 2nd ed. Chicago: Open Court, 1995.

Tollefsen, Torstein Theodor. "*Theosis* according to Gregory." In *Gregory of Nazianzus: Images and Reflections*, ed. Jostein Børtnes and Tomas Hägg, 257–70. Copenhagen: Museum Tusculanum, 2006.

Tomadakis, Eutychios I. Ἰωσὴφ ὁ Ὑμνογράφος. Βίος καὶ ἔργον. Collection Ἀθηνᾶ 11. Athens: Typographeion Adelphōn Myrtidē, 1971.

Topping, Eva Catafygiotu. "The Psalmist, St. Luke and Kassia the Nun." *Byzantine Studies/Études Byzantines* 9 (1982): 199–219.

Torrance, Alexis C. *Repentance in Late Antiquity: Eastern Asceticism and the Framing of the Christian Life c.400–650 C.E.* Oxford: Oxford University Press, 2013.

Toynbee, J. M. C., and K. S. Painter. "Silver Picture Plates of Late Antiquity: A.D. 300 to 700." *Archaeologia* 108 (1986): 15–65.

Treasures of Heaven: Saints, Relics, and Devotion in Medieval Europe. Ed. Martina Bagnoli et al. Baltimore: Walters Art Museum, 2010.

Tripolitis, Antonía. *Kassia: The Legend, the Woman, and Her Work*. Garland Library of Medieval Literature 84, ser. A. New York: Garland, 1992.

Troelsgård, Christian. "Kanon Performance in the Eleventh Century, Evidence from the Evergetis Typikon Reconsidered." In *Vizantija i Vostočnaja Evropa: Liturgičeskie i muzykal'nye svjazi: K 80-letiju doktora Miloša Velimiroviča*, ed. Nina Gerasimova-Persidskaia and Irina Lozovaia, 44–51. Moscow: Progress-Tradicija, 2003.

———. "What Kind of Chant Books Were the Byzantine Sticheraria?" In *Cantus planus: Papers Read at the 9th Meeting, Esztergom & Visegrád, Hungary, 1998*, ed. László Dobszay, 563–74. Budapest: Institute for Musicology of the Hungarian Academy of Sciences, 2001.

Tschilingirov, Assen. "Eine byzantinische Goldschmiedewerkstatt des 7. Jahrhunderts." In *Metallkunst von der Spätantike bis zum ausgehenden Mittelalter*, ed. Arne Effenberger, 85. Berlin: Staatliche Museen zu Berlin, 1982.

Tsironis, Niki. "The Body and the Senses in the Work of Cassia the Hymnographer: Literary Trends in the Iconoclastic Period." *Symmeikta* 16 (2003) 139–57.

Turner, C. H. "Notes on the Apostolic Constitutions: The Compiler an Arian." *JThS* 16 (1915): 54–61.

Turner, H. J. M. *St. Symeon the New Theologian and Spiritual Fatherhood*. Leiden: Brill, 1990.

Vailhé, S. "Saint André de Crète." *Échos d'Orient* 5 (1902): 278–87.

Valantasis, Richard. *The Making of the Self: Ancient and Modern Asceticism*. Eugene, Ore.: Cascade, 2008.

van Esbroeck, Michel. "La lettre de l'empereur Justinien sur l'Annonciation et la Noël en 561." *Analecta Bollandiana* 86 (1968): 351–71.

Velkovska, Elena. "Byzantine Liturgical Books." In *Handbook for Liturgical Studies*, vol.1, *Introduction to the Liturgy*, ed. Anscar J. Chupungco, 225–40. Collegeville, Minn.: Liturgical Press, 1997.

———. "The Liturgical Year in the East." In *Handbook for Liturgical Studies*, vol. 5, *Liturgical Time and Space*, ed. Anscar J. Chupungco, 157–76. Collegeville, Minn.: Liturgical Press, 2000.

Velimirović, Miloš. "The Byzantine Heirmos and Heirmologion." In *Gattungen der Musik in Einzeldarstellungen: Gedenkschrift Leo Schrade*, ed. Wulf Arlt, 192–244. Bern: Francke Verlag, 1973.

Ventrella, Gianluca. "L'etopea nella definizione degli antichi retori." In *ΗΘΟΠΟΙΙΑ: La représentation de caractères entre fiction scolaire et réalité vivante à l'époque impériale et tardive*, ed. Eugenio Amato and Jacques Schamp, 179–212. Salerno: Helios, 2005.

Verghese, Annamma. "Kaiserkritik in Two Kontakia of Romanos." In *Byzantine Narrative: Papers in Honor of Roger Scott*, ed. John Burke, 393–403. Byzantina Australiensia 16. Melbourne: Australian Association for Byzantine Studies, 2006.

Vikan, Gary. *Early Byzantine Pilgrimage Art*. Rev. ed. Washington, D.C.: Dumbarton Oaks, 2010.

———. "Early Byzantine Pilgrimage *Devotionalia* as Evidence of the Appearance of Pilgrimage Shrines." *Jahrbuch für Antike und Christentum Suppl.* 20, 1 (1995–97): 377–88.

———. "Pilgrims in Magi's Clothing: The Impact of Mimesis on Early Byzantine Pilgrimage Art." In *The Blessings of Pilgrimage*, ed. Robert Ousterhout, 97–107. Urbana: University of Illinois Press, 1990.

———. "Sacred Image, Sacred Power." In *Sacred Image and Sacred Power in Byzantium*. Variorum Collected Studies 1. Aldershot: Ashgate, 2003.

Wade, Andrew. "La prière ἄνες, ἄφες, συγχώρησον: La pratique palestinienne de demander l'absolution pour la communion solitaire et quotidienne: Lex orandi pour une orthopraxis perdue?" In *Thysia aineseōs: Mélanges liturgiques offerts à la mémoire de l'archevêque Georges Wagner (1930–1993)*, ed. Job Getcha and André Lossky, 431–35. Paris: Presses Saint Serge, 2005.

Ward, Benedicta. *Harlots of the Desert: A Study of Repentance in Early Monastic Sources*. Kalamazoo, Mich.: Cistercian, 1986.

Webb, Ruth. "Imagination and the Arousal of Emotions in Greco-Roman Rhetoric." In *The Passions in Roman Thought and Literature*, ed. Susanna Morton Braund and Christopher Gill, 112–27. Cambridge: Cambridge University Press, 1997.

Wehofer, Thomas. "Untersuchungen zum Lied des Romanos auf die Wiederkunft des Herrn." *Sitzungsberichte des kais. Akademie der Wissenschaften in Wien, Phil.-hist. Klasse* 154/5 (1907): 108–20.

Weitzmann, Kurt. "*Loca Sancta* and Representational Arts of Palestine." *DOP* 28 (1974): 31–55.

Wellesz, Egon. *A History of Byzantine Music and Hymnography*. 2nd ed. Oxford: Clarendon, 1961.

Wharton Epstein, Ann. "The Rebuilding and Decoration of the Holy Apostles in Constantinople: A Reconsideration." *GRBS* 23 (1982): 79–92.

Wiley, Tatha. *Original Sin: Origins, Development and Contemporary Meaning*. Mahwah, N.J.: Paulist Press, 1989.

Winkler, Gabriele. *Die Basilius-anaphora: Editionen der beiden armenischen Redaktionen und der relevanten Fragmente, Übersetzungen und Zusammenschau aller Versionen im Licht der orientalischen Überlieferungen.* Anaphorae Orientales 2. Anaphorae Armeniacae 2. Rome: Pontificio Istituto Orientale, 2005.

———. *Das Sanctus: über den Ursprung und die Anfänge des Sanctus und sein Fortwirken.* OCA 267. Rome: Pontificio Istituto Orientale, 2002.

Wolfram, Gerda. "Der Beitrag des Theodoros Studites zur byzantinischen Hymnographie." *JÖB* 53 (2003): 117–25.

Woods, Marjorie Curry. "Weeping for Dido: Epilogue on a Premodern Rhetorical Exercise in the Postmodern Classroom." In *Latin Grammar and Rhetoric: From Classical Theory to Medieval Practice,* ed. Carol Dana Lanham, 284–94. London: Continuum, 2002.

Woods, Majorie Curry, and Rita Copeland. "Classroom and Confession." In *The Cambridge History of Medieval English Literature,* ed. David Wallace, 376–406. Cambridge: Cambridge University Press, 1999.

Woolfenden, Gregory W. *Daily Liturgical Prayer: Origins and Theology.* Aldershot: Ashgate, 2004.

Wybrew, Hugh. *Orthodox Lent, Holy Week and Easter: Liturgical Texts with Commentary.* Crestwood, N.Y.: St. Vladimir's Seminary Press, 1997.

———. *The Orthodox Liturgy: The Development of the Eucharistic Liturgy in the Byzantine Rite.* Crestwood, N.Y.: St. Vladimir's Seminary Press, 1990.

Zecher, Jonathan L. "The Angelic Life in Desert and *Ladder*: John Climacus's Re-Formulation of Ascetic Spirituality." *JECS* 21 (2013): 111–36.

Zheltov, Michael. "The Anaphora and the Thanksgiving Prayer from the Barcelona Papyrus: An Underestimated Testimony to the Anaphoral History of the Fourth Century." *Vigiliae Christianae* 62 (2008): 467–504.

INDEX OF BIBLICAL CITATIONS

ACKNOWLEDGMENTS

The time to learn new things and the people from whom I learned them: these have been among the greatest joys of the past decade. In the midst of my career's journey, as I took what Susan Harvey called "the liturgical turn," I engaged in some retooling in Byzantine art and material culture, the Christianity of the middle Byzantine period, the history of liturgy, and the study of manuscripts. In this endeavor I relied heavily on the advice of colleagues and friends about what to read and about how to ponder new problems. For my art historical education I thank Betsy Bolman, Holger Klein, Glenn Peers, Linda Safran, and Heather Holian, as well as Martina Bagnoli at the Walters Art Museum, Griff Mann at the Cleveland Art Museum, Barbara Boehm at the Metropolitan Museum of Art, and Guido Cornini at the Vatican Museums. On matters liturgical I am grateful to Father Robert Taft and Sister Vassa Larin for their correspondence, and to Alex Lingas and Daniel Galadza for their guidance in both speech and email. I am supremely thankful to Father Justin Sinaites for his hospitality during my visit to St. Catherine's Monastery, for allowing me to examine manuscripts when the library was closed for renovation, and for taking and sending me photographs to study and to publish. I acknowledge further debts in my notes.

My work benefited from the generous support of the National Endowment for the Humanities in 2007–8; the Institute for Advanced Studies of the Hebrew University of Jerusalem in 2010; and the Institute for Advanced Study in Princeton in 2012–13 (funded by the NEH and the Herodotus Fund). In accord with federal policy, I certify that any views, findings, conclusions, or recommendations expressed in this book do not necessarily reflect those of the National Endowment for the Humanities. In fact they are all my own, as are any mistakes or howlers you may find in these pages.

I thank Brouria Bitton-Ashkelony and Lorenzo Perrone for their invitation to Jerusalem and for organizing a stimulating environment for discussion, curiosity, and exploration, and I am indebted to Yonatan Livneh for finding books and articles in libraries throughout Israel.

In Princeton, I thank Patrick Geary for his thoughtful welcome and his willingness to number me among his medievalists. Kirstie Venanzi and Karen Dowling worked tirelessly fetching materials hither and yon on short notice, making this stay in Central New Jersey even more intellectually busy than my previous sojourns, and affording me many hours to wander the Institute Woods rather than Firestone Library.

The University of North Carolina at Greensboro provided release time for my research and awarded me faculty grants and travel allowances from the Kohler Fund and from the Dean's Fund for travel to museums around the country and abroad. I thank Gaylor Callahan and Patrick Kelly of Jackson Library's Interlibrary Loan Department, a lifeline for all scholars on campus; our Departmental Administrative Assistant Pat Bowden for logistical support and wise perspective; my Department Head Bill Hart for bearing the brunt of my absence in the midst of a budget crisis; and my most supportive Dean, Tim Johnston, who has fostered the scholarship of discovery in the College of Arts and Science at UNCG for much of my tenure.

Over the years, I delivered sections of this project in lectures at the annual conference of the Byzantine Studies Association of North America, the International Congress of Byzantine Studies, the Catholic University of America, Central European University in Budapest, Dumbarton Oaks, Durham University, Fordham University, the Hebrew University of Jerusalem, Rutgers University, UNCG, and the universities of Bologna, Cambridge, Chicago, Oxford, and South Carolina. In each venue interlocutors asked smart questions and offered suggestions for how to expand or hone my inquiry. Discussions made this book richer and broader. Many hosts offered warm hospitality and delicious eats, delighting this wayfaring foodie.

Parts of this book were previously published in different form. Sections of Chapters 1 and 2 appeared as "Romanos the Melodist and the Christian Self in Early Byzantium," in *Proceedings of the 21st International Congress of Byzantine Studies, London, 2006*, vol. 1, *Plenary Papers*, ed. Elizabeth Jeffreys (Aldershot: Ashgate, 2006), 247–66. The second half of Chapter 2 appeared as "The Internal Lives of Biblical Figures in the Hymns of Romanos the Melodist," *Adamantius* 19 (2013): 290–302. An earlier version of Chapter 4 appeared as "The Liturgical Creation of a Christian Past: Identity and Community in Anaphoral Prayers," in *Unclassical Traditions*, vol. 1, *Alternatives to the Classical Past in Late Antiquity*, ed. Richard Flower, Christopher Kelly, and Michael Stuart Williams, *Cambridge Classical Journal* Supplementary Vol. 35 (Cambridge: Cambridge Philological Society, 2010), 58–71. An earlier version of Chapter 5 appeared as "The *Great Kanon* of Andrew of Crete, the Penitential Bible, and the Liturgical Formation of the Self in the Byzantine Dark Age," in *Between Personal and Institutional Religion: Self, Doctrine, and Practice in Late Antique Eastern Christianity*, ed. Brouria Bitton-Ashkelony and Lorenzo Perrone, Cultural Encounters in Late Antiquity and the Middle Ages 15 (Turnhout: Brepols, 2013), 57–97. A section of Chapter 6 appeared as "Authorial Voice and Self-Presentation in a Ninth-century Hymn on the Prodigal Son," in *The Author in Middle Byzantine Literature: Modes, Functions, and Identities*, ed. Aglae Pizzone, Byzantinisches Archiv (Berlin: DeGruyter, 2014).

At the University of Pennsylvania Press, I am indebted to Jerry Singerman, my editor and friend, and his assistant Caroline Hayes; Alison Anderson, project editor; and Sister Mary Jean of the Community of St. Mary, copyeditor. Henry Hilston prepared the index. I thank my colleagues on the Divinations series board, Daniel Boyarin and Virginia Burrus, for their encouragement, patience, friendship, and interchange.

Over the years, this work has benefitted especially from my conversations with Thomas Arentzen, Brouria Bitton-Ashkelony, Peter Brown, Mary Cunningham, Antonia Giannouli, Mayke de Jong, John Gager, Ellen Haskell, Itzik Hen, Laura Lieber, Ophir Münz-Manor, Margaret Mullett, Charlie Orzech, Lorenzo Perrone, Philip Rousseau, Alice-Mary Talbot, and Frans van Liere, many of whom read and remarked on more than one chapter.

Georgia Frank, Susan Harvey, and Stratis Papaioannou read the entire manuscript offering perspectives that both expanded and tempered my conclusions. I can think of no better critics, except perhaps for Gene Rogers, who also read most of this lovingly along the way. But to him I am chiefly grateful for being my husband. Dedicating to him the book of my forties can convey but a small portion of my love.